D1572527

Public Life
in Toulouse
1463–1789

Public Life in Toulouse 1463–1789

From Municipal Republic to Cosmopolitan City

ROBERT A. SCHNEIDER

CORNELL UNIVERSITY PRESS

Ithaca and London

THIS BOOK IS PUBLISHED WITH THE AID OF
A GRANT FROM BRANDEIS UNIVERSITY.

First published 1989 by Cornell University Press.

International Standard Book Number 0-8014-2191-8
Library of Congress Catalog Card Number 89-42880
Printed in the United States of America

*The paper in this book is acid-free and meets the guidelines for
permanence and durability of the Committee on Production Guidelines
for Book Longevity of the Council on Library Resources.*

For my parents

Contents

Figures and Tables

Acknowledgments

I am happy to acknowledge the people and institutions that aided in the research and writing of this book.

Funding for research in France came from several sources: the French government (Bourse Chateaubriand); the Center for Western European Studies and the Department of History, both of the University of Michigan, Ann Arbor; a grant-in-aid from the American Council of Learned Societies; and Brandeis University (Mazar and Sachar grants). Like so many other historians, I am indebted to the services of several archives and libraries in Toulouse, whose staffs I have burdened over the years. My heartfelt thanks go to them, especially Geneviève Maillard and Christian Cau, of the Archives Municipales de Toulouse; Robert Nadal, of the Archives Départementales, Haute-Garonne; and Christian Peligry, of the Bibliothèque Municipale de Toulouse. Frequently, a quiet day in the archives turned into a free-wheeling historical seminar, and I would like to acknowledge those confreres who turned the lonely enterprise of research into a pleasant collective endeavor: Barbara Beckerman-Davis, M. Genestie, Rémy Papillaut, Sister Marguerite-Marie Shibano, Kay and Paul Solon, Jack Thomas, and others. The Thomas family, Annie, Jack, and Laura, opened their Blagnac home to me summer after summer, for which I am eternally grateful.

An earlier version of this book was read by Raymond Grew and the late James Vann. Charles Tilly was an important intellectual influence on and a helpful reader of that first version. It was also read by Barbara Diefendorf. Several colleagues at Brandeis offered their comments on the book in manuscript, and I here acknowledge their help: Rudolph Binion, Samuel Cohn, James Kloppenberg, and Bernard Wasserstein. I also thank students in my spring 1987 graduate seminar for commenting on the manuscript. Robert Forster was kind enough to read it on short notice and offered much-needed support. John Ackerman of Cornell University Press has been all that a first-time author could wish for in an editor. I thank Joanne S. Ainsworth for her diligent copyediting.

My greatest debts are to two historians whose advice and support have been unstinting and invaluable. David Bien has been a part of this project from inception to completion. To him I owe what thoughtfulness I have managed to bring to bear on the study of early modern history, although I am well aware that the product falls far short of his example. Philip Benedict has shared with me his encyclopedic knowledge of the ancien régime, prodded me to reconsider many issues, and extended his support at several crucial moments. Needless to say, none of the readers of the manuscript is responsible for any of the book's errors or excesses.

My friends and family, though generally mystified as to what I have been up to these years, have played an important role in the book's development. A displaced Gascon, François Dutreuilh, tutored me in "la sociabilité toulousaine." Jack Thomas, another fellow traveler in the byways of Toulouse and its past, has continued to offer his fellowship at long distance. John Pacheco will not recognize a friend's appreciation of his deep Catholic spirituality in the book's treatment of religion, but it is there nevertheless. Stuart Klawans gave an earlier version of the book the benefit of his consummate writer's eye. Eleanor V. McLaughlin was an essential helpmate in the production of that first version. My friends of "Shlocke Alley" now might understand why on so many evenings I refused a second glass of wine. Paul Gootenberg has been both friend and colleague during a difficult time. Sarah L. G. Mitchell has made that difficult time considerably less so. My parents have been there all along.

ROBERT A. SCHNEIDER

North Cambridge, Massachusetts

Abbreviations

ADH-G	Archives Départementales, Haute-Garonne
AMT	Archives Municipales de Toulouse
AN	Archives Nationales
Arch. hosp.	Archives hospitalières
BIC	Bibliothèque de l'Institut Catholique de Toulouse
BMT	Bibliothèque Municipale de Toulouse
BN	Bibliothèque Nationale
ADM	*Annales du Midi*
HGL	C. Devic and J. Vaissette, *Histoire générale de Languedoc*, 13 vols. (Toulouse, 1889)
MASIBL	*Mémoires de l'Académie des Sciences, Inscriptions et Belles-Lettres*
RHT	*Revue Historique de Toulouse*

PART ONE

Introduction

Prelude

To begin this study of public life in an Old Regime city, let us turn to one of the earliest critics of the rising metropolis. Jean-Jacques Rousseau despised life in the big city. His preference for the country and small town is well known; what is less appreciated is that his dislike of contemporary urban life not only was based on prejudice, temperament, and a hopelessly idealized view of his native Geneva, but that it derived also from a penetrating critique of contemporary city ways. Rousseau's critique can be found in his *Lettre à Monsieur d'Alembert sur les spectacles,* a tract concerned for the most part with the theater and whether its establishment would have a corrupting or salutary effect on the morality of his fellow Genevans. Rousseau, of course, saw the theater as a Trojan horse bearing decadence and vain amusements into his happy *polis.* But in the course of the *Lettre* he enlarged upon his subject by delivering a characteristically scathing portrait of the metropolis, blaming it for ruining morals, destroying intimacy, and subverting honest relationships. For Rousseau, the big city was itself a theater, its citizens actors whose roles were not defined by work, affection, and the necessities of mutual dependency, but were rather inspired by deception, frivolity, and the desperate pursuit of fame. The big city was "full of scheming, idle people without religion or principle, whose imagination, depraved by sloth, inactivity, the love of pleasure, and great needs, engenders only monsters and inspires only crimes; in a big city . . . *moeurs* and honor are nothing because each, easily hiding his conduct from the public eye, shows himself only by his reputation and is esteemed only for his riches."[1]

1. Jean-Jacques Rousseau, *Politics and the Arts: Letter to M. d'Alembert on the Theatre,* trans. A. Bloom (Ithaca, 1968), pp. 58–59. Richard Sennett has taken the same passage from Rousseau as a point of entry into a very interesting discussion of manners and

3

In Rousseau's estimation Geneva, his cherished birthplace, alone among European cities preserved urban living as an edifying experience. He depicted it as a small city where people knew one another, where activities were useful, pastimes innocent, and amusements healthy. The felicity of existence there was sustained by a sociability rooted in family, work, and the fellowship of simple entertainment. Though Calvinist, his Geneva was not devoid of pleasures. In particular, he pointed with approbation to the men's clubs, or *cercles*, and to public festivals as two forms of conviviality that were at once morally salubrious and enjoyable.[2]

Toward the end of this book I investigate the culture of eighteenth-century Toulouse; there, in a sense, we shall discover that Rousseau was right. Not that I will take his part in condemning the quality of big-city life in the Age of Enlightenment; rather, it will become obvious that in its public culture and forms of sociability, the eighteenth century represented a new era. It was the beginning of the era of the cosmopolitan city. This means not that the city had grown in any significant fashion—indeed, Toulouse's demographic growth lagged far behind the countryside's—nor that the city was physically transformed in dramatic ways. Instead, the changed character of eighteenth-century Toulouse was apparent in the scale of its public ceremonies and festivities, the cultural concerns of its elite citizens, and the kinds of sociability which then emerged. In each of these domains there was something new, at least in comparison with the sixteenth and seventeenth centuries—a newness most apparent in the frivolity and enlarged scale of festive life and in the cosmopolitanism that began to characterize the cultural activities of the elite.

The demonstration of this newness occupies only a portion of this book, which is largely devoted to a reconstruction and analysis of urban public life in the sixteenth and seventeenth centuries. Until the eighteenth century, the dominant religious and civic activities, although not, to be sure, those of Rousseau's imagined happy commune, were yet infused with a spirit of localism and social commitment. The city and its populace largely defined the vistas of the old

public conduct in the Old Regime in his *The Fall of Public Man* (New York, 1978), pp. 118–19.

2. On Rousseau and Geneva see Robert R. Palmer, *The Age of Democratic Revolutions*, vol. 1 (Princeton, 1959), pp. 111–19; and G. Vallette, *Jean-Jacques Rousseau, genevois* (Geneva and Paris, 1911).

urban elite's cultural activities, and did so until the eighteenth century, when a new spirit of cosmopolitanism took hold. This, in brief, is my main thesis, although in the course of an episodic account of the evolution of public life and culture over three centuries, I shall have occasion to modify and qualify the argument.

This claim may contradict some present understandings of the relationship between elites and their local communities in the early modern period. It has been asserted in several studies that as early as the sixteenth century urban elites began to consider themselves corporately and socially apart from the populace they governed.[3] Indeed, one scholar has posited that growing social distance as a distinguishing characteristic of the Robe nobility as opposed to traditional nobles of the Sword.[4] Insofar as I emphasize the ties between ruling elites and the lower orders, this book contradicts this assumption and suggests that neither the early emergence of a distinct upper-class culture nor the growth of corporate solidarity among ruling elites precluded such ties. Of course, the emergence of cultural forms confined to the elite cannot be ignored and I necessarily touch on some of them. But because the development of those forms has been widely accepted in the study of early modern culture (although questions remain about its precise timing and course), its treatment here is muted. It does have a place in what follows, but only as a reminder that the cultural preoccupations of the urban elite were often torn in two directions— toward both the concerns of the community and considerations of a more cosmopolitan sort. This elite culture will finally take center stage in the eighteenth century, when it more or less defines for the first time the range of dominant, nearly exclusive cultural interests of the upper class.

This book, which grows out of research into the public life of a provincial city, bears on other questions of interest to historians. First, it has become nearly ritualistic in the study of early modern French society to begin with a meditation on the conflicting views of Boris Porschnev and Roland Mousnier, and I make no exception here.

3. See on this theme George Huppert, *Les Bourgeois Gentilhommes: An Essay on the Definition of Elites in Renaissance France* (Chicago, 1970), chap. 12; Jonathan Dewald, *The Formation of a Provincial Nobility* (Princeton, 1980), pp. 16–68; Ralph Giesey, "State-Building in Early Modern France: The Role of Royal Officialdom," *Journal of Modern History* 55 (1983): 191–207.

4. Giesey, "State-Building in Early Modern France," p. 197.

Greatly simplified, their differences hinged on the question whether seventeenth-century French society was composed of classes or orders—whether, that is, people organized themselves in homogeneous, horizontal groupings around material interests, or whether they remained tied to each other in vertical hierarchies—peasant to lord, artisan to magistrate. Porschnev maintained that early modern society was fundamentally a society of classes, its nature confirmed by the fact that in moments of social conflict feudal landowners and bourgeois officials closed ranks against the threat from the laboring populace of peasants and artisans.[5] Mousnier, by contrast, objected vigorously to Porschnev's views and insisted that ties of loyalty between social unequals were stronger than class or material interests.[6] Begun as a discussion of the origins of revolt, the debate quickly focused on social structure.[7]

There is much that is valuable in Porschnev's work, especially the evidence he introduced demonstrating the extraordinary number of uprisings that swept France in the decades before the Fronde. But even Marxist historians have admitted that his depiction of these revolts as resulting entirely from lower-class mobilization is incorrect; and most would now be willing to concede that along with divisions of class early modern society was also structured "vertically," or in other ways that fostered solidarities among people of different classes.[8] The emphasis on such vertical ties has been Mousnier's enduring contribution, and most accounts of early modern France adopt his notion of *fidélités* as a fundamental feature of the social order. But as with Porschnev, there has been criticism of Mousnier's formulation too, especially of his insistence that the formal category of "orders" was the primary unit of social organization in the ancien régime.[9]

5. Boris Porschnev, *Les soulèvements populaires en France de 1623 à 1648* (Paris, 1963).
6. Roland Mousnier, "Recherches sur les soulèvements populaires en France avant la Fronde," *Revue d'Histoire Moderne et Contemporaine* 4 (1958): 88–113; *Les hiérarchies sociales de 1450 à nos jours* (Paris, 1969).
7. For a review of this controversy, see J. H. M. Salmon, "Venality of Office and Popular Sedition in Seventeenth-Century France," *Past & Present*, no. 37 (1967): 21–43; P. J. Coveney, ed., *France in Crisis, 1620–1675* (Totowa, N.J., 1977), pp. 1–63; and William Beik, *Absolutism and Society in Seventeenth-Century France: State Power and Provincial Aristocracy in Languedoc* (Cambridge, 1985), pp. 6–18.
8. A. D. Lublinskaya, *French Absolutism: The Crucial Phase, 1620–1629* (Cambridge, 1968).
9. Salmon, "Venality of Office and Popular Sedition"; Robert Mandrou, *Classes et luttes des classes en France au début du XVIIe siècle* (Messina and Florence, 1968); Beik, *Absolutism and Society*, pp. 6–9.

In the course of my investigation I noted that there seemed to be a problem not adequately addressed by either Porschnev or Mousnier. Focusing mostly on the social composition of revolts and legal conceptions of the social hierarchy, they were less interested in the patterns of social interaction between people in other, less extraordinary or more informal circumstances. Several other historians have indeed sought to reconstruct those patterns. Yves-Marie Bercé, a student of Mousnier, extended the analysis by examining popular celebrations, festivals, and more routine events for evidence of social solidarity at the village level.[10] There is also the study of sociability, pioneered by Gabriel Le Bras and developed by Maurice Agulhon, which takes as its focus voluntary associations of various sorts and offers a view of social interactions at some distance from the formal hierarchy.[11] Much of the original research for the present book stemmed from my interest in sociability in an early modern urban context. In particular, I was interested in discovering whether patterns of sociability changed and, specifically, whether they changed from a configuration in keeping with Mousnier's conception of a vertically articulated social structure to more horizontal, class-bound associations.[12]

This question in turn suggested another area of investigation among historians of early modern Europe, that of popular culture and religion. One of its established themes is the developing split between elite and popular cultures in the early modern period. Peter Burke, for example, concludes his *Popular Culture in Early Modern Europe* with a section on the "withdrawal of the upper classes," in which he explains that "by 1800 . . . the clergy, the nobility, the merchants, the professional men—and their wives—had abandoned popular culture to the lower classes, from whom they were now separated, as never before, by profound differences in world view."[13] Burke's formulation offers only one approach to the split between popular and elite cultures, an analysis deepened by such scholars as Marc Soriano, Robert Muchembled, and Natalie Zemon Davis.[14] But

10. Yves-Marie Bercé, *Fête et révolte: Des mentalités populaires de XVIe au XVIIIe siècle* (Paris, 1976); and *Histoire des croquants*, 2 vols. (Paris, 1974), 1:206–26.
11. Gabriel Le Bras, *Etudes de sociologie religieuse*, 2 vols. (Paris, 1955), 2:423–62; Maurice Agulhon, *Pénitents et francs-maçons dans l'ancienne Provence* (Paris, 1968), and "La sociabilité, la sociologie et l'histoire," *L'Arc*, no. 65 (1976): 76–84.
12. See my Ph.D. dissertation, "Urban Sociability in the Old Regime: Religion and Culture in Early Modern Toulouse" (University of Michigan, 1982).
13. Peter Burke, *Popular Culture in Early Modern Europe* (New York, 1978), p. 270.
14. Marc Soriano, *Les contes de Perrault, culture savante et traditions populaires* (Paris,

to my knowledge, this theme has never been considered relative to Mousnier's characterization of the social order, although both examine, in part at least, those vertical connections transcending divisions of class—Mousnier focusing on the social ties, Burke and others assuming an early, unifying culture that eventually gave way to cultural division. The parallelism is even more apparent if an evolutionary element is added to Mousnier's schema whereby these vertical ties break down by the eighteenth century;[15] for this, then, mirrors the roughly contemporaneous "withdrawal" of the upper classes from the realm of popular culture. Taken together, in short, these discussions suggest a general shift from close connection between the higher and lower orders to separation, both culturally and socially.

This shift is indeed the starting point for the present book, which is entirely devoted neither to the evolving patterns of social relations nor to the emergence of a distinctively elite, as opposed to popular, culture, although it deals in part with each of these themes. In all, four themes are explored, some overlapping and one or another accorded more prominence in a given period than the others. The first is the way the form and content of public life were embedded in social conditions and concerns, especially those of the city and its populace. This is to say that civic culture and religious activities were not merely entertainments, spectacles, or socially irrelevant spiritual expressions (if they ever are). Rather, they were instrumental in the rule, mobilization, and reform of urban society. The second theme involves associational life and how it promoted contact between the upper and lower classes. The third is the local, as opposed to national, cast of official urban culture. Finally, there are the various ways popular and elite culture overlapped, although that matter will not be treated at length. In each of these themes we shall also observe an evolution:

1968); Robert Muchembled, *Culture populaire et culture des élites dans la France moderne, XVe–XVIIIe siècles: Essai* (Paris, 1978); Natalie Zemon Davis, *Society and Culture in Early Modern France* (Stanford, 1975), pp. 227–62. See also, among other works, Robert Mandrou, "Cultures populaires et savantes: Rapports et contacts," in J. Beauroy, M. Bertrand, E. Gargan, eds., *The Wolf and the Lamb: Popular Culture in France,* Stanford French and Italian Studies 3 (Stanford, 1977); Carlo Ginzburg, *The Cheese and the Worms,* trans. J. Tedeschi and A. Tedeschi (Baltimore, 1980); James Van Horn Melton, "From Image to Word: Cultural Reform and the Rise of Literate Culture in Eighteenth-Century Austria," *Journal of Modern History* 58 (1986): 95–124; and David Garrioch, *Neighborhood and Community in Paris, 1740–1790* (Cambridge, 1986), chap. 5.

15. For Mousnier's own formulation, see *La société française de 1770 à 1789* (Paris, 1967), pp. 1–2.

from commitment to detachment, from social mixing to associational segregation, from localism to cosmopolitanism, and from aspects of a common culture to a separation between elite and popular cultures. And in each of these areas this evolution leads to the eighteenth century, when, as I have already suggested, the city and its culture were dramatically transformed.

These, then, are the themes to be studied in the context of the early modern city. This book is thus as much about the city of Toulouse from the late fifteenth century to the eve of the Revolution as it is about the evolution of its public life. Indeed, the central focus of Part II will be how public life was marked by representations of the city itself, by its various self-images, especially that of the so-called municipal republic. But this book is not a full history of Toulouse or a social study in the manner of the *Annales'* approach of "total history." It rather focuses on ruling elites and how they defined themselves vis-à-vis three elements: the city, the crown, and the urban populace. The principle of selection favors politics broadly considered: the politics of intercorporate rivalry, the politics of ruling the urban populace, and increasingly over the centuries, the politics of dealing with the crown. Why should a consideration of politics take precedence over other realities? The answer is that for the most part the concern in this book is with the city's official culture and the cultural activities of the elite, where the pursuit and preservation of political power were never far from view. One feature of the early modern French elite which perhaps distinguishes it from modern upper classes is that it was dominated by officers, functionaries, and others who had a role in administration and governance: for the most part they were members of the royal, provincial, or municipal bureaucracies. Thus, a range of political concerns permeated the cultural activities of the elite, especially in the sixteenth and seventeenth centuries, when society was ruled, managed, and reformed as much through culture, religion, and religious institutions as through the formal deployment of secular political power. For this reason, the history of the municipality's political life is essentially inseparable from the account of its cultural evolution. Indeed, these twin considerations form the basis of most of what follows.

To enter into the public life of an early modern city is thus to encounter a range of activities and experiences, some the purview of elites, others entailing the participation of a range of the populace. Some were political in nature, while many were religious exercises or symbolic expressions. As noted, my investigation will follow the various contours of Toulouse's public life from the Renaissance to the Enlightenment, focusing primarily on elites as they defined themselves in relationship to three elements. First is the city itself. Every city's culture is rich in self-representations—its history, myths, and traditions; its ceremonies and symbols; its civic institutions bound to promote its privileges and defend its honor. But there are vicissitudes in every city's sense of itself, and in the early modern period these moved unmistakably in the direction of diminished civic pride and self-consciousness. This is what we shall observe in Toulouse. While sixteenth-century public life remained faithful to the myth of the municipal republic and to a range of local traditions and ceremonies, by the eighteenth century most of these symbolic expressions had lost their vitality. And this shift was the result largely of a changed orientation of city elites, of their eventual alienation from Toulouse's traditions and culture, and their adoption of more cosmopolitan ways.

What promoted this change leads to the second element that local elites confronted. This was the crown and its increasing intrusion into local affairs, that is, state formation. The concept of state formation, however, must be broken down into several components. The imposition of centralized, royal authority is only one aspect of the process, although perhaps the most dramatic and certainly the most conspicuous. Local elites usually resisted this imposition, and ruling corporations frequently competed for royal favors or developed opposing strategies for coping with the crown's intrusion. On some occasions authority coalesced on the local level as a reaction to its consolidation at the center. On others civil strife arose in the wake of the collapse of royal authority; indeed, this is one view of the outbreak of the religious wars. Thus from a local perspective, state formation took a variety of forms and provoked a variety of responses. Here I shall concentrate on the cultural forms and responses, where the variety was just as great. But two modes seemed to characterize the relationship between elite cultural life and the growth of royal authority. In the sixteenth and seventeenth centuries, largely as a matter of resisting or otherwise coping with the newly intrusive centralized power, the cultural interests of elites remained grounded in the political exigencies and social realities of urban life. In the eighteenth century, by which time the political relationship of urban elites to the crown had changed, resistance gave way to identification. And public life, at least as defined by the elite, largely lost its connection with the social realities of the city. This, I will suggest, was one result of the success of absolutism and perhaps one precondition for the outbreak of the Revolution as well.

Elites had to cope not only with an intrusive monarchy but also with the populace they governed—the third element that defined their actions and interests. This book is not a demographic or social history of Toulouse; it does not pretend to reconstruct the early modern urban experience and all its problems—demographic change, rural migration to the city, religious strife, revolt, economic dislocation, and the like. But no study of public life in the Old Regime can ignore the social realities that made urban existence so turbulent and precarious. These realities form part of the background of what follows. In particular, I focus on how forms of public life were instrumental in dealing with social problems, especially those of poverty and revolt. For a thesis of this study is that in the sixteenth and seventeenth century public life remained grounded in social affairs, while in the eighteenth century such social grounding was lost with the advent of new forms of public life—cosmopolitanism for the elites, a mass culture based upon entertainment and spectacle for the rest of the populace.

Finally, a word should be said about the structure of this book. Although the work covers *la longue durée*—three hundred years of public life—it does not do so in the manner of most studies of this temporal breadth. Most such studies follow one series of documents or one social experience as the basis of their analyses and reconstructions. In contrast, I have drawn on a range of documents, evidence, and experiences in order to present an episodic account of the dominant and most visible forms of public life in Toulouse from the late fifteenth century to the eve of the Revolution. Despite its episodic form—the chapters present snapshots of public life in different periods—I strive to present an underlying structure of public behavior. This structure was defined by the features I have already described: a public life grounded in the social affairs of the city and marked by multiple ties between elites and the general populace. And it was a structure that would change by the eighteenth century, thus suggesting some important implications for the nature of public authority in pre-revolutionary France.

1

Early Modern Toulouse

A Roman outpost since the second century B.C., Toulouse served ancient Gaul as an important way station on the trading route connecting the Atlantic with the Mediterranean—a route that would be retraced with the construction of the Canal du Midi in the late seventeenth century. After the Roman period Toulouse began its modern rise to prominence as a pilgrimage site. As early as the fifth century Christians gathered to pray before the tomb of Toulouse's first martyr and bishop, Saint-Saturnin, but it was the Pilgrimage of Compostella, popularized in the eleventh century, that established Toulouse as a permanent refuge on the medieval religious circuit. The *Guide du pèlerin de Saint-Jacques* of the twelfth century gave Toulouse as a major step on the route to Compostella, and even though the Via Tolosana was not the sole path through southwestern France, it offered a bridge for crossing the Garonne River as well as churches and inns for harboring sojourners. From the early Middle Ages down through the Old Regime, throngs of pilgrims, many sporting the seashell and staff of Saint James, converged upon Toulouse each June from throughout the Christian world.[1] In the early modern period the faithful continued to flock to Toulouse to partake of the spiritual resources only an urban center could offer. They came to hear celebrated preachers, such as the blind Oratorian Père Le Jeune, who moved the assembled at the cathedral with his Lenten sermons in

1. Jean Coppolani, *Toulouse: Etude de géographie urbaine* (Toulouse, n.d.), p. 41; Michel Fracisque, "Le pèlerinage de Saint-Jacques de Compostelle," *Revue des Pyrénées* 10 (1898): 164.

1648; or they journeyed to witness religious spectacles, such as the processions on Corpus Christi Day in the sixteenth century, in which hundreds of hooded, barefoot penitents marched, some flagellating themselves; or they might have traveled from far off to pray at the miraculous Augustinian shrine, Our Lady of Pity, which was reported to heal everything from broken bones and cancer to hemorrhoids. When Thomas Wentworth, the future earl of Strafford, stopped at Toulouse in 1611, he remarked his "great contentment" upon viewing hundreds of uncorrupted mummified bodies in the crypts of the Cordeliers' convent; and when Mrs. Cradock, an English visitor of the late eighteenth century, found herself barred from these same crypts because of her sex, she yet managed to cajole an obliging monk to fetch a sample cadaver for her inspection, much to her satisfaction.[2]

In large part, then, our interest in Toulouse will also be its religious life and attractions, but this should not blind us to its more fundamental role as a market town and regional entrepôt, for even those who came to pray usually came also to trade. Situated on both banks of the Garonne on the frontier between Languedoc and Gascony, Toulouse received wood, clay, wool, leather, furs, olive oil, and other primary products from the Pyrenees, northern Spain, and the Mediterranean basin, sending them downstream by way of the Gironde toward Bordeaux, where they entered the international market. From the later fifteenth to the mid-sixteenth century, Toulouse was also a world center for the processing of pastel pigment, the preferred source of blue dyestuff at the time. Cultivated in the nearby region of the Lauragais, the harvested pastel was brought to Toulouse for fermentation and extraction and then crushed into a heavy, putrid substance called *coquagnes*, whose distinctly unpleasant odor permeated much of the city.[3] Toulouse was also a regional entrepôt for grain, for the city is surrounded by some of the richest grain-growing lands in

2. On Le Jean see Raoul Allier, *La Compagnie du Saint-Sacrement à Toulouse* (Toulouse, 1914), p. 21. On Corpus Christi processions see Simon de Peyronet, *Recueil des ordonnances synodales et autres*, vol. 2 (Toulouse, 1669), p. 832. Testimonies on the miracles performed by the Virgin in the Augustinian convent are found in ADH-G, E 1017, "Notre-Dame de Pitié." On Strafford, John Stoye, *English Travellers Abroad* (New York, 1968), p. 68; on Mrs. Cradock, *Journal de Madame Cradock: Voyage en France (1783–1786)*, trans. O. Delphin-Balleyquier (Paris, 1896), pp. 175–76; Arthur Young, *Voyages in France during the Years 1787, 1788, 1789*, ed. J. Kaplow (Garden City, N.Y., 1969), p. 28.

3. Philippe Wolff, *Histoire de Toulouse* (Toulouse, 1974), pp. 223–36; Gilles Caster, *Le commerce du pastel et de l'épicerie à Toulouse, 1450–1561* (Toulouse, 1962).

all of France. Its *halle aux grains*, constructed in 1202, was still in use in the nineteenth century. And another thirteenth-century edifice, the Bazacle Mills, perched on the left bank of the Garonne, was the marvel of visitors from throughout Europe.[4] In 1599, Thomas Platter, a well-traveled Swiss medical student, called these mills the "most remarkable that one could hope to see in all Christendom," and estimated that they could "provide more than enough flour each day for a hundred thousand persons."[5]

He also remarked that Toulouse "enjoys . . . privileges so considerable . . . which it defends with such care and jealousy, that it might be called a Republic."[6] Platter's rather inflated judgment probably reflected the substantial fiscal concessions the city had recently received from the crown in return for its recognition of Henry IV following the Wars of Religion. But, like other Old Regime towns, Toulouse did indeed have its charters of privileges and liberties that it had won in the course of the Middle Ages from its feudal overlords, the counts of Toulouse. The most important and long-lasting of these privileges, secured in the twelfth century, granted the medieval commune the right to self-government by elected consuls. At the beginning there were twenty-four of these *capitouls*, but by the early fifteenth century their ranks had been reduced to eight, each elected by one of the city's administrative districts, known as *capitoulats*, for a term of one year. The capitouls were the sovereign judicial and legislative authorities of the medieval city, as yet unrivaled by ecclesiastical officials or royal magistrates and, within the town walls at least, the equal of any prince, count, or other feudal lord. By the year 1200 they were the political masters of "la République toulousaine," the memory of which has been celebrated through the centuries as the city's golden age.[7]

The golden age, however, proved to be short-lived. A stronghold of the Cathar heresy, Toulouse was besieged three times during the Albigensian crusade and finally capitulated to the papal forces led by

---

4. Coppolani, *Toulouse*, pp. 46–47.

5. Thomas Platter, *Journal of a Younger Brother*, trans. S. Jennett (London, 1963), p. 245.

6. Ibid.

7. On this period and the capitouls in particular, see Wolff, *Histoire*, pp. 94–103; *HGL*, 3:790–92; Roger Limouzin-Lamouthe, *La commune de Toulouse et les sources de son histoire* (Toulouse, 1932); John Mundy, *Liberty and Political Power in Toulouse, 1050–1230* (New York, 1954).

Simon de Montfort in 1219. The city was devastated in the attack and subsequently stripped of many of its newly won liberties. And yet it emerged from the trauma of the crusade with an expanded regional role that would ensure its future as a provincial capital. Under the terms of the Treaty of Paris, which ended the crusade, Toulouse became the home of a university, the Dominican Inquisition, and four mendicant orders. An ecclesiastical community of church officials soon came to dominate the city, and in 1317 a former student at the university, Pope John XXII, ordered the reorganization of the diocese under the authority of the archbishop of Toulouse. At the outset of the Albigensian crusade it was Pope Innocent III's stated design to transform what he called a "foyer of pestilence" into a "holy city." He succeeded: Toulouse was at last, and would remain, the preeminent religious center in the region and a bastion of Catholic orthodoxy.[8]

With the mid-fourteenth century came renewed hardship and crisis for the city, as for all of Europe; but while Toulouse was racked by revolt and plague, it was spared the brunt of the Hundred Years' War. In fact, from that prolonged conflict the city emerged with additional privileges, for its position on the frontier of English-held Gascony prompted several royal concessions, some granted personally by Charles VII when he entered the city in 1420. In 1444 a parlement was established in the city and in 1459 the crown conferred nobility on the consulate. Henceforth, all capitouls and their descendants were noblemen.[9] The fourteenth century also saw the creation of an institution that would endow Toulouse with a reputation as a haven for the muse. In 1324, seven local poets founded the Consistoire du Gay Savoir, a sort of late-medieval literary academy that sponsored a poetry tournament each May. The contest, the Jeux Floraux, or Floral Games, was named for the gilded bouquets awarded to the winners. (The games continue to be celebrated to this day and claim title to being the world's oldest literary competition.) The Consistory of Gay Science was conceived as the institutional heir to the chivalric culture that had flourished in the Midi during the thirteenth century, though in fact the poetry of the Floral Games usually lacked the passion, sensuality, and drama of troubadour lyricism. What it did preserve and encourage, however, was the production and popularity of poetry in Occitan, Gascon, and Provençal, at least until the sixteenth

8. Wolff, *Histoire*, pp. 126–34; *HGL*, 6:217–588; Coppolani, p. 42.
9. Wolff, *Histoire*, pp. 183–222.

century, when the Francophonic vogue of the northern Renaissance overtook the games.[10]

At the end of the fourteenth century, Toulouse was still recovering from the Black Death of 1347, which had mortally stricken nearly a third of its inhabitants. The medieval city, prosperous, though not rich, shared only marginally in the revival of the European economy in the late Middle Ages and had little of the economic luster of the northern Italian cities or other international commercial, manufacturing, and banking centers, such as Augsburg, Antwerp, Lyons, and Troyes. The city was host to a large and cosmopolitan student body drawn to Toulouse because its university taught Roman law. The capitouls, still the political masters of the city, were increasingly rivaled by the growing ecclesiastical officialdom: the archbishop and his entourage, the canons of the Cathedral of Saint-Etienne and the Basilica of Saint-Sernin, the theologians of the university, the priors of the many religious orders, and the Office of the Inquisition. There was also a handful of royal officials in the city—the *viguier, juge mage,* and the officers of the *sénéchal.* The feudal aristocracy, however, was not a dominant element in the urban social hierarchy, largely because the Albigensian crusade had ruined the region's *noblesse de race.* A survey of the population in 1398 revealed that of the 2,246 heads of family whose professions could be identified, only 72 were living from their properties, and only a handful of these were noblemen. If the patriciate of medieval urban society was usually composed of the traditional aristocracy or great merchant families, Toulouse was a city whose upper crust was somewhat thin by comparison.[11]

Circa 1500: A New Elite

Toulouse's social composition would change dramatically in the second half of the fifteenth century. A convenient demarcation date is 1463, a catastrophic year for Toulouse, for it was then that a great fire raged for twelve days in its southern section, destroying many of its wooden buildings and leveling whole neighborhoods. What was a

10. Joseph Anglade, *Origines du Gai Savoir: Receuil de l'Académie des Jeux Floraux* (Toulouse, 1919); François de Gelis, *Histoire critique des Jeux Floraux* (Toulouse, 1912); *HGL*, 9:429–32; Camille Chabaneau, ed., *Origine et établissement de l'Académie des Jeux Floraux* (Toulouse, 1885).

11. Wolff, *Histoire*, p. 201.

disaster for most Toulousains proved a boon for others: speculators bought up whole lots of ruined properties, and foreigners, encouraged by a special royal edict, flocked to the city to take advantage of new economic openings.[12] Much of the subsequent rebuilding utilized bricks fashioned from the red clay that the Garonne had deposited along its alluvial plain centuries before. That distinctively colored brick, already used to construct many churches and convents in the Middle Ages, gave Toulouse the hue that still characterizes it today. Even then it was known as *la ville rose*. As the city went from wood to brick, other transformations were reshaping it socially. For many of those brick dwellings were the *hôtels*, or town houses, of wealthy merchants and royal magistrates, whose rise to prominence in the late fifteenth and early sixteenth centuries created a Renaissance city out of the medieval commune.

Toulouse's newfound wealth was based on the pastel plant, cultivated east and south of the city. Until the mid-sixteenth century and the discovery of indigo, pastel (also known as woad) was the only source of indelible blue dye. Thus, with the rising European textile trade, the city found itself with a local industry whose product was in demand throughout the continent. From a mere regional entrepôt, Toulouse became the pastel capital of the world in the space of a generation.[13] And from diverse and often foreign origins arose wealthy *pastelier* families, such as the Bernuys, Assézats, and Boyssons, whose splendidly tasteful Renaissance hôtels still grace the old city. The construction of their town houses represented the first large-scale building effort of a private and secular nature in the city's history and gave it a new face as well. In the richer quarters, at least, small houses and shops were destroyed to make room for these large, distinguished domiciles, several of which were constructed by Nicolas Bachelier, master mason and a student of Michelangelo.[14] The pasteliers amassed immense fortunes. One of the richest, Jean de

12. Wolff, *Histoire*, pp. 221–22, 246; Pierre Saliès, "Le grand incendie de Toulouse de 1463," *Mémoires de la Société Archéologique du Midi de la France* 30 (1964): 131–66, and 32 (1964): 70–85; M. Bastide, "Un exemple de reconstruction urbaine: Toulouse après l'incendie de 1463," *ADM* 80 (1968): 7–26.

13. Wolff, *Histoire*, pp. 223–36; Caster, *Le commerce du pastel.*

14. On the new hôtels see primarily two comprehensive works on Toulouse architecture: Jules Chalande, *Histoire des rues de Toulouse*, 3 vols. (Toulouse, 1920–29), and Robert Mesuret, *Evocation du vieux Toulouse* (Toulouse, 1960); as well as the thesis by Remi Papillaut, "Les hôtels particuliers au XVIe siècle à Toulouse," *Mémoire de fin d'études à l'école d'architecture de Paris-Belleville* (Paris, 1986). On Bachelier see, Henri

Bernuy, was personally responsible for a large share of the ransom paid to the emperor for the release of Francis I in 1525. The sons of the pasteliers, educated at the university, turned their interests to non-commercial endeavors: some became humanists, others were elected to the capitoulat, a few purchased offices in the parlement. A Bourse des Marchands was established in 1549 to represent the interests of the merchants, whose European-wide contacts brought new ideas and a measure of cosmopolitanism to the provincial capital.[15]

The era of pastel prosperity did not last. In 1560 the industry collapsed, the victim of a series of bad harvests that indebted merchants to the point of bankruptcy. The outbreak of the religious wars in 1562 forestalled a timely recovery, and by the time peace was restored to Toulouse, indigo had replaced pastel as the preferred source of blue dyestuff. Toulouse never regained its prominence as an international commercial center; it became again a regional entrepôt for grain and an administrative capital for the religious and political affairs of upper Languedoc. The end of the trade meant the end of an era for Toulouse: The Renaissance city existed no longer.[16]

But the passing of the pastel trade did not relegate the city to obscurity. A royal parlement, established in Toulouse in 1444, the second in the realm after the Parlement of Paris, ensured its position as a provincial capital down to the Revolution. The Parlement of Toulouse, officially the king's court of justice in Languedoc, was an administrative institution as well as a judicial body.[17] Having only a handful of magistrates at its founding, the parlement grew steadily over the years. In the mid-sixteenth century there already were over fifty councilors and three presidents. By the end of the seventeenth century the sovereign court's ranks had swollen to nearly 130 members, including 9 *présidents à mortier*, 8 *présidents aux enquêtes* and *requêtes*, 112 *conseillers*, 2 *avocats généraux*, and 1 *procureur général*.[18]

Graillot, *Nicolas Bachelier, imagier et maçon de Toulouse au XVIᵉ siècle* (Toulouse, 1914).

15. Guilliame Catel, *Mémoires de l'histoire du Langedoc* (Toulouse 1633), p. 199; F. Astre, *Essai sur l'histoire et les attributions de l'ancienne bourse de Toulouse* (Toulouse, 1934).

16. Wolff, *Histoire*, pp. 229–36; Caster, pp. 207–65.

17. Wolff, *Histoire*, pp. 236–40; F. Astre, "Introduction à l'histoire du Parlement de Toulouse," *MASIBL*, 7th ser., 4 (1872): 285–305; André Viala, *Le Parlement de Toulouse et l'administration laïque, 1420–1525 environ,* 2 vols. (Albi, 1953), vol. 1, passim.

18. Jean-Claude Paulhet, "Les parlementaires toulousains à la fin du XVIIᵉ siècle," *ADM* 76 (1964): 37–51.

Other royal courts of justice were established or expanded in the city during the sixteenth century; to the *sénéchal* were added twenty-four councilors in 1519, and a *présidial* was created in 1522 with twenty--two, spawning in the city a subpopulation of several hundred lawyers, barristers, clerks, scribes, and other minor functionaries who served the courts.[19]

The emergence of both the pasteliers and the royal magistrates created a new urban elite, a group of privileged families of wealth and power that quite rapidly transformed Toulouse in the early sixteenth century. This elite also gradually transformed the surrounding countryside, for the wealth of the city went largely into the land. Like their counterparts throughout Europe, the pasteliers ultimately preferred to invest their fortunes in the countryside, often to the detriment of their commercial enterprises. The *robins* (noblemen of the royal courts) too turned their financial interests toward the land, styling themselves great seigneurs, and many grew rich in the grain trade.[20] By the eighteenth century, as Robert Forster discovered, "wheat was a gentlemen's commodity in Toulouse."[21] Through the sixteenth and seventeenth centuries, these merchant and officer landowners were together responsible for the land consolidation at the expense of small-scale peasant proprietors, a movement that Emmanuel Le Roy Ladurie has documented for lower Languedoc.[22] In the process they dispossessed many traditional noble families of patrimonial estates and thus added the title of seigneur to their names. By the mid-seventeenth century, this urban conquest of the land was complete. A survey conducted by a royal officer in 1674 revealed that in the diocese of Toulouse, the officeholding class owned 42 percent of the seigneuries. Within a twelve-mile radius of Toulouse, city dwellers possessed nearly three-quarters of the domains, the majority owned by officeholders. One village alone was divided among sixteen absen-

---

19. Wolff, *Histoire*, pp. 234–36.
20. Janine Estèbe, "La bourgeoisie marchande et la terre à Toulouse au seizième siècle," *ADM* 76 (1964): 458–67; Michèle Thoumas-Schapira, "La bourgeoisie toulousaine à la fin du XVIIe siècle," *ADM* 67 (1955): 312–29.
21. Robert Forster, *The Nobility of Toulouse in the Eighteenth Century* (Baltimore, 1960), p. 23.
22. Emmanuel Le Roy Ladurie, *Les paysans de Languedoc*, 2 vols. (Paris, 1966), vol. 1, passim, and "Sur Montpellier et sa campagne aux XVIe et XVIIe siècles," *Annales: ESC* 12 (1957); Gaston Roupnel, *La ville et la campagne au XVIIe siècle: Etude sur les populations du pays dijonnais* (Paris, 1955); Viala, *Le Parlement de Toulouse*, 1:260.

tee landlords, all Toulousains, including a president, three councilors, and two lawyers of the court.[23]

But our interest is primarily in the role of this new elite in the city, not the countryside. On the most fundamental level, the arrival of the pasteliers and parlementaires rearranged the urban social hierarchy. Whereas previously its aristocratic ranks had been somewhat thin, the city was now graced with a substantial, wealthy, and powerful group of families. The pasteliers' first claim to prominence was, of course, based on their wealth, although many subsequently were ennobled through the capitoulat. Of the thirty-six pastelier families listed by Gilles Caster, their historian, about a third became capitouls in the late fifteenth and sixteenth centuries. On the other hand, only a few purchased offices in the parlement.[24] Recruitment into the parlement proceeded along several social lines: some magistrates were from the traditional nobility; others were from the ranks of the royal officialdom in Paris or from royal courts in the region, especially the sénéchal; a few were from merchant families.[25] Although there were notable cases of intermarriage between pastelier and parlementary families—the most significant for the city was the union of the wealthy Bernuys with a Robe dynasty, the Dufaurs—the two elite milieus remained somewhat separate.[26]

But they remained still more distant from the urban society they dominated, for both the pasteliers and parlementaires, who constituted a new Toulousain elite, were largely foreign to the city. This was especially true of the pasteliers, many of whom were Spanish merchants lured to Toulouse by the lucrative trade in dyestuff. The Boysson, Bernuy, and Beauvoir families were all from Burgos; the Lopez clan was from Saragossa; the Cheverrys were Basque in origin. It is likely too that some of these Spanish merchants were "New Christians," that is, converted Jews. Even those pasteliers of French extraction were rarely native to the city itself: the Lancefoc family was Bordelais, while the Assézats came from Rouergue. The very nature of the trade made it an international endeavor, putting pasteliers in touch with bankers, agents, and merchants in Spain, London, Lyons, Strasbourg, and Antwerp and bringing foreigners to the city to serve

23. Georges Frêche, *Toulouse et la région Midi-Pyrénées au siècle des lumières (vers 1670–1789)* (Paris, 1974), pp. 467, 478.
24. Caster, pp. 387–94.
25. Viala, 1:235–40.
26. Wolff, *Histoire*, p. 244.

the great pastel firms. One street was for a time virtually an Italian enclave.[27] The magistrates of the parlement, by contrast, were not ordinarily foreign. There were even a few native Toulousains in the first generation of the court's existence. But a majority came from outside the city. Most were from the Midi, several were recruited from the Parisian officialdom, and at least two were Italians.[28]

Once installed in the city, this new elite rapidly began to change the very shape of urban life. The most striking change was architectural. We have already seen that when the pasteliers and parlementaires constructed their town houses, they introduced a new style of building, indeed a new style of living, into the city. By the end of the sixteenth century at least fifty-four of these hôtels had been built, most in the southern part of the city, clustered on a few streets in the capitoulat of the Dalbade.[29] What was distinctive about the hôtel was that, unlike other private domiciles, it insulated its inhabitants from the street with a large courtyard surrounded by a high wall pierced by an imposing, usually ornate gate. Most such town houses were quite large; those built by the Assézat and Bagis families displaced five houses each. With their several stories, their towers and inner courtyards—the Hôtel Assézat had two such courts—the hôtels constituted a world unto themselves amid the crowded, often rude city. And the face they presented to the city spoke of the wealth and taste of their proprietors. The Italian influence was evident in the facades, with classical proportions and antique figurines.[30] By the mid-sixteenth century, the classical architectural style was established as a quasi-official standard for the city, and the capitouls took to citing the commentaries of Vitruvius and Alberti as guides to new urban construction.[31] But the Spanish influence was also apparent, most notably in the hôtel of Jean de Bernuy, a reminder of his Iberian origins and a standing affront to many humanists, such as Jean de Boysson, who criticized the building for deviating from the principles of Alberti.[32]

27. Caster, pp. 84–85; Coppolani, p. 97.
28. Viala, 1:232–40; L. Delaruelle, "Un président au Parlement de Toulouse, Jacques Minut (+ 1536)," *ADM* 35 (1923): 137–53.
29. Coppolani, p. 85; Chalande, *Histoire des rues de Toulouse*, 1:76–80, 431–35.
30. Jules de Lahondès, *Les monuments de Toulouse* (Toulouse, 1920), p. 407 and passim; Wolff, pp. 255–64.
31. AMT, BB 274, "Annales manuscrits de la ville," 1549–50, p. 118.
32. Clémence-Paul Dubrat, "L'influence espagnole sur le décor des hôtels toulousains de la renaissance," *ADM* 66 (1954): 129–42.

More important than such architectural monuments was the social transformation this new elite effected in the city. In short, by the mid-sixteenth century, and increasingly so in the next century, whole sections of Toulouse evolved from largely mixed neighborhoods of craftsmen, tradesmen, and a few notables to more homogeneous quarters in which an elite of noblemen, officers, lawmen, and wealthy merchants predominated. Part of the story can be told in numbers. In the sixteenth and seventeenth centuries, the number of houses in the city declined steadily, as smaller dwellings were destroyed to make room for the hôtels and large homes of the privileged. In 1478 there were 4,703 urban properties; in 1571, 4,025; in 1633, 4,109; and in 1678, 3,516. In the capitoulat of the Dalbade, a favorite quarter of officers and merchants, the decline was even more precipitous, from 643 in 1478, to 409 in 1633.[33] Some of this decline can be explained by the erection of religious edifices; but for the most part it was private construction, a sort of early modern "gentrification," which was responsible for the transformation of whole sections of the city into residential havens for the new elite.

A closer look at the evolution of property holding in the capitoulat of the Dalbade from the late fifteenth century to the late seventeenth illustrates this process in detail. Situated in the southern half of the city on the banks of the Garonne, the Dalbade became in the sixteenth century a community of robins and lawmen. In the fifteenth century its social composition was quite different. For example, the Rue Saint-Remesy, located in the heart of the district, was, in the late fifteenth century, a street inhabited almost entirely by butchers—*mazelliers* in Occitan—along with, apparently, several prostitutes and a handful of notables. By the mid-sixteenth century the Robe takeover of the street was nearly complete, and indeed, most of the houses still lining Rue Saint-Remesy date from that period.[34]

The entire capitoulat followed this trend, though not everywhere so dramatically. In the early modern period, Toulouse's urban settlement was arranged in islands of buildings called *moulons,* clusters of anywhere from five to twenty houses. A moulon was thus a true neighborhood, for its constituent edifices formed a block of houses, some facing each other, others side by side. The urban land survey, or cadastre, carried out periodically for tax purposes, noted the names

33. Coppolani, pp. 85–86.
34. Chalande, 1:57–61.

and occupations or titles of proprietors by moulon. Thanks to a series
of excellent cadastres for 1478, 1555, 1571, and 1678 we can follow
rather closely the evolution of property holding in Toulouse.[35] First it
should be noted that as a source the cadastre has both its advantages
and disadvantages. On the one hand, it affords a close look at patterns
of property holding moulon by moulon and thus can yield a portrait of
actual neighborhoods. Without such a source, we might have to rely
on parish records, which would merely present us with a list of
names—those whose births, marriages, and deaths were recorded by
the parish clergy—without any sense of whether those listed lived
near one another or even in the same parish. The Dalbade, for example, included in its jurisdiction the island of Tounis, a large parcel of
land in the Garonne almost exclusively inhabited by boatmen, fishermen, artisans, and laborers. Formally a part of the Dalbade, this
lower-class neighborhood, both socially and geographically separated
from mainland residents, might be classed as simply belonging to the
extended community of the capitoulat—if, that is, we were forced to
view the capitoulat as an undifferentiated whole. The cadastre, drawn
up as it was by moulons, saves us from this mistaken conclusion. The
obvious disadvantage of the cadastre is that it lists property holders
only, not residents. It can be assumed that in many if not most cases
the proprietor and resident were one and the same—though the
assumption must remain open to some doubt, since rental properties
were widespread in the early modern city. But despite this limitation,
the four cadastres can at least demonstrate the evolution of property
holding across two hundred years, from 1478 to 1678, and thus suggest
the changing character of the city's social composition by
neighborhood.

This is what we can observe in maps 1–4. The popular character of
the Dalbade in the late fifteenth century is evident from the first map,
but by 1550 the capitoulat had already changed dramatically. Indeed,
one of the striking aspects of the four cadastres is how rapidly the
social composition of the Dalbade was transformed, a finding in keeping, however, with the known rapid influx of magistrates and lawmen in the early sixteenth century.[36] The capitoulat continued to

35. The records from these cadastres are to be found in AMT, CC 14, 21, 48, 76, 77.
36. For neighborhood segregation by occupation in other French cities, see Philip
Benedict, *Rouen during the Wars of Religion* (Cambridge, 1981), pp. 26–31; Jean-Pierre
Bardet, *Rouen aux XVIIe et XVIIIe siècles* (Paris, 1983), pp. 238–41; Richard Gascon, *Grand
commerce et vie urbaine au XVIe siècles: Lyon et ses marchands* (Paris, 1971), pp. 435–50. On

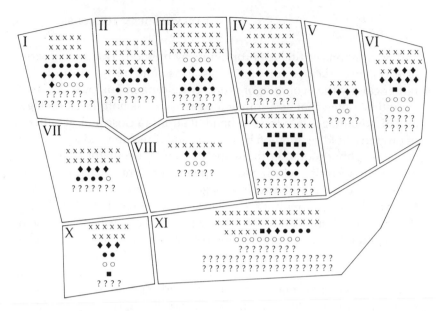

MAP 1. Capitoulat of the Dalbade: Moulons 1–11, 1478

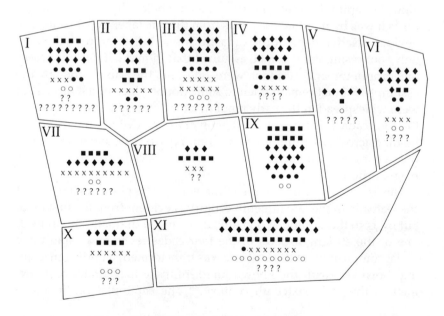

MAP 2. Capitoulat of the Dalbade: Moulons 1–11, 1555

■ *noble:* capitoul or former capitoul, "noble," seigneur, baron, coucilor in the parlement or sénéchal, procureur du roy, trésorier de France

◆ *law officer or lawman:* procureur, licencier, bachellier, avocat, practicien, greffier, huissier, notaire, notaire royal, receveur

● *merchant:* marchand, banquier, "bourgeois"

x *artisan:* artisan (by trade), hoste, travailleur

○ *other:* church or municipal property, sergeants, priests, students

? *unknown:* not given, illegible, "heirs of"

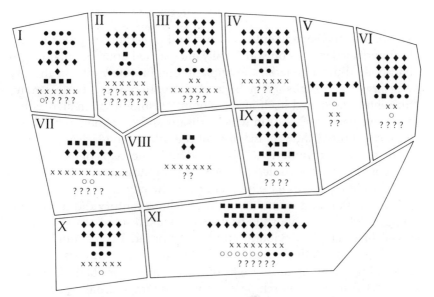

MAP 3. Capitoulat of the Dalbade: Moulons 1–11, 1571

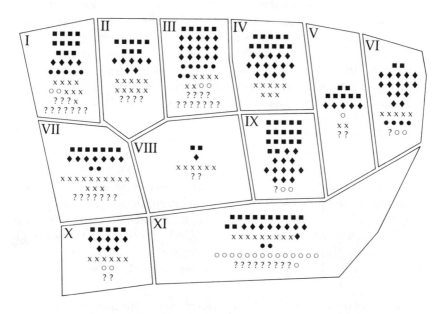

MAP 4. Capitoulat of the Dalbade: Moulons 1–11, 1678

evolve into the seventeenth century, and in certain moulons the officer and legal classes only gradually encroached upon popular neighborhoods. But in general, the implantation of a new elite in the city was largely accomplished by the mid-sixteenth century. Furthermore, this elite established itself in the city in a fashion that created rather exclusive neighborhoods in which artisans and craftsmen, who otherwise constituted the vast majority of the urban populace as a whole, were in a distinct minority. This is evident in the maps of the Dalbade and could be demonstrated as well for the capitoulats of Saint-Etienne and La Pierre, the other elite sections of the city.

The creation of a new elite in the sixteenth century did more than gentrify whole neighborhoods; it also provoked some concern for the social hierarchy, its stability and proper order. Even though social mobility was relatively high—and obvious to contemporaries—the prevailing image of society was of a fixed and immutable hierarchy embedded in an overarching cosmology divinely ordained. How to save the appearance of such a timeless hierarchy was thus a widespread concern, and nowhere was this concern more evident than in the sumptuary laws issued by the parlement in the course of the sixteenth century. Such laws governing consumption, especially of luxuries, and the wearing of silks and other finery were not peculiar to Toulouse; indeed, a concern was widespread in France for what was perceived to be a rampant disregard for the sartorial privileges of the elite, a disregard that was, of course, symptomatic of the more fundamental social and economic changes of the times. But the tendency toward conspicuous consumption and extravagance was particularly great in a metropolis such as Toulouse, where newfound wealth promoted previously modest families into the ranks of the well-to-do. In 1550 the parlement issued an edict that forbade nonnobles from wearing clothing of silk.[37] Was this edict prejudicial to the pasteliers? Not likely, for by then most pastel families of note had made their way into the capitoulat and were thus ennobled. Another edict was issued in the 1570s, this one decrying "the confusion of ranks in this disordered society whose diverse classes indiscriminately wear robes of

_____

the growth of the administrative class in sixteenth-century Montpellier, see Frederick M. Irvine, "From Renaissance City to Ancien-Régime Capital: Montpellier, ca. 1500–ca. 1600," in Philip Benedict, ed., *Cities and Social Change in Early Modern France* (London, 1989).

37. AMT, BB 274, p. 128; Germaine de Lafaille, *Annales de la Ville de Toulouse depuis la reunion du comté à la couronne*, 2 vols. (Toulouse, 1687), 1:156.

silk . . . and coats of different colors."[38] Urban society remained "disordered" despite such prohibitions that are in fact evidence of the desire of the ennobled—parlementaires, capitouls, and wealthy merchants posing as great seigneurs—to ensure their new status and the privileges it entailed.

Ideally, and on a somewhat more elevated plane, the distinctiveness of new sixteenth-century elites was evident also in their daily behavior and demeanor. It is always difficult to assess change in people's comportment in the past, especially when what was prescribed was something as elusive as refinement and courtesy, or heightened piety and morality. But that new and more rigorous standards for comportment were not only prescribed by moralists and churchmen but acknowledged by a large segment of the elite in the sixteenth century cannot be doubted. Here the textbook distinctions blur between such contradictory movements as the Renaissance and the Counter-Reformation, for both were imbued with a sense of the ideal and perfect, not only in the realm of art or spirituality, but also in the more mundane dimension of human behavior and social interaction. Both promoted what Norbert Elias has called "the civilizing process."[39]

Whether or not new elites of sixteenth-century Toulouse were any more "civilized" than previous generations of notables must remain an open question. Certainly they were no less violent, as their behavior in the religious wars amply demonstrates. But they were instilled with an image of themselves as a true elite, not simply more wealthy or powerful than the commonfolk, but morally and spiritually superior. This was certainly the case with the officials (especially the magistrates of the parlement), who were held up as paradigms of restraint, virtue, and wisdom, men worthy of comparison with Hebrew judges and Roman senators. Such was the portrait sketched by La Roche-Flavin, an officer in the Toulouse court in the latter sixteenth century. His *Treize livres sur les parlements de France*, something of an *Il Cortegiano* for robins, was one of several handbooks for the *parfait magistrat*, collections of prescriptions for the model official of the day.[40] Magis-

---

38. M. E. Cibiel, "Les arrêts somptuaires du Parlement de Toulouse," *MASIBL*, 7th ser., 2 (1878): 248–66. On sumptuary laws in general see also Henri Baudrillart, *Histoire du luxe*, 3 vols. (Paris, 1880), 3:441–42.

39. Norbert Elias, *The Civilizing Process*, trans. E. Jephcott (New York, 1978).

40. La Roche-Flavin, *Treize livres sur les parlements de France* (Toulouse, 1621); Colin Kaiser, "Les cours souveraines au XVIe siècle: Morale et contre-réforme," *Annales: ESC* 37 (1982): 15–31.

trates were to refrain from talking of subjects "light, lowly, or ridiculous," even in private. They were to refrain from attending public dances, from gambling or card playing. Hunting, a proper pastime for "kings, princes, and great lords," was deemed inappropriate for the grave and decorous magistrates. They should avoid "indiscreet and disrespectful people," especially the kind who gathered at outdoor theaters and comedies. They were to be modest and correct in their dress and person, never adorning themselves with jewels or ornaments, masques or makeup, perfume, or even wigs. Nor were they to allow themselves exaggerated or crude gestures, such as immoderate laughter, deep sighs, pronounced groans, or "involuntary noises." And, among other bits of advice, La Roche-Flavin warned against eating "onions, leeks, or other bad smelling and strong things."[41]

The capitouls' description of themselves was similarly elevated. The pages of the "Annales de la ville" (a yearly account written by the outgoing capitouls) in the mid-sixteenth century are filled with allusions to Greek and Roman legislators, with references to themselves as "magistrates and moderators of the Republic," whose every action was guided by the wisdom of Plato, Solon, and the like.[42] Increasingly in the sixteenth century, the standards for elite behavior were cast also in pious terms, particularly as religious reform and the combat against heresy became the order of the day.[43] Both the magistrates of the parlement and the capitouls made a point of attending daily mass as a group, and many individual officials founded or patronized religious orders and lay confraternities. It was frequently the case in the sixteenth and seventeenth centuries that such lay officials distinguished themselves by their orthodox devotion, surpassing even the clergy as spiritual leaders of the laity, especially when it came to Christian charity. But this is to get ahead of our story, for one of the themes pursued in the following chapters is the evolution of expressions of elite self-consciousness: how, from the early sixteenth to the late eighteenth century, religious and cultural forms served as a vehicle for Toulouse's elites to identify and assert themselves as a class of people separate from, and superior to, the general urban populace. Here I must emphasize, first, that this process was set in motion in the early

41. La Roche-Flavin, *Treize livres sur les parlements*, pp. 566, 592–98, 648–709.
42. AMT, BB 275, p. 420.
43. M. V. Fons, "Coûtumes religieuses de l'Hôtel de Ville de Toulouse," *Mémoires de la Société Archéologique du Midi de la France* 11 (1874): 82–107.

sixteenth century, when a new elite appeared on the scene, thus transforming the city in fundamental ways, and second, an important qualification, that the establishment of the new elite did not preclude patterns of interaction between upperclass Toulousains and the urban populace. Quite the contrary.

Urban Society

The large officialdom of Toulouse dominated the city throughout the early modern period, especially after the collapse of the pastel industry diminished the merchant community. This is one reason the urban social order remained essentially stable throughout the Old Regime, at least after the mid-sixteenth century. This feature, true of many cities, might strike the modern observer as paradoxical. We are accustomed to viewing the city as a generator of change, a center of revolutionary developments, whereas we see the countryside as sunk in tradition and presumably resistent to the changes thrust upon it by urban modernity. In the Old Regime this pattern was in fact often reversed. It was in the countryside where, socially and economically at least, revolutionary changes were taking place: it was there that population growth was most pronounced, that landholding patterns were rapidly changing, that industrialization was first emerging. By contrast, the Old Regime city slumbered in a sort of social and economic late Middle Ages. Despite the movement and even turmoil that superficially characterized early modern urban life, there it was a matter of "plus ça change, plus c'est la même chose."

Demographically the city experienced its ups and downs, but its overall population remained fairly stable over the course of the Old Regime. Before the Black Death of 1347, it numbered between 35,000 and 40,000 inhabitants. The plague reduced that figure by about a third, but by the end of the fifteenth century it had more than regained its former population and reached beyond 50,000. A time of troubles began in the mid-sixteenth century—religious warfare, economic decline, renewed outbreaks of the plague—and the population sank to about 40,000. There it remained until the eighteenth century, when it regained its former level, reaching by some estimations 58,000 on the eve of the Revolution. Even then, while the overall demographic growth of France was in the range of 30 percent between 1715 and 1789, and that of the province about the same,

Toulouse grew by a mere 16 percent.[44] Fourth among French cities in the sixteenth century, Toulouse still had the appearance of a large metropolis, at least by the standards of the time. In the early seventeenth century both a local historian and a foreign visitor judged it the second in the realm.[45] But in the last century of the Old Regime Toulouse's demographic growth lagged behind that of France's manufacturing centers and port cities. By the mid-eighteenth century the provincial capital ranked only ninth among the cities of the realm.

Still, the bustling metropolis could yet evoke exaggerated estimates of its size: just before the Revolution several observers placed the population at 80,000.[46] These inflated assessments probably reflected the thousands of transients and strangers always found in a regional capital such as Toulouse. The city was regularly swollen with day laborers and other temporary immigrants, and legions of the rural destitute seeking sustenance would periodically choke its streets. During the religious wars, the city served as a haven for Catholic refugees from Protestant strongholds, and in times of plague it was transformed into a hospice for the sick and dying seeking cures and comfort, both medical and spiritual. The city also attracted a steady stream of routine visitors: petitioners to the several royal courts; traders, peddlers, and traveling journeymen drawn to the economic metropole; adolescent villagers looking for employment; itinerant students, pilgrims, preachers, and healers seeking opportunities and adventures of other sorts. On occasion a nobleman and his unruly entourage would also storm into town, cluttering the streets with their horses, sometimes exchanging blows with the locals, and generally making a nuisance of themselves. Formal entries of various officials and dignitaries were frequent, from the new archbishop or First President to foreign princes or ecclesiastics who, with their exotic retinues and strange dress, were themselves objects of great curiosity. Finally, at least once during each reign the royal court entered

44. On Toulouse's population, see Wolff, *Les estimes toulousaines des XIVe et XVe siècle* (Toulouse, 1956); Coppolani, pp. 56–59, 97–104; Wolff, *Histoire*, pp. 335–42; E. Roux, "La population de Toulouse de 1600 à 1650" (Mémoire maîtrise, Université de Toulouse, 1969–70); Bernard Bonnery, "L'évolution démographique toulousaine de 1650–1700" (Mémoire maîtrise, Université de Toulouse, 1967).

45. The local historian was Guilliaume Catel, *Mémoires de l'histoire du Languedoc*, p. 114. The visitor was a German traveler, Abraham Golnitiz; see Pierre de Gorsse, "Toulouse au XVIIe siècle vue par un érudit dantzikois," *L'Auta*, April 1941, p. 68.

46. For examples of such inflated estimates, see ADH-G, C 287; *Affiches et annonces de Toulouse pour l'année 1782*, p. 90.

the city in an elaborate and costly procession and momentarily transformed the provincial capital into a theater of homage.

A truly complete portrait of urban life would, of course, include all
of these itinerant and transient social elements and thus would appear as crowded and varied as a vast and bewildering mosaic. Leaving aside most of these foreigners, marginals, and transients, however, we need to concentrate for a moment on two subgroups in the
early modern city. These are students and the poor. For these very
different social elements, though marginal and usually foreign to the
city, often played an important role in its public life. Moreover, their
shifting presence during the early modern period contrasts sharply
with the general depiction of Toulouse's relatively changeless social
order.

The University of Toulouse attracted students from throughout
western Europe, especially after its reform in 1470 and its subsequent
rise to prominence as one of the continent's centers for the study of
Roman law. Indeed, a large and diverse community of young scholars
and their illustrious professors were essential ingredients in the
emergence of a Renaissance culture in the early sixteenth century. It is
difficult to determine how many students then inhabited Toulouse, if
only because these young men were usually itinerant scholars on the
European university circuit. One oft-cited estimate places the community at 10,000, others at 4,000.[47] Whatever their precise number, they
loomed large on the urban scene. Students were ubiquitous participants in the city's festive life and played a crucial role in the religious
wars, often as leading combatants in the bloody events. They were
among the most pious of the city's inhabitants, making up nearly half
of the members of the Company of Blue Penitents, and some of the
most criminal as well, committing much of the violence and theft that
routinely marked urban life. But after the sixteenth century the university entered a period of decline, and its student ranks thinned considerably. Competition from new French and Spanish universities and
collèges robbed it of matriculants, and with the Counter-Reformation's
dominance in the city, Toulouse proved less hospitable to an often
boisterous, somewhat cosmopolitan student community. Although
the university revived somewhat in the eighteenth century, its student
body never attained its former size: on the eve of the Revolution there
were not more than a thousand students in the city. Their diminished

47. On the University of Toulouse, see below, Chapter 2.

presence is one feature that distinguishes seventeenth- and eighteenth-century Toulouse from the city in the preceding era.

As for the poor, it is tempting to see them as merely a permanent feature of the urban landscape. The poor, after all, "are always with us" and indeed their presence in great numbers was a persistent blight on the early modern city. In times of famine and epidemic their ranks were especially swollen by hordes of indigent migrants from the countryside. The pages of the eleven volumes of the city "Annales" give numerous, sometimes eloquent, testimony to the crushing presence of the poor in Toulouse.[48] Condemnations of the "great multitudes of the Poor," or, less kindly, of "vagabonds and people without repute" (gens sans adveu), were a constant refrain. In 1555 more than 1,600 homeless poor were confined in the city hospitals.[49] In 1604 the capitouls noted that while there were ordinarily 5,000 to 6,000 poor within the city limits, their numbers had recently grown to nearly 14,000.[50] Ten years later there were 2,000 registered indigents.[51] And during the plague year of 1631 a list of the poor drawn up by the capitouls was 5,000 names long.[52] "Their cries interrupt the sleep of the night," noted one source, referring to the numerous homeless indigents who huddled in the streets and plazas.[53] In 1647 the crowds of beggars and vagabonds were described as creeping vermin infesting homes and churches.[54] During the great subsistence crises that struck the entire realm in the last years of Louis XIV's reign, Toulouse was overwhelmed by an army of the starving and desperate, whose numbers were so great that the excess from the general hospital had to be confined in the city mills.[55] In 1782 the "Annales" noted that "the city was overflowing with people from the countryside."[56] A few years later the hospital was again filled to capacity, with 2,600 indigents and 1,360 foundlings.[57]

48. AMT, BB 274–84.
49. AMT, BB 274, p. 186.
50. AMT, BB 276, p. 94.
51. AMT, BB 277, p. 335.
52. AMT, BB 278, p. 325.
53. Barnabé Farmien de Rozoi, Annales de la ville de Toulouse, 4 vols. (Paris, 1771–76), 4:349.
54. "L'aumône générale. Les désordres que causent les pauvres dans Tholose," reprinted by Abbé Lestrade as "L'aumône générale à Toulouse au dix-septième siècle," in Mélanges Léonce Coutre: Etudes d'histoire meridionale (Toulouse, 1902), pp. 282–83.
55. AMT, BB 282, pp. 192–93.
56. AMT, BB 284, p. 278.
57. M. F. Buchalet, L'assistance publique à Toulouse au dix-huitième siècle (Toulouse, 1904), p. 52.

One might make an argument for a permanent "culture of poverty" in the Old Regime, but in fact there were periods when the problem of indigency pressed even harder on the city than in others. We should note two such periods. Recent local studies of the late fifteenth and early sixteenth centuries suggest that it was then that the rootless, itinerant poor attained unprecedented proportions. Several social and economic changes conspired to throw people into the ranks of the impoverished: demographic increase and the price revolution, land consolidation and parcelization, enclosures and other aspects of agrarian commercialization. For Languedoc, Le Roy Ladurie has documented some of these trends and their contribution to social immiseration in the countryside. But the same result followed from similar causes in other Western European lands on the eve of the Reformation. In short, whatever the reasons, indigency in the countryside, and thus the migratory pressures of the poor on urban centers, were particularly severe at the end of the Middle Ages.[58] It will be important to recall this rise in social misery when we examine the municipality's attempts to reform the instruments of poor relief during the sixteenth century.

While the rural poor continued to flock to Toulouse throughout the early modern period, it was in the eighteenth century that their presence reached crushing proportions. The dimensions and causes of this later wave of indigency are discussed in Chapter 9. For now it is important to note one of the essential traits of urban social life in the Age of Enlightenment—the flood tide of indigent immigrants. As in earlier periods, changes in the countryside caused by the spread of commercial agriculture fostered this migratory wave. But another, unprecedented factor aggravated it. This was the end of the Malthusian cycle that heretofore had limited population through what economists call demographic wastage—death. In the eighteenth century, however, with a better food supply and more efficient provisioning, the cycle was broken. Peasants continued to suffer hard times, but they did not die in vast numbers; rather, many took up a life of vagrancy. And many made their way to the big city. One researcher has calculated that Toulouse received 37,000 immigrants, most of

58. Le Roy Ladurie, *Les paysans de Languedoc*, pp. 263–79. For other regions and countries, see Guy Bois, *Crise du féodalisme* (Paris, 1976), pp. 106–11; Keith Wrightson and David Levine, *Poverty and Piety in an English Village: Terling, 1525–1700* (New York, 1979); B. Geremek, "La populazione marginale tra il medioe e l'erà moderna," *Studi Storici* (1968): 623–40; Peter Blickle, *The Revolution of 1525*, trans. T. Brady and E. Midelfort (Baltimore, 1981), p. 77 and passim; C. Lis and H. Soly, *Poverty and Capitalism in Pre-Industrial Europe* (Atlantic Highlands, N.J., 1979), chap. 4.

them indigents, during the century between 1695 and the Revolution.[59] This invasion of the rural poor in the eighteenth century contributed to the instability and social division that characterized public life in the decades before the Revolution.

Whether the poor "belonged" to urban society seems to have been a genuine question. In a sense they did, insofar as a delegation of municipal poor—suitably costumed and well-behaved—was often included in general processions, and thus acknowledged as having a place in the urban hierarchy. But in great numbers, as the foreign, "shameless" indigents who increasingly threatened the social peace, they were viewed as expendable outsiders, suitable only for banishment or confinement. In the eighteenth century, the "Annales" begin to distinguish two classes of city dwellers—the *habitants* and the *bas peuple*, the latter marked by their poverty and a propensity toward disorder and revolt.[60] The distinction is a valid one for the Old Regime as a whole, in fact just as valid as other descriptions of the early modern social hierarchy, such as a society of orders or classes. In this sense, the poor served a function in establishing a social and psychological boundary for the division of urban society into two groups: people of property—a category that could include everyone from powerful magistrates to humble craftsmen—and the poor. This was, to be sure, a shifting boundary, for in economic hard times many of those same craftsmen, having fallen into the ranks of the indigent, would find themselves beyond the social pale. The distinction was especially relevant in times of social tensions and revolt, when people of property and position found themselves confronted by a usually impoverished and often hungry crowd.

But if these "habitants," like the "bourgeois" of old, could psychologically join ranks in the face of a social threat from below, in most times they were quite alert to the social distinctions that divided them. Like other early modern cities, Toulouse was arranged in a complicated and overlapping social hierarchy, the general outlines of which remained fairly constant throughout the period. At the apex of

---

59. Coppolani, p. 103. On the influx of poor migrants from the countryside in the eighteenth century, see Emile Bonnet and Bernard Mariotto, "Les passagers et les étrangers à Toulouse au XVIIIe siècle" (Mémoire maîtrise, Université de Toulouse-Mirail, 1974); and Jean Rives, "L'evolution démographique de Toulouse au XVIIIe siècle," *Bulletin d'Histoire Economique et Sociale de la Révolution Française*, 1968, pp. 85–146.

60. AMT, BB 283, p. 523.

urban society was the parlement, with its numerous councilors and several presidents. The parlementaires were rivaled locally in prestige and power on one side by the archbishop and other members of the high clergy, including the canons of the chapters of the Cathedral of Saint-Etienne and the Basilica of Saint-Sernin, and on another by the capitouls. Below these high officials was another layer of the officialdom: the councilors of the sénéchal, présidial, and other royal courts. Next in descending order was the university, with its privileged professors and theologians, and then the leading religious orders, such as the Dominicans, the Franciscans, the Augustinians, and the Jesuits. The lower clergy, divided between regulars and seculars, were also an important element in the city, although the curates and monks were themselves overawed by the ecclesiastical hierarchs, veritable church potentates who marked the city with their wealth and pomp. There followed one of the most numerous groups in the city: the lawyers, barristers, and *praticiens*—the lawmen who pullulated in the provincial legal center—most of whom were attached to a court. The roll for the *capitation* (the new head tax) in 1695 lists 228 lawyers, 264 barristers, and 132 praticiens.[61] Even greater in number were the variety of minor officers and functionaries, both lay and ecclesiastic. Some of these men were attached to the Hôtel de Ville, others to the royal courts or to various ecclesiastical institutions. They were the *huissiers, greffiers, commis, secrétaires, commissaires, contrôleurs,* and the like, to whom could be appended such civil servants as the soldiers of the city's militia. Apart from this world of governmental employees and lawmen, and occupying an ambiguous position in the social hierarchy, was the mercantile community, whose members ranged from wealthy bankers and big merchants to petty tradesmen and peddlers. As noted earlier, after the collapse of the pastel trade in the mid-sixteenth century, merchants never again attained the prominence and number they had once enjoyed, except perhaps during the eighteenth century, when Toulouse's commercial life revived slightly. At the end of the seventeenth century the intendant Basville despaired that "there is hardly any commerce [in Toulouse], for the talents of its inhabitants are not suited to it." And he offered the standard explanation for the city's economic languor: "the religious convents occupy half the city, the privileges of the capitoulat, which confer nobility,

61. Robert Senot, "Analyse du rolle de la capitation de Toulouse (1695)" (Mémoire maîtrise, Université de Toulouse-Mirail, n.d.), pp. 160–62.

inhibit the growth of commerce, as is the case with the parlement. All of the children of the large merchants prefer to become noblemen or procure an office rather than continue in the businesses of their fathers."[62]

By far the most numerous element in urban society was the *artisanat*, the members of Toulouse's more than sixty craft corporations, who dominated the city's working class. Over 40 percent of the occupations listed on the capitation roll were those of craftsmen. The largest contingent devoted itself to the fabrication of apparel, to food supply, and to transport, and it catered mostly to the consumption needs of parlementary households, religious orders, students, and travelers—that is, people who had to be fed and clothed above all.[63] This was not the laboring population one finds in Pierre Deyon's Amiens or Pierre Goubert's Beauvais, with their armies of textile workers, for very few were industrial workers manufacturing goods for export beyond Toulouse.[64] Like the officialdom, the craft community was traditional in structure and customs, with nearly all of its trades organized in corporations and confraternities, each with its privileges and monopolies, each with its internal hierarchy of masters, *bailles*, and journeymen, each with its saint days, processions, and masses. To be sure, there were many simple workers—*travailleurs, ouvriers*, and the like— outside the corporate community who in fact constituted an unprivileged segment of the laboring class. But even those tradesmen not organized into guilds, such as fishermen, roof workers, and porters, were often grouped in religious confraternities and thereby endowed with a special identity.

The atmosphere of Toulouse was thus conservative, aristocratic, enclosed, and not a little pretentious, with social relations limited by the strictures of privilege and corporate jealousy, and affirmed in the endless ceremonies that marked public life. The inhabitants of the city lived in the shadow of imposing institutions—the parlement, the Hôtel de Ville, the great religious convents, the university, the archbishop's palace—and the haughty men who ran them. And these were the same sorts of men who would run the city until the Revolution. What were the relations between those who ruled the city and

---

62. Lamoignon de Basville, "Mémoire de Languedoc" (1697), pp. 176–77; BN, Fonds Français, 11398.

63. Senot, "Analyse du rolle de la capitation," p. 56.

64. Pierre Deyon, *Amiens, capitale provinçale* (Paris, 1967); Pierre Goubert, *Beauvais et les beauvaisis de 1600 à 1730* (Paris, 1960).

those who merely lived and worked in it—between, that is, elites and ordinary people? One might assume, given the wealthy and powerful who came to dominate the city in the early sixteenth century, that such social relations were characterized by haughtiness and distance on the part of the elite and a combination of fear, loathing, envy, and obsequious respect on the part of their inferiors. Surely the rich and poor, the privileged and powerless, moved in two separate worlds. After all, notions of rank and privilege permeated every aspect of life in the Old Regime, from where one sat in church or marched in processions to considerations of marriage and tax assessments. But what may seem paradoxical from a modern perspective is how a punctilious concern for distinctions of rank did not imply an understanding of the social order that excluded ordinary people. Privilege adhered to many, not only to the elite. Master artisans, for example, knew themselves to be socially inferior to the royal magistracy and were reminded of their low status in myriad ways, yet they maintained their own corporate privileges and were normally included in public processions and other civic ceremonies along with members of the ruling elite. In processions of a religious sort, corporations of artisans frequently carried the city's many holy relics. That was a burden, to be sure, especially since these objects of veneration were housed in heavy reliquaries of gold and silver, but it was an honor as well.[65] Artisans were, in short, members of Toulouse's official community, worthy of handling the city's sacred treasure.

In addition, no sort of snobbery or elitism could disguise the economic ties that bound craftsmen to their social superiors, for elites relied on the labor and services of the common people—the artisans and craftsmen who built their houses, supplied their households, and fabricated their clothing. Despite the pronounced social differences that separated, for example, a magistrate from a tailor, ties could develop between them which, if not as intimate as the relationship between Molière's Monsieur Jourdain and his tailor, at least momentarily pierced the barrier of class. Elites needed artisans and tradesmen, although their need may have been mixed with a measure of fear and disdain. An anonymous mid-sixteenth-century poet of Toulouse, a woman who surveys the city's craftsmen in a tone both ironic and condescending, conveys the attitude in her verses. Butchers never sell their meats for much, she notes; they almost give them

65. See, for example, AMT, BB 278, p. 385.

away. Haberdashers are courteous and helpful, never coarse. Coal dealers, millers, mule drivers and carters, boatmen, fishermen, and innkeepers—all deserve our praise. "And their faith never wavers / They are quite loyal in this City."

> Item les gentils Bolengiers,
> Qui font leurs pains petiz et legiers,
> Affin ne nous facent dangiers,
> Comme chose poisante et utille:
> Sont fort loyals en ceste Ville.
>
> Item Cousturiers, Chaussetiers,
> Barbiers, Orfevres, Pelletiers,
> Et brief, de trestous les mestiers,
> Qui sont (je crois) plus de cent mille:
> Sont fort loyals en ceste Ville.[66]

Whether artisans were indeed "quite loyal" is somewhat beside the point. Perhaps the question should be turned around: how loyal were elites to their city? For it was only elites who really had a choice in the matter: they could choose to identify with the city and its populace or not; they could choose to participate in enterprises relating to the reform and management of urban society or not. Whether and how they did—and the cultural forms their social engagement could take—is largely the theme of what follows. For now, the issue can be illustrated by the changing nature of elite behavior in the face of the greatest perennial danger facing the early modern city—the plague.

To be sure, at the first sign of epidemic disease those who could usually sought safety beyond the city walls. In 1561, the capitouls noted with relief: "the aforesaid contagious disease only attacks poor people. . . . let God in his mercy be satisfied with that. . . . The rich protect themselves against it."[67] The protection the rich found was in flight, for nearly all possessed country properties, which served as life-saving refuges in times of epidemic; it was the well-to-do who could heed the advice of the sixteenth-century Toulousain physician Oger Ferrier: "Three words against the plague are more useful than craft: Flee quickly, go far, and don't hurry back."[68] The fate of the rest

66. J. B. Noulet, "De la prétendue Pléiade toulousaine," *MASIBL*, 4th ser., 3 (1853): 312–13.

67. Cited by Fernand Braudel, *Capitalism and Material Life, 1400–1800*, trans. M. Kochan (New York, 1975), p. 49.

68. T. Porte, "Esprit social et charité: Le tiers-ordre dominicain à Toulouse au XVIIe siècle," *ADM* 70 (1958): 163.

of the populace in time of plague was, of course, quite different. For the most part their lot was to remain trapped in the infected city, there to be subjected to the desperate, often cruel policing measures administered by the authorities and the makeshift, equally desperate treatments applied by a procession of physicians, surgeons, apothecaries, disinfectors, alchemists, and outright charlatans. In short, there was no more crucial distinction between elites and ordinary people, between the rich and poor, than their very different experiences in times of plague.[69]

Members of parlement were usually among the first to take flight at any hint of plague, a privilege sanctioned by both edict and tradition. There is, however, evidence that this custom underwent some modification in the mid-sixteenth century. In 1474 the court fled to Revel and then to Gaillac; in 1502 the rapidly spreading contagion forced the magistrates from Toulouse to Muret, Lavaur, Gaillac, and finally Granade, all in the course of only a few weeks. In 1521 the parlement resolved at first to remain in the infected city, but the magistrates' courage proved short-lived and in a few days they made a hasty retreat to Lavaur. Eight years later, however, there were signs of change. Half the sovereign court stayed in the city despite a very serious threat of plague. And in 1556, during a bout of the epidemic that struck 4,500 houses and killed 200 people a day, the magistrates refused to take their customary leave.[70] Germain de Lafaille, a local chronicler, claimed that henceforth the court made a point of not abandoning the city in times of plague, and there is evidence that this was indeed so.[71] In the 1580s Henry III attempted to encourage royal officers to remain in service during epidemics by promising that if they died from the disease their survivors would inherit their offices.[72] Though he endorsed the strategy of flight, La Roche-Flavin also argued that a "senator" who lost his life while serving during the plague deserved to be considered a martyr, just like those killed in combat against the infidel.[73] In 1630 the Parlement of Toulouse registered a royal ordinance calling for the selection of thirty councilors who were assigned to remain in the infected city for a three-month

69. For a more extended treatment of this issue, see Schneider, "Urban Sociability in the Old Regime," chap. 2.

70. Victor Fons, "Le Parlement du Toulouse en temps d' épidémie," MASIBL, 7th ser., 10 (1878): 39–51. See also AMT, BB 274 and passim.

71. Lafaille, Annales, 2:183.

72. La Roche-Flavin, p. 784.

73. Ibid., p. 785.

period.[74] Throughout the plague of 1628–32, the deadliest in the
city's history after the Black Death, First President Le Masuyer and six
other magistrates distinguished themselves not only by refusing to
abandon the populace even during the customary vacation period,
but also by ministering to the sick and poor alongside surgeons,
apothecaries, and priests. Le Masuyer eventually perished from the
disease.[75] The capitouls who served in 1632 penned the following
inscription over their portraits in the "Annales": "We have lived
amidst the people and in combat against the plague. But to live is
nothing if the scourge is not vanquished." During that epidemic,
three capitouls had been fatally stricken.[76]

What do these responses to the plague tell us about elites' relationships to urban society? On the one hand, it is clear that their
mobility and wealth afforded them the life-saving means to flee the
city, which is one more illustration of the social chasm that separated
them from the common people. On the other, however, there is an
indication that for those in positions of authority, especially the parlementary magistrates, their duties and responsibilities called for a continued presence in the city, despite the danger. In this sense, ruling
elites were torn between privilege and responsibility—between the
ability to escape the infected city and the need for their presence there
as the ultimate guarantors of law and order. The point, I would suggest, transcends the context of the plague. For despite their high
status and their rather haughty view of the populace beneath them,
ruling elites such as the parlementaires, capitouls, and other officers
did not remain entirely aloof from the social realities of the city.

But beyond their growing sense of obligation, there was another
reason for their social commitment: the rivalry between ruling corporations, especially the capitouls and parlement. The parlementaires,
as relative newcomers, took an increasing interest in the social affairs
of the city because they needed to demonstrate their legitimacy locally, their rightful place in the city, especially vis-à-vis the capitouls,
whose role as municipal governors was based on several centuries of
service. Competition between the two corporations took various
forms, some symbolic and ceremonial. One civic ceremony was
known as the Redde, a ritual visit by officials to the city's prisons

74. HGL, 11:180.
75. Wolff, Histoire, p. 299.
76. AMT, BB 278, p. 329; Joseph Roucaud, La peste à Toulouse: Des origines au dix-
huitième siècle (Toulouse, 1918), p. 213.

during which they would check on the inmates' condition and judicial status. The capitouls traditionally undertook the Redde each Saturday in the company of several assessors and notaries. In the sixteenth century, the parlement joined in the practice, only it limited its
ceremonial visits to four yearly.[77] It was not that the prisons were in
themselves so important, for in the Old Regime detention was mostly
reserved for those awaiting trial and debtors, not convicted criminals.
But the prisons were symbols of justice, and both the parlement and
the capitouls claimed the city as their legal jurisdiction; this was one
source of conflict between them. In order to demonstrate that their
judicial powers extended to the city, the magistrates entered its prisons—thereby claiming the inmates as their wards—just as the capitouls had been doing for generations. They even visited the prison at
the Hôtel de Ville, the stronghold of the capitouls; and, like the king,
from time to time they granted pardons to inmates. The magistrates
realized that if they were successfully to challenge the capitouls, they
were going to have to do so on the latters' own turf, in the social
world of the city.

But no group of officials could ignore the social realities of their
city, if only because their physical presence was often crucial in ensuring domestic calm and order. The city's police force, the Guet, was
quite small; until its reform and enlargement in the eighteenth century it numbered no more than forty men, ill-armed and only inter-
mittently deployed. Such a force was perhaps capable of providing
the muscle to clear crowds and quell disturbances, but it was hardly
sufficient in size and character to instill in the populace a sense of
obedience and deference necessary for domestic tranquility—something that in any case, in any time and place, is rarely the result of
policing and force alone. For this, the collective presence of ruling
officials—capitouls, parlementaires, and others—was obligatory.
Thus, when the populace grew restless, when famine threatened,
when heretics or indigents clamored at the city gates, or when criminal justice had to be meted out, it was then that officials would assemble, robed and accompanied with as much fanfare and ceremony as
could be mustered, and attempt to impose their authority as the
people's governors, the city's protectors, and the hierarchy's defenders. Authority was personal in the Old Regime city, and time and

77. On the Redde, see Antoine Tournier, *Reiglement et ordre des affaires de la maison de
la ville et cité de Toulouse* (Toulouse, 1558), pp. 18–22; La Roche-Flavin, pp. 250–57, 649.

time again its imposition entailed a confrontation between magistrates and the crowd.

The nature of relationships of elites with their city and its populace is of primary concern in this book. These complex relationships were modified under the influence of several factors, from civic humanism and the Counter-Reformation to the exigencies of political and social control in an urban milieu. The creation of a new elite in the sixteenth century did not necessarily preclude vertical social ties and local commitment. Rather, this elite continued to play a role as the governors of their city, the rulers of its populace, although the nature of that role changed as the city's political and social life evolved, which is why we shall be following the course of Toulouse's history across three centuries down to the Revolution. Let us begin our investigation with the city newly transformed in the early sixteenth century and with its many-faceted culture of the Renaissance.

PART TWO

Public Life in the
Municipal Republic

2

A Renaissance City

Though a university city renowned for its culture and learning, Toulouse proved notoriously inhospitable to new intellectual trends and often lived up to its reputation as a foyer of intolerance—a reputation given currency by a number of literati, from the humanist-printer Etienne Dolet in the sixteenth century to Voltaire in the eighteenth. The vitality of its university was rivaled by the watchfulness of the Inquisition, a relic of the Albigensian crusade yet capable of casting a pall over local intellectual life. But the university itself represented a barrier to antischolastic learning, for its faculty was still under the sway of the Dominican fathers. Thus it was that the Renaissance progressed only with much struggle in Toulouse, before being cut short by the Wars of Religion in the latter part of the sixteenth century.

Despite these institutional and intellectual obstacles, a Renaissance culture did flourish for a time in the city in a number of guises. One was the linguistic transformation of urban culture. Not until 1539, with the edict of Villers-Cotterets, was French declared the official language of the realm, but long before then it had made serious inroads in the capital of the Midi.[1] As early as the late fifteenth century many official documents were being written in *langue d'oïl* rather than Latin; between 1500 and 1537 the statutes of the city's craft confraternities were redrafted in French, as were the registers of the major clerical chap-

---

1. J. B. Noulet, *Essai sur l'histoire littéraire des patois du Midi de la France* (Paris, 1859); C. Brun, *Recherches historiques sur l'introduction du français dans les provinces du Midi* (Paris, 1923); Robert Lafont, *Renaissance du sud* (Paris, 1970), p. 28.

ters.[2] Most significantly, in 1513 the Floral Games decreed French, not Occitan, the preferred poetic language of the literary forum.[3] Still, the progress of Frenchification was uneven. In the first half of the sixteenth century the statutes of several lay confraternities were printed in Occitan.[4] It was not until 1533 that a native of Toulouse wrote a poem in French, and as late as 1564 complaints were voiced that no French poets could be found to enter the Floral Games.[5] Indeed, the persistence of Occitan in the face of the official embrace of French is striking and represents more than a case of cultural lag. In fact, literary Occitan underwent a revival in the sixteenth century, a revival running parallel to the process of Frenchification.[6] Both were features of the Renaissance in Toulouse.

Another local aspect of the Renaissance was the transformation of both the Floral Games and the Consistory of Gay Science, the institutional sponsor of the annual poetry festival. The adoption in 1513 of French as the official poetic language of the games has already been noted, but this was only one concession to northern humanism. It was also in 1513 that the consistory was rebaptized the Collège de la Science et de l'Art de Rhétorique, and then too that the old troubadour style of versifying was forsaken in favor of the *ballade* and the *chant royale*, two poetic forms emanating from the northern school of *rhétoriquères*.[7] Despite this modernization, in a few decades the Floral Games were apparently considered behind the times, at least according to Joachim Du Bellay, who in his *Deffence et illustration de la langue française* (1549) condemned the tournament of Toulouse—as well as that of Rouen—for "corrupting the style of our language and serving only as a testimony to our ignorance."[8] Stung by this reproach,

2. Lafont, *Renaissance du sud*, p. 28; Arnaud du Bourg, "Coup d'oeil historique sur les diverses corporations de Toulouse," *MASIBL* 13 (1883–85): 258–96, and 14 (1886–89): 52–91, 240–58; Brun, *Recherches historiques*, p. 202.

3. F. de Gelis, *Histoire critique des Jeux Floraux* (Toulouse, 1912), pp. 74, 351.

4. See, for example, *Los estatutz de la tresque devota, nobla, antiqua Confrayria de la grada conception de Nostra Dama mayre de Nostre Senhor Jhesu Chryst, fundada en la devota et antiquissima gleys de la Daurada de Tholosa* (Toulouse, 1515). In 1509 the statutes of the tailors' confraternity were also newly issued in Occitan (BMT, MS 2434).

5. Marie-Madeleine Mouflard, *Robert Garnier, 1545–1590: La vie* (La Ferté-Bernard, 1961), p. 222.

6. Lafont, pp. 32–50.

7. Gelis, *Histoire critique*, pp. 57–85.

8. Lafont, p. 30.

amounting to a charge of barbarism by a leading court figure, the literati of Toulouse hastened to appease the Parisian poets by awarding a prize bouquet to Ronsard at the Floral Games in 1554.[9] More important, they embraced Ronsard as their literary model, and what followed was a generation of poets *à la Pléiade*.[10] With this, the transformation of the Floral Games from a provincial haven for Occitan poets to an outpost of courtly verse was virtually complete.

Perhaps the most conspicuous feature of the local Renaissance was the architectural transformation of the city, evident in the scores of hôtels constructed by wealthy pasteliers and parlementaires. But these men of wealth and power, constituting, I have suggested, a new elite in sixteenth-century Toulouse, did more than exhibit their cultivation in brick; they also patronized humanist scholars and gave their sons a taste for the new learning. The offspring of three prominent pasteliers, Jean de Boysson, Jean Bernuy, and Pierre Assézat, became leaders in the local humanist community.[11] Within the parlement as well there was a coterie of jurists who sought to apply humanistic scholarship to the practice of law. Most of these magistrates had ties to the university, and nearly every lawman of the city had completed his legal studies there.[12] The most prominent among the legal humanists, Jean de Coras, was both a councilor in the parlement and a professor at the university, as was another humanist of note, Estienne Forcadel.[13] Indeed, it was the university, more than anything else, which put Toulouse on the map of European humanism, and which served as both the center of humanistic activity in the city and the arena in which many of the local struggles over humanism were played out.

9. Ibid., p. 31; Gelis, *Histoire critique*, p. 109.

10. John C. Dawson, *Toulouse in the Renaissance* (New York, 1921), pp. 46–87. F. de Gelis, "Les poètes humanistes des Jeux Floraux," *MASIBL*, 11th ser., 7 (1919): 45–68; "Les Jeux Floraux pendant la Renaissance," *MASIBL*, 11th ser., 6 (1918): 141–61; and "Quelques poètes des Jeux Floraux," *MASIBL*, 12th ser., 12 (1924): 21–46. Mouflard, *Robert Garnier*, pp. 76–77.

11. Irene Q. Brown, "Politics and Renaissance Educational Reform: Toulouse and the Founding of Its Municipal College," (Ph.D. diss., Harvard University, 1969), p. 88.

12. Viala, *Le Parlement de Toulouse*, 1:242.

13. On Coras, see Natalie Zemon Davis, *The Return of Martin Guerre* (Cambridge, Mass., 1983), pp. 93–103; and A. Gordon Fell, *Origins of Legislative Sovereignty and the Legislative State*, 3 vols. (Cambridge, 1983–86), 1:25–47. On Forcadel, see Charles Oulmont, "Estienne Forcadel: Un juriste, historien et poète vers 1550," *Revue des Pyrénées* 19 (1907): 547–83; and Fell, *Origins*, 3:312–23.

Legal Humanism

Founded in the thirteenth century, following the Albigensian crusade, the University of Toulouse was one of the great centers of learning in western Europe, attracting students from as far away as Germany, Poland, and England. Most came to study civil law, for which the university, since its reorganization in 1470, was renowned. Civil law then meant Roman law and principally the Justinian Code, one of the main subjects of humanistic scholarship. It is thus not surprising that the University of Toulouse, with its prestigious law faculty and cosmopolitan student body, should have become a center for legal humanism in France, especially since the Sorbonne theologians had banned the study of Roman law in Paris.[14] Nearly every humanist of note passed through the university, and the names of some of Toulouse's more illustrious students make up an honor roll of French humanism, including Etienne Dolet, Louis Le Roy, Jacques Cujas, Michel de l'Hôpital, Guy Du Faur de Pibrac, Estienne Pasquier, Jean Bodin, Michel Servetus, Rabelais, and probably Montaigne.

As large and illustrious as this university community was, in the 1530s several of its most important members began to feel the heat of official repression, in part for maintaining ties with notable humanists in the reform camp. A visit from Marot just after his release from prison did not place Jean de Boysson, one of the university's most renowned humanists, in a favorable light in the eyes of the Inquisition. Nor did his meeting with Luther's lieutenant, Melanchthon, as the latter was passing through Toulouse on his way to Marguerite de Navarre's court at Nérac. Jean de Pins, the chief patron of the Toulouse humanists, also fell under suspicion for his correspondence with Erasmus, although the parlement was forced to suspend its proceedings when it discovered that the nature of the exchange was nothing more threatening than the Dutch humanist's request for a copy of Josephus's *The Jewish Wars*. In 1531, however, following the persecution of two reform-minded monks, the Inquisition turned on the professors. Two of them, Mathieu de Pac and Otho, managed to escape to Italy. Not so fortu-

---

14. Pierre Mesnard, "Jean Bodin à Toulouse," *Bibliothèque d'Humanisme et Renaissance* 12 (1950): 35. In 1553, a royal decree declared the University of Toulouse the best in the realm for the study of jurisprudence: *HGL*, 12:553. On the university see Antoine Deloume, *Aperçu historique sur la Faculté de Droit de l'Université de Toulouse* (Toulouse, 1900); and René Gadave, *Les documents sur l'histoire de l'Université de Toulouse* (Toulouse, 1910).

nate, Jean de Boysson was arrested, saw his house and property confiscated, was forced to pay a fine, had his head shaven, and suffered the added humiliation of having to make a public abjuration of his "errors." After this ordeal, he too fled to Italy. Less fortunate still was one of Boysson's colleagues and former students, Jean de Catuce, who in 1532 was burned at the stake.[15] It was this round of persecutions, affecting more than a score of students and professors alike, several consigned to the flames, which prompted Rabelais's Pantagruel to quit Toulouse in disgust "that they did cause burn their regents alive like red herring."[16]

By 1533 the atmosphere had apparently changed, for Boysson and Mathieu de Pac were again teaching at the university. If the city had indeed become more receptive to the humanists, it probably had something to do with Francis I's visit in the summer of that year. The king journeyed to Toulouse to fulfill a vow made during his captivity in Madrid to undertake a pilgrimage to the relics at Saint-Sernin upon his release.[17] Francis's devotion aside, he was also acknowledging his gratitude to Jean Bernuy, the Toulouse pastelier who fronted his ransom to the emperor. Bernuy was not only wealthy, he was also an important patron of local humanists, his son ranking among them. It is thus likely that the king extended his gratitude to his host's friends— the Toulouse humanists still smarting from the sting of official persecution and in desperate need of protection. Francis endowed two new chairs at the university, on whose occupants were bestowed the title of *chevalier des lois*. Perhaps more important, he let it be known that his kingdom would remain open and hospitable to all men of talent.[18] The Day of Placards was still a year away.

No sooner had the king left, however, when the peace was again shattered in the university community. On this occasion, the conflict was precipitated by the words and behavior of the brilliant and headstrong Etienne Dolet, a student at the university since 1531. Dolet was twenty-four when he arrived at Toulouse, a professional student, so to speak, having already studied in Italy, where he had become an accomplished Ciceronian. Soon he was among the leaders of the

15. On this round of repression, see Wolff, *Histoire*, pp. 266–68; Rozoi, *Annales*, 3:348; Lafaille, *Annales*, 2:76–77.
16. François Rabelais, *Gargantua and Pantagruel*, 2 vols., trans. T. Urquhart and P. A. Motteux (1693; London, n.d.), p. 162.
17. Caster, *Le commerce du pastel*, p. 327.
18. Boysson, *Un humaniste toulousain*, p. 71; Lafaille, vol. 2, preuves, 13.

French *nation*, the fraternity of students from the north, and it was in this capacity that Dolet delivered his two orations in 1533, both broadsides against the city for its provincialism and backwardness.[19] Seizing upon the fact that the king had, for unknown reasons, cut short his visit, Dolet drew the following conclusion: "What the reputation of Toulouse is for culture, for politeness of manners, for civilization, the recent departure from the city the king of France has shown. He came, he saw, he departed. The vulgarity, the rudeness, the barbarism, the fooleries of Toulouse drove hence the glory of France."[20]

Given such words and his position as the most vocal defender of the nations—now under attack by the authorities—it is not entirely surprising that Dolet shortly found himself imprisoned, only to be released owing to the efforts of his influential humanist allies: Pins, Boysson, and First President Jacques de Minut. Insult was added to injury when Dolet next met with defeat in the Floral Games, losing in the literary competition to a third-rate hack noted for his misogynist verses. Dolet was stubborn by nature, but he knew when the game was up and quit Toulouse for good in 1535.[21] This was, of course, hardly the end of his troubles: in 1546 he was executed in Paris for the crimes of heresy, blasphemy, and sedition.[22]

Of what importance were these contests and conflicts? After all, a generation later the city would be consumed by religious warfare, making such disputes between local humanists and their enemies seem like petty scholastic squabbles. But they were important in several respects. For one, they serve as a reminder that in France, at least, the spread of humanism almost always met with resistance, especially since it coincided and was often confused with the beginnings of the Reformation. For another, the divisions that emerged in Toulouse over humanism carried over into the period of religious warfare. One of the fault lines running throughout the sixteenth century was that which divided those Catholics in the officialdom who inclined toward toleration and accommodation in the confessional struggle from their more militant colleagues who favored an all-out

19. On Dolet in Toulouse, see Dawson, *Toulouse in the Renaissance*, pp. 147–87; Henri Jacobet, "Les dix années d'amitié de Dolet et de Boyssone (Toulouse 1532–Lyons 1542)," *Revue du Dix-Septième Siècle* 12 (1925): 1–32; and R. C. Christie, *Etienne Dolet: The Martyr of the Renaissance: A Biography* (London, 1899), chap. 4.
20. Quoted in Dawson, *Toulouse in the Renaissance*, p. 171.
21. Dawson, pp. 174–76; L. De Santi, "La réaction universitaire à Toulouse à l'époque de la Renaissance," *MASIBL*, 10th ser., 6 (1906): 27–68.
22. Christie, *Etienne Dolet*, pp. 443–61.

holy war against heresy. The campaign against humanism in the city reveals the early stages of this division, when cosmopolitan scholars, in many ways the predecessors of the politiques, chafed under the repressive rule of the Inquisition, the university, and the parlement. Finally, the repression of the 1530s explains why a whole generation of young Toulouse humanists abandoned the university in favor of a scholarly sojourn in Italy.

Indeed, from 1538 to 1552 the names of forty-five Toulousains can be found on the rolls of the University of Ferrara alone.[23] The University of Padua, however, was the preferred place of exile, one of the major centers of legal scholarship in Europe, and it was there that the beleaguered humanists of Toulouse regrouped.[24] The legal scholar and physician Pierre Bunel was forced from Toulouse in 1533 and found refuge in Padua, and he was accompanied by several voluntary exiles, among them Arnaud Du Ferrier, Jacques Du Faur, Guy du Faur de Pibrac, Jean Daffis, Antoine de L'Aulo, and Jean de Coras, all future members of the parlement, and all (except for Coras) one day affiliated with the politique party. It is tempting to see here, in the exile of these like-minded young men, the formation of a cohesive ideological group through their collective experience abroad, much as Michael Walzer saw for the Marian exiles two decades later.[25]

In any case, by the early 1540s most of these humanists had found their way back to Toulouse. Owing in large part to their return, the university enjoyed a period of preeminence in legal studies during the next two decades. Arnaud Du Ferrier taught there before entering first the Parlement of Toulouse and then the sovereign court at Paris, where he occupied the position of First President. It is likely too that Jean de Boysson was still on the faculty in this period. Estienne Forcadel, a poet and historian as well as a leading jurist, taught both civil and canon law. Jacques Cujas, considered by many of his contemporaries as the leading legal scholar of the sixteenth century, held a position at the university until 1554 when, for reasons that still remain obscure, he lost to Forcadel in a competition for a chair. Pierre de Grégoire, known for his anti-Machiavellian writings, was also on the faculty, as was the Portuguese scholar, Antoine de Govéa, a

23. Irene Q. Brown, "Politics and Renaissance Educational Reform," p. 152; Emile Picot, "Les françaises à l'Université de Ferrare," *Journal des Savants* 67 (1902): 80–102, 141–58.
24. Irene Q. Brown, pp. 151–52.
25. Michael Walzer, *The Revolution of the Saints* (New York, 1976), pp. 92–113.

noted participant in a long debate over the powers of the magistracy. Certainly the most popular professor was Jean de Coras—best-known today as the investigator into the strange case of Martin Guerre—who, after stints at the universities of Valence and Ferrara, returned to Toulouse as a magistrate, only to perish at the hands of Catholic assassins in 1572. Coras's course on Roman law was said to have attracted four thousand students. Finally, Jean Bodin, not a member of the faculty but a formidable intellectual presence at the university nevertheless, studied in Toulouse from 1554 to 1559. All of these scholars were not merely colleagues; in most cases they also shared the same patrons.[26]

But what intellectual principles did they share? Despite some important differences among them, all belonged to a scholarly tradition that strove to rescue Roman law from the linguistic and historical misinterpretations that threatened to render it both obscure and irrelevant.[27] Eventually, this critical endeavor led to the entire reworking of French civil law—a shift in its footing from the Roman corpus to

---

26. On these scholars, see Eduard Fremy, *Un ambassadeur libéral sous Charles IX et Henry III, ambassade à Venise d'Arnaud du Ferrier* (Paris, 1880); Boysson, *Un humaniste toulousain;* Clement Tournier, "L'humaniste toulousain Jehan de Boyssonne," *RHT* 10 (1923): 241–53; Oulmont, "Estienne Forcadel"; Donald Kelley, *The Foundations of Modern Scholarship,* pp. 112–15, and *François Hotman: A Revolutionary's Ordeal* (Princeton, 1981), pp. 181, 191; Lafaille, 2:151; Mesnard, "Jean Bodin à Toulouse"; Pierre Mesnard, "La place de Cujas dans la querelle de l'humanisme juridique," *Revue Historique de Droit Français et Etranger,* 4th ser., 28 (1950): 521–37; Myron Gilmore, *Arguments from Roman Law in Political Thought, 1200–1600* (Cambridge, Mass., 1941), chap. 2; Davis, *The Return of Martin Guerre,* pp. 94–103; Fell, *Origins,* 1:25–33, 39–42; 3:297–364. Presented here is a rather sketchy view of Toulouse's university milieu, one that will highlight its cosmopolitan elements and its vulnerability in the face of local reaction. For a full account of intellectual life in the first half of the sixteenth century, one should consult Irene Q. Brown; two articles by Joan Davis ("The Libraries of Some Protestants of Toulouse in 1572: Cultural Influences and Calvinism," *Bibliothèque d'Humanisme et Renaissance* 41 [1979]: 555–66, and "Student Libraries in Sixteenth-Century Toulouse," *History of Universities,* vol. 3 [Amsterdam, 1983], pp. 61–86); and Barbara Beckerman-Davis's recent dissertation, which promises to provide the most detailed view of late-fifteenth- and early-sixteenth-century Toulouse. Unfortunately, I have not been able to consult her dissertation.

27. Cujas, for example, disdained any departure from the study of Roman law for the sake of examining French customs (see Mesnard, "La place de Cujas,"), whereas Coras seemed eager to turn his legal acumen on issues of the day (Davis, *The Return of Martin Guerre,* p. 100). And Bodin broke with the lot of scholars when he raised history above the law as the ultimate source of political wisdom. See, especially on Bodin, John L. Brown, *The "Methodus ad facilem historiarum cognitionem" of Jean Bodin: A Critical Study* (Washington, D.C., 1939); and Julian H. Franklin, *Jean Bodin and the Sixteenth Century Revolution in the Methodology of Law and History* (New York, 1963).

the principles of universal law and history.[28] But at Toulouse in the period under consideration, the emphasis was still on the critical study of Roman law. The study of Roman jurisprudence was valued in France not only because in much of the country it served as the basis of the legal system but primarily because it offered definitions of public power in keeping more with the emerging reality of a strong monarchy than with the fading feudal order.[29] This is not to say that all legal humanists embraced the principle of a supreme monarch (although the case of Bodin suggests that the tradition contained a built-in bias in that direction). Many were concerned with the public powers of magistrates as distinct from the monarch—the question of whether they too possessed attributes of *imperium*.[30] What cut across such differences was a common concern to expand the legal basis of the public order, of the realm of the French state as opposed to imperial, ecclesiastical, or private interests. One notable example of the practical exercise of this concern was Jean de Coras's treatise of 1557 against the legitimacy of clandestine marriages, written in support of a royal edict issued the previous year.[31]

This concern was also that of the politiques, although they did not assume that name until the second decade of the Wars of Religion. Most of the politiques were Catholic, though supporters of a Gallican—that is, national—church. Nearly all believed in the necessity of a strong, even supreme, monarch; and to a person they were willing to submerge confessional differences for the sake of preserving the integrity of the realm.[32] In addition, humanists ranked among the most prominent politiques, including Bodin and Montaigne. So it

28. Bodin was the scholar most responsible for this departure, hence his importance; see John L. Brown, *The "Methodus,"* p. 37 and passim; and Franklin, *Jean Bodin.* But another group of scholars also strove to free French law from Roman, imperial, and ecclesiastical authority, ultimately discovering a basis for national law in the French past and in native and local traditions. See Kelley, *Foundations,* and George Huppert, *The Idea of Perfect History* (Urbana, 1970).

29. William F. Church, *Constitutional Thought in Sixteenth-Century France* (Cambridge, Mass., 1941), chap. 2; Gilmore, *Arguments from Roman Law,* chap. 2.

30. Gilmore, p. 50.

31. See Davis, *The Return of Martin Guerre,* p. 100; Jean de Coras, *Des mariages clandestinement et irreveremment contractes par les enfans de famille aua deceu ou contre le gré, vouloir et consentement de leurs Peres et Meres . . .* (Toulouse, 1557); Fell, *Origins,* 1:31.

32. On the politiques, see J. E. Neale, *The Age of Catherine de Medici* (New York, 1943), pp. 84–85; Mark Greengrass, *France in the Age of Henri IV* (London, 1984), pp. 8–10; Lucien Romier, *Catholiques et Huguenots à la cour de Charles IX* (Paris, 1925), pp. 215–16; Quentin Skinner, *The Foundations of Modern Political Thought: The Reformation* (Cambridge, 1978), pp. 249–54.

was with the humanists of Toulouse. Jean de Pins, an early patron of humanism in the city, was well known for his advocacy of a tolerant papal policy when he served as ambassador in Italy.[33] Arnaud Du Ferrier, once a member of the faculty of law at Toulouse, ranked among the early politiques in the Parlement of Paris.[34] In Languedoc, the Montmorencys led the politique party, and they too were patrons of humanists:[35] Estienne Forcadel, the legal scholar at the University of Toulouse, wrote a panegyric history of the noble family, *Montmorency Galois*, published in 1576.[36]

Among the most important patrons of humanism in Toulouse were the Dufaurs, who were also one of the leading politique families in the realm. The Dufaurs were robins with Gallican leanings. Nearly every Toulouse humanist of note benefited from their patronage.[37] Both Bunel and Cujas served as tutors of the Dufaur children. Bodin dedicated his *Methodus* to Guy Du Faur de Pibrac and singled out the Dufaur family as "friends of learning" in his *Discourse* of 1559. Guillaume Le Sueur, another commentator on the case of Martin Guerre, acknowledged the Dufaurs' patronage, calling them "a house surpassing all others in the region for its singular erudition, integrity of life, splendor and honor."[38] The Dufaurs were also involved in local affairs:[39] for several generations they had served as chancellors of the Floral Games, and in the 1550s they were in the forefront of efforts to establish a municipal collège. Arnaud Dufaur was elected to the capitoulat in 1561, and another member of the family occupied the position of juge mage. It was mainly through the Dufaurs as well that a humanist-pastelier axis was formed in the city: Géraud Boysson, a pastel merchant, married the daughter of Michel Dufaur, who himself was the second husband of the daughter of Jean de Bernuy, the wealthiest of the pasteliers.

33. J. de Pins, "Autour des guerres. Une ambassade à Venise et à Rome (1515–1525), Jean de Pins, évêque de Rieux," *Revue d'Histoire Diplomatique* 61 (1947): 215–46.

34. Fremy, *Un ambassadeur libéral*; Irene Q. Brown, p. 251.

35. Greengrass, *France in the Age of Henri IV*, p. 9.

36. Oulmont, "Estienne Forcadel," p. 557.

37. On the Dufaurs, see Alban Cabos, *Guy Du Faur de Pibrac* (Paris, 1922).

38. Davis, *The Return of Martin Guerre*, p. 95. On the ties between these Toulouse humanists and the Dufaurs, see Mesnard, "Jean Bodin à Toulouse," pp. 49–50; Cabos, *Guy Du Faur de Pibrac*, pp. 18–19; Fell, *Origins*, 1:25–47; 3:297–364. Boysson ("Un Humaniste Toulousain") notes that L'Hôpital, Ferrier, Jacques Dufaur, Jean Daffis, Bunel, and Boysson were known as the "six amis," pp. 34–35.

39. On the Dufaurs in Toulouse, see Cabos, pp. 10–13, 43; Irene Q. Brown, pp. 78, 82, 244–45; Rozoi, 3:427; and M. Contrasty, "Une illustre maison toulousaine. Les Dufaur, seigneurs de Saint-Jory," *RHT* 2 (1915–19): 253–71.

By far the most illustrious of the Dufaurs was Guy Du Faur de Pibrac—known simply as Pibrac—distinguished both as a public servant and humanist. Pibrac was a poet whose *Quatrains,* modeled on the psalms and designed as pedagogic verses for children, remained popular through the eighteenth century. He spoke Greek and Latin, was a disciple of Ronsard, a close friend to Baïf, and a leader of Henry III's Palace Academy.[40] In his youth, Pibrac had studied at Padua, along with his brother and the other Toulouse exiles, but his most important friendship was with another young French scholar studying in Italy, Michel de L'Hôpital, the acknowledged leader of the *politiques* and the future chancellor of France. The Dufaurs and the L'Hôpitals had a history of close association: Pibrac's uncle was a member of the L'Hôpital circle in Paris, and Michel stayed in the Dufaur household while a student at the University of Toulouse. It was through the Dufaur family, and especially Pibrac, that the *politiques' chef de file* maintained a following in Toulouse. Both Forcadel and Coras dedicated treatises to Michel de L'Hôpital, as did Le Sueur. Boysson attended his wedding. There was also a faction within the Toulouse parlement which followed L'Hôpital, including Arnaud Du Ferrier and Michel Dufaur.[41] In short, the influence of France's leading *politique* family was one of the factors uniting the city's fragile and besieged humanist community.

Harried as they were, the humanists yet attempted to leave their mark on the city—to apply their humanist principles in an urban setting. In 1559, just three years before the storm of religious warfare broke, Jean Bodin delivered a public oration entitled "Discourse to the Senate and People of Toulouse on the Education of the Young in the Republic," in which, as spokesman for his humanist friends, he argued for the creation of a municipal school. Such a school had been talked about for years but never realized, despite the support it received from the capitouls, the church hierarchy, and even the crown.[42] Bodin's "Discourse" was, in fact, the last attempt to approach public

40. Cabos; Henry Guy, "Les quatrains de Pibrac," *ADM* 15 (1903): 449–68; Frances Yates, *French Academies of the Sixteenth Century* (London, 1947), pp. 104–10.

41. On these ties, see Cabos, p. 40; Boysson, *Un humaniste toulousain,* pp. 34–35; Deloume, *Aperçu historique,* p. 114; Davis, *The Return of Martin Guerre,* p. 94; Fell, *Origins,* 1:33.

42. Jean Bodin, "Discours au sénat et au peuple de Toulouse sur l'éducation à donner aux jeunes gens dans la République," in Pierre Mesnard, ed., *Oeuvres philosophiques de Jean Bodin* (Paris, 1971), pp. 33–65. On the municipal collège, see Irene Q. Brown; Raymond Corraze, "Le collège de l'Esquille au XVIe siècle," *MASIBL,* 8th ser., 3 (1936): 67–92, and "Le collège de l'Esquille," *MASIBL,* 12th ser., 14 (1941): 213–38.

education from a strictly humanistic perspective; in succeeding years it would be left to the Jesuits, with somewhat different principles in mind, actually to establish a collège at Toulouse. Bodin's argument balanced humanistic sentiments with an appeal to municipal pride, reminding the city fathers of the honor and gain that would result from the education of their children. He paid homage to Toulouse's reputation for art and erudition but noted too those local elements antagonistic to new learning—a reference to the repression of the 1530s as well as a dark hint of the forces of intolerance currently gathering in the city. His plan was simple: a school for the young emphasizing languages and history, but also including some mathematics and science. Such a school, he argued, would complement the existing faculties of theology and law at the university and prepare future students for these higher studies as well. One of Bodin's more radical proposals was that the school be open to all, rich and poor alike, and that the city provide scholarships for those deserving and talented students lacking means.[43] This was one way, he and other humanists argued, education could provide the basis for a common culture. And indeed, the notion of a common culture and its benefits emerges as a fundamental theme of his appeal—the need to instill the young with an education that would promote the spirit of entente in a society fraught with divisiveness and faction.[44] The problem was, in Bodin's view, twofold: the complete lack of education, creating widespread ignorance and "error"; and a reliance on private education (that is, in the household), breeding a dangerous variety of opinions. "How," he asked, "has such a proliferation of errors invaded the human mind?"

> Whence the multiplication of sects? Why are there so few whose convictions are in agreement? Why are there so many parties, not only opposed to each other, but who do not even listen to one another . . . if it is not that each places its honor in following its sect and the master who founded it. . . . Thus originate all the disastrous tempests, hatreds, disputes, rivalries, enmities, complaints, accusations, factions; thus, finally, these plots, civil wars, the pillage of cities, the subversion of the State, the assassination of illustrious men.[45]

Here Bodin made reference not only to the religious wars in Germany, just ended in 1555 with the Peace of Augsburg, but also to the

43. Bodin, "Discours au sénat," p. 59. This point is emphasized by Irene Q. Brown in her study of the municipal collège of Toulouse.
44. Bodin, "Discours au sénat," p. 58.
45. Ibid.

persecution and rioting that had troubled many French cities, including Toulouse, in recent years. And one did not have to be a Nostradamus to see that in 1559 France was ripe for religious war, especially since the Treaty of Cateau-Cambrésis, concluded with Spain that same year, left the crown and nobility free to engage in mutual slaughter. Given the enormity of the conflagration that was about to break, and the social and confessional differences deepening daily, Bodin's panacea seems feeble indeed. But this was not the first time, nor certainly the last, that education was prescribed as a cure for social ills, and it was entirely in keeping with the humanist agenda. "All these evils will no longer be feared by the State," he concluded, "if . . . in each city, the young people receive an education and a common doctrine."[46]

The municipal collège, however, was not to be, at least not on the terms Bodin and his fellow humanists envisioned.[47] Bodin left Toulouse the next year, in 1560, certain that his failure to interest the city fathers in his educational enterprise portended worse things to come for him and his friends. And he was right: the start of the religious wars in 1562 entailed a purge in the parlement of all those magistrates espousing a tolerant policy toward Calvinism.[48] The university was also the scene of open combat.[49] The politiques would have to wait until after the Saint Bartholomew Day's massacres in 1572 to reassert themselves in the city. In Toulouse, a generation of humanism had come to an end.

Why were the Toulouse humanists so unsuccessful? Why did they and their allies prove so vulnerable to official repression? After all, most were prominent men with positions in either the university or parlement, and many enjoyed the patronage of wealthy pasteliers. One explanation points to the city's imposing ecclesiastical establishment, the archbishop, the Inquisition, and the many religious orders, but even here there were reform-minded clergymen favorably inclined toward the humanists.[50] Another implicates the parlement, which, under Henry II, was given the task of rooting out heresy.[51] A

46. Ibid.
47. Corraze, "Le collège de l'Esquille." For a study of the general decline of humanistic secondary education in France, see George Huppert, *Public Schools in Renaissance France* (Chicago, 1984).
48. Lafaille, 2:240.
49. Gadave, *Les documents sur l'histoire de l'université*, passim.
50. Lafaille, 2:19, 25; Rozoi, 3:296–98, 313; Irene Q. Brown, p. 156.
51. Wolff, *Histoire*, p. 224.

further explanation, however, relates to the social position of the humanists themselves and their somewhat ambiguous relationship to local society. Take the case of Etienne Dolet, who suffered both imprisonment and literary failure in Toulouse. Dolet's position was that of leader of the French nation and this suggests not only a reason for his vulnerability but also a pattern afflicting other humanists. The French nation was composed of students from the north, a distant, foreign *pays* in the eyes of Toulousains. When the parlement and capitouls began to police the student community,[52] it was thus easy for them to take aim at these foreigners and their most conspicuous leader—who, moreover, publicly insulted the city and mocked its language and customs. In short, Dolet was an outsider who lacked support in the city, while the forces arrayed against him were solidly entrenched in both the faculty of theology, with ties to the ecclesiastical establishment, and the Floral Games Consistory, an institution whose traditions he openly flouted. Dolet's predicament was that of other humanists as well. It has been suggested, for example, that the reason why both Cujas and Bodin failed to secure permanent positions at the university was precisely their lack of local support.[53] Jean de Coras undermined whatever local goodwill he might have had by savagely criticizing the capitouls as "ignorant men, without learning or experience."[54] And the Dufaurs, though a prominent local family with years of municipal service, were increasingly drawn into national and even international affairs, and thus neglected their ties to the city. But such broad vistas were part and parcel of the humanist experience: most humanists of Toulouse, even those born and bred in the city, spent time abroad, and all identified with a culture that was international in scope. Moreover, the pasteliers, who had many ties with the humanist community, were similarly cosmopolitan in orientation: not only did they range far and wide in their business dealings, but, as noted before, most were originally foreign to the city. It was thus not only what the humanists represented and espoused which drew the ire of the conservative authorities, both lay and ecclesiastic, but also their status as "outsiders" which provoked the resentment of their fellow townsfolk, leaving them isolated and vulnerable.

52. Gadave, p. 134.
53. Mesnard, "Bodin à Toulouse," p. 51; Franklin, pp. 60–61.
54. Lafaille, 2:261.

The Municipal Republic

Although the humanists were all cosmopolitans, cosmopolitanism itself cannot serve as a blanket description of the Renaissance in Toulouse. For there was another face of the Renaissance in the city, one whose profile was less well defined than the intellectual movement we have been considering, but whose importance is central to a social understanding of urban culture in the sixteenth century. This other Renaissance was one whose vistas were primarily local.

Just as the university created a milieu for legal humanism, so the Hôtel de Ville provided a focus for this local Renaissance and especially its political agenda. And just as many humanists increasingly spoke of the French monarchy and state as equal to the nations and empires of antiquity, so did local scholars and officials see their city in similarly elevated terms. For them, Toulouse was not simply a large, wealthy city; it was a municipal republic. Of course, like other French cities in the sixteenth century, Toulouse was neither an independent state nor was its government representative; but this did not prevent writers and municipal officials, especially those schooled in the tenets of civic humanism, from referring to their city as a true republic, worthy of comparison with city-states, both ancient and modern. Thus, in large part, what we are dealing with in this "local Renaissance" is a myth of the city and its government, a myth supported by both the intellectual aspirations and political interests of municipal elites. This myth, however, was not entirely a fantasy, for in many respects the early sixteenth century was a time when municipal government achieved a high degree of self-consciousness, prompting very real reforms and innovations. Let us first examine the reality behind the myth of a municipal republic and then its more symbolic expressions.

The era of Toulouse's municipal autonomy effectively came to an end in the thirteenth century, with the Albigensian crusade, but the independence of the capitoulat as a governing institution endured until the reign of Louis XIV. Established in the twelfth century, the capitoulat had evolved over the centuries into an eight-man body, each capitoul elected for one year, and, since the fifteenth century, each ennobled by his service.[55] The promise of automatic nobility

55. On the capitoulat from its establishment until the late fifteenth century, see Roger Limouzin-Lamouthe, *La commune de Toulouse et les sources de son histoire* (Toulouse, 1932); and Wolff, *Histoire*, pp. 183–222.

View of Toulouse in 1515 (from Nicolas Bertrandi, *De gesti tholosanorum*, Bibliothèque Municipale de Toulouse)

Jacques Boulevene, "The Four Functions of the Capitouls," sixteenth century (Musée des Augustins)

made municipal service an attractive opportunity for upwardly mobile men, especially for the pasteliers, who entered the town council in great numbers. In theory, the capitoulat was to be composed of a mix of lawyers, lesser noblemen, and merchants, but in practice, after the sixteenth century, merchants were usually excluded or underrepresented. The capitulary election took place in several stages during November and December of each year. The procedures for the election were established in the fourteenth century and, with some adjustments, left intact until the late seventeenth. On November 23 the outgoing capitouls each selected six candidates; this group of forty-eight nominees was then halved by a company of former capitouls. The viguier and sénéchal named the final eight, who took their oath of office on December 13. Usually the elections were less than tidy civic exercises: chicanery and bribes were routine, and the magistrates of the parlement, as well as other urban notables, managed to meddle in the process, even though they were formally barred from the proceedings.[56]

Men were eager to secure election to the capitoulat not only because they could earn noble status for themselves and their descendants but also because the position conferred real powers. Collectively, the capitouls, as custodians of the Hôtel de Ville, controlled a major source of patronage in the city, for in their hands were over a hundred municipal jobs, ranging from secretaries, councilors, archivists, lawyers, and surgeons, to corps of guards, street cleaners, town criers, musicians, painters, and soldiers.[57] In addition, the capitouls depended upon a large contingent of appointees known as the *dizainiers*, who served as the link between the Hôtel de Ville and the populace. Each dizainier was responsible for a moulon of houses, whence the name, which probably referred to a block of ten buildings. The dizainiers were something like ward heelers, and served on an ad-hoc basis: they aided in the house-by-house inspection that went into drawing up the cadastre, for example, or carried out the periodic searches for nonresident poor in order to facilitate their ex-

56. Victor Fons, "L'organisation municipale à Toulouse du temps des capitouls," *Recueil de l'Académie de Législation de Toulouse* 26 (1877–78): 19–84; Marie-Louise Ribe and Michelle Ribe, "La décadence de l'autonomie municipale toulousaine pendant les dernières années de la Ligue (1594–96)" (Mémoire maîtrise, Université de Toulouse-Mirail, 1974).

57. One document from 1571 lists 164 municipal appointees: AMT, BB 113, Rubrique de Police, 1570–71.

pulsion from the city. The position of dizainier was not full time. Most who held it were craftsmen or laborers who received compensation for their municipal services in the form of tax relief and most certainly profited as well from routine corruption. The number of dizainiers for the city and the suburbs was as high as four hundred.[58]

Beyond this considerable patronage, the capitouls also had formal control over four crucial areas of municipal life: justice, police, "reparations" (the maintenance of public buildings and thoroughfares), and the city's several hospitals, each area the specific responsibility of a pair of town councilors. As a measure of the vitality of municipal government in the early sixteenth century, it is worth a brief look at how the capitouls managed then to extend their powers in each of these domains.

In the Old Regime, the notion of "police" had a wider meaning than in current usage. It related to the preservation of public order and included such concerns as food supply, the regulation of markets, sanitation, protection against fire, public ceremonies, and the policing of the poor, especially vagrants and beggars, as well as the pursuit of criminals. The capitouls saw in themselves the ultimate guarantors of public order and strove to emulate the well-policed republics of antiquity. A constant refrain in the "Annales" was their vow to "purge, clean, disinfect their Republic not simply of lazy vagabonds, and disreputable people but also gamblers, taverngoers, bullies, thieves, tricksters, abjurers, blasphemers of the name of God, lewd people, and every other kind of bearer of vice."[59] Moreover, there is every indication that, starting in the 1530s, the capitouls began seriously to act upon this vow, taking steps to rid the city of its large vagabond population. But they strove as well to care for the deserving poor, for they were convinced, as the "Annales" noted in 1539 (citing the "Oracle of Apollo"), that "every Republic renders itself immortal through generosity and that Sparta perished only because of avarice."[60] From 1532 to 1543 they undertook what appears to have been a series of unprecedented solicitations for the nourish-

---

58. Fons, "L'organisation municipale," and M. E. Lamouzèle, "Quelques fonctionnaires municipaux de Toulouse à la fin du dix-septième siècle," *Bulletin de la Société Archéologique du Midi de la France* 32 (1932). On the dizainiers, Christian Cau, *Toulouse, l'organisation municipale* (Toulouse, 1983). For a list of dizainiers, see the records for the collection of the taille in 1549–50, which gives the name of each dizainier and in many cases his occupation: AMT, CC 784, 297, 697, 867.

59. AMT, BB 274, p. 268.

60. Ibid., p. 40.

ment of the city's indigent. In 1532, 111 residents of the Daurade contributed to this effort; in 1537, the entire parlement, as well as other secular and ecclesiastical bodies, cooperated.[61] The capitouls also took new measures to deal with the ever-present threat of plague. In 1515 they created the office of Capitaine de la Santé, followed by the establishment of a Bureau de Santé, or Health Board, sometime later.[62] The city militia was reformed as well: in 1518, the Famille de Guet, or Watch, was established, which served as the major force for public order throughout the Old Regime. And in 1556 the capitouls expanded the Watch's duties to include round-the-clock patrols of the city.[63] During this same period the town council addressed the problem of prostitution in a novel way. Heretofore tolerated in a number of "public houses," the capitouls decided in 1527 to limit such commerce to one building, the Château Vert, which was purchased and maintained by the city. In 1557 even this limited toleration of the *filles de joie* was deemed unacceptable and the Château Vert closed.[64] Three years later, it was discovered that some prostitutes, still plying their trade, had apparently found refuge in several convents.[65]

The capitouls' reforming zeal was also evident in their approach to the city's hospitals. There were nine separate institutions devoted to the care of the sick and the confinement of the poor, each with its own administration, most under the control of a church foundation. In 1505 the capitouls moved to consolidate these into five hospitals under one municipal administration, a move in keeping with the actions of many authorities in the pre-Reformation and Reformation

61. AMT, GG 963, 964, 965, and Lafaille, 2:74. For municipal charity in 1555, see AMT, BB 274, p. 173.

62. Lafaille, 2:2; Antoine Tournier, *Reiglement et ordre des affaires de la maison de la ville et cité de Tolose* (Toulouse, 1558), pp. 94–97; Antoine Noguier, *Histoire tolosaine* (Toulouse, 1556), p. 130; and AMT, BB 247, p. 108.

63. Lafaille, 2:13–14; Tournier, *Reiglement et ordre des affaires*, pp. 77–86. On the Guet in general, see E. Lamouzèle, *La Famille de Guet à XVIIe et XVIIIe siècles* (Toulouse, 1906), and Maryse Ughetto, "La vie sociale du Guet de Toulouse" (Mémoire maîtrise, Université de Toulouse-Mirail, 1972). Health boards were commonly established in the early sixteenth century: Montpellier in 1506; Troyes in 1517; Grenoble in 1554. See J. N. Biraben, *Les hommes et la peste en France et dans les pays européens et mediterranéens*, 2 vols. (Paris, 1976), 1:139–40.

64. Jules Chalande, "La maison publique au XVe et XVIe siècles à Toulouse," *MASIBL*, 10th ser., 11 (1911): 65–86; also, Catel, *Mémoires*, pp. 187–89; and Leah L. Otis, *Prostitution in Medieval Society: The History of an Urban Institution in Languedoc* (Chicago, 1985), for background.

65. AMT, BB 274, p. 264.

era, when the secularization of ecclesiastical institutions was the order of the day. In 1514 work was completed on a new hospital called the Saint-Sébastien, located on the right bank of the Garonne on the periphery of the city, which was conceived as a special hospice for plague victims, who until this time had been dispersed among the other institutions of confinement. And in 1525 the capitouls turned their attention to the city's orphans and foundlings, housed then in the hospitals, and tried as well to involve the craft corporations in the older boys' education.[66]

"Magnificence is a proper and appropriate virtue for princes or administrators of Republics," noted the "Annales" of 1549, citing passages from Cicero and from Aristotle's *Ethics*.[67] Accordingly, the capitouls strove to beautify their town, taking as their model none other than the quintessential Renaissance city, Florence.[68] True, they admitted, Toulouse suffered by the comparison, for many of its neighborhoods were somewhat "malformed and deserted," but this should only spur the city to correct the structural infelicities of its "gothic" past. In a sense, they were merely trying to make the city's public appearance—its buildings and thoroughfares, many suffering from decades of neglect—a less shabby backdrop for the sumptuous hôtels that had recently transformed whole neighborhoods. But throughout they were guided by classical tenets culled from the writings of Vitruvius and Alberti, cited in their "Annales" as proclaiming that "uniformity, symmetry, and due proportion render things delightful to see and beautify every human creation."[69] Construction and repair proceeded on several fronts. In 1506 the cordon of defensive walls around the city was finally restored and completed.[70] In 1540 work was begun on the Pont Neuf, a project that took over a century to complete.[71] That same year the public wells were repaired, an essential enterprise in a city chronically plagued by fire.[72] In 1549 a fountain in the Place Saint-Etienne was also restored as a public

66. On these early-sixteenth-century reforms see L. Saint-Charles, "Archives de l'Hôtel Dieu et de la Grave," 5 vols. in manuscript, ADH-G, vol. 1; Barbara Beckerman-Davis, "Poverty and Poor Relief in Toulouse, 1474–1560" (typescript, 1985).

67. AMT, BB 274, pp. 104–5.

68. Ibid., p. 119.

69. Ibid., p. 118.

70. Lafaille, 1:301.

71. In the 1540s and 1550s, the "Annales" contained a report on the progress of the construction of the Pont Neuf nearly every year (AMT, BB 274, passim).

72. Ibid., p. 47.

The capitouls in 1516 (Archives Municipales de Toulouse)

The capitouls in 1554 (Archives Municipales de Toulouse)

source of water.[73] And throughout the first decades of the sixteenth century, the successive capitouls labored on transforming their once run-down Hôtel de Ville into a showcase of the city's wealth and taste.[74] Some efforts were even made to straighten and enlarge several major thoroughfares, though Toulouse would remain plagued by its sinewy, nearly impassable streets at least until the eighteenth century, when a new spirit of urbanism began to reshape the cityscape.[75] Still, by 1550 the changes had been so great, boasted the capitouls, that someone returning to life who had died thirty years earlier "would think he was in another city."[76]

The increase in the capitouls' authority in the realm of justice was less dramatic than in the three other areas, but here too, where they were increasingly contested by the parlement, they could still boast of significant advances. In 1530 and 1546 royal decrees confirmed the capitouls' right to adjudicate all cases concerning public order.[77] And in 1554 the king granted them the right to prosecute all crimes of heresy in the city, thus eclipsing the power of the Inquisition.[78] They quickly used this as a warrant to investigate several religious orders. If the capitouls' powers of justice can be measured by the introduction of new instruments of punishment, the early sixteenth century was surely a time when their authority was both greater and more severe: in 1508 they constructed the infamous "cage," which served to submerge "blasphemers and ribalds" in the waters of the Garonne, sometimes to the point of drowning.[79] And in 1523 they had the city's pillory moved from a peripheral spot near the municipal walls to the centrally located Place Saint-Georges.[80] They also imposed harsher measures on thieves, hanging no fewer than eighteen on one day in 1544 and parading their corpses throughout the city for the public's edification on a gruesomely novel, wheeled scaffold.[81]

Despite such evidence of the capitoulat's expanded powers and reforms in the first half of the sixteenth century, it would be a mistake simply to conclude that municipal government was enjoying a period

73. Ibid., p. 105.
74. Henri Ramet, Le Capitole et le Parlement de Toulouse (Toulouse, 1926), pp. 32–48.
75. AMT, BB 247, p. 120.
76. Ibid., p. 118.
77. Déloume, Vue de Toulouse au XVIe siècle. Les capitouls, p. 47.
78. Catel, Mémoires, p. 200.
79. Ibid., p. 191.
80. AMT, BB 274, p. 175; Lafaille, 2:175.
81. Ibid., p. 69; Lafaille, 2:134.

of unchallenged autonomy. For precisely at this moment the rivalry between the capitoulat and the parlement began, a corporate contest that would mark urban politics throughout the Old Regime. On at least six occasions in the first half of the century, the capitouls found themselves under the heavy hand of parlementary interference. In 1513, 1519, and 1524, the parlement unilaterally selected the new capitouls, in each case because the sénéchal had attempted to impose its nominees on the Hôtel de Ville. In 1527 the royal magistrates simply "broke" the capitulary election for reasons that remain unclear, just as they would do in 1562, when the pretext was the heretical views of several capitouls. On two other occasions, the parlement ordered the sitting capitouls to remain in office another year because crucial projects, in one case a new cadastre, had not yet been completed.[82]

Even these actions, however, did not necessarily mean that the capitoulat was succumbing to the parlement or that municipal government was becoming a plaything for royal officials. To be sure, the growth of the parlement did threaten both the Hôtel de Ville politically and its magistrates socially. But it would be a mistake to view the relationship between the two institutions as merely a zero-sum game. For one thing, the parlement's interference in municipal elections was sometimes nothing more than an effort to protect the town council from the meddlesome influence of the sénéchal; it was, in other words, not so much a matter of the magistrates' imperious policy toward municipal government as an extension of their ongoing competition with another royal court. For another, while the parlement as a body did increasingly flex its superiority over the capitouls, the magistrates as individuals never became members of the town council, although lawyers and barristers associated with the court did.[83] Finally, the parlement had a formal role in municipal government and not simply as a rival corporation, for several parlementary delegates, including the First President, served as permanent members of the Conseil des Bourgeois, which functioned as a kind of council of notables for the city.[84] As elite residents of Toulouse, they had an interest in preserving what independence and privileges the city still enjoyed,

---

82. Lafaille, 1:323; 2:16, 17, 46, 65, 156.
83. Lafaille, 2:144; Déloume, *Vue de Toulouse au XVIe siècle*, p. 35. On these conflicts and the general state of municipal government in the sixteenth century, see Robert A. Schneider, "Crown and Capitoulat: Municipal Government in Toulouse 1500–1789," in Benedict, *Cities and Social Change in Early Modern France*.
84. Fons, "L'organisation municipale à Toulouse," p. 37.

and they realized that this presupposed a reasonably robust municipal government, one that could maintain the loyalty of a cross section
of urban notables and not be sacrificed to corporate rivalries. The
benefits of such cooperation across corporate lines were obvious to all
concerned, and were demonstrated rather dramatically in 1549, when
the collective efforts of Toulouse's elite secured for the city a renewal
of its century-long exemption from the royal taille.[85]

Like the French revolutionaries over two centuries later, the municipal elite of sixteenth-century Toulouse "performed the task of their
time in Roman costume and with Roman phrases."[86] But one gets the
impression that the capitouls' performance was more than merely
theatrical. "The Seigneures of the Capitole represent the Image of the
Roman Senate," they proclaimed in 1549, somewhat redundantly.[87]
Their identification with Rome and the recent vintage of this identification are most strikingly revealed in the subtle shift in the name by
which the seat of municipal government came to be known in the
early sixteenth century. Throughout the Middle Ages, the Hôtel de
Ville and its ruling body were called the *capitulum*, meaning "chapter" in Latin. Then, in 1522, the city's scribe, Pierre Salamon, accomplished a lexical sleight-of-hand, changing one letter, adding another,
and "capitolium" was the result—a reference to the religious and
political center of ancient Rome. So successful was this transposition
that the most sophisticated of Toulouse's historians in the seventeenth century, Guillaume Catel, believed that the name dated from
antiquity, thus proving the capitouls' ancient lineage.[88]
    Such mythologizing, of course, was precisely the intention.
Toulouse had always been independent, and its rulers owed their
legitimacy not to the king but to their connection to the Roman consuls:
such was the view promoting the myth of "la République toulousaine." The city's first modern historian, Nicolas Bertrandi, whose *Les
gestes des tolosains* was published in Latin in 1517, argued that while
Charles VIII confirmed the municipality's privileges, and in particular
the powers of the capitouls, in 1495, its liberties actually were granted

    85. AMT, BB 247, p. 237; Wolff, *Histoire*, 232.
    86. Karl Marx, *The Eighteenth Brumaire of Louis Bonaparte*, in *Works* (Moscow, 1968), p.
97.
    87. AMT, BB 247, p. 104.
    88. Ramet, *Le Capitole et le Parlement*, p. 11; E. Roschach, *Les archives de Toulouse*
(Toulouse, 1891), p. 49; Catel, *Mémoires*, pp. 125, 183.

by the Roman emperor Theodonius and predated the monarchy.[89]

Indeed, this concern for proving Toulouse's antiquity and the venerability of its privileges spurred several local humanists to study their city's history. Local history was a growth industry in the sixteenth century, and its growth, usually encouraged by municipalities or other regional entities such as provincial estates, was as much a part of the Renaissance as the study of Roman law or the history of the Franks.[90] In 1555 Bertrandi's book was translated into French, and the following year another history of the city was published, *Histoire tolosaine*, by Antoine Noguier, who dedicated it to the capitouls. Both Bertrandi and Noguier had close ties to the Hôtel de Ville.[91] Both emphasized Toulouse's antiquity: Noguier claimed that Toulouse was more ancient than Rome, having been founded by Tolus, Noah's grandson, while Bertrandi placed its origins during the time of the biblical Deborah. Both repeated the myth of Virgil's stay at the city's university, where his failure to secure a chair supposedly caused him to retire to Rome and write the *Aeneid* as an act of consolation.[92] And, despite the fictional nature of much of their texts, both Bertrandi and Noguier based their histories upon research into documents only recently put in order by the capitouls. In 1507 the *Liber testamentorum* was begun, an official collection of charters and other important documents relating to the city's privileges and liberties. In 1518–19 the clerks of the Hôtel de Ville accomplished the first reform of the city's archives, rescuing a whole roomful of manuscripts, maps, and registers from rot and worms, and classifying them for consultation. And from 1525 to 1528 construction was completed on a special chamber in the Hôtel de Ville to store the city's treasure of archives.[93] Perhaps the capitouls' most notable act of historical consciousness was their decision in 1524 to draw up a narrative of the important events of each year, a legacy of their accomplishments and an invaluable source for future historians, including the present one. In ordering such a record, the capitouls were expressing their faith in history: just as "the knowledge of things past, of Hebrew and Greek texts as well as those

89. Nicolas Bertrandi, *Les gestes des tolosains et d'autres nations de l'environ*, trans. G. de la Perrière (Toulouse, 1555), p. 124.

90. See the comments by J. G. A. Pocock in his introductory chapter, "The French Prelude to Modern Historiography," in *The Ancient Constitution and the Feudal Law* (New York, 1967), pp. 18–21 and passim; and Kelley, *Foundations*, p. 133.

91. Roschach, *Les archives de Toulouse*, pp. 40–43.

92. Bertrandi, *Les gestes des tolosains*, pp. 6, 12; Noguier, *Histoire tolosaine*, pp. 5, 45.

93. Roschach, pp. 45–49.

in Latin, is greatly necessary to us," so their "Annales de la ville," inspired, they claimed, by the advice of Cicero, would serve to instruct future generations in the accumulated wisdom of governing their republic.[94]

The "Annales de la ville," the printed histories of Bertrandi and Noguier, and two other texts, one by Antoine Tournier, a capitoul, another by Guillaume de La Perrière, an officer of the city and Bertrandi's translator, form a corpus of works testifying to a pronounced strain of civic humanism within the circle of scholars and officials orbiting the Hôtel de Ville in the early sixteenth century.[95] Beyond a belief in the myth of "la République toulousaine," its antiquity and independence, this intellectual position was marked by two interests. One was to establish the capitouls as magistrates of the highest order, worthy of comparison with both the senators of antique Rome and the gentlemen officers of contemporary France. What distinguished the capitouls was their sense of public duty and their willingness to sacrifice their personal interests for the public good. Their honor resides, proclaimed the "Annales," in voluntarily "halting their own business, suspending their commerce, abandoning all particular affections, and putting aside their cherished projects in order to augment the Republic, following the precepts of Plato, Aristotle, Xenephon, and other philosophers."[96]

The other concern was for the unity of the republic, a unity ideally based upon more than the sum of its parts. The diversity of a republic's many citizens must be transformed into a unity "of consent and will," noted Tournier in words that presaged Rousseau.[97] The "Annales" went even further, declaring that a republic, like the family, must be united by true amity, without which it risks "inevitable ruin."[98] This ideal of unity was not without ambivalence, especially toward the lower orders, for it did not really embrace the poor, who

---

94. AMT, BB 247, p. 42. A first volume of the "Annales" covers the period from the early fifteenth to the early years of the sixteenth century, but its accounts are much briefer than the subsequent volumes and the text is in Latin.

95. Guillaume de La Perrière, *Le mirroir politique* (Lyons, 1555); Tournier, *Reiglement et ordre des affaires*. See also G. Dexter, "Guillaume de La Perrière," *Bibliothèque d'Humanisme et Renaissance* 17 (1955): 56–73. For the influence of civic humanism and the "ethic of public responsibility" on the city councillors of Paris, see Barbara Diefendorf, *Paris City Councillors in the Sixteenth Century* (Princeton, 1983), p. 300.

96. AMT, BB 247, p. 50.

97. Tournier, *Reiglement et ordre des affaires*, p. ii.

98. AMT, BB 274, p. 113.

were barely tolerated in the city, sometimes treated with solicitude, sometimes with severity. Nor did it necessarily include the laboring classes, although La Perrière, in constructing an ideal hierarchy of urban society, was careful to rank artisans and laborers as members of the republic because of the crucial services they rendered.[99] It was rather an ideal in the Platonic sense; not a sociological blueprint, but more a vision of the city as a harmonious whole. This was the same concern voiced by Bodin in his "Discourse" of 1559, when he argued that in providing a common education for its youth, the city would overcome the factionalism and contest blighting urban life.[100] It was, of course, one of the dominant themes of humanism to hold up the ideal of a society governed by peace and concord; but it was the particular burden of the governors of the municipal republic to transform this image into a reality, however impossible that task might have been. One still somewhat symbolic measure was to do away with the distinction between *bourg* and *cité*, a remnant of the medieval divisions of Toulouse into two separate settlements.[101] By the first years of the sixteenth century, the capitouls were no longer identified as representing either the bourg or cité.[102] To the followers of civic humanism the very notion of the city implied a unified entity. "The city," wrote La Perrière, "which is to say the unity of citizens, is the most perfect society of all others."[103]

It was more than civic humanism, however, that promoted this concern for municipal unity. For it was precisely in the early sixteenth century that social, political, and cultural forces began to place new strains on the city's social fabric, thus transforming the ideal of a unified municipal republic into an urgent political preoccupation. From below came the challenge of the burgeoning poor and a restless populace of near poor; from outside came foreigners who forced their way into the city's social order. The municipal governing elite itself was increasingly fraught with competition and conflict, especially as the parlement began to contest the capitouls' autonomy. The university attracted young scholars whose new ideas and aggressive cosmopolitanism challenged the city's cultural establishment. And, starting

99. La Perrière, p. 165.
100. Bodin, "Discours au peuple."
101. Philippe Wolff, "Civitas et burgus. L'exemple de Toulouse," *Die Stadt in der europäischen Geschichte*, Festschrift Edith Ennen (Bonn, 1972): 200–209; Catel, pp. 129–38.
102. Fons, "L'organisation municipale à Toulouse," p. 23.
103. La Perrière, p. 11.

in the 1530s, the element of religious heresy was added to the cauldron of urban conflict, contesting not only the church's control of spiritual life but also the city's identity as a bastion of Catholic orthodoxy. As is often the case in history, a principle was raised to an ideal precisely when it was most threatened. In the early sixteenth century the principle was that of a unified city, or the myth of the municipal republic.

Expressions of Toulouse's identity as a self-conscious municipal republic, endowed with a highly developed sense of local patriotism, can be found in several domains during the Renaissance, some of them ceremonial. One ceremony was particularly revealing in this respect, the display mounted on the occasion of Charles IX's royal entry into Toulouse in 1564, for it demonstrates clearly the vitality of the spirit of localism in sixteenth-century public life.

On the surface it would seem that a royal entry represented the antithesis of all that was particular and local. The focus, after all, was on the king, and the tendency in the course of the Old Regime, especially under Louis XIV, was to efface particular features of the cityscape in favor of an artificial theater—a theater of homage—rendering a given town virtually indistinguishable from others on the royal *tour de France*.[104] This is indeed what we see in much of the entry that greeted Charles in 1564.[105]

The procession was orchestrated by Etienne Duranti, then a capitoul, later to serve as First President of the parlement, still later, in 1589, to die at the hands of a Holy League crowd for his royalism. Duranti was also a scholar, a close reader of Bertrandi's history, among other books, and his learning is evident throughout the organization of the entry, which represented a full flowering of Renaissance imagery and allusion. At the very start of the procession, for example, at the gate of Arnaud Bernard, the king was greeted with an arch of triumph, the base of which was decorated with scenes of the martial exploits of Alexander and Augustus.[106] There was also a por-

104. Daniel Fabre, "La fête éclatée," *L'Arc*, no. 65 (1976): 65–75.

105. There are several accounts of the entry of 1564, including that found in the "Annales de la ville" for 1564 (BB 274, pp. 337–72) and another in Lafaille, 2:70–82. I will cite from the account in the "Annales," which has been reproduced with notes in V. E. Graham and W. M. Johnson, *The Royal Tour of France by Charles IX and Catherine de Medici, Festivals and Entries* (Toronto, 1979), pp. 252–78. See also Roschach, "Documents inédits sur le voyage du Roi Charles IX à Toulouse," *MASIBL*, 9th ser., 7 (1895): 20–46.

106. Graham and Johnson, p. 243.

trait of Apollo proclaiming in Latin a line of Petrarch, "Blessed is the city which listens to one herald."[107] Within this larger arch was a smaller one, which framed a crowned figure of Monarchy standing triumphant over both Aristocracy and Democracy. Duranti explained this symbolic affirmation of the crown's supremacy with references to Salon, Cicero, Plato, Herodotus, Demosthenes, and other classical writers.[108] There followed nine other arches, marking the king's progress through the city, most of them extolling the virtues of Charles; his father, Henry II; Catherine de Médicis; and other members of the royal family. On a seemingly frivolous note was a tableau of the "Nymphs of the Garonne" expressing in song their joy that the king had arrived, like Neptune, to calm the tempestuous winds and waters, which in fact was an allegorical reference to the first round of religious warfare in the city just two years before.[109]

What is surprising is that despite this surfeit of obsequious theatricality, much of the entry was still devoted to Toulouse, its history and culture. Superficially the ceremony may have been High Renaissance, but a palimpsest of the city was apparent nevertheless. At the second stop of the entry, at the gate of Posonville, for example, were erected several tableaux and statues depicting the origins of Toulouse and in particular the legend of the Delphic treasure of gold—"that curses those who steal it"—supposedly buried at the bottom of a lake in the Roman period.[110] The display at Saint-Sernin was consecrated to Charlemagne, Charles IX's namesake, but here also was a local point of reference, for Charlemagne's body was among the basilica's storehouse of holy relics.[111] At the Rue de la Porterie a pictorial review of the medieval counts of Toulouse and their battle victories greeted the king. There too stood the figure of Mercury, which the annalist was careful to explain in local terms: "According to the astrologers, the planet Mercury governs this city, and as Mercury is considered to be first in letters, so it is that the Toulousains are thus talented and dedicated in letters."[112] At the Place La Pierre, a central marketplace, the theme again was the special virtues of the city, especially those of "Commerce and Letters." Here reigned Clémence

107. Ibid., p. 255.
108. Ibid., p. 256.
109. Ibid., p. 249.
110. Ibid., pp. 257–58.
111. Ibid., p. 259.
112. Ibid., p. 262.

Isaure, the legendary founder of the Floral Games. A placard proclaimed Dame Clémence as the city's source of both wealth and poetry. "Isaure loaded our native Toulouse with riches and, upon dying, established rewards for the muses."[113] A pun was made linking Clémence Isaure's name with Charles's quality of clemency, but for the moment it was the local patroness of poetry, and not the king, who dominated the scene.

Other features of the city were highlighted during the entry—the Garonne River and its riches, the Bazacle Mills, "unparalleled in all France," distinguished Toulousains of the past.[114] The organization of the entry thus struck a balance between monarch and city: Toulouse flaunted its identity and traditions even as it welcomed and paid homage to its king. But such a ceremonial balance was unique to the sixteenth century. The next king to enter Toulouse, Louis XIII in 1621, was greeted by an entirely different display. Gone was any evidence of Toulouse, which along the processional route was completely obscured by scaffolding and tapestries. Gone were the references to the city's ancient and medieval past, its natural gifts and literary reputation. Gone too was Clémence Isaure. The entry of 1621 succeeded in effacing any original feature of Toulouse; it was merely *a* city, one which still greeted its king with much pomp and magnificence but with nothing of its own.[115]

Like the royal entry of 1564, the Floral Games also exhibited a tendency to celebrate localism in the spirit of the Renaissance. The consistory's turn toward the French language and northern poetic modes in the early sixteenth century has already been noted. Curiously, however, other aspects of the annual tournament, especially the considerable ceremony that attended the games, inclined in the opposite direction. The Floral Games were Toulouse's Maytime festival, falling at the end of a period of intense ceremonial activity, from the popular and profane rituals of carnival in late winter, to the solemn religious processions staged during the Lenten and Easter season.[116] It was a civic festival. The eight capitouls, the seven *mainteneurs* of the Collège de Rhétorique, and an army of municipal officials led the proceedings, which consisted of a series of processions between the

113. Ibid., p. 266.
114. Ibid., pp. 263–64.
115. Alard, *Entrée du Roy à Tolose* (Toulouse, 1622).
116. On the festivities of the Floral Games, see primarily F. de Gelis, *Histoire critique des Jeux Floraux* (Toulouse, 1912), and Dawson.

Church of the Daurade, where the prize bouquets were displayed, and the Hôtel de Ville, where the poetry contests were held. Dignitaries and commonfolk alike shared in the ceremonies, which dominated the city for three days; while the poets were holding forth at the Hôtel de Ville, Toulouse's neighborhoods would break out in fête. The streets, plazas, and buildings were festooned with flowers, and, in keeping with the chivalric spirit of the occasion, bouquets were distributed to women attending the games. The celebration climaxed with a great banquet, a veritable gargantuan repast, at which feasted not only the city's leading citizens but also the scores of minor officials and their friends. Before this, however, one tradition had to be affirmed: the homage to the reputed patroness of the Floral Games. Legend had it that in 1323 a chaste, devout, and learned lady, one Clémence Isaure, bequeathed her property to the city to establish an annual poetry contest. In fact, the legend is without basis, as later antiquaries were sadly forced to admit: Clémence Isaure never existed. Moreover, there was no mention of her at the public festival until the sixteenth century. No matter; throughout the early modern period she was hailed as the guardian of the muse at Toulouse and a link with the chivalric past. Even Etienne Dolet and Jean Bodin, who both had some cutting things to say about local traditions and customs, sang her praises. Her statue stood in the courtyard of the Hôtel de Ville, and as we have just seen, when Charles IX entered Toulouse in 1564, the figure of Clémence Isaure greeted him on behalf of the city. Every year the Floral Games ended with a eulogy to Dame Clémence, who was popularly recognized as a sort of municipal saint.[117]

All of this might be taken as yet another illustration of the so-called waning of the Middle Ages, insofar as the Floral Games were a creation of the fourteenth century and, moreover, grew out of the troubadour culture of an even earlier time. To be sure, the festival was authentically medieval in origin and cherished by the city precisely for this reason. The existing evidence, however, suggests that the tournament was not merely a relic or vestige from a distant past but, rather, attained its greatest popularity only in the sixteenth century. It was then that its ceremonial lavishness peaked, and then too that the figure of Clémence Isaure first appeared. Her statue at the Hôtel de Ville, for

117. On Clémence Isaure, see Gelis, *Histoire critique*, pp. 171–269; Dawson, p. 15. On the historical critique of the legend, see Catel, pp. 396–402, and *L'origine des Jeux Floreaux par le feu Pierre de Caseneuve. Par M. Medon* (Toulouse, 1659).

example, was erected only in 1557. And the first use of her full name was in 1549 in a prize ballad written by one Saint-Anian. It has been suggested that until the sixteenth century "Dame Clémence," in the context of the Floral Games, actually referred, not to Clémence Isaure, but to the Virgin Mary, who was regarded as the patron of the poets of the Consistoire du Gay Savoir.[118] Indeed, many of the submitted poems were allegorical hymns to the Virgin. In the late Middle Ages, Mary was often called Clémence, a reference to her role as the Mother of Mercy. Only in the early sixteenth century was the surname Isaure affixed to Clémence, and a new female figure emerged, one who embodied the Marial qualities of chastity and beneficence, but who draped them in secular robes. This may explain why Dolet and Bodin took care to pay homage to Clémence Isaure, for she represented a sort of Platonic ideal for poets, like Petrarch's Laura, Dante's Beatrice, and Le Charon's Charité, offering a secular alternative to the Virgin Mary. And unlike the Virgin, she was a female figure who was strictly local and thus could serve as an emblem of the city and its culture. What must be stressed is that this was an emblem that grew out of a sensibility connected to the Renaissance.[119]

So did a classical proverb associated with Toulouse, one discovered in the early sixteenth century and subsequently cited with some regularity. A brief digression on this particular proverb illustrates how classical erudition could be put at the service of local culture. The

---

118. M. Noulet, "De Dame Clémence Isaure, substituée à Notre-Dame la Vierge Marie comme patronne des Jeux Littéraires de Toulouse," *MASIBL*, 4th ser., 2 (1852): 191–225.

119. On the identification of the city with the Floral Games and Clémence Isaure, see de la Perrière, pp. 196–97. Clémence Isaure was not the only female image to emerge in the early sixteenth century as an emblem of the city. There were at least three others. One was the statue of a woman placed on the summit of the newly refurbished Hôtel de Ville, who soon became known as "Dame Toulouse" (Roschach, *Les archives de Toulouse*, p. 60). Another similar image appeared on the first page of the volume of the "Annales de la ville" beginning in 1532 (AMT, BB 247, frontispiece). There was also a living woman among these emblematic female figures. During the banquet at the Hôtel de Ville honoring King Charles in 1564, a capitoul boasted of the singular marvels and beauties of Toulouse, foremost among them a magistrate's wife known as the Belle Paule, a woman of extraordinary beauty, whose mere presence in public attracted crowds of admirers (Gabriel Minuit, *De la beauté . . . avec la Paule-Graphie ou description des beautez d'une dame tholosaine nommée la Belle Paule* [Lyons, 1587], p. 220 and passim). It was this same woman who had been selected by the municipal fathers to present Charles's grandfather with the keys to the city in 1533 (Rozoi, 3:354). She was something like the queen of the town and her legendary beauty continued to find a place in the city's official folklore well into the seventeenth century.

proverb, that of the "Gold of Toulouse," featured prominently in the royal entry of 1564. At the gate of Posonville, Charles was greeted with a tableau depicting a lake in the city environs during the time of the Gauls. Across the tableau was written: *Ecce Tolosanum infaelix raptoribus aurum* ("Behold the gold of Toulouse that curses those who steal it"). Another panel explained the proverb and the legend giving rise to it, drawing upon the writings of Strabo, Justin, Cassius, and Cicero. The Tectosages, the people who inhabited southwestern Gaul, once took possession of the sacred treasure of the Delphic temple in Toulouse but subsequently suffered a terrible fate, just as the Oracle had warned. They thus "sank their ill-gotten booty in the depths of the lake now called the Lake of Saturn." Some years later the Roman general Caepio, having conquered Toulouse, laid claim to the gold, and he too met misfortune for this theft. Thus it is that the gold of Toulouse "ever brings ill luck to robbers."[120]

I have discovered a series of references to the proverb in various texts and other representations; indeed, it surfaced with some regularity in the course of the sixteenth and seventeenth centuries, appearing as a minor leitmotiv in Toulouse's popular history. One of the first citations in modern times was in Erasmus's *Praise of Folly* (1511).[121] Guillaume Budé also cited it in one of his works. Both Bertrandi and Noguier discussed the legend as an actual event in Toulouse's history, and stressed, as the 1564 entry also stressed, that the Delphic temple was on the site of the current Church of the Daurade. Noguier suggested that the Romans invented the proverb to explain their defeat at the hands of the Gauls of Toulouse.[122] Clearly, at least for the scholars of Renaissance Toulouse, the proverb was a source of municipal pride, especially because it affirmed both the city's antiquity and its importance in Roman history. A student of Toulouse's popular culture, a self-styled Rabelaisian who published a compendium of local customs and expressions in the 1580s, also found the proverbial legend of interest.[123] Here is one case of a curiosity of historical erudition finding its way into rather popular texts. In a poem of praise to Pèire Godolin,

---

120. The proverb and the legend behind it are discussed in Graham and Johnson, pp. 257–58, nn. 10–16.

121. Desiderius Erasmus, *The Praise of Folly*, trans. John Wilson (Ann Arbor, 1958), p. 124.

122. Bertrandi, *Les gestes des tolosains*, p. 31; Noguier, *Histoire tolosaine*, pp. 31–39.

123. Claude Odde de Triors, *Les joyeuses recherches de la langue Tolosaine* (1578; Paris, 1847), p. 12.

the early seventeenth-century Occitan poet was jocularly accused of having availed himself of the hidden gold, whence his considerable talents.[124] The proverb again surfaced in a carnivalesque text written in the early seventeenth century by a lawyer of the parlement. *Le dialogue du mardy gras* between Fat Tuesday and Thin Tuesday was a mock dialogue where the more miserable of the disputants recalls the pilfered treasure as the explanation for his misfortune.[125] The seventeenth-century Toulousain historian, Guillaume Catel, also devoted several pages to a critical discussion of the various accounts of the legend.[126] In an appendix to his *Annales de la ville* (1701), the city's syndic Germain de Lafaille included a fifteen-page "dissertation" on the gold of Toulouse in which he calculated the precise value of the treasure and the exact date of its theft.[127] By the eighteenth century, the legend had become something of a curiosity, the subject of antiquarian speculation, though still a source of municipal patriotism. A painting exhibited at the local artistic salon in 1765 (although completed in 1685) illustrated the historical episode that gave rise to the proverb as one of the central events of Toulouse's past. And when the capitouls ordered the reorganization of the municipal archives in 1730, the annalist noted that such documents were precious to the city, since they contained proof of its liberties and privileges; they should be guarded like the "gold of Toulouse."[128]

As these references suggest, the proverb was exploited in a rather pointed political fashion, particularly in the royal entry of 1564 but elsewhere as well. An explanation takes us back to another royal visit, that of Francis I in 1533. During his sojourn at Toulouse, the king prayed before the relics at Saint-Sernin, just as he had vowed to do while a captive in Madrid. Apparently he coveted as well, for he asked the city if he could have a precious stone stored among the relics to present as a gift to Pope Clement VIII.[129] What kind of stone this was or whether it was a relic of sorts is not clear. In any case, the capitouls, indignant at the request, swore that such a treasure would

124. J. G. D'Astros, "A Mossur Godolin avocat à Tolosa," in Philippe Gardy, ed., *Le Ramelet mondin et autres oeuvres* (Aix-en-Provence, 1984), p. 209.

125. François Roussel, *Le dialogue du mardy gras de Carneval, avec le mardy maigre de Caresme, aux masquez curieux de nouvelles masquées* (n.p., n.d.).

126. Catel, pp. 117, 429–30.

127. "Dissertation sur l'or de Toulouse dans une lettre écrite par Monsieur Lagni à l'auteur de ces annales," in Lafaille, 2:329–44.

128. AMT, BB 283, p. 278.

129. Lafaille, 2:89.

never be taken from their city, citing the proverb of the gold of Toulouse in their defense. But to no avail—Francis made away with his stone and apparently was never the worse for it. Still, the episode stuck in the memory of Toulousains, and when Francis's grandson visited their city in 1564, he was reminded of the proverb and its lesson, perhaps as a warning against another royal appropriation. But it is likely that a rather different message was intended, for by then Toulouse, like other French cities, had suffered several royal challenges to its traditional independence. In particular, the crown had recently burdened the city with new taxes and financial demands.[130] In light of this, it seems hardly a coincidence that during his entry Charles was confronted by a placard proclaiming in Latin, "Toulouse has always been free," a visual reminder of the city's claim to autonomy.[131] My suggestion is that the proverb was put to use as part of a ceremonial display that, besides vaunting the traditions and virtues of the city and its culture, also contained various reminders of its long history of independence and autonomy, now called into question. From this political protest, couched in erudite terms, the proverb subsequently entered the city's culture, both official and popular.

A concern for the city's political integrity and freedom increasingly preoccupied Toulousains throughout the early modern period. It was in the early sixteenth century when this concern began to take shape and, consequently, when expressions of municipal republicanism were asserted most strenuously. Such expressions took various forms, some drawing upon Renaissance erudition and imagery, and I would suggest that the sentiment of localism which pervaded both the ceremony of the Floral Games and the royal entry of 1564 derived in part from the vitality of municipal independence and a concern for its preservation. Thus there is nothing inimical to Renaissance culture in localism, just as there was nothing ipso facto cosmopolitan about humanism. J. G. A. Pocock has commented on a "sixteenth-century species of romanticism," meaning a renewed interest in customary and feudal law and local traditions.[132] Whether civic pride and municipal patriotism were romantic notions or not is beside the point; the fact is that for many sixteenth-century Toulousains their municipal republic was not only a reality, but a reality worth defending.

130. Lafaille, 2:24, 62, 69.
131. Graham and Johnson, p. 256.
132. J. G. A. Pocock, *The English Constitution and the Feudal Law* (New York, 1967), pp. 19–20.

A Rabelaisian Renaissance?

The Hôtel de Ville, the Floral Games, and the university were all contexts for the development of forms of Renaissance culture in early-sixteenth-century Toulouse. There was yet another context, this one less defined, more amorphous, and somewhat popular in its social orientation. It bred a type of linguistic erudition which fostered a revival of literary Occitan and an appreciation for vernacular expression and wisdom. Such learning gravitated toward popular sources for its inspiration and thus relied upon those social elements that could bridge the gap between popular urban culture and literate society. In an era when rich pasteliers and haughty magistrates dominated both the city's official life and its culture, when the private town house served as a fortress of polite sociability well insulated from the ruder aspects of urban living, where could such social elements have been found? The answer takes us full circle back to the university and the boisterous student community it hosted.

The student population of Toulouse was quite large in the sixteenth century, and it loomed large in the city's public life. It was also diverse, with young scholars from throughout Europe. The diversity of the student community had an organizational expression in its various "nations" (regionally based fraternities).[133] There were many different nations, each representing a separate region or province; clusters of these nations formed supernations or alliances, according to geographical origin of the students. These alliances and nations served students in a number of ways: they provided housing, "safe" taverns, a messenger service to families and other universities, protection from the authorities and other rival student groups, as well as a milieu for sociability and a vehicle for participating in the city's ritual life. The nations were hierarchically structured, with a leadership consisting of priors, subpriors, and other officials. Many of these leaders were quite mature in years, sometimes thirty or older. And it was common to find students in their late twenties as well. Thus the average student was not necessarily a wet-behind-the-ears adolescent, but more likely a streetwise young man, hard-bitten by his years on the European university circuit.[134]

133. Dawson, pp. 89–104; Gadave.
134. Dawson, pp. 104–20; Gadave; Marie-Madeleine Mouflard, ed., *Liber nationis provinciae provinciarum: Journal des étudiants provenciaux à l'Université de Toulouse (1558–1630)*, 2 vols. (La Roche-sur-Yon, 1965).

The nations were not the only associations of young men in the city. In fact, they were part of a fabric of associations made up of assorted bands of single men who in many ways controlled and defined ritual life in the city, at least at street level. We are most familiar with these male groups in small towns and villages, where they went under the names of youth abbeys, kingdoms of youth, *bachelleries,* and the like.[135] In a large metropolis such as Toulouse, with a less homogeneous youth population, these groups were naturally more diverse. Some were comprised of craft workers, such as the *compagnonnages,* underground, illicit syndicates of journeymen on the *tour de France.*[136] Others were associations of apprentices, or the "good friends" forming the entourage of a great noblemen. Still others were more informal or ephemeral groupings, such as the young men who annually animated the rites of carnival, or the "gentle companions" of Pèire Godolin, Toulouse's most famous bard.[137] Perhaps closest to the nations among these groups was the Basoche, a confraternity of the many law clerks who gravitated to Toulouse because of its parlement and other courts. Like other brotherhoods, the Basoche had its own traditions and rituals: it annually elected a king, participated in public ceremonies, and also staged its own funeral processions.[138] During carnival these learned barristers-to-be presented themselves as the confrérie des Baisés-Cus, the Confraternity of Kiss-Ass. The explanation for this unusual name is quite simple: like the students, the law clerks were fond of lifting the purses of passersby. Their goal, however, was not gain but sport, for they would happily ransom back the purse for a mere kiss on the rump.[139]

As a member of a nation, a student belonged to an urban subculture of young men, a world of taverns, streetcorners and brothels, neigh-

135. See especially Natalie Zemon Davis, *Society and Culture in Early Modern France,* pp. 97–123, and Jacques Rossiaud, "Prostitution, Youth and Society in the Towns of Southeastern France in the Fifteenth Century," in *Deviants and the Abandoned in French Society,* ed. R. Forster and O. Ranum (Baltimore, 1978), pp. 1–46.

136. On the compagnonnages, see Emile Coornaert, *Les compagnonnages en France du moyen âge à nos jours* (Paris, 1966); Etienne Martin Saint-Léon, *Le compagnonnage* (Paris, 1901); and William Sewell, Jr., *Work and Revolution in France* (Cambridge, 1980), pp. 47–50.

137. On Godolin and his circle, see below, Chapter 4.

138. La Roche-Flavin, *Treize livres sur les parlements,* pp. 239–40; Vaisse-Cibiel, "Note rétrospective sur la basoche toulousaine," *MASIBL,* 6th ser., 4 (1868): 221; J. Lestrade, "Les gâteaux de la basoche," *RHT* 2 (1915–19): 147–48; Michel Cassan, "Basoches et basochiens à Toulouse à l'époque moderne," *ADM* 94 (1982): 263–76.

139. Cassan, "La fête à Toulouse," p. 109; Mme de Noyer, *Lettres historiques et galantes de deux dames de condition* (Amsterdam, 1738), p. 279.

borhood festivals, charivaris, and carnival—that is, the world of Rabelais. It was also a violent world. The nations themselves were a source of constant violence: they fought among themselves over issues of honor, precedence, and turf; they clashed with artisans and other groups; they routinely accosted wayfarers and had elaborate protection schemes for defrauding them; they fought with the authorities or rioted against their professors. From 1486 to the start of the religious wars, the nations were the object of fifty-nine decrees, ordinances, and other edicts issued by the authorities concerning violence, the carrying of weapons, or illicit assemblies.[140] In 1533 a student was killed during combat with the city guard.[141] In 1535 two hundred students battled the guard in the streets. That same year the students were aided in their struggles by the noblemen who accompanied the king of Navarre to the city, and the authors of the municipal "Annales" commented that in one of these bloody contests two members of the guard "were cut to pieces like the flesh of a dumb beast and afterwards perished."[142] In 1540, angered at the symbolic punishment accorded to one of their peers, over a hundred students rioted, and in the process set a university building ablaze. Following this incident, which drew four thousand armed townspeople into the streets, one student was hanged and several others burned in effigy.[143]

Much other violence remained hidden from the authorities or was the result of long-standing feuds between rival nations and thus did not necessarily concern the officialdom directly. The level of routine violence in the early modern city was great, and students partook of this rough-and-tumble urban world as much as artisans and other elements of the common people. But, as the examples I have cited indicate, the years following 1533 marked a period of heightened conflict between the authorities and the nations. The reason for this is quite simple: in 1533 the parlement, aided by the capitouls, launched a campaign to eliminate the nations.[144] Once tolerated as an internal aspect of the university and even sanctioned as a corporate body, the nations were henceforth viewed as illicit and illegal—a standing threat to the public peace and seedbeds of heretical beliefs as well. It

140. Gadave; Sophie Cassagnes-Brouquet, "La violence des étudiants à Toulouse à la fin du XVe et au XVIe siècle (1460–1610), *ADM* 94 (1982): 247–62.

141. Gadave, p. 133.

142. Ibid., p. 140; Lafaille, 2:100; quotation from Dawson, p. 125.

143. Lafaille, 2:213–14; AMT, BB 274, pp. 41; Gadave, p. 148.

144. Gadave, p. 134.

was this open attack on the nations that provoked Etienne Dolet, in his capacity as a leader of the French alliance, to lock horns with the authorities. And it was the intellectual and social challenge represented by an autonomous student culture that provided the backdrop to the official repression of humanism at the university from 1528 to 1533.

This student culture also provided a link with the city's popular culture, for the university students comprised a literate community that yet belonged to the world of the common people: theirs was a youth culture immersed in a larger urban popular culture. In addition, we might consider that the relationship between these two cultures in the mid-sixteenth century entailed a dynamic principle: students increasingly identified with the world of the common people as a result of the official campaign against their nations. For this campaign effectively branded student culture as illicit, casting it into the urban underworld so as to exclude the nations once and for all from the corporate community of the elite. It is telling to note, in considering this suggestion, that the appearance of a popular Occitan literature followed by only a few years the start of the campaign against the nations, and that most of the texts have been ascribed to student authors.

Indeed, perhaps the most remarkable feature of Renaissance culture in Toulouse was the revival of literary Occitan. I have already noted the penetration of French into the Midi in the first part of the sixteenth century, but this tells only half the story of the linguistic revolution of the Renaissance. For some literati a recovery of the vernacular meant the adoption of Occitan, not French;[145] and most humanists at least acknowledged an interest in the variety and originality of native expression. In their efforts to create a living French, even the poets of the Pléiade counseled turning an ear to vox populi.[146] As might be expected, Rabelais's novel is brimming with popular proverbs and the rustic expressions of non-French-speaking peasants. Montaigne (like Blaise de Monluc) frequently employed "gasconisms" in his Essays, for

145. Lafont, *Renaissance du sud*, pp. 13–50; Noulet, *Essai sur l'histoire littéraire des patois*.
146. James B. Atkinson, "Naïveté and Modernity: The French Renaissance Battle for the Literary Vernacular," *Journal of the History of Ideas* 35 (1974): 179–98. On the more general subject of the relationship between vernacular expression and French literati in the sixteenth and seventeenth centuries, see Davis, *Society and Culture*, pp. 225–67.

which he was criticized by Estienne Pasquier, but Pasquier too favored the "naive" quality of the vernacular as a fundamental source of modern French.[147]

What we see in the sixteenth century, however, is not merely an ethnolinguistic interest in Occitan, but the revival of literary Oc, a movement that has been dubbed a veritable Occitan Renaissance.[148] In Toulouse this turn toward the literary possibilities of Occitan was in part a reaction to the recent Frenchification of official culture, especially in the Floral Games. In the Midi as a whole it was also an outgrowth of attempts by both Calvinists and Catholics to proselytize in the native tongue. Several local printers specialized in the production of books in Occitan or Gascon. Some of these texts were religious tracts, such as the translated sermons of the famous Franciscan Olivier Maillard or the Gascon psalms of Pey de Garros.[149] Jean de Coras possessed a copy of the latter, evidence of an interest in the possibilities of vernacular expression in the highest circles of the humanistic elite.[150] Others were poems and prose works dealing with the popular customs of the city, or irreverent, humorous discussions of sex, courtship, and marriage. Most of these latter texts have not survived, although we do know their titles, which hint at the nature of this literature: *The Farce of those Girls who go to the Garonne; The Women of Toulouse want to marry-off their daughters; Incomparable Recipes for making Women Happy, Joyful, Agreeable, Pretty and Beautiful.*[151]

One work that has survived provides a fuller view of this mid-sixteenth-century efflorescence of Occitan literature in Toulouse. *Las ordenansas e costumas de libre blanc* is a text shrouded in obscurity: its publication date is unclear (about 1555) and its authorship is in doubt.[152] It was most certainly composed by a student, someone,

147. See Montaigne's own confession, "My French is corrupted, both in pronunciation and in other respects by the barbarism of my home soil," in his essay, "Of Presumption," *The Complete Essays*, trans. D. Frame (Stanford, 1958), p. 194.

148. Lafont, *Renaissance du sud*.

149. [Maillard], *La confession generala de fraire Olivier Maillart: En lengatage de Tholosa* (Toulouse, 1502); André Berry, "Les psaumes de Pey de Garros," *Bulletin de la Société Archéologique du Gers* (1965): 319–51, 499–525.

150. Christian Anatole, "Echo des poésies de Pey de Garros au XVIe siècle," *Revue des Langues Romanes* 82 (1976): 119–27; Charles Pradel, *Lettres de Coras, celles de sa femme, de son fils et de ses amis* (Albi, 1880).

151. Odde de Triors, *Les joyeuses recherches*, p. 11; Lafont, *Renaissance du sud*, p. 34.

152. *Las ordenansas et coustumas del libre blanc, observadas de tota ancianetat, compausadas per las sabias femnas de Tolosa et regidas en forma deguda per lor secretary. Imprimadas nouvellament a Tolosa per Jac. Colomies imprimeur.* An edition, edited by Noulet, was

moreover, familiar with both the language of the city and its folkways. The *Libre blanc* purports to be the ordinances and customs of Toulouse's midwives—"What one ought to do at baptisms and *fêtes.*" It is really much more. It offers advice on a range of subjects, many within the purview of midwifery: "A nursing woman should not show her breast, lest someone cause her grief by giving her the evil eye. . . . Do not throw away the umbilical cord of a baby, for it is good against scurf. Do not let it be eaten by the cat, because the child, thinking that he is dreaming, will then wet his bed day and night. . . . A wetnurse should not eat or drink while the baby is suckling, otherwise he will grow up more gluttonous than a German."[153] It even suggests techniques for bearing a child with certain desirable traits—"a son equipped with a large member, stiffer and harder than a bone, . . . a girl [with] lips as soft and plump as nice crepes, both above and below."[154] If a couple wanted a boy, they only needed to follow the *Libre blanc's* advice: "[The woman] will wear stitched into her underclothes the right foot of a crow. Or, when her husband mounts her, she will squeeze both fists, press her heels together and close her eyes, and if resolved in her purpose . . . she will conceive a male child, provided the husband shafts her well."[155]

Although concerned for the most part with pregnancy, childbirth, and nursing, the *Libre blanc* ranges far and wide with its wisdom, offering counsel on predicting plague or rain, telling the future, thwarting jealousy, ensuring a successful wedding night, exorcising spirits, doing laundry, securing husbands for widows, and choosing godparents. It even cautions against eating butter or cheese during Lent, warning that those who do will sprout ears "at least as long as a rabbit's."[156]

The "ordinances" of the *Libre blanc* are the stuff of popular culture, familiar to students of the folkways and customs of ordinary people in preindustrial Europe. But it is the popular culture of a particular city—of Toulouse, whose landmarks and features are an integral part of the text. The midwives are enumerated according to street and

published in Montpellier in 1878. I have used a French translation currently being prepared for publication with extensive commentary by Daniel Fabre and his colleagues at the Centre National de la Recherche Scientifique, Institut méridionale à Toulouse. I am grateful to them for allowing me to consult their unpublished text.

153. "Les ordonnances et coutumes du livre blanc" (typescript), pp. 1–2, 4, 5, 10.
154. Ibid., p. 11.
155. Ibid., p. 12.
156. Ibid.

neighborhood and listed by name; mention is made of local rituals, shrines, convents, and churches. Even two Augustinian brothers, specialists in prayers for infertile women, are named.[157]

It should be stressed too that the *Libre blanc,* though culled from popular sources, was drafted by a man of letters. Whoever its author was, his enterprise was in keeping with the Renaissance interest in popular proverbs and vernacular expression. But we have here not a man filled with reverence and respect for the folk wisdom he was drawing upon—a sixteenth-century version of the tape-recorder-in-hand field enthnographer. Quite the contrary, the author deliberately deforms and exaggerates popular expression, rendering much of it absurd and laughable. The tone throughout the *Libre blanc* is one of mockery, though without a hint of viciousness. In short, we are in the territory of Rabelais, where the language of carnival and the marketplace is fashioned into literature, while still preserving the essential playfulness and polymorphous character of popular expression.

This same Rabelaisian spirit also motivated another man of letters of Toulouse to take up the study of the city's native language and its curiosities. Claude Odde de Triors was originally from Dauphiné, but while studying at the university of Toulouse he became an enthusiastic student, even a champion, of the language and customs of his adopted city. He modeled his *Joyeuses recherches de la langue toulousaine* (1578) after Erasmus's *Adagiorum Chiliade,* a collection of proverbs, but the example of Rabelais is evident as well. It is a rambling, irreverent, virtually indecipherable commentary on a handful of local expressions and the author's labors in hunting them down. He acknowledges the help he received from many "doctors"—of the taverns and streetcorners of the city, that is—and he also notes the salutary effect of wine on his research.[158] In addition, Odde de Triors cites the titles of a number of contemporary Occitan texts that have not survived but that afford further proof of a vibrant literature in the true vernacular of the city. His familiarity with the *Libre blanc* is detailed, and one senses that all of these texts form a sort of underground literature that circulated among Occitan cognoscenti.[159] The text of *Les joyeuses recherches* is sprinkled with Latin citations from classical authors, popular expressions in the Toulouse vernacular,

157. Ibid., p. 8.
158. Odde de Triors, *Les joyeuses recherches,* p. 9.
159. Ibid., pp. 10, 19.

references to contemporary humanists, and allusions to other works, especially those of Rabelais. Much, however, is deliberately and comically garbled, as when he pays tribute to "un livre de la république de Boudin" (*boudin* = blood sausage).[160] But an occasional note of seriousness is sounded, as when the author expresses the hope that his research into the language of the city might prove "good and useful for the republic."[161]

That a man of letters given to literary slumming should have addressed the needs of his republic, if only in an aside, suggests a unity of concerns not evident in my general presentation of the Renaissance in Toulouse. I have emphasized the cultural variety within the city's erudite community in the first half of the sixteenth century—a tripartite Renaissance of legal scholars, civic humanists, and Occitan literati. But if these men of letters were not of one mind, as they certainly were not, they yet stood on common ground at least part of the time. While the legal scholars, for example, were largely preoccupied with issues that transcended the city, they did display an interest in educating the city's youth as a means of fostering civic unity. And those literati responsible for the Occitan Renaissance raised the oral expression of their city to a literary form, thus textually reproducing a living community of speech. In short, the common ground was the city, as both ideal and reality, as both a community and a set of institutions. The myth of "la République toulousaine" stands at the center of the local Renaissance and was its legacy to the period that followed. What would be its fate in the turmoil and internecine conflict that were the Wars of Religion?

160. Ibid., p. 18.
161. Ibid., p. 12.

3

A Holy City

As we have seen, violence and contention were no strangers to early modern urban life. Thus one cannot blame the Wars of Religion, which began in Toulouse as in all of France in 1562, for shattering a civic calm that in truth never really existed. Nevertheless, the outbreak of religious warfare did factionalize the city for nearly four decades, raising organized violence to a legitimate instrument of urban politics, unleashing the forces of the crowd, and adding an element of fanaticism, even savagery, to public life as well. It is said that the religious wars of the sixteenth century ended the civic consensus enjoyed by the cities of France since the late Middle Ages.[1] If this was indeed the case, it must also be said that the Renaissance city, at least as we have reconstructed it, was itself torn in several directions. The so-called municipal republic barely contained a whole range of latent contradictions which, when an organized Protestant challenge appeared, precipitated an open breach in the urban social fabric. What ensued was not only two generations of unprecedented violence but also a period during which Toulouse was more at the mercy of forces beyond its walls than in any other time in its history, at least since the thirteenth century.

One might conclude from this that the history of the religious wars in the city was the national experience writ small, that the local conflict was merely a manifestation of the great confessional struggle being played out on a much larger stage. Recent local studies have

1. Bernard Chevalier, *Les bonnes villes de France du XIVe au XVIe siècle* (Paris, 1982).

90

shown how misleading this view is, and what follows is an attempt to depict the conflict in the context of the city and in particular to high-light the forms and patterns of mass mobilization that it entailed.[2] What we shall discover is a city in which many traditional social boundaries gave way to new associational patterns drawing upon the entire range of the urban populace. And while many features of the local Renaissance succumbed to the pressures of religious conflict, the sense of Toulouse as an autonomous provincial capital persisted, forming, in fact, a basis of the Holy League's ascendancy in the city.

Religious Riot and Repression, 1562–1572

Every year from 1563 to 1791, in what was one of the longest con-tinual ceremonies in all of Old Regime France, the official orders of Toulouse would assemble each May 17 for a solemn general proces-sion commemorating the city's "deliverance" from a Huguenot take-over. On that day in 1562, after almost two months of religious vio-lence, several hundred members of the Reformed church were forcibly driven from the city. As events turned out, Toulouse re-mained a bastion of Catholic orthodoxy in an otherwise largely Prot-estant Midi and soon emerged as a national center of the ultra-Catholic Holy League. But despite the successful purge of nearly all the city's Calvinists in the 1560s—and the cold-blooded murder of most of the rest in 1572—street fighting and mass devotional displays continued to mark public life for the balance of the century as rival parties of royalists and militant Catholics contended for local supremacy.

Protestant sentiments made little headway in Toulouse until 1530, when Lutheranism found a handful of adherents inside the walls of the mendicant orders and among the humanists at the university. The latter included several of the students and professors persecuted by the authorities and banished from the city in 1532. Most of the humanists, however, merely flirted with Reformed ideas while still remaining loyal to Catholicism, although that of a decidedly Erasmian stripe. It will be recalled, for example, that Jean de Pins, the most important patron of the local humanist community, was a correspon-dent of Erasmus. But others were professed Protestants, some of

2. See especially Benedict, *Rouen during the Wars of Religion.*

whom, most notably the magistrate and legal scholar Jean de Coras, owed their support to Jeanne d'Albret, queen of Navarre. Perhaps what is most notable about religious life in Toulouse in this period is how modest the Protestant community actually was, despite the presence of such cosmopolitan elements as the humanists, the university community, and the pasteliers. In the case of the latter, there is the likelihood that their Reformed sympathies were tempered by a Nicodemite caution, a common stance for prudent businessmen in confessionally torn communities in the sixteenth century.[3] One formidable obstacle to Reformed thinking was the Dominican Inquisition, established in Toulouse after the Albigensian crusade in the thirteenth century. But even here there were cracks in the defense of orthodoxy: on September 10, 1538, the Inquisitor of the Faith himself, the Jacobin Louis Rochette, was strangled and burned at the stake as a Protestant.[4]

Copies of Calvin's *Institution chrétienne* first appeared in Toulouse in 1536, and it was in the 1540s that the struggle against the Reformed faith began in earnest. In 1548 Henry II charged the parlement to form a *chambre ardente* composed of a president and twelve councilors to prosecute heretics, thus establishing the magistrates as the supreme defenders of the faith in the province.[5] In the course of the 1540s the parlement conducted trials against two hundred suspected Huguenots, of whom no fewer than eighteen were burned at the stake.[6] This prosecutory zeal, however, was based less on the parlementaires' religious sentiments than on their attachment to the crown, which remained strong at least until the collapse of monarchical authority with Henry's untimely death in 1559. Even before then there appeared some renegades among the magistrates: in 1554 two councilors fled to Geneva and were burned in effigy in Toulouse.[7] And in 1562, thirty-seven parlementaires signed a document charging twenty-

---

3. On Nicodemite businessmen, see Robert M. Kingdon, "Christopher Plantin and His Backers, 1575–1590," *Mélanges d'histoire économique et sociale: Hommage au Antony Babel* (Geneva, 1963).

4. Raymond A. Mentzer, Jr., "The Inquisitor as Heretic: The Pre-Reformation at Toulouse," *Wascana Review* 9 (1974): 156–65.

5. Lafaille, *Annales*, 2:175; Wolff, *Histoire*, p. 224.

6. Wolff, *Histoire*, p. 223; and Mentzer, "Heresy Suspects in Languedoc prior to 1560: Observations on Their Social and Occupational Status," *Bibliothèque d'Humanisme et Renaissance* 39 (1977): 561–68.

7. Jean-Baptiste Dubédat, *Histoire du Parlement de Toulouse*, 2 vols. (Paris, 1885) 1:397.

five of their colleagues with heresy.[8] Some of the accused were merely politiques before the letter, moderate Catholics more interested in civil peace than confessional purity. These were the humanists and their fellow travelers whom we encountered in the last chapter. Others, however, were convinced Calvinists.

During the 1550s the size of Toulouse's Calvinist community increased steadily, and in 1558 the first Reformed church was established outside the city gates. Estimates of the number of Calvinists in Toulouse just before the confrontation of 1562 range from four thousand to twenty thousand, although the lower figure is probably closer to the truth. On February 7, 1562, five thousand Huguenots gathered in an open-air service, where they had to be guarded by a militia of one hundred soldiers, for by then violence between the two religious communities had become routine. Both sides were armed; itinerant Catholic preachers daily inflamed the populace against the Calvinists, who had recently taken control of a number of towns perilously close to Toulouse. To the psalm-singing of the Calvinists, Catholics responded with mass processions, public prayers, and citywide fasts. At the Dalbade, a man caught singing the psalms during the Lenten service was stoned to death, his body then dragged to the parlementary palace. At Saint-Sernin a merchant interrupted a preaching Jacobin with the cry, "You lie, you sneaking monk!" He was slaughtered on the spot. Toulouse was ready for a showdown.[9]

Nearly two months of religious violence began on April 4, 1562, at the burial of a Calvinist women in the Saint-Michel faubourg. Although her parents and confessor insisted she died a Catholic, her husband proceeded to have her interred in the Huguenot cemetery. What began as a struggle over a woman's corpse quickly escalated into a pitched battle between Catholics and Protestants. The tocsin was sounded, and a general cry went out to slaughter the Huguenots. Several score of both faiths were killed in the fighting.[10]

The following day President Manscencal managed to arrange a

8. Lafaille, 2: 240; Dubédat, *Histoire du Parlement*, 1:397–98. On the divided court, see also Mark Greengrass, "The Anatomy of a Religious Riot in Toulouse in May 1562," *Journal of Ecclesiastical History* 34 (1983): 380; and *Histoire ecclésiastique des églises réformées au royaume de France*, ed. G. Baum and E. Cunitz, 3 vols. (Paris, 1885), 3:8.

9. On these events, see AMT, BB 247, pp. 99–100, 188, 190; Lafaille, 2:150, 200–15; Wolff, *Histoire*, pp. 273–75; Davis, *Society and Culture*, chap. 6.

10. Greengrass, "Anatomy of a Religious Riot," p. 373.

truce whereby the Calvinists would disarm and withdraw to the faubourgs. Although ostensibly willing to entertain these terms, the Huguenot leaders secretly harbored more ambitious plans: having made contact with the prince of Condé, they aimed with his support to seize control of the Hôtel de Ville on May 17. Their plans, however, were intercepted and passed on to the Catholic governor and warrior, Blaise de Monluc, who informed Manscencal of the Huguenot plot. The parlement at once met in an emergency session, purged its own ranks of Calvinist sympathizers, and took steps to fortify the Hôtel de Ville. All that this accomplished was to force the Huguenots' hand, and on the morning of May 13 the city awoke to discover the town hall transformed into a Calvinist fortress.[11]

The Catholics were quick to respond: they occupied the parlementary palace, seized the powder stored in the Bazacle Mills and requisitioned all the silver in the city. The parlement ordered all Catholic combatants to mark their clothing and houses with white crosses and the remaining faithful to display lighted candles in their windows. The populace was up in arms: weapons and munitions began to pour into the city, while civilian militias were organized in each confessional camp. With the arrival of troops led by aristocrat warriors such as Joyeuse, Monluc, and Terride, the Catholics began their assault on the enemy's stronghold in the northern part of the city. The Huguenots had at their disposal over a thousand troops as well as the allegiance of at least one student nation. Promised reinforcements from regional noblemen failed to arrive, however, and the Protestants proved no match for the ever-growing Catholic army. They hung on nevertheless, and the parlement, in a desperate attempt to dislodge them, authorized the torching of the Saint-Georges quarter, destroying more than two hundred houses. It appears that on May 17 another truce was arranged between the two factions under which the Calvinists would relinquish their control of the Hôtel de Ville and retire from the city unmolested. During the day groups of them trickled out the city gates; by nightfall many remained behind to celebrate a last holy service in their erstwhile fortress. Some, it was reported, sang Protestant hymns from the rooftop of the Hôtel de Ville. As the last contingent filed out of the city, defiantly chanting the psalms in French while they marched, Catholic troops, joined by armed peasants alerted by the tocsin and

11. *HGL*, 11:382–85; Greengrass, "Anatomy of a Religious Riot," pp. 375–78; J. Garrisson-Estèbe, *Protestants du Midi (1559–1598)* (Toulouse, 1980), pp. 22–28.

eager for a slaughter, set upon them. Fighting continued throughout the night, leaving about 100 Catholics and 200 Protestants dead.[12]

The number of casualties for the weeks of religious rioting was estimated by a contemporary at 4,000—a figure that seems greatly exaggerated until one recalls that fighting was nearly continuous during the whole time. Much of the violence, especially by the Calvinists, was ritualistic: the desecration of churches, the shattering of images, and the like. It was said that one Protestant woman made a point of her contempt for the mass by defecating on a church altar. And some of the atrocities committed by Catholics had a ritual, purifying dimension insofar as the corpses of a number of their victims were thrown into the Garonne or mutilated in a systematic fashion. Undoubtedly among the leading combatants in both camps were the university students, who were well prepared for street fighting and urban guerrilla warfare, even better than the noble warriors, whose horse-mounted tactics and cumbersome armor rendered them relatively ineffective in Toulouse's narrow streets and alleys. Ordinary Catholics, who might have displayed some reluctance to attack their neighbors, were called upon to participate in a "holy war" and given dispensation in advance for the taking of a heretic's life. A few, to be sure, took advantage of the occasion to settle personal scores or pillage the property of the rich. The sumptuous town house of Jean de Bernuy, for example, was sacked by a Catholic crowd and one of his daughters raped despite the fact that the wealthy pastelier was not a declared heretic.[13]

But the confessional conflict was not primarily a war of rich against poor. In fact, the Catholic and Calvinist communities of Toulouse, though not mirror images of each other, were quite similar in social composition. In the days leading to the final confrontation in May, both groups sent representatives to the Hôtel de Ville to negotiate a truce, and their delegations offer a comparison between the constituencies of the two confessions. Merchants, officials, and the liberal professions dominated the Protestant delegation but accounted for only 45 percent of the Catholic group. The Catholic party was more popular in makeup, with 39 percent recruited from artisans as com-

---

12. *HGL*, 11:386–92; Greengrass, "Anatomy of a Religious Riot," pp. 387–88.

13. Greengrass, "Anatomy of a Religious Riot," pp. 384–89; *Histoire ecclésiastique*, 3: 20–36; *Histoire de M. G. Bosquet sur les troubles advenus en la ville de Tolose l'an 1562* (Toulouse, 1595), published in *Recueil de pièces historiques aux guerres de religion de Toulouse* (Paris, 1862), pp. 50–80.

pared with 17 percent for the Protestants.[14] From the persecutions that
followed the violent days of May we get a clearer image of the Calvinists. Most were artisans, but over 35 percent were from the liberal
professions and nearly 15 percent were merchants.[15] Most important,
the organizational structures of the warring parties were also matched.
Each depended upon inspiration or support from far-off leaders: Condé and Théodore Bèze for the Calvinists, the Guises and the papacy for
the militant Catholics. Each relied on the military aid of local noblemen; each organized their combatants in armed militias; each drew
upon the fighting traditions of the student nations; each was inspired
by the zeal of its clergy, although the Calvinist pastors seemed to play a
more decisive role as leaders than their Catholic counterparts. And
each faction, at least for a time, depended upon leadership from an
element of the city's officialdom: the Calvinists looked to the capitouls,
several of whom in 1562 were of the "new religion," while the parlement quickly took charge of the Catholic defense of the city.[16] The
court's loyalty to the Catholic church was clearly related to the magistrates' positions as royal officers whose legitimacy depended upon the
stability and integrity of the realm. While some individual magistrates,
both in Toulouse and elsewhere, embraced Calvinism, the sovereign
courts as institutions were if anything more firmly Catholic than even
the crown.[17] The capitoulat's kinship with Calvinism is more puzzling.
Perhaps it was due to the presence of several pasteliers or the humanist
Michel Dufaur among the town councilors. More likely it reflected the
capitouls' concern to defend both their own privileges and those of the
city in the face of growing royal power represented by the parlementary magistrates, whose ranks and prerogatives had increased enor-
mously in the preceding decades. Elsewhere, Protestantism proved
adaptable to the cause of urban autonomy, especially when this meant
investing civic power in lay hands.[18] Such a cause was dear to the
partisans of the Hôtel de Ville, with their myth of the municipal
republic. In any case, in 1562 the parlement "broke" the election of the

14. Wolff, *Histoire*, p. 274.
15. Joan Davies, "Persecution and Protestantism: Toulouse, 1562–1575," *Historical Journal* 22 (1979): 38.
16. Lafaille, 2:213.
17. David Parker, *The Making of French Absolutism* (New York, 1983), p. 37.
18. Bernd Moeller, *Imperial Cities and the Reformation*, trans. E. Midelfort and M. Edwards (Philadelphia, 1972); and Steven E. Ozment, *The Reformation in the Cities*, (New Haven, 1975).

Antoine Rivalz, "The Expulsion of the Huguenots," eighteenth century (Musée des Augustins)

current capitouls, replacing them with men whose Catholic allegiance was above suspicion.[19] Henceforth, the leadership of the opposition to ultra-Catholicism would shift to a faction of moderate magistrates within the parlement—the growing party of local politiques.

The persecution of Toulouse's Calvinists did not end with their expulsion from the city on May 17. Later that year more than 120 of them were sentenced to death, and throughout the decade their property was subject to confiscation as well. Among these victims was one capitoul and five former town councilors.[20] It appears that in the fall of 1568 a nocturnal pogrom was staged in which four hundred to five hundred Huguenots were murdered, their bodies dumped into the Garonne.[21] Sixteen high officers, many from the parlement, were placed under arrest, and an equal number fled to Montauban and Castres.[22] That year also saw the formation of one of a series of local "crusades," an early manifestation of the Sainte Union, or Holy League, that was soon to dominate the city.[23] But in Toulouse, as elsewhere in France, the coup de grace for the Huguenots came in 1572, during what Michelet called the "Season of Saint Bartholomew."

In the capital of the Midi the season's slaughter started late, in October, over a month after the Parisian massacre. On the evening of October 3, two merchants—the Delpeches, father and son—arrived from Paris with orders "to kill all," or so they claimed. For several weeks the remaining Huguenots of the city had been under lock and key, some in the convents of the Jacobins and Carmes, others in the municipal prison. Beginning in the evening, a group of self-appointed executioners led by the Delpeches brought the prisoners from their cells one by one and slaughtered them in their tracks. The number of victims was between two hundred and three hundred. Among them were three councilors of the parlement, whose corpses, draped in their official robes, were later hanged from a large tree that stood before the parlementary palace. It was in such an ignominious fashion that Jean de Coras met his end. Unlike the Saint Bartholomew massacres in Paris and other provincial towns, this one was not marked by a popular outbreak of violence or by an orgy of indiscrimi-

19. Lafaille, 2:250.
20. Lafaille, 2:241.
21. Davies, "Persecution and Protestantism," p. 35.
22. Lafaille, 2:290–91.
23. On the league in 1568, see Lafaille, 2:291; and *HGL*, 11:509–10 and 12:1247.

nate slaughter and the mutilation of bodies. In Toulouse, the killing
was organized, systematic, and cold-blooded.[24]

It was not, however, an enterprise planned and carried out with
the support of the entire municipal officialdom, for a faction of elites
opposed the executions. The First President of the parlement attempted to halt the slaughter, and on hearing of the massacres in
Paris the duc de Joyeuse—the future leader of the league in the
Midi—cautioned the Catholics of Languedoc "to do nothing."[25] In
fact, three groups were entangled in the bloody events of 1572: the
Huguenot victims, the band of assassins and their supporters, and a
party of moderate Catholics opposed to the massacre. The leader of
the latter group was probably Jean-Etienne Duranti, avocat général of
the parlement, who, as First President in 1589, would be assassinated
by a crowd of extreme Catholics for his royalist and politique sympathies. We saw evidence of this party of moderate Catholics among the
handful of magistrates who were willing to come to terms with the
Calvinists in 1562; by 1572 they had grown in number, and it is more
than likely that the Saint Bartholomew executioners had in mind
terrorizing these parlementary politiques as much as eliminating their
hapless Huguenot captives.

The assassins of 1572 numbered about twenty-five; they included
the merchants Delpeches, a president and a councilor of the parlement, a captain of the city guard who was the son of a councilor,
several other merchants and "bourgeois," a handful of artisans, and a
large contingent of students. The schoolboy executioners, drawn
mostly from the Provence nation led by its prior La Tour, were probably inspired as much by a hatred for their rival nationaires, who
happened to be Huguenots, as by religious passions. Several years
after the Saint Bartholomew massacre in Toulouse, the secretary of
the Provence nation reflected on his older colleagues' role in the
event: "And certainly if I say that the principal ones who conducted
the massacre were students, it will be with great regret. For it is a
pitiable thing to hear of the sons of Minerva, humane and kind, being
transformed into sons of Mars, cruel [and] bloody, seeing that they
could thus proceed to the deaths of so many people."[26]

24. Janine Estèbe, *Tocsin pour un massacre: La saison des Saint-Barthélemy* (Paris, 1968),
pp. 152–54; *HGL*, 11:545 and 12:33–5.
25. *HGL*, 11:544–45.
26. Quoted in Dawson, *Toulouse in the Renaissance*, p. 137.

Apart from the three councilors of the parlement and two officers of the sénéchal, neither the identities nor the precise number of victims is known. From a list of Huguenots detained by the capitouls in the month before the massacre, however, Joan Davies has identified the occupations of ninety-seven: more than half were officers, lawyers, or other members of the liberal professions; nearly a third were artisans of one kind or another; and the remainder were merchants.[27] There is no proof, only a likelihood, that these detainees became the victims of the night of October 3–4. In any case, the existing evidence supports the conclusion that both those who died and those who killed represented a cross section of urban society. Here, as in other religious riots, bands of artisans, students, merchants, and notables confronted one another as victims and executioners.

The Lineaments of Catholic Allegiance

As serious as the Huguenot threat was to Toulouse, the fact is that those of the "new religion" ultimately did not stand a chance in the city. Outnumbered and isolated from their potential support in the region, they were overwhelmed militarily and then persecuted mercilessly. Even when their coreligionists elsewhere were enjoying the relative toleration offered by several royal edicts, the Calvinists of Toulouse were made to chafe under the rule of the parlement, which often refused to abide by the crown's will in matters of faith.[28] More important in the long run was the fact that the urban populace's attachment to Catholicism remained strong, not only rendering it impervious to the appeal of Calvinism but also instilling in it a crusading zeal. Sixteenth-century historians have long puzzled over the appeal of Calvinism, but until recently much less thought has been given to the basis of ordinary people's attachment to Catholicism, especially before the Counter-Reformation. What kept the common people bound to their faith? What made them look upon heresy as a threat to the very soul of their community?

The question is obviously very large and complex, but one starting point is to appreciate the extent to which signs of the sacred perme-

---

27. Davies, "Persecution and Protestantism," p. 38.
28. Pierre Delattre, ed., *Les établissements des Jésuites en France depuis quatre siècles,* 5 vols. (Enghien, 1949–57), 4:1286.

ated the urban community, indeed marked the very cityscape, so that a rejection of Catholicism would have been tantamount to a rejection of the city itself. Toulouse was saturated with churches, chapels, convents, monasteries, and other religious institutions; moreover, during the period of the religious wars the number of ecclesiastical institutions increased notably as new orders were created and others sought refuge from Protestant persecution in the Catholic stronghold. In 1566 the Jesuits arrived in Toulouse from Pamiers; in 1569 both the Chartreux and the Cordeliers established themselves in the city, the former fleeing Saix, the latter Ile-en-Jordain; and in 1582, First President Duranti arranged for the installation of the Capuchins.[29] By the end of the sixteenth century, Toulouse's ecclesiastical establishment was unusually large, at least in the opinion of the well-traveled Swiss medical student Thomas Platter, who in 1599 noted his astonishment at the number of churches within the city walls.[30] Counting the institutions of the regular clergy alone, there were more than 25 religious orders for men and women in sixteenth-century Toulouse, each with its own convent or chapel, each with its own distinctive habit, each too with special devotions that emphasized a particular aspect of the universal faith.[31]

The number of churches and convents was thus matched by their diversity—not so much the architectural diversity appreciated by the present-day tourist as a diversity of representations of the holy within their walls. One found, of course, the same mass in every church and chapel, but people looked upon religious edifices as repositories of sacred mysteries as well as ritual spaces, and here there was an array of offerings. For each church, chapel, and convent housed different shrines, relics, and other holy things that people could turn to in need and that the populace looked upon with respect and awe. The convent of the Minimes, for example, harbored a fourteenth-century chapel dedicated to Saint Roch, the patron of pestiférés, which attracted a stream of supplicants during epidemics. In the suburbs was located another shrine to Saint Roch, one presumably serving poorer plague victims.[32] At the Augustines stood a miraculous statue of the Virgin, whose powers were thought to have relieved a range of suf-

29. Lafaille, 2:296; Delattre, Les établissements des Jésuites 4:1274; HGL, 12:1473.
30. Platter, Journal of a Younger Brother, p. 245.
31. Catel, Mémoires, pp. 147–269; M. L'Abbé Cayre, Histoire des evêques et archevêques de Toulouse (Toulouse, 1873).
32. Roucaud, La peste à Toulouse, pp. 92–93; Rozoi, 4:461–64.

ferers from the region.[33] The most cherished icon in the city was the Black Virgin in the Church of the Dalbade. Normally this twelfth-century Byzantine figurine stood on the parish church's main altar, but in times of collective calamities it would be borne in procession by crowds of clergymen and lay people and brandished before the threatening fire, floods, or even the unseen plague. The Black Virgin's processional role was captured in a popular Occitan expression: "Le, nostro Damo la Negro que se passejo" (Our Black Lady who walks).[34] Some churches were renowned merely for certain mysteries—the cathedral, for example, for possessing, along with the body and head of its patron, Saint Etienne, an ampoule of his blood, which reputedly increased and decreased with the phases of the moon; or the crypts of the Cordeliers convent, which contained hundreds of mummified bodies "miraculously" preserved.[35] In the convent of the Jacobins was to be found one of the most cherished relics in all of Christendom, and one especially meaningful for a university town: the body of Saint Thomas Aquinas.[36]

Undoubtedly the most singular religious edifice, a source of sacred power as well as civic pride, was the Basilica of Saint-Sernin, long a resting spot for pilgrims on their way to Compostella. This twelfth-century Roman Gothic structure, located at the northernmost part of the city, housed the city's repository of holy relics, stored in the basilica's choir—a sacred treasure that included the body of Charlemagne as well as the remains of nearly thirty saints and martyrs. Some were of local origin, including the early bishops of Toulouse, Saints Sernin and Exupère; others were from far away, such as Saint Edmond of England. There were also the partial remains of six apostles. All were venerated by the populace. Toulouse had been a repository for holy relics by virtue of its position as a major way station

33. ADH-G, E 1017, Notre-Dame de Pitié.

34. T. R. Caussette, *Notice sur Notre-Dame la Daurade à Toulouse* (Toulouse, 1874). The Black Virgin of the Daurade was the prefered votive among the populace. Witness a sort of competition between the Holy Sacrament and the Virgin during a large fire in 1672: the archbishop first bore the holy wafer before the conflagration, but to no effect; then the Black Virgin was brought out, and according to one account, a great arrow of flames fell from the sky and extinguished the fire. See J. Lestrade, "Notes historiques, extraits des registres des notaires de Toulouse," *RHT* 1 (1914): 500.

35. Catel, pp. 161–63, 217.

36. C. Douais, *Documents sur l'ancienne province de Lanquedoc*, 2 vols. (Paris and Toulouse, 1904), 2:xxxvi.

on the route to Compostella; by the early modern period the choir of
Saint-Sernin was hailed by many as one of the holiest spots in all of
Christendom. No visitors, not even Protestant tourists, could pass up
a glimpse of its holy treasure.[37]

While Toulouse may have been particularly rich in sacred objects,
the city was certainly not unique in this respect. Medieval Christianity left a legacy of diverse manifestations of the sacred—the pan-
orama of saints, shrines, relics, and the like that provided the faithful
with a range of possible contact points with the church.[38] Such diversity constituted part of the medieval church's great appeal, especially
for many ordinary people for whom a celestial God was a distant,
abstract figure. But it also drew the criticism of the reformers and
many humanists, who saw the cults of saints and relics as distracting
people from the religion of Christ. Since Catholic reformers later
joined in this critique, such cults may be mistaken for mere medieval
vestiges, aspects of the so-called waning of the Middle Ages. What
we see in Toulouse is rather that the diversity of representations of
the sacred was both preserved and intensified in the first half of the
sixteenth century.

To illustrate, let us look more closely at Saint-Sernin's treasure of
relics. To be sure, these relics had been the objects of great devotion
throughout the Middle Ages; they were the single most important
source of Toulouse's reputation as a holy city. But starting in the late
fifteenth century both municipal and church officials approached
them with increasing solicitude. For example, the first real inventory
of the relics was undertaken in 1468; that of 1489 was even more
thorough and there followed four more inventories between 1502 and
1524. As a result, the relics were rescued from the neglect of centuries
and made presentable to the faithful, something done annually on
Holy Thursday. The inventory of 1502 precipitated a legal contest
between the basilica chapter and the city over the proprietorship of
the relics: it was then decided that they were part of the city's patrimony and were henceforth treated with even greater official in-

37. On these relics, see Bertrandi, *Les gestes des Tolosains*, pp. 13–14; Raymond
Dayde, *L'histoire de St. Sernin: ou, l'incomparable trésor de son église abbatiale de Tolose*
(Toulouse, 1661); Alphonse Bremond, *Histoire de toutes les saintes reliques conservées dans
l'insigne Basilique le Saint-Saturnin* (Toulouse, n.d.); C. Douais, *Documents*, 2:ix–xxxvi,
104–74.
38. A. N. Galperin, *Religions of the People in Sixteenth-Century Champagne* (Cambridge,
Mass., 1976), p. 70. For Spain, see William A. Christian, Jr., *Local Religion in Sixteenth-
Century Spain* (Princeton, 1981), chap. 2.

terest.[39] Indeed, during the plague of 1528 the city turned to them for protection, and when the epidemic subsided, the capitouls made an offering of thanksgiving to the relics in the form of a wax image of the city.[40] What could better emblemize the city's identification with these holy remains? The heightened interest in them is evident in other respects. In 1509 the statutes of the Confraternity of the Holy Bodies, the brotherhood of caretakers of the relics, were renewed.[41] In 1511 the remains of three saints were "elevated"—that is, placed in reliquaries—in a great ceremony ordered by the city.[42] In 1526 the pope granted Toulouse a jubilee every five years in honor of the "Corps Saints de Saint-Sernin," and there followed another ceremony, a massive procession of the relics which included all of the city's official bodies, from the magistrates, capitouls, and clergymen to representatives of the artisan community.[43] In 1533, as has been noted several times, Francis I made a pilgrimage to the city to pray before the holy treasure.[44] During the 1530s the architect Nicolas Bachelier constructed a large arched gateway leading from the city directly into the crypts that stored the relics.[45] In 1562, when the Protestant menace was most threatening, when religious objects and holy places were daily desecrated, it was through the public display and adoration of the relics that Catholic officials hoped to resanctify and protect their city.[46] And in 1564, on the occasion of Charles IX's visit to the city, a capitoul boasted to the young king that there were "four singular and beautiful things in Toulouse," chief among them the holy relics of Saint-Sernin.[47] In short, it was in the first half of the sixteenth century that these relics—and the cult of saints they represented—became the chief focus of public devotion.

People did not have to visit the crypts of Saint-Sernin or other churches and chapels to gaze upon holy objects and figures, however; they were confronted by them on nearly every streetcorner. In the early modern city signs of the sacred were never far from sight.

39. Douais, *Documents*, pp. ix–xix, 106–7.

40. Lafaille, 2:65–67; Dayde, *L'histoire de St. Sernin*, p. 342.

41. DAMT, GG 788, Confrérie des Corps Saints de Saint-Sernin, 1533; Douais, *Documents*, p. xxiv.

42. Lafaille, 1:314–16.

43. Ibid., 2:62.

44. Ibid., 2:88–89.

45. Douais, *Documents*, p. xiii.

46. Lafaille, 2:239.

47. Gabriel de Minuit, *De la beauté . . . avec la Paule-Graphie ou description des beautez d'une dame tholosaine nommé la Belle Paule* (Lyons, 1587), p. 218.

Scattered throughout Toulouse were a dozen or more large crosses, some constructed during the Middle Ages, but some of more recent origin.[48] Several of these crosses were considered the special preserve of a particular neighborhood, such as the one standing in the Place Mage, whose residents lighted a lamp before it each Saturday.[49] These were urban shrines denoting in most cases miracles or other holy events: as recently as 1525 a miracle reportedly occurred on the spot sanctified by the Holy Crucifix in the Place du Salin.[50] Another cross, that of Saint Carbes, commemorated the deaths of two Catholic noblemen during the religious wars; it was a sixteenth-century equivalent of the "Ici est tombé" plaques, marking a fallen partisan of the Resistance, found today on the streetcorners of many French cities.[51] These crosses were not the only holy markers in the city. Looking down on people from buildings and gates at nearly every turn were statues of the Virgin and various saints.[52] Following the inspirational preaching of a Cordelier friar in 1518, the capitouls were moved to mount marble reliefs on each of the city gates—frescos depicting bevies of angels supporting the words, "Nom de Jesus."[53] In that same year they instituted the practice of having town criers circulate during the night; these four réveilleurs not only thoughtfully shouted out the hour to slumbering Toulousains but also called upon those now rudely awakened to "pray to God for the souls of the departed!"[54]

All of this is not to say that the populace's Catholic fervor was mounting, nor that it was less vulnerable to the Protestant challenge. All that can be said is that public signs of the sacred were increasing in the early sixteenth century and that the city's official concern for religious matters was becoming more explicit. This was, of course, in large part a reaction to the problem of heresy, which, noted the "An-

48. Catel, pp. 190, 193, 204, 211, 233.
49. Ibid., p. 204.
50. Lafaille, 2:57; Rozoi, Annales, 3:328.
51. Catel, p. 190.
52. Jules de Lahondès, Toulouse chrétienne: L'église Saint-Etienne (Toulouse, 1890), p. 158. See also Lahondès, "Les statues de la Vierge au Musée de Toulouse," Mémoires de la Société Archéologique du Midi 16 (1908): 270–87.
53. Lafaille, 2:13. On this preacher, see M. F. Godfroy, "Thomas Illyricus, prédicateur et théologian, 1484–1528" (Thèse de doctorat, 3e cycle, Université de Toulouse-Mirail, 1984).
54. Abbé Salvan, Histoire générale de l'église de Toulouse, 4 vols. (Toulouse, 1861), 4:18. Catel notes that in 1527 an image of the virgin "with a representation of the son" was found buried in a ditch near one of the city gates. Subsequently a special chapel was constructed to honor this image (p. 236).

nales" in 1549, threatened to divide the city like the "rent robe of
Jesus Christ."[55] After 1562 the city's identification with the faith was
complete: the city as a corporate whole, and not simply the ecclesiastical establishment, took up the defense of the church, something
epitomized in the annual procession of May 17 commemorating the
"deliverance" of Toulouse, which soon became as much an emblem
of the city as the more secular Floral Games, and a mark of its Catholic
militancy as well. But although this civic religious fervor was primarily a strategic reaction to Protestantism, it also drew upon the
Renaissance ideal of a unified urban polity: in 1564 the capitouls
employed for the first time the denomination "la République chrétienne" for their city.[56]

Beneath this mantle of religious and civic unity, however, was
another reality, that of a city in which representations of the sacred
remained diverse and varied. This contradiction would remain a feature not only of urban religiosity but, more generally, of civic life
throughout the early modern period. For urban society was increasingly fragmented corporately, leading often to the "corporate
individualism" which, Tocqueville claimed, thwarted concerted social
action in the Old Regime. The tension between unity and diversity was
most apparent in the mass ceremonial displays periodically mounted
by cities on holy days, for civic occasions, or in times of collective
danger: the general procession. Here the city as a whole, from the
varied officialdom and ecclesiastical orders to artisan guilds and even a
delegation of the poor, took to the streets in an elaborate ceremony that
in Toulouse could involve the participation of more than five thousand
people—over one-tenth the settled population. The general procession was meant to be the quintessential expression of municipal unity,
but by its very composition and nature it invited incidents that undermined this purpose. Putting rival corporations in the street and asking
them to conform to a fixed rank and order risked having the public
ceremony degenerate into a shoving match between normally decorous officials. General processions "broke down" in such a fashion
with regularity in the Old Regime—sometimes remaining stalled for
hours as embarrassed officials frantically tried to placate the entangled
disputants while thousands of other participants waited in the
streets.[57]

55. AMT, BB 247, p. 99.
56. Ibid., p. 332.
57. See, for example, the procession on the Feast of Saint John in 1584 when the

The fragmented nature of urban society and its relationship to the diversity of expressions of the sacred was most apparent in the organization of the craft community. By the middle of the sixteenth century there were nearly sixty artisan corporations in Toulouse, each recognized by the capitouls as having jurisdiction over a trade or craft, and each, too, sanctioned by the church as a religious body, endowed with a patron saint, and consigned a chapel in one of the city's parish churches or convents. Each craft corporation was thus also a confraternity; indeed, members were hardly conscious of any distinction between the two. We can see evidence of this blurring of the sacred and profane in the articles the arquebusiers presented to the authorities when they sought to create an elite of masters and constitute themselves as a sworn guild. Their petition first details a series of religious obligations, expresses fidelity to their patron, Saint Eloy, promises to contribute to the upkeep of a chapel in the Cordeliers' convent, and includes plans to hold special masses and stage public processions. Only then does the document get down to the business of setting restrictions on apprentices, defining the standards for the mastership, and asserting their claim to a monopoly on the fabrication and sale of firearms within the city.[58]

Membership in religious brotherhoods bound artisans to their faith but did so in a fashion that tended to promote identification within their particular confraternity rather than the larger community of Christians. They also were a powerful force fostering the cult of saints, for each confraternity assembled under the patronage of a saint and periodically paraded his banner or statue through the streets during its confraternal processions. These craft confraternities were not free-floating associations, however—devotional cells with no ties to the ecclesiastical establishment. In fact, craft brotherhoods were rather closely associated with the regular clergy. Although some confraternities were sponsored by parish churches, most were protected by the monks and friars in the city's religious orders, not the secular clergy. (See Table 1.) Artisans possessed or were consigned chapels in monastic churches, their services officiated by the monks

---

sénéchal tried to march ahead of the capitouls, "to the great scandal of the people" (AMT, BB 275, pp. 353–54). On the tension between unity and diversity in the public procession, see Mervyn James, "Ritual, Drama and Social Body in the Late Medieval English Town," *Past & Present*, no. 98 (1983), pp. 3–29.

58. A. du Bourg, "Coup d'oeil historique sur les diverses corporations de Toulouse," *MASIBL* 14 (1886–89): 77.

TABLE 1

Affiliations of craft confraternities with religious orders and parish churches in the sixteenth century

Craft or trade	Religious order	Parish church or other church
Weavers		Saint-Etienne
Shearers	Visitation	
Velour makers	Frères béguins	
Drapers	Grands Carmes	
Tailors	Bénédictins	
Furriers		Saint-Sernin
Ragmen	Augustins	
Bonnet makers	Carmes	
Hatters	Carmes	
Fullers	Couvent de Saint-Trinité	
Spinners	Carmes	
Carders	Carmes	
Tanners	Augustins	
Metalworkers	Frères prêcheurs	
Gelders	Carmes	
Shoemakers	Carmes	
Bootmakers	Augustins	
Gilders	Couvent de Saint-Croix	
Skinners	Augustins	
Purse makers		Saint-Rome
Barber-surgeons	Frères prêcheurs	
Provisioners	Frères prêcheurs	
Bakers	Carmes déchaussés	
Tavernkeepers	Carmes déchaussés	
Candlemakers		Daurade
Apothecaries	Frères mineurs	
Masons	Augustins	
Carpenters	Couvent de Saint-Etienne	
Latheworkers		Saint-Rome
Embroiderers	Frères prêcheurs	
Edge-tool makers	Augustins	
Blacksmiths		Daurade
Gunsmiths		Daurade
Goldsmiths	Frères prêcheurs	
Needle makers	Grands Carmes	
Lantern makers	Carmes	
Saddlers		Daurade
Fiddlers	Carmes	

Source: Du Bourg, "Les diverses corporations de Toulouse," MASIBL, 13 (1883–85): 257–96; 14 (1886–89): 52–91, 240–58.

and brothers of the regular clergy, and their statutes approved by a priest of the order. Humanists and reformers might have railed against the supposed sloth and ignorance of the monastic clergy. But most artisans had reasons to take a kinder, more appreciative view of their frocked neighbors and patrons, who frequently played an integral part in the confraternal life of craftsmen. The statutes of the tailors of Toulouse, for example, issued in 1509, stipulated that on the eve of the feast day of their patron, Saint Luke, both masters and workers would gather in a procession to vespers service accompanied by their sponsors, the Benedictine friars.[59] Members of the confraternity of shoemakers, sponsored by the Augustinian order, could count on twelve of the brothers in attendance at their funerals, at least according to the regulations of 1550.[60] The fishermen of the city depended upon a regular order for spiritual support of their livelihood: each May the Benedictines carried out a ritual known as the *baignade de la croix*, in which they would dip a long metal cross into the waters of the Garonne to ensure its fecundity.[61] In short, the regular clergy was the arm of the church closest to the common people not only as sponsors of craft confraternities but for other reasons as well; for in this pre-Tridentine era the parish clergy was often ill equipped to deal with the needs of the faithful. During the epidemic of 1585, for example, the capitouls thanked the Jesuits and Capuchins for aiding plague victims "physically as well as spiritually," while the rest of the city's clergy had done little to help the stricken population.[62] Before the poor-relief reforms of the seventeenth century, the religious orders were an important source of alms, and their role as the major public benefactors of the city's laboring classes disposed artisans to look toward the monasteries and convents for material, as well as spiritual, support.[63]

59. Du Bourg, "Les diverses corporations de Toulouse," *MASIBL* 13 (1883–85): 266.
60. Ibid., p. 269.
61. In the eighteenth century, Pierre Barthès mentions this custom as being an annual event in Toulouse and notes its venerability as well ("Les heures perdues de Pierre Barthès," BMT, MS 699–706, passim).
62. Roucaud, *La peste à Toulouse*, p. 84.
63. On the ties between the laity and the clergy, especially the regular clergy, in an urban setting, see Natalie Zemon Davis, "Protestants and Printing Workers of Lyon: A Study in the Problem of Religion and Social Class during the Reformation" (Ph.D. diss., University of Michigan, 1959), pp. 121–24; and John MacManners, *French Ecclesiastical Society under the Ancien Régime: A Study of Angers in the Eighteenth Century* (Manchester, 1960), p. 134.

The example of the artisan community—its organization into craft confraternities and their close association to the regular clergy—highlights the advantages of a diverse and fragmented pattern of sacred representations. For just as the artisans were divided into many different corporations, each with its own identity, so was the church similarly broken down into separate parts, both symbolic and associational, thus allowing the two domains to mesh like matched sprocket wheels. If, however, this arrangement was one source of the common people's allegiance to the church, it struck some humanists and most reformers as less than ideal. Even the crown issued an edict in the 1530s aimed at banning certain craft confraternities, although this prohibition remained a dead issue.[64] The fractured organization of religious life at mid-century can thus be juxtaposed to the ideal of a united faith and city, an ideal central to the tradition of civic humanism, as we have seen. Does it follow, to simplify grossly, that the forms of urban religious life and the Renaissance were at odds, that the contradiction between the diversity of the sacred in the city and the myth of the municipal republic remained unresolved? In fact, the patterns of religious association began to evolve in the sixteenth century toward broader, less fragmented forms, and such an evolution eventually served as a basis for the citywide association that was the Holy League.

Brotherhood and Militancy

Craft confraternities were not the only lay brotherhoods in the city. There were also many nonvocational confraternities, those assembling people sharing a devotion for a particular saint or holy figure, or those dedicated to the maintenance of a parish church or chapel. Documentation on these before the seventeenth century is sparse, but it appears that in the mid-sixteenth century at least twenty such brotherhoods were active in Toulouse, a few dating to the thirteenth century, when the newly formed Dominican and Franciscan orders inspired the formation of kindred lay associations. Some were dedicated to saints, such as the Confraternity of Saint Anne in the Cathedral, the Confraternity of Saint Germiers in the Church of the Dalbade, and the

---

64. Howell A. Lloyd, *The State, France, and the Sixteenth Century* (London, 1983), p. 39.

Confraternity of Saint James, the association of pilgrims to Compostella.[65] There were several Confraternities of the Souls in Purgatory; and the Church of the Daurade had a committee of laymen, the
Confraternity of the Work, which served as a sort of board of trustees
for the secular affairs of the parish.[66]

At least thirteen new lay associations were founded in Toulouse in
the sixteenth century, including six confraternities, three Jesuit-sponsored congregations, and four penitential companies. All but one of
the confraternities were dedicated to either Jesus or Mary, as opposed
to the saints, and thus emphasized those devotions increasingly
favored by Catholic reformers. Four were founded between 1540 and
1559, suggesting that they were established in response to the Protestant challenge. All of the confraternities were large and recruited their
members from a mix of professions and occupations. The statutes of
the Confraternity of the Sacred Conception of the Virgin Mary, published first in Occitan in 1515 and then in French in 1523, include a
membership list of seventy-two clerical confrères and seventy-two
laymen, the latter drawn from the high and low officialdom and
merchants.[67] The Confraternity of Saints Roch, Fabian, and Sebastian
had at least five hundred members in the sixteenth century.[68] Founded in the 1560s, this association, composed primarily of artisans, also
included some officials, functionaries, and merchants, and it even
accepted women (table 2 and figure 1). It was rare to find a craft-based
confraternity that drew workers from a variety of trades, for the associational patterns of the artisan community were primarily corporate.
It was also rare to find a confraternity that drew members from both
the upper and lower classes, that is, a lay association that was both

65. ADH-G, 4G115, Chapitre de Saint Etienne, chapels et confréries; Lahondès,
Toulouse chrétienne. L'eglise Saint-Etienne, p. 158; ADH-G, E 997, "Confrairie de St.
Germiers établie en 1455, renouvelle en 1470"; ADH-G, E 1604, "Statuts de la vénérable
Confrairie Sainct-Jacques Establie en Tholose, 1513."

66. ADH-G, E 1047, Table de Purgatoire, Saint-Etienne; Lahondès, *Toulouse chrétienne*, p. 157; Jean de Chabanel, *De l'estat et police de l'église Nostre-Dame dite la Daurade à
Tolose* (Toulouse, 1625), pp. 40–45; ADH-G, E 1022 (Table de Purgatoire de l'église St.
Agne); ADH-G, E 1001, Confrérie de l'oeuvre; R. D. Julien, *Toulouse chrétienne, histoire
de la paroisse Notre-Dame la Dalbade* (Toulouse, 1891), pp. 82–94.

67. *Los estatutz de la tresque devota, nobla, antiqua confrayria de la grada conception de
Nostra Dama mayre de Nostre Senhor Dieu Jhesu Chryst, fundada en la devota et antiquissima
gleys de la Daurada de Tholosa* (Toulouse, 1515); *Les statutz, ordonances et establissements de
la saincte, et tres devote Confrerie de dieu à l'honneur de la Sacrée Conception de la glorieuse
Vierge Marie fondee en al saincte et anticque Esglise de la Daurade de Tholose ensemble la teneu
de lau ctozisation et confirmation dy ceulx* (Toulouse, 1523).

68. ADH-G, E 861, Confrérie des Saints Roch, Fabien et Sébastien.

TABLE 2
Memberships of sixteenth-century confraternities

	Sacred Conception (1523)	Notre Dame (1563)	Assumption (1553)	Corps Saints (1533)	Saints Roch, Fabian and Sebastian (1568–1600)	Blue Penitents (1578–1600)
Nobles and high officers	20	15	15	2	2	47
Lawmen and low officers	8	12	45	17	14	145
Capitouls	4	2	0	0	0	0
Merchants and "bourgeois"	32	38	21	15	7	125
Free professions	6	2	4	11	0	0
Artisans	0	0	15	15	71	1
Clergy	72	0	0	0	3	115
Women	0	0	0	0	31	0
Students	0	0	0	0	0	638

Sources: Les statutz . . . da la sainte et tres devote confrérie de dieu à l'honneur de la Sacrée Conception de la glorieuse vierge . . . (Toulouse, 1523); AMT, GG 812, Confraternity of Our Lady of the Daurade; Statuts de la Confrérie de l'assomption . . . (Toulouse, 1553); AMT, GG 788, Confraternity of the Holy Bodies of Saint Sernin; ADH-G, E 861, Confraternity of Saints Roch, Fabian, and Sebastian; BIC, R MS 40, "Livre des Pénitents Bleus."

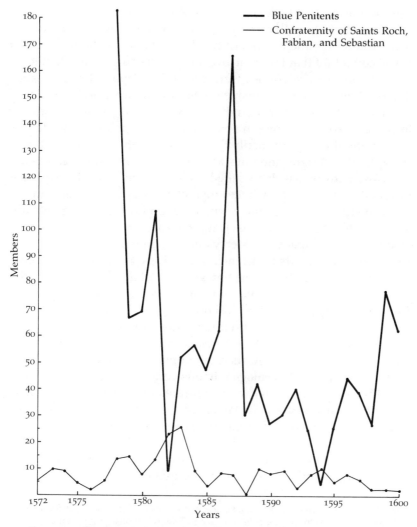

FIGURE 1. Enrollments in two sixteenth-century confraternities, 1572–1600

occupationally and socially mixed. But the new confraternities of the sixteenth century represented a departure from the traditional patterns of religious sociability, guided as they were by the ideal of a broad community of the faithful. The preamble of the Confraternity of the Assumption, founded in 1553, voiced the concern that Christians too often were "disunited," having fallen prey to the same "sectarianism" that bedeviled pagan philosophers. Unity is the goal of nature and should be the purpose of religion as well, noted the text. And it is in the confraternity where Christians "united in their faith" could find that fraternal love and charity surpassing all other.[69]

These new confraternities were primarily supported by the cathedral or other prominent parish churches in the city. But the Society of Jesus was also active in founding new lay associations. When the Jesuits arrived in Toulouse in 1566, they immediately set to the task of influencing the laity, primarily through the creation of two lay brotherhoods, the Congrégation des Messieurs and the Congrégation des Artisans, both of which recruited widely.[70] The latter in particular included men from the whole range of the city's crafts and trades. Unfortunately, there is little documentation on these congregations for the sixteenth century. This is not the case for another new brotherhood, the Company of Mercy, also founded by the Jesuits in Toulouse in 1570.[71] Its ranks included a cross section of urban notables—members of the parlement and sénéchal, the capitouls, the canons of both Saint-Etienne and Saint-Sernin, as well as other officers and clergymen. Unlike most other lay groups, this confraternity had a particular mission: its brethren undertook periodic visits to the city's prisons to see that their inmates were adequately clothed and fed and properly treated. As its name implies, the Company of Mercy strove to demonstrate a magnanimous concern for convicted criminals, thus allowing its high-born confrères to dramatize their public authority as custodians of the law. In fact, this confraternity took up a traditional task of the officialdom known as the Redde—the ceremonial visit of mercy to the city's prisons which the capitouls were customarily bound to undertake weekly, and the magistrates four times yearly.[72] Perhaps because of the influence of the Jesuits, per-

69. *Statuts de la Confrérie de l'assumption Nostre-Dame, Vièrge, mére de Jésus Christ, instituée en l'eglise métropolitaine Saint Estienne en Tolose* (Toulouse, 1553), not paginated.

70. Delattre, 4:1304. Delattre notes that the records of the Congrégation des Artisans are deposited in the Archives des Jésuites de Toulouse; this, however, turns out not to be the case. For the Congrégation des Messieurs, see also *Règles, coutumes et prières de la Congrégation des Messieurs érigée à Toulouse dans la Maison Professe des Pères de la Compagnie de Jésus* (Avignon, 1760).

71. *Statuts de la Confrérie de la Miséricorde, établie à Toulouse pour le soulagement des pauvres prisonniers, l'an 1570* (Toulouse, 1808); Léon-Pierre Raybaud, "Le bureau de la miséricorde de Toulouse aux XVIIe et XVIIIe siècles," *Mélanges Roger Aubens*, Recueil de mémoires et travaux publié par la Société d'Histoire du Droit et des Institutions des Anciens Pays de Droit Ecrit, fasc. 9 (Montpellier, 1974), pp. 665–82.

72. On the Redde, see above, Chapter 1.

haps also because of the turmoil and insecurity brought on by the religious wars, this duty was, in the late sixteenth century, assumed by a lay confraternity, one, moreover, that had a far wider membership than the two ruling corporations. In other words, it had become a shared responsibility of a cross section of the city's elite, now organized under a religious banner.

It should come as little surprise that in a time of confessional conflict religious associations predominated, eclipsing or even supplanting those of a secular or civic nature. These associations had a role in stimulating Catholic fervor, in mobilizing the populace to even more militant action; and in the process they fostered patterns of interaction between a wide range of social classes and took also the whole city as their terrain. Perhaps the most successful and novel of such associations were the penitential companies, which made their way from Italy to France in the early sixteenth century, in part through the efforts of the Jesuits. By the latter part of the century there were hundreds of these companies in scores of cities and towns—mostly in the Midi, where penitential piety proved particularly popular.[73] And in 1575 and 1576, when the city, having rejected the royal Edict of Beaulieu, was increasingly leaning toward ultra-Catholicism and anti-royalism, four penitential companies were installed in Toulouse.[74]

With the penitents we cross the threshold dividing primarily devotional confraternities from those whose purpose was to animate Catholic militancy in the context of the religious wars. With the penitents we enter the arena of crusading Catholicism. Not that the penitential companies lacked devotional concerns; indeed, virtually everything about them spoke to a specific style of Catholic devotion, the regime of mortification. Moreover, they persisted long after the religious wars, serving as a major forum for religious sociability for the rest of the Old Regime. But in the course of the confessional struggle, their

---

73. The penitential companies in France have attracted a great deal of scholarly attention in recent years. See, among other works, Maurice Agulhon, *Pénitents et francs-maçons de l'ancienne Provence* (Paris, 1968); Marc Venard, "Les confréries de pénitents au XVIe siècle dans la province ecclésiastique d'Avignon," *Mémoires de l'Académie du Vaucluse*, 6th ser., 1 (1967): 55–79; Benedict, *Rouen during the Wars of Religion*, pp. 190–208; Andrew Barnes, "*De Poenitentibus Civitatis Massaliae*: The Counter-Reformation, Religious Change, and the Confraternities of Penitents of Marseille, 1499–1792," (Ph.D. diss., Princeton University, 1983). I have analyzed aspects of the penitential ceremony in my article "Mortification on Parade: Penitential Processions in Sixteenth- and Seventeenth-Century France," *Renaissance and Reformation* 10 (1986): 123–46.

74. Delattre, *Les établissements des Jésuites*, 4:1286.

purpose clearly was to mobilize the urban populace to resist any compromise with the Huguenots; some served as devotional fronts for the Holy League. The penitential companies functioned on several levels, serving several purposes, some contradictory. They fostered a regime of strict discipline that only the few could maintain, yet they were also mass organizations. They were at once devotional confraternities and, in the context of the religious wars, politically militant associations.

There were four penitential companies in Toulouse: the Blues, Whites, Blacks, and Grays, known thus because of the color of their hooded robes, or *cagoules,* which entirely covered the wearer's face and head, leaving only slits for the mouth and eyes. Whenever they appeared in public or gathered for their devotions the penitents donned the cagoule. Such was the scene in late November 1576 at the Blue Penitents' inaugural outing: fifty-six shrouded figures, walking barefoot, ranged in double file behind a large, rough-hewn cross upon which hung a crown of thorns; each carrying a large yellow candle in one hand and an oversized book in another. Some flagellated themselves as they marched, or at least wore their whips—emblems of their severe devotional regime—hanging at their waists. The procession startled the populace with its novelty and reportedly caused children to cry out in terror. As they marched, the Blues chanted in unison hymns of the Passion "in a devout and lugubrious tone."[75]

The statutes of two sixteenth-century penitential companies have survived, those of the Whites and the Blues.[76] Many of these statutes are typical of confraternities in general: they govern the initiation of new members and the "research" into their morals; they outline the procedure for the election of officers and the holding of meetings; and they address the penitents' duties of charity, devotion, and participation in public processions. Individual penitents were urged to visit "the poor in the prisons and the pensionnaires in the hospices, giving according to their means to each," while girls "in dire need" were

75. This first procession is described in Jean-François Thouron, *Histoire de la Royale Compagnie de Messieurs les Pénitens Bleus de Toulouse* (Toulouse, 1688), pp. 10–13. See also AMT, BB 275, pp. 195–96.

76. The statutes of the sixteenth-century Blue Penitents are located in the BIC, R MS 61, "Livre des statutz de la Compagnie de St. Hieriosme . . . esrigee en l'année MDLX-XV." The documents of the White Penitents have been deposited in a private archive, but most have been reproduced by Marguerite Pecquet, "La Compagnie des Pénitents Blancs de Toulouse," *ADM* 84 (1972): 213–24.

singled out for special care, provided with dowries, and persuaded "to live honorably."[77]

In addition to these concerns for public welfare, the companies' statutes also addressed aspects of their penitential devotions. The penitential garb was strictly regulated; each White Penitent was to wear a white robe, "symbol of innocence and mortification," belted with a cord and embroidered on the left shoulder with an insignia of the five wounds of Christ.[78] The Blues were commanded to say five Paters and Aves Marias upon rising and to "examine their conscience" every evening.[79] Attendance at penitential meetings and processions was mandatory—something rarely stipulated by other confraternities.[80] The Whites welcomed females as penitents—again, somewhat rare for confraternities—although women were forbidden to appear in public processions or to meet with their male confrères.[81] And members were warned "to keep the silence which ought to be strictly observed about their organization," "to tell no one what is done" in their chapel. Among the company's elected officials, in fact, was an officer "du silence," who enforced the rule of secrecy.[82] This penchant for mystery was no doubt related to the precise nature of the company's regime of "discipline." As for this, the documents only make mention of the devotions that took place in the White Penitents' chapel during an all-night vigil the eve of Good Friday: "and each one according to his good wishes will receive the discipline, though with discretion. And so that aid can be given rapidly to the disciplined, two of their brethren will put themselves at their disposal in order to care for them as is necessary."[83]

The statutes of the White Penitents revealed another concern, that for the public display of irreverence in particular and profane celebrations in general. The penitents were warned, for example, to stay away from "dances"—a reference, it would seem, to the many popular festivals held in the city—and urged instead "to spread the light over everyone as models of devotion and piety."[84] A company with a high concentration of artisans and tradesmen, the Whites had to wage a

77. Pecquet, p. 218. See also BIC, R MS 61, statute 16.
78. Pecquet, p. 216.
79. BIC, R MS 61, statute 8.
80. Pecquet, p. 217.
81. Ibid., p. 219.
82. Ibid., pp. 216–17.
83. Ibid., p. 220.
84. Ibid, p. 218.

silent war against pastimes having an irresistible appeal even to the most devout. The period of the greatest temptation was carnival, when all was permitted, when the "world was turned upside down." The White Penitents' strategy to combat this temptation was ingenious— they simply kept their members preoccupied with devotional exercises. During the three days before Ash Wednesday, the penitents were required to make frequent visits to their chapel, where the Eucharist was exposed. And on Mardi Gras itself, when the popular celebration was at its peak, they were virtually kept captive in the chapel day and night. Their twenty-first regulation reads: "and so as to be prepared to flee the orgies that take place that day, as well as the other seductions and vanities of the world, they will be all assembled together and listen to the exhortations made after the meal in the chapel by the learned preacher." The regulation concludes ominously, "Those who do not attend will be punished."[85]

The four penitential companies of Toulouse shared a commitment to militant Catholicism and a devotional orientation toward severity. They all practiced, or at least advertised, their regime of mortification, but some were more strict than others in this respect. The Whites and Grays, for example, seem to have taken their exercises quite seriously, while the Blues were noted for a certain laxity.[86] Perhaps this difference was related to the social composition of the companies. The Blues were dominated by the upper class: at the founding of the company in 1576 the elite of the city and region were assembled, including the ecclesiastical and parlementary hierarchy, the nobility, and the high officialdom. In contrast, the Whites and Grays, having a large contingent of artisans and shopkeepers, were rather democratic in their recruitment.[87] The several companies also had different sponsors. Among the founders of the Blues were the Jesuits, especially Père Augier, a champion of penitential piety throughout France.[88]

---

85. Ibid., p. 221.
86. Pecquet, "La Compagnie des Pénitents Blancs de Toulouse," p. 220; for the Grays, ADH-G, E 940; P. E. Ousset, "La Confrérie des Pénitents Bleus de Toulouse," *RHT* 11 (1942): 278.
87. Ousset, p. 80; Thouron, *Histoire de la Royale Compagnie,* p. 10; BIC, R MS 40, "Livre des Pénitents Bleus: Registre des inscriptions depuis 1577." On the social composition for the other penitential companies, see primarily the seventeenth-century membership rolls; there is every indication that the same social mix prevailed at their founding (ADH-G, E 929 [Pénitents Blancs]; E 934 [Pénitents Gris]; E 942 [Pénitents Noirs]).
88. Thouron; Delattre, 4:1281.

The Whites had for their chief patrons the Franciscan order of the city, in whose chapel their statutes were first drawn up and agreed to in 1575.[89] It is more than likely that in sponsoring different penitential companies, these two orders—one old and well established in the city, the other the newest soldiers for Christ—were competing for influence among the laity.

There were thus differences and even some competition among the penitential companies—a kind of associational segregation within what was yet a single devotional movement. In this sense they did not entirely escape the organizational fragmentation we have noted as a fundamental feature of religious sociability in the city. By the late 1580s the differences between them seemed to take a political turn. The Blacks celebrated the funeral of the assassinated duc de Guise and were clearly lined up behind the league, while the Blues remained Royalist in sympathy.[90] But in the 1570s, at least, the penitents did comprise a single movement, and one which, most significantly, drew on virtually the whole range of the urban populace—from high churchmen and aristocrats to artisans and tradesmen. Until the period of the religious wars, such a wide recruitment pattern was rare, and this suggests a new trend in devotional association—both an outgrowth of the extraordinary mobilization occasioned by the confessional strife and a contributing factor in its continuation. The penitents also marked themselves as members of a spiritual elite, a select group of Christians who embraced a devotional regime of penance, physical mortification, and exemplary charitable works. This was not, however, an elite restricted to the upper classes or ruling hierarchy. The penitential companies were quite large, much larger, in fact, than other lay confraternities. In 1578, barely four years after their founding, more than 350 penitents filed past Catherine de Médicis during her visit to the city; and while few membership rolls have survived for the sixteenth century, those of the Blue Penitents show more than 1,000 enlistees by the end of the century, over half of them students (see figure 1 and table 2).[91] Thus the penitents can be likened to an army of the faithful—a volunteer army comprised of a self-selected yet open elite, which appeared in public equipped with

89. Pecquet, "La Compagnie des Pénitents Blancs," p. 213.
90. J. Contrasty, "Les prédicateurs du XVIᵉ siècle à Sainte-Marie de la Dalbade à Toulouse," RHT 34 (1947): 84; Thouron, p. 57.
91. AMT, BB 275, p. 259; BIC, R MS 40, "Livre des Pénitents Bleus."

instruments of their rather special devotion and garbed in uniforms denoting the militancy of their faith.[92]

That Toulouse's penitential companies were part of a more general movement of Catholic militancy cannot be doubted, for the year of their founding, 1576, also marked the creation of one of a series of Catholic "leagues" in the city.[93] Toulouse was not alone. Throughout France that year Catholic forces united in the first Holy League, the sworn goal of which was to prevent the ascension of the Protestant prince Henry of Navarre to the throne.[94] But the populace of Toulouse had long been trained in the ways of organized confessional militancy. As early as 1563, the year following the Calvinist debacle in the city, and again in 1568, the citizenry was enrolled in leagues devoted to preserving the religious purity of the realm.[95] Both leagues were created with the approval of parlement; both were animated by a consortium of Catholic warriors, high churchmen, and urban officials; both involved the taking of an oath. The oath of 1563 warned that those "of whatever dignity" who refused to swear would "be considered rebels"—and both called upon the faithful to make their houses and clothing with white crosses.[96] The league of 1568 (or crusade, as it was called) also received Rome's blessings in the form of a papal bull issued in March of that year.[97]

The third Catholic league in the city, that of 1576, was the largest yet. Like the earlier associations it was part confraternity and part army, combining prayers, sermons, and religious zeal with the concerns of a military undertaking. The articles of the association summoned, in the "name of the Holy Trinity and the precious body of Jesus Christ," all men capable of bearing arms to come to the defense of "our Catholic religion, apostolic and Roman, which has nourished

92. Schneider, "Mortification on Parade."
93. AMT, BB 275, pp. 213 ff.; "Association facte entre les manantz et habitans de la ville et viguerie de Thle et dioceze de l'estat ecclesiastique et de la noblesse que du tiers etat," in Jean Loutchitsky, ed., *Documents inédits pour servir à l'histoire de la réforme et de la Ligue* (Kiev, 1875), pp. 19–25. The original document is in AMT, GG 828, the last fourteen pages of which are filled with the signatures of those subscribing to the association.
94. For a good summary, see J. H. M. Salmon, *Society in Crisis*, pp. 234–75.
95. Lafaille, 2:254; Rozoi, 2:75–80. Lafaille, 2:291 and *preuves*, pp. 62–64; AMT, BB 274, pp. 422–23.
96. Quotation from Rozoi, 2:75–80; also quoted in Robert Harding, *Anatomy of a Provincial Elite* (New Haven, 1978), pp. 57–58.
97. *HGL*, 12:1247.

us and our ancestors and in which we wish to live and die."[98] Those
who answered this call were guaranteed payment and exemption
from taxation.[99] They also swore to carry out their holy enterprise
faithfully "without regard for friendship, family, or other alliance," a
proviso that clearly marked the league as transcending normal ties
and allegiances, or rather as a higher form of allegiance based upon a
sworn commitment to defend the faith.[100] It was to remain a secret
association as well, a rather surprising stipulation considering its size,
for the signers of the articles of the 1576 league included not only
members of the officialdom but also representatives of the city's crafts
and trades.[101] More than four thousand people attended a convoca-
tion of the league at the Jesuits' church the following year.[102] Unlike
the national Holy Leagues, which until 1588 remained an association
of Catholic militant elites, the league of Toulouse was popular from
the very start. And in 1589 it would prove insurrectionary as well.

Toulouse's Holy League

Reflecting on the events that followed the assassination of the
Guises in December 1588, an obscure scribe of Bar-sur-Seine noted in
his memoirs that France had two capitals during those turbulent
months, Paris and Toulouse. But while the League takeover of Paris
has long held the attention of historians, until recently little notice has
been paid to provincial insurrections, in particular that of Toulouse.
There a well-established tradition of Catholic militancy culminated in
a full-scale uprising that consumed the entire city for over a year.[103]
We have seen evidence for the steady buildup of Catholic mobilization in the city, especially as inspired by the penitential companies
and the several leagues created in the 1560s and 1570s. The year 1586
saw the creation of yet another militant association, which, like the

98. "Association faicte . . .," in Loutchitsky, *Documents inédits pour servir à l'histoire
de la réforme et de la Ligue*, p. 23.
99. Ibid., p. 22.
100. Ibid., pp. 24–25.
101. Ibid., p. 25.
102. Delattre, 4:1286.
103. Edmond Bruwaert, ed., *Mémoires de Jacques Carorquy, greffier de Bar-sur-Seine* (Paris,
1880), p. 17, quoted in Henri Drouot, "Les conseils provinciaux de la Sainte-Union
(1589–1595)," *ADM*, 65 (1953): 430. See, however, Mark Greengrass, "The *Sainte Union*
in the Provinces: The Case of Toulouse," *Sixteenth Century Journal* 14 (1983): 469–96.

earlier "crusades," claimed the allegiance of both the officialdom and the ordinary people, especially members of the craft community. In 1589, a generation of ultra-Catholic propaganda and mobilization climaxed in a final outburst of confessional hatred that took as its target not so much the Calvinists, whose presence in the city had been effectively eliminated during the "season" of Saint Bartholomew, but rather those moderate or politique Catholics whose faith was suspected of being more Royalist than Roman.

As in Paris, it was Henry III's desperate attempt to recover his royal authority by ordering the assassination of the brothers Guise at the Estates General in Blois that precipitated the League takeover of Toulouse. On January 3 news of the Guises' demise reached Toulouse. Three days later two League delegates—Etienne Tournier, scion of a parlementary family and a former capitoul, and Urbain de Saint-Gelais, bishop of Comminges—regained the provincial capital. Upon their arrival a full council of urban officials was convoked. There, Jean Daffis, vicar-general and provost of the Cathedral of Saint-Etienne, proposed the creation of an executive committee of eighteen officials to take charge of the city. The new ruling body, a sort of Committee of Public Safety before the letter, was composed of six clergymen, six magistrates of the parlement, and six bourgeois, the last of whom were all former capitouls.[104] As Mark Greengrass has pointed out, despite its menacing cast, the Council of Eighteen did not really supplant or overturn the existing urban officialdom, for all its members were drawn from the traditional elite; moreover, its very composition recalled the Conseil des Bourgeois, a group of eighteen town notables that customarily exercised great authority in the Hôtel de Ville.[105]

But there was more to the politics of the League-dominated city than what transpired within the officialdom, for the crowd, always a factor in a period of confessional strife, claimed center stage at this moment of crisis. The first assembly of the Eighteen in January 1589 was attended by six hundred armed craftsmen and laborers, and subsequent meetings of the town officials also had to contend with pressure from the street. The Hôtel de Ville remained open to these popular lobbyists, and the streets were the scene of ever-escalating mass demonstrations.[106] Etienne Tournier and Saint-Gelais were the masters of

104. HGL, 11:770.
105. Greengrass, "The Sainte Union in the Provinces," pp. 481–82.
106. HGL, 11:773.

the crowd, and they were aided by several fiery preachers, including François Richard, the provincial of the Minims; De Doiard, a priest from Cugnaux; and Odard Motte, a Jesuit.[107] New confraternities also played a prominent role in mobilizing the faithful: the Confraternity of the Holy Sacrament, a popular association of League partisans in Toulouse and other cities, staged several violent processions at crucial points during the insurrection; and it is likely that other militant confraternities were also established.[108] In short, the mobilization of the city's populace was general, complete with mass processions, barricades in the streets, incendiary preaching, and images and placards vilifying Henry III and the politique governor, Montmorency-Damville. "The gentlemen of the long robe became soldiers," wrote Saint-Gelais, "leaving the robe to take up arms. The boutiques entirely closed in order to arm the merchants and other workers; the wisest among the schoolboys closed their books to arm themselves, and mounted guard day and night. Priests and monks doffed their square bonnets and left their brevaries, their robes, and their habits to don armour and appear with arquebuses and poleaxes."[109]

But what was the point of the uprising? On one level it allied Toulouse with those forces in the nation opposed to Henry III and the likely succession of Henry of Navarre. On another, however, it further pitted the city not only against the politique governor Montmorency-Damville but also against his rival in the region, Guillaume de Joyeuse, who ostensibly led the Catholic party. Despite the fact that his family owed its prominence to the favor of the Valois, Joyeuse eventually declared for the League in mid-1589; but this did not make him any more acceptable to the Toulousains, who saw in him an "outsider," an agent of the crown, and a man willing to compromise the purity of religion for the preservation of his power in the region. And they were right, for Joyeuse was a reluctant leaguer at best, hardly a partisan of the Guises and their cause. Both Montmorency and Joyeuse had their allies within the city, and these were the real enemies of the uprising, which thus took on the character of a defense of the city from the pretensions of regional magnates whose political ties and aspirations were national.[110]

107. Ibid, p. 772; Contrasty, "Les prédicateurs du XVIe siècle," pp. 77–84.
108. Greengrass, "The *Sainte Union* in the Provinces," p. 474.
109. *Advertissement particulier et veritable de tout ce qui s'est passé en la ville de Tholose, depuis le massacre . . .* (Paris, 1589), p. 11.
110. *HGL*, 11:770 and passim.

Chief among Joyeuse's agents in the city were First President Etienne Duranti and his brother-in-law, Jacques Daffis, the avocat général of the parlement.[111] Duranti and Daffis did have several allies, especially in the sovereign court. They were the descendants of those humanists, politiques, and moderate Catholics we have encountered throughout the sixteenth century—but their numbers were few and dwindling, and they were hardly strong enough to persuade the parlement to oppose the popular revolt. Shortly after the Eighteen took power, Duranti, Daffis, and their friends were stripped of their public duties.

Duranti was too closely identified with the crown and too conspicuously anti-League to remain unmolested for long.[112] Although a Royalist, his Catholicism was hardly lukewarm; in fact, it was largely through Duranti's efforts that the Jesuits, the Capuchins, and the Cordeliers settled in Toulouse, and he also was a leading sponsor of both the Blue Penitents and the Confrérie de la Miséricorde. But such pious patronage counted for little in the minds of the leaguers, who held his royalism and an apparent taste for luxury against him. On February 1, Duranti was arrested, and a week later, after League leaders intercepted a letter from the avocat général pleading for assistance from the Royalist governor Mantignon, Daffis was also placed in custody. League justice proved summary: four days later Duranti was taken before an armed mob to answer for his "treason" and, while stammering some words in his defense, was shot in the chest. The crowd then dragged his body to the Place Saint-Georges, the customary spot for executions, and hoisted it up with a portrait of Henry III attached. "The king was so dear to you, here you are now with him!" chanted the crowd, which then proceeded to sack his home and extensive library and hang his manservant as well. Later, Daffis too was taken from his cell and murdered.

Despite Duranti's close ties to the Queen Mother, it took the king more than two months to respond to his assassination: on May 15 the

111. The following narrative is based on several sources: *HGL*, 11:770–92; Dubédat, *Histoire du Parlement de Toulouse*, 1:489 and passim; *L'advertissement de tout ce qui s'est passée en la ville de Tholose*; Greengrass, "The *Sainte Union* in the Provinces."

112. Duranti was in communication with the royal court and shared his fears about the Toulouse uprising with the Queen Mother. See "Lettre du Président Duranti à la reine mère sur une tentation des ligueres pour s'emparer de Toulouse," in *HGL*, 13:1439. He was also a local humanist of some repute, having orchestrated the entry for Charles IX in 1564 (see Graham and Johnson); Estienne Forcadel dedicated one of his works to Duranti (C. Oulmont, "Estienne Forcadel," p. 554).

crown declared Toulouse guilty of treason and formally deprived the city of its parlement. The majority of the magistrates, however, led by President de Paulo and the councilors Vézian and Bertier, refused to abandon their offices and attempted to play a leading role in the insurrection. But the real master of the city was the bishop of Comminges, Saint-Gelais, who was made governor of Toulouse by popular acclamation.

Upon the assassination of Henry III on August 1, 1589, events in Toulouse again changed course. The League openly rejoiced at the downfall of the hated king and publicly hailed his assassin, Jacques Clément, with masses and processions. But while antiroyalism had reached a peak among the populace, negotiations were taking place between Montmorency and Joyeuse to bury their regional rivalry, thus ending aristocratic support for the Toulouse insurrection. Within the city, the sénéchal registered their truce, and the parlement raised no objections. In addition, several prominent leaguers and members of the Eighteen also engaged in secret negotiations with Joyeuse to hand over control of the city to him and to eliminate Saint-Gelais, who by then had become the virtual dictator of Toulouse.

The bishop of Comminges, however, would have none of this. In the fall of 1590, along with President de Paulo and the ever-present mendicant preachers, he led the populace in a prolonged and violent campaign against Joyeuse and his designs. On the first of October, Saint-Gelais preached in the Church of the Dalbade; brandishing a sword in one hand and a crucifix in another, he called upon the people to arm themselves for Jesus Christ. As an organized expression of this most frenzied phase of the insurrection, a new confraternity was formed under the name of Corpus Domini, which included thousands of ordinary inhabitants turned Catholic militants. On October 2, Saint-Gelais and de Paulo led an armed procession of the Corpus Domini that stormed through the city, pillaging the Joyeuse palace at its finale.

The fury of the people, however, was ill spent, for such violent displays only convinced those elites who formerly had supported the popular League that Toulouse must be pacified at all costs. By mid-November, Joyeuse's army was at the city gates, and it was apparent that Toulouse could not long resist a siege. The city finally surrendered to Joyeuse, and Saint-Gelais was allowed to escape to his diocese in the Pyrenees. But the populace did not remain tranquil for long. When the parlement began to administer justice, after nearly a year of revolt, several quarters of the city stirred with renewed discontent. Etienne Tournier, one of the leaders of the insurrection, seized control of the island of Tounis, a section of the city primarily inhabited by boatmen, who had been enthusiastic partisans of the league. He urged Saint-Gelais to return and assume leadership of the people once again. This time, however, the radical leaguers were without the support of the parlement, and the rest of the urban officialdom, even such former members of the Eighteen as de Paulo and Bertrand, turned against the insurgents. Tournier fled, Saint-Gelais never regained Toulouse, and the other leaders were promptly executed.

The League takeover of Toulouse marked a decisive chapter in the city's history and was also a formative experience in the genesis of a local movement for Catholic reform. In addition, it offers a point of comparison with insurrections in other French cities and with the explanations historians have adduced to account for both the initial success and the ultimate failure of the Holy League. All students of the events of the late 1580s agree that the insurrectionary leaguers in Paris and elsewhere can no longer be seen as the rabble that historians once held responsible for the violence and excesses of the day.[113] And indeed, the League of Toulouse, with its ruling council of Eighteen, its parlementary spokesmen, its clerical street preachers, and those solid members of the city's craft community who served as its foot soldiers, was a movement which, sociologically speaking at least, drew upon the respectable levels of urban society. The mobilization of the city was general during the League takeover, as it was in the preceding years of religious warfare, and although many Toulousains refused to participate in and opposed the insurrection, the line separating them from their rebellious neighbors was not drawn by class.

113. Recent works on the league emphasizing the broad base of its participants include J. H. M. Salmon, "The Paris Sixteen, 1584–94: The Social Analysis of a Revolutionary Movement," *Journal of Modern History* 44 (1972): 540–76; Elie Barnavi, *Le parti de Dieu: Etude sociale et politique des chefs de la Ligue parisienne, 1585–1594* (Brussels and Louvain, 1980); Robert Harding, "Revolution and Reform in the Holy League: Angers, Rennes, Nantes," *Journal of Modern History* 53 (1981): 379–416; Robert Descimon, *Qui étaient les Seize? Mythes et réalités de la Ligue parisienne (1585–1594)* (Paris, 1983); Philip Benedict, *Rouen during the Wars of Religion*; Greengrass, "The *Sainte Union* in the Provinces." For a good review of this literature, see Barbara B. Diefendorf, "Recent Literature on the Religious Conflicts in Sixteenth-Century France," *Religious Studies Review* 10 (1984): 362–67.

How, then, are we to understand the League and in particular its appeal to city dwellers? One explanation has been offered by Henri Drouot, who in his magisterial history of the League in Burgundy analyzed the apparent social division in the officialdom between the insurrectionaries and the others, who upheld the municipal order. Drouot found that among the leaders of the League of Dijon was a preponderance of lesser officials and lawyers who, he suggested, were acting upon their resentment of the officer elite, especially the parlementaires, for supposedly blocking their upward mobility in the officialdom.[114] Though suggestive and plausible, Drouot's findings have not been confirmed in other cities where the league took power, except perhaps Paris.[115] No such split occurred among the combatants in Rouen, Nantes, Angers, or Rennes.[116] And in Toulouse as well, the partisans of the League ranged from parlementaires and lower officials to the clergy and elements of the common people. There, the only apparent social division was between the insurrectionaries on the one hand and the regional magnates, Montmorency and Joyeuse, on the other. But this hardly marks the League takeover in Toulouse as antiaristocratic, since several of its leaders were at least nobles of the Robe.

Another way to understand the League in Toulouse is to see it as an urban phenomenon rooted in the traditions of municipal autonomy and corporatism. This is the approach of Robert Descimon in his prosopographical study of the Parisian "Sixteen." In it he argues that the urban League was essentially a religious confraternity infused with a reborn civic consciousness and raised to the level of a municipal organization. Descimon sees such urban forms as essentially medieval in origin, and thus frames the League as a sort of revived commune.[117] Interesting as his thesis is, he does not present much proof for it. But the evidence we have encountered throughout the sixteenth century suggests that Descimon's interpretation could be applied effectively to Toulouse, where the tradition of a municipal

114. Henri Drouot, *Mayenne et la Bourgogne: Etude sur la ligue en Bourgogne, 1587–1596*, 2 vols. (Paris, 1937), 1:43–55, 334–43.

115. Salmon, "The Paris Sixteen, 1584–94"; Denis Richet, "Aspects socio-culturels des conflits religieux à Paris dans la seconde moitié du XVIe siècle," *Annales: ESC* 22 (1977): 779. Descimon, *Qui étaient les Seize?* pp. 273–80, does not see such professional blockage as relevant to the Paris league's ascendancy.

116. Benedict, *Rouen during the Wars of Religion*, pp. 182–89; Harding, "Revolution and Reform in the Holy League."

117. Descimon, *Qui étaient les Seize?* pp. 62–65, 281–85, 295–96.

republic was not merely a half-forgotten idea but a still vital myth.

There were indeed several formative antecedents to the city's embrace of the League and the insurrection of 1589. One takes us back to what I have called the local Renaissance—the myth of the municipal republic and the tradition of civic humanism. Despite the secular cast of this tradition, it did prove useful to urban officials in an era of religious warfare, especially when the task of defending the faith fell primarily to them. And the notion of a unified city, first voiced in more secular tones, seemed to influence the scope of new religious associations as well. The League also drew upon prior experience of urban institutions that had come to maturity only in the early sixteenth century (the Guet and the Bureau de Santé) and that had the capability of mobilizing the resources of the city against collective danger. The League's center of gravity in Toulouse was the Hôtel de Ville; it was there, and not at the parlement or the archbishop's palace, that the committee of Eighteen sat, and though parlementaires and clergymen were members of the League junta, they exercised their authority within the confines of the city hall. It would be misleading to say that the League captured the Hôtel de Ville, for this gives the impression of a split between the municipal officialdom and the leaguers when, in fact, most urban officials were partisans of the insurrection. But in transforming the seat of municipal authority into an insurrectionary headquarters the League did inherit those powers and capabilities that were already part of the arsenal of urban government. Thus, rather than look forward to the Committee of Public Safety for a historical analogy to the urban League, we can glance backward to the newly acquired policing powers of the sixteenth-century city as a source of the Eighteen's ability to mobilize the populace in a moment of danger. For example, nothing resembles the League takeover more than the battery of emergency measures periodically instituted to combat the plague—the closing of the city gates, the monitoring of the populace, the public prayers and processions ordered by the authorities, and the creation of a special committee to govern the city. The sixteenth-century city had learned to galvanize its policing powers in moments of crisis whether natural or manmade, and the League insurrection was the beneficiary of this apprenticeship.

The League also benefited from the ties that traditionally bound ordinary people to the regular clergy. It has been noted that most craft confraternities in the city were sponsored by monastic orders, and we have seen that mendicant preachers in particular were instrumental in leading the crowd during the insurrection. While much of the populace was undoubtedly affected by the growing Catholic fervor in the city, it is likely that the common people were disposed to accept the leadership of the street-preaching monks precisely because of the preexisting ties between the craft community and the religious orders. But what of the relationship between the city and the regular clergy? Here too there is evidence of an evolution toward concerted action. In 1569 a visiting preacher suggested that several of the city's religious orders band together. The town council approved this suggestion and 2,000 livres were allocated to purchase a building for the unified order.[118] Whether this project was ever realized is not known, but the idea behind it is what matters. Then in July, the capitouls approached the four mendicant orders with a dual request: first they wanted them to offer their prayers to God on behalf of the people; then they asked that each order name several from their midst to serve militarily "against the enemies of the Catholic faith." Nearly sixty monks were thus conscripted for the cause, armed, and supplied with munitions.[119] In other times the city's religious orders proved to be a fractious and recalcitrant lot, often at odds with the civil officials and disputatious among themselves. During the religious wars, however, they subordinated these differences, locked arms with the lay officialdom, and helped unite the city in the cause of militant Catholicism.

The League also derived much of its strength from the series of confraternities and militant associations founded in Toulouse since mid-century. In a sense, these were another form of apprenticeship for the populace in the ways of general mobilization. There were three layers of such associations. First were the several new lay confraternities that drew their memberships from throughout the city and among a wide range of occupations. Then there were the four penitential companies, which recruited even more widely, combining a special devotional regime with a crusading spirit. Finally there were the four "leagues," those of 1563, 1568, 1576 and 1588, each a militant association of inhabitants sworn to preserving the Catholic purity of the realm, each assembling thousands in its ranks. During the insurrection itself, the populace was organized in yet another association, the Confraternity of the Holy Sacrament, with Urbain de Saint-Gelais

118. Lafaille, 2:296.
119. AMT, BB 275, p. 257.

at its head. The 1580s was also a time of increased demonstrations of public devotion, exercises drawing upon the entire populace. General processions were frequent. That of 1587 was particularly novel: all the inhabitants of the city marched in double file, women following men, to the Basilica of Saint-Sernin, where a mass was said for the "protection of France and the City," and then proceeded in the same fashion to the chapel of Saint-Roch in the suburbs for another mass.[120] Saint Roch, of course, was the patron saint of plague victims, suggesting a psychological association between the city under siege during the plague and this moment of heightened Catholic militancy. This procession was followed by another ceremony in which the city granted dowries to many young girls to enable them to marry.[121] Devotion to the relics of Saint-Sernin continued and, indeed, became the centerpiece of public piety. In 1582, 1586, and 1588 the remains of Saint-Exupère were elevated; it was by no means coincidental that the saint in question was an early bishop of Toulouse and that his elevation was staged precisely when the city was most concerned with its autonomy and independence.[122]

The forms of the League's mobilization of the populace are worth stressing; indeed, they are crucial to understanding this chapter's place in the broader thesis of this book. Before the mid-sixteenth century, the religious organization of the city was diffuse and decentralized—in keeping, I would suggest, with the corporate fragmentation of urban institutions. The challenge of Calvinism and the need to shore up the popular faith, however, added another level of association to the city's religious organization. First in large-scale voluntary associations—lay confraternities writ large—then in the structure of the urban league itself, a new terrain for religious mobilization was carved out: that of the entire city. It would not be going too far in fact to claim that the city itself became one religious organization, a holy community (in Bernd Moeller's words); one in which even the structural divisions between laity and clergy, town council and parlement, were dissolved in a new insurrectionary committee.[123] The perceived sacred integrity of the city at this moment was perhaps illustrated best by the people themselves, in a ritualistic act carried

120. Lafaille, 2:401.
121. Ibid.
122. Douais, *Documents*, 2:xxiii–iv.
123. Moeller, *Imperial Cities and the Reformation*.

carried out at the finale of the mass procession of the Corpus Domini, led by Saint-Gelais in September 1589. After pillaging the palace of the royal governor, the duc de Joyeuse, the crowd marched to the house of Saint-Gelais and baptized its walls with holy water.[124] To destroy the residence of a magnate who threatened the city's autonomy was one thing, but to anoint a new leader and to sanctify his undisputed authority over a city in revolt was quite another. It symbolized Toulouse's unity, however ephemeral, and it also exemplified the sacred nature of that unity.

124. *HGL,* 12:1459, "Discours de la révolte des liguers de Toulouse contre Joyeuse."

Interlude

4

A Libertine Moment

French history in the years following the Wars of Religion followed several somewhat different paths. Politically, there was the triumphant ascension of Henry IV and the rather remarkable calm that set in during his brief reign. Religiously, there was both the settlement of the Edict of Nantes and the first beginnings of the Catholic Renaissance, a movement that ultimately prepared the way for French acceptance of the Counter-Reformation. And intellectually there was the growth of free thought, skepticism, and other forms of what René Pintard called "le libertinage érudit."[1] It is this last movement that will interest us in this "Interlude." Indeed, a coterie of free thinkers, adventuresome aristocrats, poets, and their assorted hangers-on momentarily managed to flaunt their presence in early seventeenth-century Toulouse, this bastion of religious orthodoxy. In fact, these "libertines" reigned only briefly, for their activities were soon cut short by the wave of Catholic devotion that was quickly overtaking city elites. But their presence is worthy of examination if only as a reminder that the stage of public life could be seized by various elements and put to various uses. In this case, the spotlight will be turned on the region's great aristocrats—on such magnates as Blaise de Monluc, Montmorency-Damville, and the Joyeuses—who led a resurgent local aristocracy in postbellum Languedoc. Though relative outsiders to the city, these aristocratic *grands* saw in public displays and local culture a means of projecting their political power and social legitimacy.

1. René Pintard, *Le libertinage érudit dans la première moitié du XVIIe siècle* (Paris, 1943).

A Resurgent Aristocracy

After years of denouncing him as a heretic, a scourge upon France, and worse, the city of Toulouse finally recognized the ascension of Henry of Navarre to the French throne in return for several concessions, agreed to in 1596 in the Edict of Folembray, which formally ended the religious wars in Languedoc.[2] Not only were the crimes committed by the leaguers, in particular the murders of Duranti and Daffis, pardoned, but the city was granted special privileges as well, including the right to harbor the Jesuits, who were otherwise expelled from the realm. Most important, Toulouse gained an exemption from the taille for one hundred years.

As much as was conceded to Toulouse, the crown granted even more to the Joyeuse family, the erstwhile leaders of the League in Languedoc. There were more than a hundred articles in the Edict of Folembray relating to the Joyeuses. The king granted Anne de Joyeuse the position of marshal of France which included a permanent, personal retinue of one hundred men and a two-year dispensation from taking the oath he would normally be obliged to swear to the crown. Joyeuse was also accorded the charge of lieutenant-governor of Languedoc. This title, shared with his rival, the duc de Ventadour, made the two of them the second-ranking noblemen of the province below the prince, Henry II de Montmorency. By other terms of the edict, Ventadour and Joyeuse continued to convene separate provincial estates, just as they had done during the religious wars, when each led a different faction. They therefore benefited from the right to levy taxes and enjoyed considerable subsidies from the provincial estates in return for their influence at court. In addition, the king conceded Joyeuse particular authority over the towns of Narbonne and Carcassonne and supplied him a regiment of five hundred infantry and thirty arquebusiers for his guard. The Duke's brother, Cardinal Joyeuse, was assigned the prestigious position of protector of the affairs of France in Rome and was confirmed as patron of several important abbeys. He was also made the archbishop of Toulouse, thus affirming the Joyeuse family as a major provincial force both politically and ecclesiastically. Warlords associated with them during the religious wars were each granted command of a company of soldiers and were left unpunished for their rebellious

2. *HGL*, 11:861–62.

actions. Even the most obstinate and lawless among them, the Sieur de l'Estrange, was confirmed as governor of Puy and endowed with added privileges and provisions. Finally, in a secret clause, the Edict of Folembray was sweetened with an outright financial bribe from Henry IV to Joyeuse to secure his loyalty.

Joyeuse was not the only aristocratic magnate of Languedoc to receive added privileges and lavish grants from the crown. Blaise de Monluc was also persuaded to lay down his arms in exchange for a royal stipend; and in all, the royal minister Sully recorded, Henry IV dispensed 32,142,981 livres in bribes to recalcitrant nobles.[3] After Henry's death the royal dole became notably more generous, for the regency of Marie de Médicis was not strong enough to prevent aristocrats from helping themselves to the royal treasure. In 1611 the amount distributed to aristocrats in pensions was 4 million livres, double the sum of the previous year.[4]

The power and privileges of the provincial nobility following the Wars of Religion, however, did not rest entirely on royal munificence. Magnates such as Joyeuse, Ventadour, and Monluc continued to control the fiscal and military levers of the province for several reasons. First, as we saw with the example of Joyeuse, their military strength remained undiminished largely because the crown lacked the effective authority to demilitarize them. Second, these aristocrats and their clients maintained a firm control over the province's fiscal machinery. In 1620 the estates of Languedoc, in addition to granting Montmorency and his family the usual salaries and gifts, voted him 30,000 livres for extraordinary expenses, 123,000 livres for the cost of his troops recently deployed to suppress an uprising, and an additional 10,800 livres for "his great services." This last amount was earmarked for his *utensiles des estrangers*, a company the estate delegates knew no longer existed.[5] These payments were not purely gratuitous, however, for the provincial notables depended upon Montmorency as their broker and spokesman at court. Finally, Rohan's Huguenot offensive in the 1620s renewed the governors' military vocation, bringing them again the privileges and opportunities of warlords. Not only did they receive extraordinary sums and supplies, but they were able to distribute the

3. Harding, *Anatomy of a Provincial Elite*, p. 106.
4. V. L. Tapié, *France in the Age of Louis XIII and Richelieu* (New York, 1974), pp. 70–71.
5. J. Russell Major, "The Crown and the Aristocracy in the Renaissance," *American Historical Review* 69 (1983): 641–42.

spoils of war to secure clients and placate their friends as well. In 1628, in addition to their usual "gratifications," the provincial estates voted 30,000 livres to Montmorency and 20,000 livres to the duc de Ventadour for their expenses in the campaign against Protestant holdouts. And in 1629, when Montmorency subdued the Huguenot stronghold of Lumas in the diocese of Béziers, he was able to turn the captured chateau over to his father's bastard son Annibal in compensation for the destruction of the latter's fortress in Mous.[6]

The resurgence of the aristocracy was not merely a provincial phenomenon but characterized all of France in the period following the religious wars and particularly after the assassination of Henry IV. Several factors were responsible for this development. The most important was the wars themselves, which, owing to the collapse of royal authority, restored many noblemen with their traditional military and political powers as local warlords. And these powers were maintained as long as the crown had to rely upon aristocrats and their followers as the mainstay of the French army in wars abroad. To this must be added a heightened consciousness among aristocrats of their status and prerogatives, an outcome in part of the Renaissance with its emphasis on honor and heroism, and in part of the social and political challenge presented by the rising Robe class. Finally, there was the death of Henry IV and the ensuing period of regency, with all the weaknesses at the center and the renewed ambitions among the great normally attendant upon a royal minority.

The aristocratic resurgence took many forms, some reflecting the problem of reclaiming a feudal role in a society where feudalism had in any meaningful sense of the term long passed from the scene. There was thus a recrudescence of aristocratic violence—brigandage, dueling, and the like—as well as a series of cabals, conspiracies, and revolts against the crown, which plagued the regime from the 1620s through the Fronde, many involving members of the royal family. In Languedoc, Montmorency's doomed revolt in 1632, undertaken with the connivance of the king's brother, was only one of the more notorious of these, ending as it did with the execution of the young and admired governor in Toulouse that same year. But in other ways aristocrats were clearly attempting to respond positively to the changing order

---

6. *HGL,* 11:1032–33. On the resurgence of the aristocracy in this period from a comparative perspective, see Stuart Wolff, "The Aristocracy in Transition: A Continental Comparison," *Economic History Review* 18 (1970): 520–31.

and to recover a sense of their collective identity. In the cahiers of the nobility of Languedoc drawn up for the Estates General of 1614, for example, there was a proposal for establishing an academy and a collège to instruct and train young noblemen of the province.[7] And between 1618 and 1620 a new association emerged in Languedoc, the Order of the Knights of Saint Mary, a brotherhood that assembled individual aristocrats who, a generation earlier, had been mortal enemies in the confessional strife.[8]

There were two camps of libertines in early seventeenth-century France. One was strictly intellectual in orientation, the philosophical descendants of Montaigne and his skeptical, somewhat epicurean view of the world. These thinkers, men such as Charron, La Mothe le Vayer, and Gabriel Naudé, were at the heart of "le libertinage érudit." The other camp of libertines consisted mostly of those young noblemen who seemed to make a vocation of flouting convention, especially during the regency of Anne of Austria, when noble conspiracy, intrigue, and license were in the very air, particularly at the royal court and in the leading Parisian salons.[9] But the capital of Languedoc also harbored a community of libertines, drawn from both camps. It was to his friends in Toulouse, after all, that Cyrano de Bergerac's fictional hero immediately traveled after his descent from his lunar excursion and from whence he departed for another to the sun.[10]

The Toulouse libertines were led by the prince, Henry II de Montmorency. Montmorency was indeed the leading figure in the province, especially following the extinction of the Joyeuse line with the death of its last scion, Anne de Joyeuse, in 1605. Son of the chief of the politique party in the south during the religious wars, governor of the province, a cousin of Louis XIII, the brother-in-law of the prince of Condé, and related through marriage to Marie de Médicis, Montmorency was a true kinglet of Languedoc. As a prince of the realm and an intimate at court, his protection was sought by many, including a number of literary figures. His interests were remarkably

---

7. *HGL*, 12:1645, "Cahiers présentés par messieurs les députés de la noblesse de Languedoc à l'assemblée des états généraux en la ville de Paris en l'année 1614."

8. E. Lamouzèle, "Une ordre de chevalerie ecclésiastique en Languedoc au commencement du dix-septième siècle," *Revue des Pyrénées* 16 (1904): 565–90.

9. On these libertines see especially G. Tallemant des Réaux, *Historiettes*, ed. A. Adam, 2 vols. (Paris, 1960); Orest Ranum, *Paris in the Age of Absolutism* (New York, 1968), pp. 132–66.

10. Cyrano de Bergerac, *Histoire comique des états du soleil* (Paris, 1662).

cosmopolitan for an uninstructed man who spent most of his adult life
on the battlefield.[11] Montmorency surrounded himself from an early
age with some of the most talented and adventuresome literati of the
day, and his personal patronage, along with that of Condé, the duch-
ess of Orléans, and the Queen Mother, was a major force in shaping
preclassical French literature. Alexandre Hardy dedicated several of
his works to Montmorency, as did Simon Ducros, Georges de Scudéry,
and Mathurin Régnier. The playwright Jean Mairet, Corneille's rival
and the first modern dramatist to employ the three unities of time,
action, and space, had fought alongside Montmorency, had served as
his personal secretary, and was a permanent member of his household
in Chantilly.[12] The leading character in Charles Sorel's *Francion* was
apparently modeled after Montmorency.[13] But perhaps he is best
remembered in the history of seventeenth-century French literature as
the friend and protector of the great libertine poet Théophile de Viau,
who found a refuge in the prince's estate after narrowly escaping the
scaffold in Paris.[14] In Toulouse, Montmorency patronized the parlementaire and poet François Maynard; the city's favorite bard, Pèire
Godolin; and the ill-fated Neopolitan philosopher-magician, Lucilio
Vanini.

Montmorency and his entourage, which included his relative the
duc de Ventadour, the comte de Clermont-Lodève, the vicomte d'Ar-
pajon, and Adrien de Monluc, the grandson of the warrior-memorist,
as well as more than a score of lesser figures, also exercised their
influence in Toulouse by sponsoring a series of entertainments in the
city, most of which were timed to coincide with carnival.[15] In the ten
years between 1614 and 1624 there were aristocratic entrées, ballets,
and other displays nearly every year. In both 1614 and 1619
Montmorency himself led the proceedings; in 1617, 1622, 1624, and
1626 it was Ventadour, the lieutenant-governor of Languedoc, or his
wife. In other years the season's entertainment was marked by the

11. Tallemant des Réaux, *Historiettes*, 1:362–64.

12. Antoine Adam, *Histoire de la littérature française au XVIIᵉ siècle*, 5 vols. (Paris, 1948–56), 1:192.

13. Alain Niderst, "Mécènes et poètes à Toulouse entre 1610 et 1630," in *Pèire Godolin*, ed. Christian Anatole (Toulouse, 1982), p. 36.

14. Henry Lancaster, *A History of French Dramatic Literature in the Seventeenth Century* (New York, 1929), 1:163; Lachèvre, *Procès du poète Théophile de Viau*, 2 vols. (Paris, 1909), pp. xvii, 20, 140, 190–91.

15. Niderst, "Mécènes et poètes à Toulouse entre 1610 et 1630," pp. 33–46.

presence of lesser regional magnates.[16] That of February 1619, offered on the occasion of the marriage between Christine de France, sister of the king, and the prince of Savoy, was indeed a carnivalesque display, replete with outlandish costumes and masks, intricate dances and several passages recited to the assembled in Toulouse's own dialect of Occitan.[17] Unfortunately, the text from the carnival of 1619 has not survived, and so for a precise image of such festivities we must move on to 1624, when the proceedings were led by the duc de Ventadour and a band of noblemen, officers, and local literati, Montmorency being absent from the scene. Those proceedings evidence a cultural moment when the interests of the aristocracy and the tastes of the populace met on the terrain of carnival.

Carnival 1624: *Le Cléosandre*

The pageant of 1624 was a fully staged theatrical production lasting two days, the text of which was published as *Le Cléosandre, ou sont rapportez tous les passe-temps du Carneval de Toulouse en 1624*. The primary author of the script was Balthazar Baro, a future member of the Académie Française and one-time secretary to Honoré d'Urfé, the author whose epic pastoral novel, *L'Astrée*, was the most popular literary work of the day.[18] There is a resemblance in fact between *Le Cléosandre* and *L'Astrée*, for both use the pastorale to present a dissection of the ways of love, its pleasures and pitfalls. Baro had assistance in the writing from Godolin, Monluc, and, among others, Pierre Caseneuve, the historian of the privileges of Languedoc; Guillaume de Catel, a historian and magistrate; Boissière, a lawyer and a writer of epigrams; and Gabriel Barthélemy de Gramand, another regional historian and a president in the parlement.[19] They were joined in

16. Ibid.

17. BN, MS fr. 24450, fos. 264–75: "Les réjouissances et magnificences faites à Toulouse par M. de Montmorency et entre autres deux courses, l'une de la Quintaine et l'autre de la Bague, l'an 1619."

18. On Baro see Lancaster, *A History of French Dramatic Literature*, 1:355–56.

19. Pierre de Caseneuve, *Le franc-alleu de la province de Languedoc establi et defendu* (Toulouse, 1645); Guillaume de Catel, *Mémoires de l'histoire de Languedoc* (Toulouse, 1633); Bossière, *Les devises de Monsieur de Boissière, avec un traitté des reigles de la devise, par le mesme autheur* (Paris, 1654); Gabriel Barthélemy de Gramond, *Historiarum Galliae ab excessu Henri IV libri XVIII quibus rerum per Gallos tota Europa gestarum accurata narratio continetur* (Toulouse, 1643).

staging and performing *Le Cléosandre* by a number of other noblemen, officials, and local men of letters, most of whom were also members of Monluc's informal libertine academy based in Toulouse.[20] Ventadour played the title role of the gentle knight Cléosandre; Monluc portrayed Cléonte, his faithful friend; and Ventadour's brother, the comte de Brions, was given, appropriately enough, the role of the knight Oléandre, Cléosandre's brother.

Le Cléosandre moves thematically in four stages. First, love is comically caricatured; second, it is more seriously abused; third, it is redeemed; and fourth, it is celebrated in conjunction with fidelity. The play opens in the country of Gascony in a typical pastoral setting west of the Garonne River on a "great mountain so high that never wind nor storm disturbs the summit." Here the supreme genie has convoked an assembly of all those "demons" charged to watch over the kingdoms of the earth. The Demon of France is called upon to speak, and after a moment's hesitation launches into a tearful account of the miseries and misfortunes that for so long have plagued his ward. "Now that the valor of that young Prince whom you favor with your affection seems to have earned for him a repose that ought never to end, let it be, Great Genie, that he will enjoy it eternally . . . with the complete assurance that he will drown the memory of his miseries in tears of joy."[21] Recognizing the justice of this plea, the genie dispatches the Demon of Peace to Cléosandre, now in a deep sleep in Toulouse.

"You slumber, Cléosandre," whispers the demon in the young knight's ear, ". . . and truly it is only just that so many vigils devoted to the service of your king should now be compensated by an agreeable sleep; but give yet some more nights that are asked of you, and if you once were watchful in hardship, be vigilant in this turn for pleasure." The demon takes flight and Cléosandre awakens with a vague intimation of his visitor's message, only to fall into an even deeper slumber, dreaming throughout the night of "Carrousels, ballets and masquerades, the infallible mark of the will that the demon had inspired in his soul."[22]

Thus is introduced a series of ballets, skits, masquerades, recita-

---

20. Monique Sabatier, "Un mécène à Toulouse, Adrien de Monluc, comte de Caraman," in Anatole, *Pèire Godolin*, pp. 47–58.

21. Balthasar Baro, *Le Cléosandre, ou sont rapportez tous les passe-temps du Carneval de Toulouse en 1624* (Toulouse, 1624), p. 4.

22. Ibid., p. 6.

tions, games, and *tableaux vivants* dragging on for two days. As with other aristocratic divertissements, the theme is buried in the length and chaos of the proceedings—a procession of bizarre and entertaining figures, each representing a facet of love and the plight of the love-struck. There is a Ballet of Fools presenting African cannibals, English hypochondriacs, madly jealous Italians, and a pair of self-centered Bohemians.[23] There follow scenes in which the demon Love is scorned and abused by shepherds and shepherdesses, Bacchus and his satyrs, and a gelder, who offers his craft as a remedy to Love's excesses; in which tennis players hurl their balls and racquets at Love, vestal virgins threaten to reduce him to ashes, and the bourgeois of the city douse him with buckets of tears lest his ardor erupt in flames and consume their homes.[24] And there is the lascivious discourse on Love delivered by Oléandre, a true libertine, who orchestrates a series of skits announcing the joys of lovemaking, the pleasure in simple abandonment, the innocence of flirtation.[25] In all of this the spectators were presented not only with words and pantomimes but also elaborate scenery and exotic costumes—a veritable kaleidoscope of colors, masks, plumage, foliage, and the like, which must have dazzled and delighted the people with its novelty and opulence. In one scene Cléosandre mounts an enormous ship fabricated entirely of Chinese satin, before which appears the figure of Triton riding four sea horses; in another, a "Knight of Tears" makes his entry, dressed in a black robe sprinkled with silver teardrops; in yet another a chariot drawn by pairs of lions, tigers, and leopards traverses the stage, accompanied by eighteen large horses, each draped in gold cloth and gray linen.[26] It is safe to assume that the people of Toulouse never witnessed such a spectacle before, not even during the opulent Renaissance entries of French monarchs the century before.

The last part of the play belongs to its hero Cléosandre, who rescues Love and restores him to his empire on the condition that he disavow infidelity. Inconstancy, not Love, is the enemy, and he announces that on the next day, February 18, at the Hôtel de Sénéchal, the lists will be open for all knights to enter a joust to disgrace the image of Inconstancy and offer propositions and devices on love.

---

23. Ibid., p. 18.
24. Ibid., pp. 21–32.
25. Ibid., p. 47.
26. Niderst, "Mécènes et poètes à Toulouse," p. 39; *Mercure françois*, 10 (1624): 364–68.

After another series of masquerades supporting the benevolent and playful aspects of love, Cléosandre reappears to close the day's proceedings triumphantly. A chant accompanies his appearance:

> Thus Inconstancy weakened
> Has no arms or help,
> And if there remains any discourse
> It is finally to proclaim:
> Long live until eternity
> Cléosandre and his resolve.[27]

The next day, the Knight of Resolve, Cléosandre—inexplicably costumed as an African—presents the following proposition: "That for whatever consideration, we should never cease to love the person we had once judged worthy of our love."[28] Finally, the day's pageant concludes with a procession through the city, merging with Toulouse's popular celebration of *férétra* and culminating in a contest in which the prize is a statue of Don Quixote tilting against windmills in the same manner that "rendered his reputation immortal."[29] The text ends with the demon taking flight and Cléosandre awakening as from a long dream. "Seeing nothing in his room but the day breaking through the windows, he gets up and dresses and sets forth in the usual exercise of his peerless piety."[30]

An analysis of *Le Cléosandre* must proceed on several levels. It was, first of all, an entertainment for the participants themselves, the noblemen, officials, and literati who wrote and performed the pageant. In this sense, its proximity to the subject of *L'Astrée* is crucial, for just as the epic novel used the form of the medieval chivalric romance as a vehicle for depicting the psychological dimensions of love and social behavior in polite society, so *Le Cléosandre* transformed the crusading knight into a crusader for love who argues, less with passion than with reason, for peace, gentleness, and fidelity.[31] Both works can be situated in the cultural movement then taking shape in France which

27. *Le Cléosandre*, p. 99.
28. Ibid., p. 104.
29. Ibid., p. 122.
30. Ibid., p. 125.
31. On *L'Astrée*, see P. J. Yarrow, *A Literary History of France: The Seventeenth Century, 1600–1715* (New York and London, 1967), pp. 43–45; Erica Harth, *Ideology and Culture in Seventeenth-Century France* (Ithaca, 1983), pp. 34–67.

coaxed the aristocratic temperament to a more acceptable notion of civility commensurate with the emerging concept of *honnêteté*. As one of the characters in *L'Astrée* proclaims, "because the lover desires nothing more than to be loved he must render himself loveable, and that which makes him loveable is also that which makes him an *honnête homme*."[32] Of course while the cult of *L'Astrée* had as its most fervent devotees the précieuses of Paris's leading salons—among them Mme de Rambouillet's famous hôtel—the cast of *Le Cléosandre*, despite its amorous theme, was an all-male affair, as befitted a theatrical effort by a band of Gascon warriors.[33]

If the production of *Le Cléosandre* can be seen as an example of a movement among the elite toward new standards of civility, as a local exercise in the fashion of *honnêteté*, it also conveyed a related message to those who witnessed the pageant. This occasion, and others like it, were opportunities for the aristocracy to demonstrate before the people those qualities of comportment and character associated with the timeless notions of noblesse, but lately more honored in the breach. On stage the "gentle knights" exhibited their skill at horsemanship and dancing, their poise when speaking and acting, their worldliness and gallantry. Elsewhere, and especially in years past, they rather displayed more menacing talents as those responsible for the violent excesses of the religious wars, for their senseless prolongation, and for the private brigandage disguised as holy battle. What we have in *Le Cléosandre* is, literally, a dramatic refutation of this image and reality. Once leaders on the battlefield, the gentle knights are now the masters and animators of the joyous, playful exercises of carnival. They emerge as human, though morally superior, beings endowed with a mission to bring contentment to the people while preaching the virtues of love and fidelity.

The specifically propagandistic nature of *Le Cléosandre*, however, was less important than its context. For while the drama is largely a fantasy, there is also an element of realism reflecting aspects of the

32. Quoted and translated by Yarrow, *A Literary History of France*, p. 43.
33. On Mme de Rambouillet, see Tallemant des Réaux, 1:442–55; Pintard, *Le libertinage érudit*, pp. 7–8. The frequenters of Mme de Rambouillet's salon would take excursions to a country chateau costumed as characters from d'Urfé's novel and would hold their rustic picnics *à l'Astrée* (David Maland, *Culture and Society in Seventeenth-Century France* [New York, 1970], p. 51). Cardinal de Retz recalled in his memoirs how he and his friends had often reenacted scenes from *L'Astrée* in their youth, engaging in guessing games to identify characters and situations from the novel (J. M. H. Salmon, *Cardinal de Retz: The Anatomy of a Conspirator* [New York, 1970], p. 35).

culture, geography, and citizenry of Toulouse. The flavor of *Le Cléo-sandre* is Toulousain; it is, after all, an account of "all the proceedings at the Carnival of Toulouse in 1624." It opens in a setting identified as lying west of the Garonne and closes with a procession including delegates from various towns and villages in Languedoc. Its characters are not only those of a fantastic order—knights, cannibals, shepherds, witches, and demons; we also meet personnages of the city—students, apothecaries, craftsmen, and bourgeois. Whole passages were written and recited in Occitan, the language of the people, and specifically in that dialect peculiar to Toulouse. Pèire Godolin, the city's most popular poet, played an important role in the pageant and was responsible for most of the recitations in the *lengua mondino*, or the language of Toulouse.

Most important, *Le Cléosandre* mirrored carnival in its prolixity and free-play, its use of disguise, masks, and exotic costumes, and its preoccupation with the trials and misadventures of love. Indeed, the pageant *was* carnival, just as other aristocratic entertainments in other years, staged also in February and March, likewise dominated the popular festival. During these years there seems to have been a marked presence of the aristocracy at carnival, and more than in the capacity of simple participants, comingling with the masses. In some instances these elites seized control of the festivities: such was indeed the case in 1619, 1624, and those other years when Montmorency's friends trooped into the city with their elaborate entertainments. And on another occasion, in 1626, three members of the parlement disguised as "hermits" enlivened the proceedings by distributing medals struck with nude images of holy figures in various positions of sexual intercourse. They were at once censured by the court for their injudicious behavior.[34]

How should we understand this carnivalesque inclination of the regional aristocracy? Its basis, I would suggest, is to be found in the political pretensions of the traditional aristocracy, a position peculiar to the first decades of the seventeenth century, when those powers accumulated during the religious wars and their immediate aftermath had not yet been challenged by Richelieu and his policy to "humble the great." In Languedoc, Montmorency's execution in 1632 would draw the curtain on the regional aristocracy's political aspirations. Such an explanation, however, does little to make the behavior of our

34. ADH-G, MS 147, "Mémoires de Malenfant," pp. 279–82.

"gentle knights" of 1624 comprehensible. But there are examples elsewhere of ruling aristocrats seizing upon carnival as a means of scoring political points, controlling the populace, or projecting their definition of the urban community. The best documented of these is the festive tradition in Renaissance Florence, where the rites of carnival routinely took the form of political pantomimes staged and orchestrated by ruling families. One persistent feature of such displays was the vaunting of chivalric, as opposed to civic, images and values on the part of elites with neo-feudal pretensions: at least under the reign of the restored Medicis in the early sixteenth century, "these celebrations appear as events to which the people came, rather than ones they made."[35] The aristocratic pageants at Toulouse were also chivalric in spirit and thus appropriate to the terrain of carnival with its amorous preoccupations. Moreover, carnival was the only urban festival open to princely elites such as Montmorency and Ventadour as a vehicle for asserting their honor and power; for all other rituals in the city's celebratory calendar were either religious in nature or strictly civic in orientation and thus unsuitable for the propaganda purposes of the high nobility, a class that lacked roots in the city. In fact, the nobility of the Sword was a bit lost when it came to participation in urban rituals; even on the occasion of the funeral procession for Henry IV in June 1610, a group of local noblemen, wanting to join in the march, was rebuffed by the parlement and told merely to appear at the mass following the public ceremony.[36] Carnival was not a problem in this sense; a free zone by definition, it was open to all— even well-healed, somewhat cosmopolitan great aristocrats, with their fancy costumes, exotic displays, and theatrical themes straight out of the chivalric tradition.

But did they not thus risk stealing carnival from the people or at least dazzling them with a pageant they could perhaps enjoy but hardly comprehend? There was certainly an esoteric strain in the libertine tradition in early seventeenth-century France, a strain reflected in Le Cléosandre itself as well as in the larger movement of free thought associated with "le libertinage érudit." And such esoterica had its adepts in Toulouse, especially among the frequenters of Montluc's libertine academy.

35. Richard Trexler, Public Life in Renaissance Florence (New York, 1979), p. 510.
36. ADH-G, MS 147, p. 43; Cassan, "La fête à Toulouse," p. 43.

L'Académie des Philarètes

The name Monluc is remembered in French literature in connection with Blaise de Monluc, the sixteenth-century warrior whose *Commentaires* is one of the best accounts of the military aspect of the religious wars. Adrien de Monluc, Blaise's grandson, is less well known but still a figure of some importance, especially as a patron of free thinkers and writers. Born in 1571, he made a propitious marriage in 1592 and thus added the titles of the count of Carmaing and governor of Foix to his name. But he was notorious in his own right as a warrior, courtier, and one of the most prominent aristocrats at the Parisian court of Marie de Médicis, where his wit and rakishness earned him and his friends, Termes and Bassompierre, the sobriquet of "Les trois dangereux." He had fought alongside Henry IV and Louis XIII, but with Richelieu's rise to power he joined those grands who endlessly conspired to eliminate the imperious cardinal-minister. Implicated in the Day of Dupes, Monluc was finally imprisoned in the Bastille in 1635, where he languished until Richelieu's death in 1642.[37]

When in Toulouse, Monluc stayed at his townhouse on the Rue des Filatiers, known to intimates as the Académie des Philarètes, or those "taken with virtue." There could be found a coterie of poets, noblemen, professional students, and assorted self-promoters, most of whom participated in *Le Cléosandre* and other carnivalesque pageants. Monluc was a generous and well-stocked host; the account for a three-month period in the spring and summer of 1616 lists 308 "divers gentilshommes, pages ou autres" who had been received in his hôtel.[38] He was the patron of Godolin, François Maynard, Mathurin Régnier, as well as Lucilio Vanini. Two important Gascon poets, Guillaume Ader and Bertrand Larade, both dedicated their works to Monluc; Charles Sorel served as his secretary.[39]

Monluc was also something of an author; in 1630 he published anonymously an assortment of stories and dialogues in a collection

---

37. On Monluc, see G. Doublet, "Un seigneur languedocien, compositeur de comédies sous Louis XIII," *Revue des Pyrénées* 8 (1896): 457–69; Frédéric Lachèvre, *Le libertinage au XVIIᵉ siècle: Mélanges* (Paris, 1920), pp. 198–204; Tallemant des Réaux, 1:231–33; Sabatier, "Un mécène à Toulouse, Adrien de Monluc."

38. ADH-G, E 48, "Rolle de la couchée des gentilshommes de Monseigneur le comte de Cramail . . . 1616."

39. Sabatier, "Un mécène à Toulouse, Adrien de Monluc," and Niderst, "Mécènes et poètes à Toulouse entre 1610–1630."

entitled *Jeux de l'inconnu*.[40] In these pieces Monluc displays an interest in language, especially in the potential for nonsense in ordinary speech and in the variety of proverbial expressions. In one selection, "La comédie des proverbes," the characters spout proverbs ad absurdum, calling into question the very meaning of such locutions.[41] In another text, *Les illustres proverbes*, he depicts a philosopher conversing with a holy man: the dialogue lapses disastrously into total misunderstanding over the simplest propositions.[42] And in "Le courtisan grotesque" he presents the amorous and military misadventures of a nobleman in which the narrative is surreally deformed through a comically arbitrary use of words.[43]

Even when Monluc turns away from the subject of language, his writing is humorous and often bawdy. In "La maigre" he mocks an unidentified lady who obviously prizes both her chastity and her all-too-meager figure: "Do not praise yourself so much for being chaste, swearing that no one has ever accomplished the work of the flesh with you. Those who see you think it simple enough, having neither flesh nor muscle, one could commit with you only sin of the bones. I defy the casuists to give it a name: Is it fornication, brutality, sodomy, or simply pollution? As for me I hardly doubt that it's a sin to couple with a skeleton."[44]

Monluc drops his scorn and misogyny when he turns to defending prostitutes from their pious attackers in "L'infortune des filles de joye." Here he is gallant, sympathetic, and obviously well informed from experience. In order to convince his readers that these are not women of luxury, he takes us on a tour of a brothel, pointing out the squalor, misery, and sickness of the place, but arguing that the *filles de joye* would be in a much sorrier state if they were denied their work. People call them lost? "What calumny is this? Can't they be found at any hour, day as well as night?"[45]

A true libertine in his life as well as his art, Monluc was not simply a parvenu or bourgeois with aristocratic pretensions like Paul Scarron or Sorel; rather, he resembled his contemporary Cyrano de Bergerac in his concern for the aristocratic standards of honor and virtue. In-

40. *Les jeux de l'inconnu* (Rouen, 1637).
41. Cited in Jacqueline Bellas, "Adrien de Monluc," *Actes de journées internationales d'étude de baroque, 1966* (Montauban, 1967), p. 51.
42. *Les illustres proverbes historiques* (Paris, 1655).
43. "Le courtisan grotesque," *Jeux de l'inconnu*, p. 61.
44. Monluc, *La maigre* (Paris, 1863), p. 41.
45. *L'infortune des filles de joye* (Paris, 1624), p. 23.

deed, Monluc had long served as a soldier and was the literary and professional bearer of one of the most illustrious names in French military history. But he seems to have worn his inherited mantle somewhat uneasily, for in his middle years at least he came to the conclusion that his was a dying breed—that the noble warrior was fast becoming a relic of the past, and a somewhat pitiful figure as well.

Monluc expressed this ambivalence toward his vocation in a short piece entitled "Le Dom Quixote Gascon," a work one literary scholar has identified as the first evidence of the influence of Cervantes' epic in France.[46] But it is a vicious satire, depicting a Gascon warrior without even a veneer of the noble idealism that makes the knight of La Mancha so appealing. Monluc's Quixote is a brute and a philistine; his palace is a tasteless mélange of ill-suited styles; life inside resembles a military barracks, even at meals: "Everything that had been placed on the table had been killed with a pistol, sword, or battle-axe, and having only been singed by the fire, seemed to accuse the murderer with the blood it spilled."[47] The Dom Quixote Gascon is unlettered; moreover, he is proud of his ignorance:

> He insists that science unmans courage, that a Gascon Gentleman should be ignorant, arrogant and fearless; and that courtesy was a result of pusillanimity; that mercy was also a baseness of the heart; that it was necessary to be cruel, insolent, and brazen . . . that treason, dissimulation, and perfidy were the marks of a good mind; that provided one were rich, strong, great, and feared it did not matter how one got that way; that philosophy was a dream, and mathematics an occupation for pedants.[48]

Dom Quixote's palace is an absurd monument to battle: there are whole rooms displaying petty mementos from past conquests, galleries stuffed with every conceivable weapon, and a hall reserved for bloody combats between disputants in law cases. The dom is particularly proud of a parcel of land—"the busiest on his grounds"—where his friends and neighbors can indulge their lust for violent sport and mutual bloodletting "without fear of Edicts or Justice."[49] Having

---

46. Henry C. Lancaster, *French Dramatic Literature (1610–1634)*, pt. 1 (Baltimore and Paris, 1929), p. 13.
47. "Le Dom Quixote gascon," *Jeux de l'inconnu*, pp. 35–36.
48. Ibid., p. 38.
49. Ibid.

completed his tour, the narrator of "Le Dom Quixote Gascon," a knightly visitor, hastens to free himself from the dom's hospitality and rides away "without looking behind him as if he had just escaped Hell."[50]

Monluc was a mainstay of the libertine community in early-seventeenth-century Toulouse, and his presence in the city ensured that libertinage would have a hearing even among magistrates of the parlement, some of whom were frequenters of his Académie des Philarètes. It appears, for example, that First President Jean de Bertier was himself a "philarète," at least for a time.[51] Most, however, were warrior-noblemen, and thus Monluc's concern for the image of the aristocratic military man touched them too. The celebration of the Gascon warrior had long been a favorite theme of regional poets even before Monluc's cynical portrayal. Shortly after the assassination of Henry IV there emerged from the pen of Guillaume Ader, a physician who had served in Joyeuse's army, an epic poem, "Lo Gentilhome Gascon," which traced the mythic life of one Henric Gascoun (actually Henry of Navarre) from his birth and childhood to the realization of his destiny as a full-blown hero—"son of war and father of soldiers."[52] Ader's literary presentation of the noble warrior conformed perfectly with what Robert Lafont has called the Gascon ethnic ideal, a sort of regional superego, which vaunted martial qualities above all others and found a personification in Henry IV, a true son of Gascony become king.[53] In Monluc's hands, however, this ideal underwent a transformation measured in the cynicism and disgust that characterized his portrait of "Le Dom Quixote Gascon." For the grandson of Blaise de Monluc the martial hero was no longer worth celebrating.

This aspect of Monluc's mentality would be merely of limited interest if it did not relate both to his other literary efforts and to his role as a patron of Toulouse libertines as well. Just as he debunked the myth of the noble warrior, so his literary exercises flouted the limits of language and the borders dividing sense from nonsense. Monluc the writer refused to conform to standard notions of meaning and order,

50. Ibid., p. 52.

51. Sabatier, "Un mécène à Toulouse, Adrien de Monluc."

52. A. Jeanroy, "Une Henriade gasconne, Le gentilhomme gascon de Guillaume Ader," Revue des Pyrénées 17 (1905): 271–91; and Felix Castan, "Une épopée baroque de 1610 et le sens de la première renaissance littéraire occitane," Actes des Journées internationales du baroque, 1964 (Montauban, 1965), pp. 131–42.

53. Lafont, Renaissance du sud, pp. 233–66.

and this refusal, like his refusal to embrace the mythology of his grandfather, set him apart—in the company, however, of those other libertines also marked by social and intellectual nonconformism. There is something about Monluc which suggests that such nonconformism had its roots in alienation, or at least in a psychological quest for a new social definition. Perhaps this is what generally characterized the regional aristocracy in the early seventeenth century, as they cast about for new ways to demonstrate their power and legitimacy.

On occasion this casting about led to trouble. A regular guest at Monluc's townhouse from 1616 to 1619 was the Neopolitan philosopher and magician Lucilio Vanini. Here we reach the high-water mark of heterodoxy in Toulouse, for Vanini was a character in the mold of his late compatriot Giordano Bruno, and his fate was the same.[54] With Monluc's backing, Vanini managed to gain the support of some of the city's leading figures, including Montmorency and Jean de Bertier, who engaged him as his children's tutor. Students, poets, and parlementaires flocked to Monluc's academy to attend Vanini's weekly lectures, and for a while there was no more popular or respected man in all Toulouse.[55]

Vanini came to Toulouse in 1616 after a two-year sojourn in Paris, where he had enjoyed the patronage of the Maréchal Bassompierre, the favor of Marie de Médicis and, for a time at least, the Sorbonne's approval of his writings. Previously he had wandered across Europe—from Germany, where he was rumored to have killed a monk, to England, where his outspokenness landed him in prison for a spell. Armed with degrees in theology, medicine, and law, he spoke with authority and wit on a wide range of topics; everywhere he went he attracted attention, followers, and usually some suspicion. It was only in Toulouse, however, that the heterodox nature of his views caught up with him.

Only two works by Vanini have survived, although he claimed to have produced tomes on physics, medicine, magic, astronomy, and the relationship between Mosaic law and Christianity. In the first of his surviving books, *Amphitheatrum aeternae providentiae*, he sets out to

54. On Vanini, see Adolphe Baudouin, *Histoire critique de Jules-César Vanini, dit Lucilio* (Toulouse, 1903); M. Gatien-Arnoult, "Note pour servir à une étude sur Vanini," *MASIBL*, 6th ser., 5 (1867): 281–94; E. Vaisse-Cibel, "Lucilio Vanini, sa vie, sa doctrine, sa mort, 1585–1619," *MASIBL*, 6th ser., 2 (1864): 113–42; Don Cameron Allen, *Doubt's Boundless Sea* (Baltimore, 1964), pp. 58–74.

55. Antoine Madrigal, "Le libertinage à Toulouse, le scandale de Vanini," in Anatole, *Pèire Godolin*, pp. 59–70.

prove the existence of God—a strange goal for a philosopher later accused of atheism. But in the course of laying out his syllogisms, it becomes apparent that Vanini is a confirmed pantheist, a position made explicit in his next book, actually four sets of dialogues, *De admirandis naturae reginae deaegue morialium arcanis*. For therein he establishes himself as the prophet of a new religion based on combined gnostic and pantheistic views of God, man, and nature. Like other Renaissance philosophers, Vanini was concerned more with knowledge and science than with religion in the orthodox sense. And like Bruno, Vanini sought to discover a means of understanding God and the universe by penetrating the timeless mysteries of nature and its laws.[56]

Although they had sanctioned his first book, it did not take the doctors of the Sorbonne long to wake up to the unorthodox nature of Vanini's philosophy, and shortly after their publication his dialogues were condemned to the flames. Vanini's retaliation took the form of a letter to the pope, in which he served notice that if he did not receive a benefice "he would in three months overturn the whole Christian Religion."[57] It is doubtful whether this threat was ever sent. Instead, Vanini sought refuge in Toulouse, where he was apparently assured a favorable reception by Monluc, Montmorency, President Bertier, and their friends.

But even with these influential supporters, Vanini's reign in Toulouse was short-lived; within a year of his arrival he was on the docket of the parlement, charged with blasphemy and atheism. And on February 9, 1619, he was burned at the stake in the Place du Salin. Because the parlement destroyed all the relevant records, except for the decree of condemnation, we can only guess why Vanini met with such a disastrous and precipitous downfall, even while in the company of some of the region's most important men. Several things, however, are clear. In the course of the trial, the parlement was divided over the validity and seriousness of the charges; several magistrates, in fact, as well as a few priests and theologians at the university, argued for clemency. Moreover, Vanini was never tortured in order to

56. "Nothing is new under the sun and this vicissitude being eternal, it must have a cause of the same nature. However, one can search for that cause only in celestial bodies, in God and in the Intelligences. Indeed, it is through the influence of celestial bodies, transmitted by the ordinary Intelligences of God, that the Laws take their birth, their growth and their end" (Quoted in Allen, *Doubt's Boundless Sea*, pp. 123–24). See also *Oeuvres philosophiques de Vanini*, ed. M. X. Rousselot (Paris, 1842).

57. Durand, *La vie et les sentiments de Lucilio Vanini* (Rotterdam, 1717), p. 80.

extract a confession. Apparently his supporters and sympathizers had at least enough power to spare him the agony of what was after all a routine feature of criminal justice in the Old Regime. Finally, the controversy surrounding Vanini's fate split the ranks of Toulouse's libertine community, and it was this split, and the betrayal by some of his friends and students, which clinched his condemnation.

What seems to have happened is this. The man responsible for pursuing the case against Vanini was Guillaume de Catel, a councilor in the parlement, who was a friend and in-law of President Bertier. Catel was also an author, whose *Histoire des comtes de Toulouse* was dedicated to Montmorency and who was among the participants in *Le Cléosandre*. Why Catel, an intimate of the same milieu that harbored Vanini, should have taken it upon himself to initiate the proceedings against the Neopolitan philosopher is anyone's guess, but it is clear that he was aided in his prosecution by another of Bertier's relatives. Thus, it is likely that what prompted Vanini's downfall was his betrayal by Bertier's entourage (where, despite the First President's identification with local free thinkers, the spirit of Catholic devotion was gaining ground), though not necessarily by Bertier himself. Still, Catel's case, which he initiated in August 1618, was not sufficiently strong to warrant a conviction, and the matter languished inconclusively into the winter until two additional witnesses stepped forward. First, the seigneur de Francon, a young nobleman who was connected to Monluc's party, attested to Vanini's blasphemous views; then Balthasar Baro, another intimate of Monluc, whom we have met as the primary author of *Le Cléosandre*, confirmed the charge.[58]

With two such testimonies the parlement could come to a conclusive verdict, and it lost no time in acting. On the morning of February 9, the magistrates declared Lucilio Vanini, also known as Julius-Caesar Vanini, guilty of "atheism, blasphemies, impieties, and other crimes," and ordered his execution for that afternoon. Dressed only in a shirt, a rope around his neck and yoked with a sign branding him an "Atheist and Blasphemer of God's Name," Vanini was led through the streets to the door of the cathedral, where he was forced to his knees and ordered to demand pardon from God, the king, and justice. Then he was bound to the stake in the Place du Salin, his tongue ripped from his mouth (the prescribed treatment for blas-

58. On the prosecution of Vanini, see Vaisse-Cibiel, "Lucilio Vanini, sa vie, sa doctrine, sa mort, 1585–1619," pp. 333–42; Dubédat, *Histoire du Parlement de Toulouse*, 2:65–71.

phemers), and strangled. Immediately, his body was consumed by the flames. Witnesses recounted that he died stoically, refusing the consolations of a Franciscan monk, and shouted out at one point, "Let us die for philosophy!" But the magistrate Gramont recorded that when the executioner placed the knife to his tongue, Vanini let out a cry like a bellowing ox. "Although he screamed that he would face death as a philosopher," commented Gramont, "he died like a beast."[59]

There is a poignant postscript to Vanini's downfall. Two days after his execution, a group of aristocrats, led by Montmorency and Monluc, presented a ballet in the same Place du Salin where Vanini had been put to the flames. The dance climaxed with a scene depicting a magician—played by Montmorency's household dwarf—being crowned with laurels in front of a sacrificial fire on an altar framed by the words, "Quand on me brûle, je triomphe." Clearly, if Vanini's aristocratic friends ultimately failed to protect him, they at least mourned him in style.[60]

What is the significance of Vanini's close association with these *grands?* On one level, their flirtation with such a heterodox thinker is an indication that the impulse toward aristocratic independence and self-assertion could take intellectual forms. By harboring Vanini, Montmorency and his friends were declaring themselves philosophical and religious outlaws, so to speak, or at least individuals unaffected by normal prohibitions. They thus demonstrate the link between "le libertinage érudit" and that tendency among young aristocrats during the regency toward free thought, scandalous behavior, impiety, and the like. But Vanini's downfall also illustrates the limits of this libertine movement: five years before the arrest of Théophile de Viau, whose long trial in 1624 cast a chill over Parisian free thinkers, the forces of repression in provincial Toulouse served notice of their intolerance with a fiery auto-da-fé. In subsequent years such intolerance would become the rule.

Pèire Godolin: The People's Bard

Two years before Vanini's execution, a collection of Occitan verses appeared under the title *Ramelet mondin.* Their author was Pèire Go-

59. Vaisse-Cibiel, "Lucilio Vanini, sa vie, sa doctrine, sa mort, 1585–1619," p. 340.
60. *Mercure françois,* 5 (1619): 120–21.

dolin, a participant as writer and actor in *Le Cléosandre* and the man who, costumed as a magician, recited some memorial verses to the Neopolitan philosopher at his mock sacrifice in 1619. If Vanini reveals the libertines of Toulouse as somewhat esoterically inclined, Godolin represents their more popular side. And if the peripatetic philosopher highlights the continental, cosmopolitan connections of aristocratic culture, with Godolin, we have a figure whose horizons were not only provincial, but deliberately and pridefully confined to the limits of Toulouse. Pèire Godolin was not only Toulouse's greatest poet, he was also the first writer in memory to claim the city's particular language—*la lengua mondina*—as his own. Other recent poets, such as Guillaume Ader and Pey de Garros, had written in Gascon, the language of the region west of Toulouse; and in general a sort of Occitan Renaissance of the second half of the sixteenth century had revived in verse and prose the Romance dialects spoken across the wide expanse of the Midi. But until Godolin, this Renaissance had bypassed Toulouse; from 1555 to 1610 there were no texts published in the lengua mondina.[61] Linguistically, the city was officially Francophonic. When Godolin abruptly appeared on the literary scene in 1610 with his homage to Henry IV, however, Toulouse found its voice.

The son of a prosperous master surgeon-barber, Godolin was born in Toulouse in 1580 and lived there until his death in 1649.[62] In fact, he strayed from the city only rarely, to take a cure at a nearby spring or to attend a gathering at a nobleman's country chateau. He was educated by the Jesuits and received a degree in law at the university. Although admitted to the parlement as a lawyer, he never practiced law but managed to earn his living as a poet. Godolin was competent in French and even submitted French verses in the Floral Games, only to be denied a prize bonquet on all but one occasion. His heart, however, was elsewhere. "Nurtured by Toulouse, it pleases me to maintain her beautiful language."

61. On Toulouse's relationship to the early phase of the Occitan Renaissance in the sixteenth century, see Lafont, *Renaissance du sud*, pp. 13–50. On Occitan language in general in this period, see Emmanuel Le Roy Ladurie, "Occitania in Historical Perspective," *Review* 1 (1977): 21–30.

62. On Godolin's life and work, see J. Lestrade, *Pierre Goudelin, ses ancestres, ses frères, ses amis* (Toulouse, 1896); Edouard Bourciez, "Le réalisme et la fantaisie dans Goudelin," *Revue des Pyrénées* 8 (1896): 258–75; Joseph Salvat, *Etude sur Pèire Godolin* (Toulouse, n.d.); Anatole, *Pèire Godolin*; Bibliothèque Municipale de Toulouse, *La vie intellectuelle à Toulouse au temps de Godolin, quelques aspects* (Toulouse, 1982). The poet's name is spelled Goudelin in French and either Goudouli or Godolin in Occitan.

If I only rarely borrow
The words of Orléans and Blois,
It is simply that the little muse
I have loved since my early years
Wishes that the Pont-Neuf and the Halle
Be my Blois and Orléans.[63]

Godolin was Toulouse's official poet, mourning the death of Henry IV in his "Stanzas to the Happy Memory of Henry the Great," or welcoming with his verses Louis XIII's visit to the city in 1621. Montmorency engaged him to write the prologues for several of his ballets staged at Toulouse and his chateau in Pézanes. Godolin was also a regular guest at Monluc's libertine academy, as well as a friend of President Bertier, whose garden outside the city walls was a popular gathering spot for the poet and his companions. But his supporters and friends were numerous, among them President Phillipe de Caminade; François de Ressiguier, a councilor; De Bertrand, juge mage of Montauban; De Loupes, a magistrate in the sénéchal; and the marquis d'Astarac, later implicated in the Cinq-Mars conspiracy.[64] Though favored by many, Godolin belonged to no one. He was frequently an honored guest in the homes and at the tables of the rich and great, but he was also a regular in the local cabarets and taverns. What we see in his poetry is a portrait of the seventeenth-century city. It is a city of parts—of neighborhoods, parishes and suburbs, landmarks and popular gathering spots. In a poem of carnival, "Intrado de May," he writes fondly of an island in the Garonne, Le Grand Ramier, a favorite haunt for him and his friends.[65] In the "Croquans," we follow a ne'er-do-well soldier as he drunkenly makes his way down the Rue de l'Empire—well known for its brothels—to an equally notorious tavern in the suburb of Saint-Agne.[66] A poem dedicated to President Bertier takes us on a tour of his property

63. "Sizain," J. B. Noulet, ed., Oeuvres de Pierre Goudelin (Toulouse, 1887), p. 337. The Pont-Neuf and Halle referred to in these lines are those of Toulouse, not Paris. Noulet's is the standard edition of Godolin's poems in Occitan. See also the collection of poems included in Salvat's Etude sur Pèire Godolin. A recent selection, with extensive notes, has been published by Philippe Gardy, ed., Pèire Godolin: Le Ramelet mondin et autres oeuvres (Aix-en-Provence, 1984). For translations into French, see Robert Lafont, ed., Anthologie des baroques occitans (Paris, 1974); and J. M. Cayla and Paul Cleobule, eds. and trans., Oeuvres complettes de Pierre Godolin (Toulouse, 1843).
64. Salvat, Etude sur Pèire Godolin, p. xxi.
65. "Intrado de May," in Salvat, Etude sur Pèire Godolin, pp. 27–31.
66. "Le Croucan," ibid., pp. 39–46.

on the outskirts of the city—a lavish garden graced with exotic flora and fauna, including a peacock and a monkey roaming free.[67] Godolin praises Toulouse's famous landmarks, such as the Bazacle Mills and the Basilica of Saint-Sernin, but he shows just as much affection for its markets and plazas, its hôtels and fountains, its streets and bridges.[68] And he inhabits this poetic cityscape with a colorful cast of characters, real and imaginary, such as Mossur Cucois, a well-known Turk living in the city; Bistobache, famous for his great mustache; Crocodil, "always alone"; and, of course, Bacchus, who at carnival reigns supreme.[69] Godolin's poetry provides us with a window on the city's popular culture and pastimes, such as the games played by young and old alike, the proverbs on everyone's lips, and the great assortment of food and drink festively consumed during carnival, which, next to the charms of the women of Toulouse, was his favorite topic.

But his city is also one with a mythic and glorious past. It was founded by Tolus, a grandson of Noah. Its language dates from the Tower of Babel, and the legendary Clémence Isaure still watches over its poetic fortunes.[70] It was also a city sure of its identity and autonomy: for Godolin, Toulouse was still a "Republica."[71] A peasant he meets from a little village to the west speaks with a Gascon accent that immediately marks him as foreign to the city.[72] In his "Stances" to Henry IV, he has a "nympho moundino"—a Toulouse nymph—salute the late king. Unlike Guillaume Ader, whose homage to Henry was from one Gascon to another, Godolin addresses the memory of the king of the French—"the beautiful flower fallen on French soil . . . the Sun of France"—and mourns him on behalf of the people of Toulouse.[73]

Indeed, Godolin's verses testify to his own and to his readers' municipal patriotism, a sentiment yet open to the notion of a larger unity of the French nation. It was a muted sort of patriotism compared with the fierce regionalism expressed by such Gascon militants

---

67. "Descripsciu de Founteno Mounrabe," ibid., pp. 112–16.

68. "Sileno as Jantis Coumpaignous," and "Stansos" in ibid., pp. 63–64, 120–21.

69. "Intrado de May," in Noulet, *Oeuvres*, pp. 197–205.

70. Cayla and Cleobule, *Oeuvres complettes*, p. 367; "A Tots," p. 31 n. 11, "A Mossurs," p. 185 n. 1, in Gardy, ed., *Le ramelet mondin*.

71. "A Touts, Dambe un Trinfle D'Abertissomen," ibid., pp. 5–7.

72. "Countro Tu, Libret, Et Per Tu," in Noulet, *Oeuvres*, p. 74.

73. "A l'urosa memoria d'Enric le Grand, invincible rei de Franca e de Navarra," in Lafont, ed., *Anthologie des baroques occitans*, p. 144.

as Ader and Garros, and it was certainly a far cry from the banner of municipal autonomy raised by the Holy League only a generation earlier. But Godolin's was the voice of authentic patriotism nevertheless, singing the praises of his city and its culture—its institutions, such as the capitoulat; its prominent citizens and commonfolk alike who shared his love for the muse; its *mignonnes toulousaines;* its carnival and Floral Games; its natural gifts; and, above all, "le boun lengatage de Toulouso," the good language of Toulouse. This last was, in fact, the underlying theme of his poetry; for Godolin, the city and its language were inseparable. The city gave rise to the spoken language with which he fashioned his verses: Godolin called his inspiration "the muse of Toulouse," and his meaning here is quite literal. But he in turn helped fashion *le lengatage de Toulouso* by turning the speech of his fellow townsfolk into literature. Some of his poems read like transcriptions of conversations and colloquies among his friends and patrons: in one, "Chansons de table," he presents the testimony of an assortment of ordinary people—a tavern owner, a sharecropper, a journeyman, a woodworker, a butter vendor—as they imbibe and socialize at a local tavern, ending each verse with the line, "Always content, let us joyously pass the time."[74] Such speech found its way into Godolin's poetry and thus into a written language. It even found its way into a dictionary; for in 1638 Godolin's friend Jean Doujat published a *Dictionnaire de la langue Toulousaine* to serve as a companion to the poet's collected works, in which the orthography and meanings of Godolin's vocabulary were canonized as a standard version of Toulouse Occitan.[75]

It would be a mistake to consider Godolin merely a rustic poet or an unlettered purveyor of popular verse. Many of his poems were packed with classical allusions and clearly addressed an erudite audience. In one, "Contra tu, libret, e per tu," he assembles references to Socrates, Diogenes, Virgil, Ovid, Horace, Plutarch, Catullus, and Empedocles, as well as citations from the writings of Petrarch, Ariosto, and Ronsard.[76] As might be expected, Rabelais, a kindred spirit, runs throughout his verses. Though humble in spirit and colloquial in style, Godolin considered himself worthy of comparison with

74. Cayla and Cleobule, *Oeuvres complettes,* pp. 286–91.
75. Doujat, *Le dicciounari moundi, Dictionnaire de la langue toulousaine* (Toulouse, 1638). See also the preface to Giles Ménage, *Dictionnaire étymologique ou origines de la langue françoise* (Paris, 1694).
76. Noulet, *Oeuvres,* p. 74.

the great poets of the day, referring at one point to his intimacy with both François de Malherbe and François Maynard. On occasion he displayed a linguistic virtuosity that surpassed theirs, as, for example, in one of his prologues to Montmorency's ballets, where he freely moves between Occitan and French to a fractured combination of the two—his own Francitan.[77] Performing before the great, the poet was half jester, half bard, and at times must have delivered his Occitan verses with a proverbial wink.

Above all, Godolin was the poet of carnival; and though he situates the festival in the classical tradition of bacchanalia, his carnival is still that of the people—hedonistic, irreverent, and bawdy—and still that of Toulouse. During carnival, Godolin's role was that of Caramentrant, that is, the personnage of Mardi Gras (Caramentrant = Entrance of Lent), or "the master of ceremonies who creates a fantastic world out of nothing."[78] More than a scribbler of verses, he was an orator, actor, and cherished bonvivant. As the seventeenth-century chronicler Germain de Lafaille recorded, "he had a marvelous grace in everything he said and did, even when he did nothing, for he only had to appear in public to excite mirth."[79] It was he who animated the festivities, adding an exotic touch when, for example, Caramentrant hails from the "Indies," blessing the festive gluttony, libation, and rites of love.[80] The people looked to him to speak for them with his verses, and sometimes he took advantage of the liberty of carnival to voice their complaints: "Poor Carnival, the people cry. Such a long time since we've seen such a meager feast!" So spoke the poet when famine threatened the region. His verses that year are marked with signs of dearth: the inflated price of grain, the watered-down wine, poultry only a gentleman can afford. Yet carnival will go on, for "to live and yawn, one becomes melancholy." Still, he adds, "the violin will sound cold if no one plays his purse."[81]

Godolin's poetry belongs to the context of carnival, but it does not simply amount to a literary gloss on a popular festival, ancillary and

77. Gardy, *Le Ramelet mondin*, p. 107 n. 12.
78. Huguette Ruel-Albernhe and Philippe Gardy, "Le thème du carnaval dans la littérature occitane," *Littérature et langues modernes* (Actes du VIe Congrès International de langues et littérature d'Oc et d'études franco-provençales, Montpellier, 1970), pp. 33–49.
79. Quoted by Noulet, *Oeuvres*, p. xv.
80. "Passatemps de Carmantrant," in Gardy, p. 121.
81. "Cançon per le jorn de Caramentrant," "Silena als jantis companhons," in Lafont, *Anthologie des baroques occitans*, pp. 211–14.

subservient to a particular ritual moment. His verses also embodied an ideal, one represented by carnival at its most civilized, and thus also elevated that ideal to a moral standard. Beyond the eat and drink and playful amorous rites, carnival meant the joy of simple fellowship, peace among men. "Thus we must recognize," he proclaims, "that Pluto's treasure, Mars's valor, Hercules' power, hardly compare to the sweetness with which carnival subdues the most savage humors."[82] Carnival was humanity at its best, purged of ill-will and want, and unburdened by preoccupations with social distinctions and divisions. He took care to address both "mossurs e menestrals"—gentlemen and artisans—in his poetry; and his "jantis companhons"—gentle companions—included epicureans of every social stripe. In carnival, of course, such intermingling was common; but in Godolin's poetry it is held up as a social model and one, moreover, which he embodied as both the great aristocracy's favorite poet and the people's most cherished bard.

Godolin, who died in 1649, was supported in his last years by an annual stipend from the capitouls. Time and fortune had robbed him of his aristocratic patrons: Montmorency had been executed, Monluc had died after several debilitating years in the Bastille, Ventadour and Bertier both turned to religion. In one sense, the capitouls' subvention was emblematic of the esteem with which Toulouse held its aging native poet. But in another it merely demonstrates the fact that by the 1640s the aristocratic libertine culture had dissolved, its few patrons having passed from the scene, leaving its chief poet and spokesman "in extreme need, having barely anything to eat."[83]

The early modern city was dominated by its officialdom, by the civil and ecclesiastical officers who pullulated in the Old Regime. Toulouse was certainly the quintessential city in this respect. There was not much room for the traditional aristocracy in this urban context, and yet we have seen how such aristocrats, led by the regional magnates among them, created a presence in the early seventeenth-century city, at a time when their power was at its apogee. That power was soon to be challenged and in a sense undermined; but while it lasted they made a point of projecting it in a number of ways, one of them through cultural manifestations on the urban scene. Their libertinage was

---

82. "Qu'es aguo qu'es?" in Lafont, *Anthologie des baroques occitans,* p. 216.
83. Lestrade, *Pierre Goudelin, ses ancestres, ses frères, ses amis,* p. 74.

Nicolas de Troy, "Portrait of Pierre Goudouli," seventeenth century
(Musée des Augustins)

indeed momentary—bounded by the religious wars of a generation previous and cut short by the movement of Catholic reform that was soon to dominate the city. The activities of these aristocrats and their hangers-on illustrate the uses of culture in the Old Regime, for it is clear that despite the frivolity of their carnivalesque pageants these can be read as exercises designed to accomplish rather serious political ends. The esoteric strand of libertinage was pronounced in Toulouse, most notably in the writings of Monluc and Vanini: here was a case of aristocrats, many of them warriors most at home in the rough-and-ready environment of the battle camp, identifying with intellectual and cultural trends of the most elite kind. Finally, and perhaps most important, despite the fact that the aristocrats we have encountered had trouble finding a place in the seventeenth-century city, they yet pitched their public displays to the general Toulousain community— seizing upon the popular festivity of carnival as their main forum, and embracing Pèire Godolin, the people's bard, as their own. Let us now turn to the lay piety and activism of the Counter-Reformation, in which, under the banner of a very different movement, such social engagement was even more pronounced.

PART THREE

Public Life and the Counter-Reformation

5

The Background to
Lay Activism

The Counter-Reformation can be said to have begun in the diocese of Toulouse only in the last decade of the sixteenth century, under the leadership of the archbishop, Cardinal Joyeuse. But even before then—before the implementation of the decrees of Trent, that is—there was already afoot a movement of Catholic renewal. For the most part this movement was connected to the religious wars and the need to shore up the city's faith as it sat uncomfortably in a sea of Protestantism. As we saw in Chapter 3, after 1562 Toulouse became a bastion of Catholic orthodoxy and welcomed within its walls a number of new religious institutions that subsequently exercised considerable influence over the populace. Chief among these were the Capuchins and Jesuits, the latter spawning special congregations for artisans and gentlemen which continued as popular agents of lay piety well into the seventeenth century. The four penitential companies were also an outgrowth of the confessional struggle; after their reform, ordered by Cardinal Joyeuse in 1593, they too persisted as a major source of religious renewal among the laity, gathering several thousand confrères within their ranks. In short, as Philip Benedict has documented for Rouen, one of the heretofore neglected currents leading into the French Counter-Reformation was the militant Catholicism forged in the course of the religious wars.[1]

---

1. Benedict, *Rouen during the Wars of Religion*. On this theme, see Denis Richet, "Aspects socio-culturels des conflits religieux à Paris dans la seconde moitié du XVIe

168   PUBLIC LIFE AND THE COUNTER-REFORMATION

But without episcopal leadership, no real reform of the church could take place. In Toulouse such leadership was supplied by Cardinal Joyeuse, who, once the wars were concluded, began to exercise his will as a reforming archbishop. Joyeuse, like other reform-minded prelates, took as his model Cardinal Carlo Borromeo of Milan, who indeed set the standard for the post-Tridentine clergy throughout Catholic Europe.[2] In 1590, even as the religious wars raged, Joyeuse called a synod of the province and published its decrees seven years later.[3] The issues treated by the synod ranged from the physical condition of the diocese's churches to the comportment and religious duties of the laity. But the central concern was for the state of the clergy and especially the obligations of priests to live in their parishes, administer the sacraments, and maintain the rule of celibacy. More important even than these synodal deliberations were the episcopal visits undertaken by Joyeuse and his vicars-general first in 1596 and 1597 and then in 1602 to 1604. What the cardinal and his entourage found in the course of their tours of the diocese was a church in disarray and disrepair. The number of parish priests had declined from 834 at the beginning of the sixteenth century to 440 in the year 1596; and over half of those surveyed were nonresident. In many parishes the sacraments were only occasionally administered and then improperly. Religious education was nonexistent. Church property, having suffered from a generation of religious warfare, was in a pitiful state, with more than a hundred churches and chapels pillaged, damaged, or entirely destroyed.[4]

Joyeuse left Toulouse for the archdiocese of Rouen in 1605, and thus it was for his successors, Louis de Nogaret and Charles de Montchal, to reconstruct the ecclesiastical province's churches and administration that had been found so lacking. Nogaret conducted 103 parish visits between 1615 and 1620; Montchal, 133 between 1631 and 1651. Like those carried out by Joyeuse, these visits were the main means for reform-minded archbishops to inform themselves not only of the state of the clergy but of the religious practices of the

siècle," *Annales: ESC* 32 (1977): 764–89; Philip T. Hoffman, *Church and Community: The Counter-Reformation in the Diocese of Lyon, 1500–1789* (New Haven, 1985).

2. André Deroo, *Saint Charles Borromée, cardinal réformateur, docteur de la pastorale, 1538–1584* (Paris, 1963).

3. Simon de Peyronet, *Statuts synodaux de la cité et diocèse de Tholoze* (Toulouse, 1597).

4. Georges Baccrabère, "La pratique religieuse dans le diocèse de Toulouse aux XVIe et XVIIe siècles," *ADM* 74 (1962): 287–88.

province's laity as well. Thus it was that the clerical "visitors," acting in the name of the archbishop of Toulouse, were furnished with printed forms designating an inquest into thirteen categories of lay misconduct, including that of separated or unmarried couples; "girls in danger of losing themselves"; heretics, excommunicants, and parishioners who failed to confess, take communion, or pay the *dîme;* and blasphemers, adulterers, concubines, and gamblers.[5] These archepiscopal visits were supplemented by the evangelizing rural missions of the Jesuits, or the Fathers of the Christian Doctrine, established in Toulouse in 1604, whose reforming zeal brought a high standard of religious duty even to those parishes where the secular clergy had not yet been reconstituted.[6] Some lay confraternities, such as the Gray Penitents, also occasionally made missionary sorties into the countryside.[7] If the pattern during the religious wars had been for groups of peasants to flock to the cities—the sites of important cathedrals and shrines—in so-called "white processions," the direction of religious commerce was reversed during the seventeenth-century, with urban clerics and lay *dévots* bearing a reformed version of Catholicism to the rustic parishes in the countryside.[8] And when they did, many were equipped with newly written catechisms in Occitan, such as J. G. d'Astros's *L'escola deu crestian idiot,* allowing them to proselytize in the peasantry's native tongue.[9]

Thus the Counter-Reformation, whatever it accomplished in terms of Catholic renewal and refurbishment, also amounted in large part to the imposition of urban religious values and standards on rural peoples. But what of the city itself? What of Toulouse? Here the process of religious reform proceeded somewhat differently, for here episcopal power confronted several barriers. While in large part supreme and uncontested in the countryside, the archbishop's office in the city was only one among many rival institutions, including the cathedral chapter, the university, several religious orders, the parlement and

5. Baccrabère, *Les paroisses rurales du diocèse de Toulouse aux XVIᵉ et XVIIᵉ siècles* (Strasbourg, 1968), pp. 61–62.

6. Abbé Cayre, *Histoire des évêques et archévêques de Toulouse* (Toulouse, 1873), p. 350.

7. C. Bégouen, "Les pèlerinages de pénitents à Notre-Dame de Garrison," *L'Auta* 41 (1931): 120–23.

8. Denis Crouzet, "Recherches sur les processions blanches—1583–1584," *Histoire, économie et société* 4 (1982): 511–63.

9. Jean-Geraud d'Astros, *L'escola deu crestian idiot* (Toulouse, 1645); P. Barthélemy Amilhat, *Tableu de la bida del parfait Crestia* (Toulouse, 1673); *La doctrino crestiano meso en rimos, per poude estre cantado sur diberses ayres . . .* (Toulouse, 1641).

PLAN DE LA VILLE DE THOLOSE

Garonne Fluvius

Toulouse, 1631 (Archives Municipales de Toulouse)

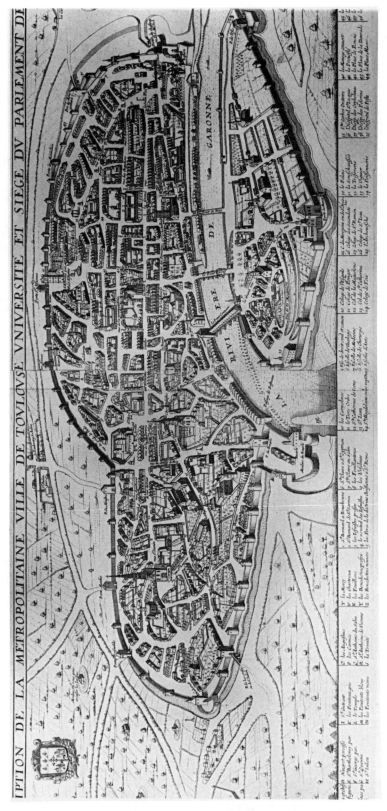

Toulouse, 1645 (Archives Municipales de Toulouse)

groups of lay dévots, each with its own vision of church reform. Archbishop's visits, for example, were never carried out with much success in the city, largely because the individual parish chapters were able to oppose episcopal intrusion.[10] The rivalry between the archbishop and the parlement was particularly intense, as illustrated in a series of squabbles in the 1630s culminating in nothing less than Archbishop Montchal's publicly excommunicating several magistrates from the cathedral pulpit.[11]

It was not the archbishop but primarily the new and reformed religious orders that first stimulated the Counter-Reformation in the city. Like Paris, Toulouse experienced a dramatic influx of the regular clergy in the early decades of the seventeenth century, an influx leading to an ecclesiastical building boom of such proportions that in 1624 the parlement was forced to prohibit further construction of religious edifices within the city walls. At least a dozen new orders and congregations were established in the first half of the century: the Recollets in 1601, the Ursulines in 1610, the Fathers of the Christian Doctrine in 1604, a congregation of Oratorians in 1618, a Third Order of Dominicans in 1603, the Jesuits' Maison Professe in 1612, the Theatines in 1621, the Carmelites in 1625, the Benedictines of Our Lady in 1623, the Dames Maltaises in 1628, the Visitation in 1646, and others. During the century as a whole, from 1590 to 1709, twenty-one new orders—seven for men, fourteen for women—were established in Toulouse, leading Lamoignon de Basville to conclude in 1698 that religious convents then occupied half the city. The intendant was exaggerating only slightly.[12]

There were two important aspects of this wave of religious establishments. First, for the most part the new orders inclined toward activism, or at least departed from the monastic tradition of reclusion. The Visitation, for example, was comprised of nuns devoted to the education of young girls, and the Sisters of Charity, an order founded by Vincent de Paul, specialized in working with the poor in the general hospital.[13] Perhaps the most influential exemplar of this turn away

10. ADH-G, G 527.

11. *Lettre d'éxcommunication de l'archevêque Montchal* (Toulouse, 1639).

12. Wolff, *Histoire*, pp. 316–19; Michel Fabry, "Carte des propriétés ecclésiastiques de Toulouse à la fin du XVIIe siècle," (Mémoire maîtrise, Université de Toulouse-Mirail, 1963); Cayre, *Histoire des évêques et archévêques de Toulouse*, pp. 347–58.

13. S. G. Douais, *La Visitation de Toulouse: Etudes, souvenirs et documents* (Paris, 1905); Wolff, *Histoire*, p. 317.

from traditional monasticism, aside from the Jesuits, was the congregation of the Oratory, founded in Paris in 1611 by Pierre Bérulle and in Toulouse seven years later. The aim of the Oratorians was to "elevate the priesthood" through a congregation that would emphasize the relationship between the secular clergy and parishioners as the focus of Catholic devotion and discipline. Thus in 1618, when a contract was signed between the Church of the Dalbade and the Oratory, the inhabitants of Toulouse were presented with a new example of priestly commitment. In the Oratory they saw a living embodiment of the Bérullian philosophy that combined rigorous Augustinianism, devout zeal, and parochial service: a community of priests who taught that a truly Christian life was possible, not only in the monastery, on retreat, or in mystical revery, but in the world of one's parish, in sacramental devotion and in service to the poor.[14] It was this last point that the Oratorian Père Le Jeune—known as Père Aveugle because of his blindness—drove home in his sermons at the cathedral on the eve of the founding of the general hospital in Toulouse. Mme de Mondonville, whom we shall soon meet as the most prominent female religious leader among the city's laity, was among those in attendance on that occasion, and it was just after Le Jeune's sermon that she sought out the priest Gabriel de Ciron to hear her confession. This was a meeting that would prove portentous for the emerging local dévot movement. Like Ciron, and like other local Oratorians as well, Le Jeune was a member of the local Company of the Holy Sacrament.[15]

This leads us to the second important feature of the new and reformed regular clergy, its manner of reaching out to the lay community, an outreach accomplished in several ways. The most routine was the practice of individual Jesuits or Oratorian priests serving as personal confessors to potential dévots or preaching in parish churches to the assembled masses. Then, too, there was the influence exercised by several regular clerics over their lay brethren in the Company of the Holy Sacrament. Most important, religious orders also sponsored special devotional groups for the laity, such as the Jesuits' congregations for artisans and gentlemen; or lay confraternities, such as the Franciscans' Confraternity of the Cordon of Saint Francis, which at-

14. Henri Brémond, *A Literary History of Religious Thought in France*, 3:133–92; R. C. Julien, *Toulouse chrétienne: Histoire de la paroisse N.D. la Dalbade* (Toulouse, 1891), pp. 255–75.

15. Shibano, "Les Débuts de la Congrégation des Filles de L'Enfance," p. 12; Raoul Allier, *La Compagnie du Saint-Sacrement à Toulouse* (Toulouse, 1914), p. 21.

tracted hundreds of women, most of them widows; or more formal societies, such as the Third-Order Dominicans, which recruited primarily among the wives of parlementaires.[16] The appeal of these societies and confraternities was great, displacing in some instances lay peoples' allegiance to their parish churches, a situation that troubled the secular clergy. The vicar-general Gabriel de Ciron, for example, was forced to admonish his brother for neglecting his parochial duties in favor of the Jesuits' Congrégation des Messieurs.[17] The laity's involvement in these groups, and in the new religious orders as well, was thus hardly passive or merely formal; many prominent Toulousains were zealous founders and sponsors of certain orders and subsequently contributed their sons and daughters to their ranks.

Such lay activism was at the heart of a Catholic Renaissance that swept the French elite in the first years of the seventeenth century. In Toulouse, this spiritual revival also coincided with the flowering of a libertine culture, described in the last chapter, thus suggesting a relationship between the two. Did free thought and irreverence in high circles help provoke a religious reaction among the righteous locals? The trial of Vanini suggests that zealous dévots were indeed active in the campaign against "libertinage," for among those who gathered testimony against him was one Marguerite de Sénaux, a founder of the Third-Order Dominicans, whose husband, the councilor Garibal (who was also a member of the Company of the Holy Sacrament), was among his more assiduous prosecutors.[18] On the other hand, that brazen libertines, piqued by what they probably viewed as pure Turtuffery, could themselves deliberately provoke the sensitivities of the dévots is illustrated by a genuine cause célèbre. One day in February 1646, the chevalier de Roquelaure—the prototype for Molière's Don Juan—rode into town with his friends, stormed a tennis court, and harassed several bystanders while shouting out insults and curses to the Virgin. Captured by the militia, he was in jail but a few

16. ADH-G, E 817, "Sensuitent les noms des confraires et confraireses du Confrairie du Courdon Sainct-François, érige au grand couvent de la regulière observance Sainct francoyse en Tholoze"; T. Porte, "Esprit social et charité: Le tiers-ordre dominicain à Toulouse au XVIIᵉ siècle," ADM 70 (1958): 161–80; Soeur Diane du Christ, Le monastère Sainte-Catherine de Sienne à Toulouse (Toulouse, 1976).
17. Shibano, "Gabriel de Ciron," p. 122.
18. Porte, "Esprit social et charité," p. 164.

days before his escape was engineered by a group of his friends, among whom were five magistrates of the parlement.[19] It can thus be imagined that in the years before the definitive triumph of Catholic piety, libertines and dévots stalked and at times provoked each other like rival gangs on disputed turf; at stake here, however, was the cultural allegiance of the elite.[20]

At stake too was the general comportment of the laity, which church officials and dévots alike were quick to condemn and strove to reform. What they confronted was a peculiarly schizophrenic city, or at least one that appeared so in the eyes of Thomas Platter. While Platter noted in 1599 that in all his travels he had never seen a place with so many churches and other religious edifices, he added that there was "frequent need of them in a town in which all sorts of scandals and impieties abound, to say nothing of the houses of ill fame that flourish in large number," frequented by men in broad daylight.[21] It seems that in the city's houses of worship the behavior was scarcely better. An archbishop's ordinance of 1619 condemned "the great and extraordinary irreverences that are daily committed in certain churches and cloisters . . . and even (which we can only say with horror) when the very august sacrament and sacrifice is raised at the altar." People spoke and gossiped during mass, strolled about, refused to kneel or doff their hats. Women, "having lost all shame and honesty," openly flirted with young men during the divine service, "which makes us greatly apprehensive that the ire of God might descend upon us."[22] A decade later matters had apparently grown worse, for an ordinance in 1633 clearly refers to sexual traffic in the churches, of those "who give and receive shameful assignations, appear as transvestites, and, disguised in the clothing of the opposite sex, dupe in this state the mendicants at the doors by scandalous actions and countenances." And again, women, "who should confine themselves within the limits of decency natural to them," were admonished for exposing "to the eyes of everyone the scandalous

19. *HGL*, 13: 241–42; René Pintard, "Les adventures et le procès du chevalier de Roquelaure," *Revue d'Histoire de la Philosophie et d'Histoire Générale de la Civilisation* 17 (1937): 1–24.

20. In 1643, two members of the parlement were among a crowd of young men who forcibly liberated from the capitouls' custody a notorious libertine who had been accused of rape. See Malenfant ADH-G, MS 149, pp. 5–7; and *HGL*, 13:149–50.

21. Thomas Platter, *Journal of a Younger Brother*, p. 250.

22. Simon de Peyronet, *Recueil des ordonnances synodales et autres*, pp. 754–58.

nudity of their bosoms, even in the confessional and at the holy table."[23]

Now there is no reason to believe that the laity's behavior, either in church or on the street, was any more scandalous in this period than in any other. But clearly it was perceived to be so by reformers of various stripes, and this perception, and the sensitivity it reveals, thus formed part of the backdrop of the local Counter-Reformation. Such was true also for the physical state of the city, its decay, and the recent misfortunes that befell its inhabitants. First among these was the plague of 1628–32, the worst since the Black Death, which left as many as 50,000 dead.[24] Then there was a region-wide famine, bringing thousands of poor—the capitouls counted 5,000—to the city in search of sustenance. "Their cries interrupt the sleep of the night," record the "Annales" in 1631; and during the day their numbers were so great as to block traffic in the cathedral plaza. The homeless poor were everywhere: they slept outside the city walls, under bridges, or in the streets; they huddled in churches, chapels, or abandoned houses; at night they crawled into the public squares, drawn by the warmth of bonfires provided by the authorities. Packs of mendicants swarmed around the town houses of the wealthy in hopes of a handout and often fought among themselves for what little food they received.[25] There evidently existed a subculture of the urban poor—documented in the proposal to the capitouls for the creation of the general hospital—in which professional pimps preyed upon young girls fresh from the countryside and sold them into prostitution for a mere ten sous; in which seasoned beggars systemically monopolized the alms intended for more deserving poor; and in which illicit marriages were struck with the mere exchange of a ring and a payment of a few coins, and broken just as easily.[26] It was the persistence of this subculture, as well as the burgeoning ranks of new poor in times of plague and famine, which drove the dévots to take innovative measures of poor relief.

To this portrait of an urban society burdened with large numbers of poor must be added the dimension of a city in a state of physical

23. Ibid., pp. 850–56. See also *HGL*, 13:149–50.
24. AMT, BB 278, pp. 279–372; Roucaud, *La peste à Toulouse*, p. 139.
25. AMT, BB 278, p. 372; Rozoi, 4:359; Wolff, pp. 303–4.
26. "L'aumône générale: Les désordres que causent les pauvres dans Tholose," reprinted in Abbé Lestrade, "L'aumône générale à Toulouse au dix-septième siècle," *Mélanges Léonce Courtre: Etudes d'histoire méridionale* (Toulouse, 1902), pp. 282–83.

collapse, for that is what is revealed in a survey conducted by the intendant Miron in 1636. Miron was the king's man, not the city's; he supervised the survey which was based on a walking tour of Toulouse's neighborhoods and an eyewitness account of the recent ravages of war, disease, and flooding. There is no reason to suspect him of exaggeration. Miron discovered that "984 houses, small plots and lands" in the city "had been ruined, destroyed, or burned." In the wealthy capitoulat of Saint-Etienne he found 135 houses abandoned or uninhabitable; in the Daurade, 215 shops and domiciles stood empty. The sole bridge that traversed the Garonne, linking the center city with the populous suburb of Saint-Cyprien and the lands beyond, was in a state of collapse, and work on a new bridge had come to a complete standstill. In the suburb of Saint-Michel several hundred hectares of land normally thick with vineyards had been left uncultivated for several seasons. The island of Tounis had been inundated repeatedly, causing the flight of three-quarters of its inhabitants, that is, the bulk of the city's dyers and textile workers. The two mills of the city, the Bazacle and the Chateau, which served not only Toulouse but the whole grain-growing region of lower Languedoc, could no longer function because flooding had caused a shift in the Garonne's normal water flow. Each neighborhood had lost several of its public ovens, which ordinary people relied upon to bake their bread. Finally, more than thirty formerly prosperous merchants had been forced into bankruptcy, causing "by their failure the ruin of a good part of the best houses of the said city."[27]

Despite such evidence, it is difficult to conclude that poverty and urban decay were somehow worse in the 1630s and 1640s than in other times (although documentation on the gravity of each is for some reason plentiful for that period). Indeed, if the much-discussed "crisis of the seventeenth century" ever visited the city and region, it likely came at the end rather than in the middle of the century.[28] Nevertheless, conditions were unmistakably grim in the century's middle decades, and further, this was a time when new royal taxes, combined with dearth, provoked popular uprisings. On several occasions in the 1630s and 1640s there were riots in the city against the salt

27. "Procès-verbal de M. de Miron sur l'estat déplorable de la ville de Toulouse," in *HGL*, 14:1–20.
28. Le Roy Ladurie, *Les paysans de Languedoc*; Georges Frêche, *Toulouse et la région Midi-Pyrénées au siècle des lumières (vers 1670–1789)* (Paris, 1974), pp. 99–107.

tax, and parts of the nearby province of Guyenne were chronically in revolt.[29] These conditions, combined with the accumulated years of neglect and decay that were the legacy of the religious wars, form the urban backdrop for the rise of a lay dévot movement, and were the problems to which many devout elites applied themselves as well. But their social activism stemmed not only from the conditions surrounding them, nor exclusively from their newfound piety. Most of the activists were first and foremost magistrates or held other positions of formal authority, and their relationship to society was thus colored by their official capacity. The particular nature of their religious activism, I suggest, was both an outgrowth of their political authority and a symptom of its limitations.

Politics and Lay Activism

To establish a connection between politics and religion has long preoccupied historians of seventeenth-century Europe, confronted as they are by the dual realities of a centralizing state and new religious mentalities. Certainly the English Revolution offers the most promising material for this project, and, indeed, there has been no shortage of attempts to draw connections between the politics of opposition to the Stuarts and the rise of Puritanism. But French historians have not been as inclined to bring religion and politics into the same analytical framework as their counterparts across the Channel, perhaps because of the elusive nature of Jansenism, which never found quite the same political expression that characterized Puritanism. One notable exception is the French philosopher Lucien Goldmann, who in his book *Le dieu caché* attempted to explain Jansenism by relating what he called its "tragic" worldview to the paralyzing effect of absolutism on the attitudes and behavior of the French officer class. The creation of a royal bureaucracy in the form of the intendants did more than displace these *robins* from their traditional role as custodians of public authority, argued Goldmann; it also rendered them helpless to protest their predicament, trapping them in a position where they both resented the crown for its threatening innovations while owing

29. On these revolts see Beik, "Magistrates and Popular Uprisings in France before the Fronde: The Case of Toulouse," *Journal of Modern History* 46 (1974); HGL, 14: 100–102 and passim; Rozoi, 4:366, 382, 426.

homage to it for guaranteeing the legitimacy of their offices. Their situation was tragic because it doomed them to inaction, condemning them to suffer their fate in a world that had passed them by. And it was in Jansenism, with its pessimism and its unorthodox theology, where they found both consolation for their predicament and a means of voicing obliquely, in religious tones, their opposition to the established order.[30]

Goldmann's thesis has had more than its share of critics.[31] His book is clearly flawed: his view of absolutism is one-sided and overestimates the power of the intendants; his sample of Jansenists is limited to the most prominent; he falsely assumes that Jansenism was primarily a Robe phenomenon; and he strains to find a link between such refined thinkers as Racine and Pascal and general Jansenist sentiments. If, however, Goldmann's thesis has been largely discredited, there is yet something worth salvaging in his approach—namely, the attempt to see in a new religious sensibility not simply an expression of political grievances but, more subtly, something of an alternative to politics itself.

This is, with some modification, what follows here. For I want to argue that in order to understand seventeenth-century lay activism we must look beyond both the Counter-Reformation and the desperate conditions of the day to the particular political circumstances of the local officialdom. Those circumstances were largely defined by the increasing intrusion of the crown into local affairs and the resulting problem of how city officials were to maintain and define their positions in the light of this intrusion. Opposition to the crown was only one possible response, a risky and unattractive one at that. Another entailed the reassertion of their legitimacy and authority, especially on the local level, where, many were convinced, the crown's policies were exacting an unacceptable cost in terms of social disorder and distress. The argument can be summarized briefly: it was in enterprises of a religious nature where local elites could assert their legitimacy as rightful officials, work to mitigate the social disorder

30. *The Hidden God*, trans. P. Thody (New York, 1964), pt. 2.

31. René Taveneaux, *Jansénisme et politique* (Paris, 1965), p. 21; Jean Delumeau, *Le catholicisme entre Luther et Voltaire* (Paris, 1971), pp. 179–80; Robert Mandrou, "Tragique XVIIe siècle, à propos de travaux récents," *Annales: ESC* 12 (1957): 305–13; Albert Hamscher, "The Parlement of Paris and the Social Interpretation of Early French Jansenism," *Catholic Historical Review* 63 (1977): 392–410.

that confronted and threatened them, and even express, albeit obliquely, their opposition to the reigning political order.

As for their opposition, it was sometimes voiced in no uncertain terms. Although one of the more obedient cities in the realm in the seventeenth century, Toulouse did participate in the general protest against the direction of royal policy during the ministries of Richelieu and Mazarin. The parlement took the lead in protesting a series of new and extraordinary taxes and especially the heavy-handed behavior of the intendants in enforcing these fiscal impositions. Such protest sometimes took on the appearance of supporting popular resistance, something widely assumed, for example, in the wake of a tax revolt in Villefranche-de-Rouergue in 1643, when the parlement issued a re- monstrance to the king and sent its agents to investigate the situation, thus directly challenging the intendants' authority.[32] In 1648, a parle- mentary delegation led by the renowned mathematician Pierre de Fermat argued before the Chancellor Séguier for the suspension of the taille in Aquitaine, warning that the enforced levy only meant in- creased hardship for the impoverished region and would likely lead to popular resistance and unrest.[33] And during the Fronde the sovereign court managed to strike up a temporary alliance with the estates of Languedoc, thus presenting the crown with the specter of a provincial opposition front.[34] The city's other main voice of opposition came from Charles Montchal, archbishop of Toulouse from 1628 to 1651. Montchal's concerns were primarily ecclesiastical. In his *Mémoires* he denounced Cardinal Richelieu for wrecking the episcopacy by ap- pointing his *créatures* as bishops, meddling in church affairs, taxing and even seizing ecclesiastical properties, and failing to persecute the Huguenots. Moreover, Montchal was a Jansenist. He was one of the sixteen bishops of the realm who approved Antoine Arnauld's *De la fréquente communion*, and signed three letters to the pope affirming his approbation of this central Jansenist tract. Montchal also refused to accept the decision that the so-called "five propositions" were hereti- cal, which later became a litmus test for Jansenism. It was in part

32. "Relation des résolutions prises au Parlement de Thoulouse en conséquence des désordres arrivés à Villefranche," in trans. Patricia Ranum and Orest Ranum, eds., *The Century of Louis XIV* (New York, 1972), p. 8; *HGL*, 13:140–43.

33. Michael Mahoney, *The Mathematical Career of Pierre de Fermat, 1601–1665* (Princeton, 1963), p. 19.

34. Beik, *Absolutism and Society*, pp. 206–15; John Miller, "Les états de Languedoc pendant la Fronde," *ADM* 95 (1983): 43–65.

because of Montchal's presence in the city that Toulouse gained a reputation for Jansenism.[35]

But this opposition, as serious as it was, ultimately foundered. There were simply too many obstacles in the way of concerted action, obstacles that thwarted the opposition at nearly every turn. To illustrate, consider the parlement and its range of actions from the 1630s through the period of the Fronde. Although not so disobedient as some, the Parlement of Toulouse did not accept every royal edict and bureaucratic innovation. On several occasions in the 1630s and 1640s it opposed new royal taxes and meddling by the intendants. It strenuously objected to the crown's creation and sale of new offices within the parlement itself.[36] But it discovered also that in these struggles the crown ultimately had the advantage, something dramatically demonstrated in 1638. In the preceding years the contest between court and crown had been lively, and the parlement succeeded in at least slowing royal intrusion into the province. In 1638, however, the king set in motion plans for creating in Nîmes a new parlement, which, by cutting the Toulouse magistrates' area of jurisdiction in half, would challenge their primacy in the region and deflate the value of their offices. Henceforth all the energies of the court were dedicated to blocking this innovation, and when negotiations with the crown had been completed in 1639 the resolution told the tale of the parlement's predicament: the proposed Parlement of Nîmes had been dropped but in exchange for the Toulouse magistrates' registration of those fiscal edicts and acceptance of those new offices that they had previously opposed. To be sure, this did not spell the end of parlementary resistance to the crown's policies, but it did serve as a lesson in the limits of such resistance and the varied strategies of royal reprisal.[37]

Another obstacle to the parlement's range of actions was division and factionalism, both in the city and within the court itself. While the court dominated the social and political affairs of the city, its domination was not uncontested. On one flank it was challenged by capitouls who still enjoyed popular support. Competition between

35. Charles de Montchal, *Mémoires de Mr. de Montchal, archevêque de Toulouse contenant des particularitez de la vie du ministère du cardinal de Richelieu* (Rotterdam, 1718). See also Beik, *Absolutism and Society*, pp. 329–30.

36. ADH-G, MS 148.

37. Ibid., p. 217; Beik, "Magistrates and Popular Uprisings," p. 598.

the parlement and capitouls was regular in the mid-seventeenth century, sometimes spilling into the streets. Several issues were involved, not least the simple question of which institution would control the city's official life, an issue largely resolved in the parlement's favor by the end of the sixteenth century but which the capitouls continued to raise nevertheless. The parlement frequently interfered in municipal elections, declaring certain candidacies invalid and sometimes circumventing the process by unilaterally naming the capitouls. For their part, the capitouls insisted in vain that the royal magistrates pay a portion of several extraordinary levies imposed on the city. The capitouls could still create difficulties for the court by appealing to the crown or provincial governor, or by mobilizing their supporters in the city, which they did in 1645, when over a thousand armed partisans of the town councilors took to the streets to demonstrate against the parlement's heavy-handed policy toward the Hôtel de Ville. In short, the capitouls clearly represented an obstacle to the parlement's freedom of action in the city and would remain one throughout the Old Regime.[38] The archbishop of Toulouse was another. Formally, the archbishop had no peer in the city; he even ranked higher than the First President in the urban hierarchy. In reality the royal court more than matched the prelate's power, at least in nonecclesiastical matters. But when the parlement began to tread on the ceremonial privileges of Archbishop Montchal in the 1630s, he reacted with violent indignation, going so far as to excommunicate several parlementaires for holding a meeting of the board of directors of one of the city's hospitals in his absence. Why should the archbishop's injured sensitivities have mattered to the haughty magistrates? The fact is that they needed his cooperation in their dealings with the crown. For example, when the court was battling the proposed Parlement of Nîmes, it was precisely the reluctance of the piqued Montchal to cooperate with the magistrates that stalled the court's campaign against the new court.[39] The successful conduct of local politics in an age of growing royal power depended upon at least the semblance of a united front among threatened institutions. Yet

38. On the mid-century competition between the parlement and capitouls, AMT, BB 279, pp. 146–47, and BB 280, pp. 151–59; HGL, 13:200 and passim; Rozoi, 4:430–35; AMT, BB 267, "Le testament syndical de Monsieur de Lafaille, ancien syndic et doyen des anciens capitouls de Toulouse"; and Beik, "Magistrates and Popular Uprisings."

39. ADH-G, MS 148, pp. 97–108, 139–73; Lettre d'excommunication de l'archevêque Montchal (Toulouse, 1639).

such unity was difficult to achieve, even within the parlement itself, for the court had to contend not only with a feisty Hôtel de Ville, and a sensitive archbishop, but with its own hotheaded members as well. During the 1640s, Bertier had his arms full with these "agitators," who nearly catapulted the Toulouse court into the ranks of the parlementary frondeurs. Short of such a precipitous course, they merely ensured that the court would be forced to deal with internal conflict at almost every turn.[40]

Local officials in the mid-seventeenth century found their position further complicated by pressures from below, by poverty-induced disorder, and even revolt. It was not only that officials felt threatened in their persons and property by a discontented populace, although this was undoubtedly the case. The "people" were more than a threat in the eyes of officials; they were also a possible source of legitimacy and power in the officials' own struggles with the crown. Local officials frequently presented themselves as the people's protectors, and although their complaints on the suffering populace's behalf may have been cynical attempts to exploit social misery for their own political ends, there was probably a certain feudal solicitude toward the lower orders in the officials' outlook.[41] Such solicitude, however, could be dangerous when it came to be seen as permission for popular resistance. This is indeed what occurred following the parlement's support of the grievances behind the tax revolt in Villefranche-de-Rouergue in 1643.[42] Once word was broadcast that the magistrates had objected to the taille, there were repercussions in the city of Toulouse itself: a boat loaded with wheat was pillaged in public view and the people "shout boldly that the tailles should not be paid, [while] others complained of so many disorders caused by the ambition of the great nobility."[43] The events of 1635, the year of the second

40. Beik, *Absolutism and Society*, p. 230. For a summary report to Colbert on the magistrates of Toulouse assessing individuals' loyalty to the crown, see Georges Bernard Depping, ed., *Correspondance administrative sous le règne de Louis XIV*, 2:111–14, 132–32.

41. As, for example, the court's claim in 1650 that it was the duty of the parlement "to take care of the urgent necessities and nourishment of the poor at a time when a delay would be fatal." This claim, as Beik points out, was used to undermine the authority of the bishops in the court's struggle with the provincial estates during the Fronde (*Absolutism and Society*, p. 212, and *HGL*, 14:380–81).

42. "Relation des résolutions prises au Parlement de Thoulouse en conséquence des désordres arrivés à Villefranche."

43. Beik, "Magistrates and Popular Uprisings"; *HGL*, 13:140–43.

most urban uprisings before the Fronde, illustrate the social pressures confronting local authorities and the need for dealing carefully with a troubled populace.[44] As news of an uprising in Bordeaux reached Toulouse in May and June, the city was rife with rumors of impending revolt. To stem the mounting disorder, the capitouls called a full assembly of the city's artisan corporations and reminded them of their sworn duty to defend king and city. First President Bertier exhorted the assembly to resist the "enemies of the state." His address was met with cries of "Vive le Roy!" Several days later an artisan suspected of fomenting sedition was arrested and condemned to die by strangulation. The victim, however, was forcibly liberated by a crowd and a general strike followed. Barricades appeared in the streets. Despite the obvious danger, the authorities did not hesitate to act: two capitouls, escorted only by their personal valets, rode through the city to calm the populace.[45] And although the city simmered with discontent for several weeks, Toulouse's populace never rose up in full revolt.

This is not to say that the personal efforts of these authorities were responsible for quelling a restless populace. In other cities, and other times, such exemplary action counted for little in the way of pacification. The point is that urban officials often found themselves having personally to play the role of police, especially since the City Watch was minuscule, not more than forty men.[46] The relationship of the authorities to the populace was thus complex and varied: sometimes they strove to placate discontent by seeming to champion popular grievances; other times they had no choice but to confront urban unrest with the weight of their authority, and hope that it would be sufficient to impose order. In any case, their already difficult situation was exacerbated by the fact that the crown held local officials responsible for any disorder in their jurisdiction and often accused them of fomenting popular discontent when they were merely trying to contain it.

In retrospect, the parlementaires' predicament appears rooted in a persisting tactical problem: surrounded on several sides by obstacles to their range of action, how were they, as the ruling aristocrats and

44. Richard Bonney, *Political Change in France under Richelieu and Mazarin, 1624–1661* (Oxford, 1978), p. 325.

45. Beik, *Absolutism and Society*, pp. 191–92; Rozoi, 4:366–67.

46. Edmond Lamouzèle, *Essai sur l'organisation et les fonctions du guet et de la garde bourgeoise de Toulouse* (Paris, 1906).

legitimate governors they held themselves to be, to maneuver? Gold-mann's answer has them seeking refuge in Jansenism, in essence withdrawing from the world of politics and seeking consolation in a refined, spiritually heroic form of religiosity. His presupposition, however, is that the officers would readily yield their raison d'être and abdicate their positions. A few magistrates did in fact "drop out" in such a fashion, but most did not. Goldmann's thesis also seems to assume that spiritual consolation led to social and political inactivity, a misreading not only of the Counter-Reformation but of some of the currents contained within Jansenism as well. That the dévots were active critics of the regime's anti-Hapsburg foreign policy is well known.[47] Many of them were also active in less dramatic ways, as agents of new forms of poor relief, for example. In short, it must not be assumed that religious piety meant a withdrawal from worldly affairs; quite the contrary, it could spur officials to social action, in-spiring them to take even more seriously their role as rulers and reformers of society. Indeed, this was the "dévot" view of local politics.

This very position was in fact articulated at the time by a leading Toulouse cleric, Etienne de Molinier, a Black Penitent and also a member of the local chapter of the Company of the Holy Sacrament.[48] In 1624 Molinier published an anti-Machiavellian tract, *A Mirrour for Christian States*, which contained a justification for the manipulation of political power from a deeply religious perspective. Molinier's advice is pragmatic and hard-headed: "To know good, and to will it, and to seek and to tend toward it, all this is not the attaynment thereof; Power is necessary for compassing what we aspire to . . . vaine the desire which cannot arrive to its ayme."[49] No justification here for withdraw-ing from the world of political action. He is also severe, counseling "that the effeminate and timorous are not proper for any matter of high nature."[50] But he goes on to suggest as well that the power of a ruler depends only marginally on force: "It is no marvell, that as the

47. Georges Pagès, "Autour de grand Orage. Richelieu et Marillac: deux politiques," *Revue Historique*, no. 79 (1937): 63–97.
48. On Molinier, see J. Contrasty, "Le prêtre toulousain, Etienne de Molinier," *RHT* 34 (1949).
49. Etienne Molinier, *Les politiques christiennes* (Paris, 1635). I have for the most part preserved the spelling and language of an early seventeenth-century translation: trans. W. Tyrwhit (London, 1635), pp. 203–4.
50. Ibid., p. 296.

swelling rage of the Sea, threatening to swallow the whole earth, breaks itself upon some sandy shore, so this tempest of a mutinous people, appeaseth itself at the approach of a disarmed person, and that opinion stayes what force, Iron, and armies were unable to stop. The esteme and opinion of this man's vertue, dissipateth all this storme."[51]

Unlike Machiavelli and Richelieu, who tailored their political wisdom to the affairs of state, Molinier addresses the concerns of smaller polities where the personal exercise and display of authority were part of a ruler's daily routine. He has in mind, not kings, princes, and ministers, but magistrates, priests, and other officials who frequently had to intervene in public disputes, face down an unruly crowd, or were themselves sometimes combatants in civil and confessional struggles. In other words, Molinier expresses a view of politics from the vantage point of the local official, the "frontline" authority. Thus his preoccupation with "mutinous people" and the like, and also his emphasis on the personal qualities of the ideal official: "Authority, Good Fortune, Courage and Eloquence," attributes "required in publick persons encountering in their pious enterprises a thousand obstacles through which they are to break."[52] What Molinier does not see as necessary is noble rank, although he concedes that a "newcomer"—meaning a nonnoble—will likely lack public respect and authority until "he has given good testimonies of his actions." More important than blood or name are "generous acts, . . . for wee do not consider man metaphysically alone . . . divided from other men, but reflect upon him in civil community and society."[53] There, "Justice, Moderation, love of the publicke, and the defense and protection of the poore and impotent doe gaine very much."[54]

A spokesman for the dévots, Molinier also clearly had in mind those robins, especially parlementary magistrates, who exercised local authority and whose claim to noblesse was based more on service and acquired virtues than blood and lineage. Like his contemporary Charles Loyseau, Molinier argued for an expanded French elite, one that included and valued the contributions and worth of the Robe class.[55] And like devout political commentators of every stripe, he

---

51. Ibid., p. 218.
52. Ibid., pp. 207–8.
53. Ibid., p. 248.
54. Ibid., p. 253.
55. Charles Loyseau, *Traité des ordres* (Paris, 1610).

was intent on repudiating the vision of *The Prince* by insisting that "the law of God is the sacred school of true political prudence."[56] But in addition, his focus on the micropolitics of local rule captures precisely the predicament of magistrates in the mid-seventeenth century, who were increasingly burdened with the dual task of resisting and accommodating the forces of social discontent.

Here is precisely where local politics and lay religiosity were joined, for if there was a theme common to the activities of the dévots it was their concern for what was generally referred to as "disorder"—poverty and vagabondage, violence and crime, public irreverence and popular celebrations of a profane sort. Foremost among their concerns was the danger of popular revolt, the ultimate social disorder. One might simply conclude that a need to reform or manage a turbulent society stood behind the activities of the dévots, that their social enterprises originated in response to social conditions. The suggestion offered here is that their efforts had more complex origins. On the one hand they arose out of a revived Catholicism and its appeal to the laity, especially the elite. But on the other, their religious commitment also derived from their political predicament. Local officials, in particular royal magistrates, found their actions through traditional channels increasingly limited in the middle decades of the seventeenth century, limited by the crown's challenge to their authority, by inter- and intracorporate rivalries, and by the danger in supporting popular grievances. Given this predicament, how were elites able to carry on as authorities in the city? In particular, how were they both to live with this status quo—since there seemed to be no political way out of it short of rebellion—and not sacrifice control over the urban populace in a period when social control was the order of the day? It was in the social activism of the lay devotional movement that this problem found its solution.

56. Molinier, *Mirrour for Christian States,* p. 4.

6

Devotion—Spiritual and Social

It is not unusual in the history of Christianity to find examples of noble military men who are abruptly converted to a life of
exemplary piety, abandoning the sword for the breviary, the career of
warrior for a regime of asceticism and service to God and church.
Certainly the most famous of such converts in the early modern period was the Basque nobleman Ignatius Loyola. But seventeenth-century France also had its share, among them the duc de Ventadour,
lieutenant-governor of Languedoc and Montmorency's brother-in-
law, whom we have already met as the leading player in *Le Cléosandre*. In the late 1620s, this one-time libertine separated amiably
from his wife (who took the vow of a Carmelite) and began a new life
as a dévot.[1] In 1627 he founded in Paris the Company of the Holy
Sacrament, a secret society of devout Catholics, which soon established chapters throughout the realm, including one in Toulouse in
1641. Ventadour's conversion thus presaged a profound and widespread movement that soon dominated the city, prompting a range of
religious enterprises from novel forms of poor relief and new confraternal associations to a renewal of Catholic devotion, especially
among the elite. The movement was at the heart of the laity's participation in the Counter-Reformation. What follows is by no means a
full survey of the local Counter-Reformation, for such a study,
though certainly warranted, would itself require a substantial mono-

---

1. On Ventadour, see Anon., *Le duc et la duchesse de Ventadour: Un grand amour
chrétien au dix-septième siècle* (Paris, 1889).

graph. Rather, the purpose here is to treat religious life at mid-century selectively, concentrating on how the movement for spiritual renewal drew elites into contact with the poor and the common people and on how it shaped the city's public life.

The dual nature of the French Counter-Reformation—its emphasis on spiritual renewal and attention to social reform—is illustrated in the relationship between two individuals who played a prominent role among the dévots in Toulouse. Gabriel de Ciron was the archbishop's vicar-general, a member of the local Company of the Holy Sacrament, and the scion of a prominent family of magistrates.[2] He served also as spiritual adviser to Mme de Mondonville, the daughter of a distinguished parlementaire, who after her husband's death became a tireless worker for the church.[3] In 1652, however, when she first met Ciron, Mme de Mondonville was still a worldly young woman of some beauty who enjoyed reading novels, attending parties, and dressing in a fashionable, even revealing manner. One day while attending mass in the cathedral, she was rather mysteriously drawn to Ciron to hear her confession. She received his absolution, but not without first suffering a scolding for her immodest attire. The meeting was momentous for her, and she records in her memoirs that during her prayers afterward she heard a voice proclaiming: "This is the man who will separate you from the world."

At her next confession, delayed for several months because of the plague, she again encountered Ciron's admonition concerning her dress, especially her bare arms, and was this time denied absolution for a week—a small price to pay, she recalls him saying, to a God "who had died completely naked for me."[4] She began to reflect on

---

2. Marguerite-Marie Shibano, "Gabriel de Ciron (1619–75), Esquisse biographique," *Revue d'Histoire de la Spiritualité* 52 (1976): 89–124; *Dictionnaire de la spiritualité*, 2:903–9.

3. On Mme de Mondonville and especially her relationship with Ciron, see Shibano, "Les débuts de la Congrégation des Filles de l'Enfance de N.S.J.C.: Les fondateurs Gabriel de Ciron et Madame de Mondonville (1619–1657)" (Thesis presented to the Ecole Pratique des Hautes-Etudes, 1977), pp. 59–60. Sister Shibano has reproduced large portions of Mme de Mondonville's memoirs, from which I will cite. Portions have already been published by Leon Dutil, ed., *Lettres inédites de Mme de Mondonville suivies de fragments de ses mémoires (1655–1697)* (Paris, 1911). See also Alphonse Auguste, "Gabriel de Ciron et Madame de Mondonville," *RHT* 1 (1914): 14–25, 129–63, 303–33; 2 (1915–19): 20–69. For other notable collaborations between female dévotes and their spiritual advisers in seventeenth-century France, see Henri Brémond, *A Literary History of Religious Thought in France*, trans. K. L. Montgomery (London, 1936), 3:446, 450, 541, 543; Orest Ranum, *Paris in the Age of Absolutism* (New York, 1968), p. 120.

4. Shibano, "Les débuts de la Congrégation," p. 69.

her mounting faith and her growing attachment to her confessor. He was stern with her, sometimes even harsh, but this she interpreted as a sign of her own resistance to the challenge that lay before her. As to his saintliness she had no doubt. On a subsequent occasion, Ciron again rebuked her for wearing a dress that exposed her arms, reminding her that "the Christian life was a continual penance." She thus had her clothes altered, adding to her dresses so-called jansenist sleeves, which she continued to wear despite the heat, the plague still threatening the region, and the headaches they brought on, for she knew that her stern-minded confessor would turn a deaf-ear to complaints.[5]

Shortly thereafter Mme de Mondonville's husband died, leaving her a childless widow at twenty-nine. She had been profoundly unhappy in marriage and experienced her husband's passing as a liberation "from the chains she had worn these long years." Later she recalled praying to God, "Now that I am all alone, make me everything to you."[6] Convention dictated that she demonstrate her grief by staying secluded at home during a long period of mourning, but Ciron counseled against such a display and directed her instead to work with the poor. "Madame," he insisted, "you must begin to lead a Christian life." Her first task was to care for the young girls in the Hôpital de la Grave, Toulouse's poorhouse—"to change their shirts and to sweep alongside some Ladies of the city who voluntarily followed my lead."[7]

Soon she was Ciron's helpmate in efforts to aid the poor, and one day received a note from him informing her that he had just been in one of the city's prisons and there "found Jesus Christ dying of cold and destitute of all help." Would she bring blankets and bouillon to a few sick prisoners? He even gave her permission to leave mass for this task.[8] They continued to work together in the city's prisons and hospitals, and as they did Ciron grew to depend more and more on her labor and learned to appreciate her extraordinary devotion to the poor. "This person, who never abandoned me," he testified, "had great sensitivity to bad odors,"

nevertheless, she had so much ardor to help the poor, and especially young girls, that she found a kind of pleasure in combing these chil-

5. Ibid., p. 71.
6. Ibid., p. 75.
7. Ibid., p. 81.
8. Ibid.

dren, which was naturally horrible to her. But as soon as she had begun this task, all the discomfort disappeared, and God graced her such that those heads so full of worms and from which pus emerged did not bother her, who was otherwise so sensitive to these things; and with a movement that was not forced, she would put her mouth to these spots on the head where there were worms and did not feel discomfort, which was the result of a truly singular grace; for I know that when she went to the hospital for the sick, merely the odor of the place prevented her from eating.[9]

Finally, on the eve of the Feast of the Immaculate Conception in 1654, Mme de Mondonville took a vow affirming her exclusive commitment to a Christian life: "My God, I renounce the world and its pomp, the devil and his incitements, the flesh and its concupiscence, giving myself to you, O my Savior, body, heart and soul, with all my understanding . . . and affection, in the extreme desire to be truly faithful to you, taking the Holy Virgin for my guardian, the 7 December 1654."[10] Henceforth, she was a *dévote* and soon became the most important female figure in the local movement of lay piety. She also became a somewhat controversial figure, the founder of a religious institution that eventually fell under the accusation of Jansenism. Gabriel de Ciron was suspected of Jansenist sympathies as well.

One does not usually associate seventeenth-century Jansenism with social activism and a commitment to charitable works. Rather, the *solitaires* of the Parisian convent of Port-Royal, at least, are remembered as quintessential dropouts from society, as eminent dévots who rejected the world in favor of a nearly monastic regime of piety, discipline, and meditation. Yet the spiritual tendencies identified with Jansenism were varied, and Mme de Mondonville's own development exemplified the apparently contradictory nature of those tendencies. For here was a women who clearly yearned for devotional purity and struggled to detach herself from the world, wanting nothing more than to submit to the guidance of her stern-minded confessor. At the same time, she eagerly embraced the cause of poor relief, demonstrating a near-pathological identification with the poor and sick, and became one of the most socially active women in seventeenth-century Toulouse.

9. Ibid. For a similar testimony from an early colleague of Ignatius Loyola, see Brian Pullan, *Rich and Poor in Renaissance Venice* (Cambridge, Mass., 1971), p. 265.
10. Shibano, "Les débuts de la Congrégation," p. 83.

More than Jansenism, however, cemented the partnership between Ciron and Mme de Mondonville, nor does that theology alone explain the dévot community in which they played the leading role. Indeed, there are grounds for rejecting the Jansenist label for their activities and spiritual inclinations; and in any case, Jansenism was only one of the movements involving a significant segment of the French devout elite. It is thus to some of the more important local manifestations of lay activism that we now must turn.

Messieurs and Compagnons

One of the more interesting, if obscure, lay groups associated with the French Counter-Reformation was the Company of the Holy Sacrament. Founded in Paris in 1627, the company soon established chapters in nearly sixty cities throughout the realm, many of which continued in activity long after the secret brotherhood's formal suppression by Mazarin in 1666. The concerns of the company's *Messieurs* (as its members were called) ranged from poor relief and the policing of public morals to the persecution of Protestants and the reform of the priesthood. Normally they took advantage of their positions in the highest circles—at court, in the parlements, in the episcopacy—to lobby for the implementation of their holy agenda, which they achieved with remarkable success. But the Messieurs were not above leaving their privileged sanctuaries and taking to the streets themselves to track down errant journeymen, round up beggars, distribute alms, reform prostitutes, inspect prison ship galleys, aid plague victims, convert Protestants, hound gamblers, invade taverns, clean up churches, and publicly rail against the "excesses" and "disorders" that were actually the pastimes and amusements of ordinary people in the Old Regime. Although the Messieurs would have been outraged by the comparison, their closest contemporary counterparts in this respect were those other meddlesome saints across the Channel, the Puritans.[11]

The local chapter of the Company of the Holy Sacrament was

11. The fundamental texts on the company are H. Beauchet-Filleau, *Annales de la Compagnie du St.-Sacrement par le comte René de Voyer d'Argenson* (Marseille, 1900); Raoul Allier, *La Compagnie du Saint-Sacrement de l'Autel: La cabale des dévots* (Paris, 1902); Emanuel Chill, "The Company of the Holy Sacrament: Social Aspects of the Counter-Reformation" (Ph.D. diss., Columbia University, 1961).

founded in 1641 when the chevalier de la Coste, Gaspard de Simiane, a Monsieur from Provence, journeyed to Toulouse, where he succeeded in "the establishment of a corps composed of a considerable number of pious persons who . . . busied themselves in works of piety . . . for the glory of God and to the great advantage of the public."[12] Who were these "pious persons"? Neither membership lists nor registers have survived, but the first historian of the company, Raoul Allier, by collecting names from the correspondence and death notices of better-documented provincial chapters, managed to assemble a membership roster that, while not nearly complete, at least gives us a sense of the scope of who the Toulouse Messieurs were. Allier listed thirty names, of whom twenty-eight can be identified. Fourteen were clergymen, including a bishop, the chancellor of the university, and an archdeacon of the cathedral. The fourteen laymen were five councilors in the parlement and sénéchal, four capitouls, three barristers and lawyers, and two other officers.[13] In short, there was a cross section of the city's civic and ecclesiastical elite among the Messieurs, including, most crucially, representatives from the capitoulat and parlement, corporations otherwise given to near incessant rivalry. It is also likely that there were more parlementaires than the handful Allier discovered associated with the company, for several, including First President Bertier, were intimately involved in the running of the new general hospital, the Messieurs' major enterprise.[14] Thus, the Company of the Holy Sacrament, among its other accomplishments, managed to assemble a wide range of ruling and frequently competing elites under a religious, albeit secret, mantle.

The Messieurs of Toulouse were active on a number of fronts in the city, especially poor relief, but one episode in their short history deserves special attention, for it shows us these highborn dévots delving into the artisan underworld in search of illicit cabals. This is the story of the confrontation between two secret societies.

In 1635, Baron Gaston de Renty, a leading member of the Paris company, who made it his practice to proselytize among the workers of the capital, discovered the existence of a secret syndicate of journeymen known as the Compagnonnage du Devoir. Scandalized by his discovery, Renty alerted his Parisian brethren, who immediately

12. Ruffi, *La vie de Monsieur le chevalier de la Coste* (1659), p. 129.
13. Allier, *La Compagnie du Saint-Sacrement à Toulouse*, pp. 143–44.
14. AMT, GG 949, passim.

set out to destroy this occult association. In short order they secured a condemnation of the compagnonnage from the Sorbonne and, with the help of a pious Luxembourg shoemaker living in Paris, Henry Buche, they established two confraternities—one for shoemakers (the brethren shoemakers), another for tailors (the brethren tailors)—expressly designed to attract workers away from the illicit syndicates, providing them with an alternative brotherhood based on Christian principles of work, obedience, and piety.[15]

In July 1650, three brethren shoemakers were dispatched by the Parisian Messieurs to their brothers in Toulouse for the purpose of establishing a provincial chapter of the pious craft confraternity. No sooner had they arrived when they discovered that Toulouse too was infested with the forbidden compagnonnages; in fact, the three brothers were approached by the masters of the shoemakers' corporation, who confessed to having been members themselves of the secret organization in their youth. And in March of 1651 these master shoemakers made a deposition before Archbishop Montchal detailing the practices and traditions of the heretofore obscure association.[16]

The compagnonnage functioned as a proto-trade union: it attempted to force masters to hire only those journeymen who were members, took actions against shops where wages and conditions were unsatisfactory, supported workers when they were ill or unemployed, and also served as a placement bureau by informing itinerant craftsmen of those towns and cities where their skills were in demand.[17] More upsetting to the dévots was the ritualistic dimension of the compagnonnages' practices, which highlight their occult character. Compagnons were furnished with passwords and rites allowing them to identify one another. But their most important ceremony

15. On this episode in Paris, see Allier, *La cabale des dévots*, pp. 193–214; Chill, "The Company of the Holy Sacrament," pp. 126–38.

16. "La condamnation du compagnonnage," May 21, 1651. This and other documents on the *compagnonnages* and the *frères cordonniers* and *tailleurs* are reprinted in the appendixes to Allier, *La Compagnie du Saint-Sacrement à Toulouse*, pp. 119–23.

17. On the early history of the compagnonnage, see Emile Coornaert, *Les compagnonnages en France du moyen âge à nos jours* (Paris, 1966); Etienne-Martin Saint-Léon, *Le compagnonnage* (Paris, 1901); Henri Hauser, "Les compagnonnages d'arts et métiers à Dijon au XVIIe et XVIIIe siècles," *Revue Bourguignonne* 17 (1907); Justin Godart, "Le compagnonnage à Lyon," *Revue d'Histoire de Lyon* 2 (1904): 425–69; William Sewell, Jr., *Work and Revolution in France* (Cambridge, 1980), pp. 47–55. A complete bibliography on the compagnonnages has been assembled by Roger Lecotté, "Essai bibliographique sur les compagnonnages et tous les devoirs du tour de France," in *Compagnonnage*, ed. Roger Dautry (Paris, 1951), pp. 271–417.

was the initiation of a new member. According to the shoemakers' testimony, their custom was to assemble in a cabaret or tavern they had secured for their private and secret meeting and carry out a mock baptismal ceremony. The initiate would choose two "godparents" from the compagnons. Standing before a table upon which was arrayed the "four elements," bread, wine, salt, and water, he swore to God and on his place in heaven that he would never repeat what he learned and what transpired at this seance. Then he took a new name, and was baptized with water by a compagnon (or sometimes a complicit priest) who intoned: "I baptize you in the name of the Father, the Son and the Holy Spirit." Now a compagnon, he would be taken aside by his godparents and initiated into the order's secrets, which he swore never to reveal, "neither to an ecclesiastic, a father, a mother, a judge, or a confessor."[18]

Confronted with this evidence, the archbishop lost no time condemning the compagnonnages. He threatened its members with excommunication if they persisted in their practices, which he judged "full of irreverence and repugnant to religion." An agent was sent from the archbishop's palace to broadcast the condemnation in the artisan community. Apparently this had some effect, for soon five journeymen shoemakers stepped forward and, avowing that the masters' testimony was accurate, promised "for themselves as well as the other compagnons of the said devoir in the present city" to desist from their ceremonies and their use of oaths.[19]

Meanwhile, the Company of the Holy Sacrament was at work establishing a local association of brethren shoemakers, whose statutes were approved by the archbishop in May 1651. Formally called the Association des serviteurs cordonniers, the brothers were similar to other craft confraternities, except that ordinary journeymen, and not masters, completely dominated the membership. The pious shoemakers declared their intention to form "a holy union and association for the greater glory of God and the assurance of our salvation, by the means of charitable and mutual assistance in our spiritual as well as corporal necessities." Among their fifteen statutes were those stipulating prayers in the morning and evening, confession at least once a month, sermons and catechism lessons each Sunday, and a bimonthly session where the brothers would kneel together and recite

18. Allier, *La Compagnie du Saint-Sacrement à Toulouse*, pp. 119–23.
19. Ibid., p. 122.

various prayers in both Latin and French. The association kept a fund from members' dues to support brothers in times of sickness; it also acted as a placement agency for newly arrived shoemakers to Toulouse to prevent them from falling into the hands of "those deceivers." And it aided shoemakers who had been dismissed or were unemployed for other reasons to find new work. Clearly, the idea of the brethren shoemakers was to prevent craftsmen from relying upon the resources of the compagnonnages in times of need, and their regulations make explicit their opposition to the underground unions: "In particular, we detest and renounce with all our heart this unfortunate practice and superstition of the so-called Compagnons du Devoir, as being a practice entirely diabolic, contrary to the Christian religion, to good morals and to the salvation of souls." Devout, charitable, and pure, the brothers were also dutiful: "We will be faithful to the masters, we will work carefully and diligently; it will not be permitted for us to talk of the masters' affairs in our assemblies, nor to discuss an increased wage, nor other things that touch upon the interests of the masters, if it is not for the glory of God and our salvation."[20]

Patronized by the archbishop, supported by the master shoemakers, and secretly directed by the Company of the Holy Sacrament, the brethren shoemakers had little trouble establishing themselves in Toulouse and attracting workers. They were engaged by the directors of the general hospital to teach their trade to the male paupers confined there, and in all likelihood they were also helpful in supplying shoes for the inmates. Henry Buche's biographer writes that the brothers were so popular in Toulouse, and their evangelizing efforts so well received by the common people, that when known members of the compagnonnages appeared in the city streets they were greeted with cries of "Down with the excommunicated!"[21] During the plague of 1652, when two brothers were mortally stricken, probably while serving the sick, their replacements were promptly furnished by the Paris association.[22] In 1655 the brothers were joined by a confraternity of brethren tailors. Both artisan brotherhoods continued in existence long after their patrons, the Messieurs, had disappeared from the scene.[23]

20. "Statutz de l'Association des Serviteurs Cordonniers à Tholose" (1651) in Allier, *La Compagnie du Saint-Sacrament à Toulouse*, pp. 130–31.

21. J. A. Vauchet, *L'artisan chrétien ou la vie du bon Henry* (Paris, 1670), p. 59.

22. Allier, *La Compagnie du Saint-Sacrement à Toulouse*, p. 52.

23. On the brethren in the eighteenth century, see AMT, GG 746.

The struggle against the compagnonnage was a remarkable chapter in the history of the Company of the Holy Sacrament and a strange one in the annals of class struggle. It was a clash between two secret societies, each in its own way pious, each acting toward its own ends sub rosa. In seeking out and attempting to destroy the compagnonnages, the Messieurs of the company had to enter the artisan underworld, a realm, one would presume, normally far removed from that of these high-born dévots. But, as extraordinary as these undertakings were, the company was not unique in seeking out the poor and lowly for its pious attentions.

Dévots and the Poor

There were many agents of poor relief in the city, for virtually every ecclesiastical body devoted some resources to the care of the poor and sick. These were complemented by the several municipal hospitals whose consolidation and secularization in the sixteenth century represented the first major reform of the means of poor relief in the early modern period. The next came in the mid-seventeenth century when, at the urging of the Company of the Holy Sacrament, the general hospital was established, thus centralizing and rationalizing official charity and making poor relief largely a question of policing the poor.

Indeed, the Messieurs' first and most important undertaking was the transformation of the Hôpital de la Grave, a large, brick edifice on the left bank of the Garonne, traditionally reserved for plague victims, into a place of confinement and a workhouse for the city's poor. On March 26, 1647, a clerical member of the company, Arnaud Baric, presented to the capitouls a detailed account of the state of the poor in the city and a plan for the creation of a hospital in which to confine them. Baric's brief was unsentimental: the poor are a threat to society, he argued. They disturb the peace, corrupt morals, and pollute the church; they are lazy, violent, completely without morals, and often a source of heresy, unable to fend for themselves yet far too numerous to be managed through simple almsgiving. A new hospital is needed, one in which "sinners will be converted by the grace of God, old people will be disposed to die well, and the young instructed in the fear of God and in public service."[24] Baric received authorization for

24. Alphonse Auguste, *La Compagnie du Saint-Sacrement à Toulouse: Notes et documents* (Toulouse and Paris, 1913), p. 61.

the general hospital immediately. The decision was not surprising, since half the sitting capitouls were members of the company. As befitting a workhouse, it was placed under the patronage of Saint Joseph, himself a craftsman.[25]

The company's campaign for the creation of a hospital then proceeded simultaneously on several fronts. The previous year Pére Le Jeune (an Oratorian and a member of the Company of the Holy Sacrament) had harangued the congregation at the cathedral on the need to take drastic measures to eliminate the ungodly stain of the poor from their city.[26] To that end, a delegate was dispatched to the cathedral canons to secure their support, and several months after the capitouls were approached, the parlement also entertained a request to approve the new institution. In December 1649, the capitouls received a letter from the Queen Mother praising their "zeal for the glory of God and the public welfare" in creating the hospital.[27] Rome's approval came in the form of a papal bull, delivered in 1652, with the royal letters patent following in 1658.[28]

The newly reformed Hôpital de la Grave was governed by a board of eighteen directors comprised of two clergy and sixteen laymen, two from each of the city's eight capitoulats. New officers were elected annually, chosen from a slate prepared by the outgoing directors, thus ensuring the control of the hospital would remain in the hands of the laity.[29] The general hospital was conceived and run as a lay enterprise, although it was, of course, an institution consecrated to the "glory of God" and staffed by priests who acted also as its collection agents in their parishes. Other employees included an "Oeconome," charged with daily finances, a controller, a porter, a clergyman, a cook, four guards, and a laundryman.[30]

Thus established, the hospital unleashed its plan of poor relief on

25. On the evolution of the image of Joseph in the early modern period, see Lynn White, Jr., "The Iconography of Temperantia and the Virtuousness of Technology," in *Action and Conviction in Early Modern Europe*, ed. T. Rabb and J. Seigel (Princeton, 1969), pp. 197–219.

26. Allier, *La Compagnie du Saint-Sacrement à Toulouse*, p. 21.

27. AMT, GG 949, fol. 10v; Auguste, *La Compagnie du Saint-Sacrement à Toulouse*, pp. 72–73.

28. ADH-G, Arch. hosp., 2E1, f. 103; Auguste, *La Compagnie*, p. 106.

29. For the period 1647–63 the breakdown of the occupations of the directors was as follows: avocats, 37%; merchants, 17%; "bourgeois," 15%; ecuyers, 24%. See ADH-G, Arch. Hosp., 2E1, passim.

30. AMT, GG 958, "Règlemens sur l'establissement d'un hôpital . . . ," pp. 4–5.

the inhabitants of Toulouse. The four guards, dressed in a special leather uniform displaying the insignia of Saint Joseph, were joined by other militiamen and dispatched to gather up "all the poor beggars and conduct them to the said hospital, there to be fed and instructed in the fear of God."[31] Guards were placed at the city gates, and *pauvres estranges*—indigents not from Toulouse—were forbidden entry unless they consented to confinement in the hospital. Those desiring to leave the institution had to submit to having their eyebrows shaved and scarified before being banished from the city.[32] The directors were careful to specify the strict segregation of hospital inmates by sex, age, and condition, for one of their grievances against the underworld of beggars was that it encouraged promiscuity between the sexes and the corruption of the young by seasoned tricksters.[33] Prostitutes were isolated in separate quarters, as were indigent priests, "hermits," and married people. Sick persons were forbidden to enter the hospital, being sent instead to the Hôpital Saint-Jacques, also located on the left bank of the Garonne. The regulations noted that an unemployed female domestic could voluntarily enter the hospital in order "to save herself from falling," a recognition of the fact that many prostitutes were former servants who had been forced into their trade by rape, trickery, or destitution.[34] By 1649 the hospital was feeding two hundred poor a day.[35]

All able-bodied males confined there were put to work: master artisans were invited to select youths suited to learn a trade; boys were sent out into the city in teams to clean the streets; girls were prepared for domestic service, and on occasion marriages were arranged for them by the directors. All poor children were trained so as "to be accustomed to work," and some efforts were made to teach them to read. Several craft guilds set up shops in the hospitals—the needlemakers, hatters, lacemakers, and carders—both to teach boys and girls a trade and to take advantage of a captive pool of cheap labor. These shops employed as many as twenty workers.[36] Among

31. AMT, GG 958, art. VIII, p. 6.

32. AMT, GG 959, Deliberations of the Conseil bourgeois and the bureau of the hospital, June 18, 1648.

33. AMT, GG 958, art. VI, pp. 6; "L'aumône générale . . . ," in Lestrade, "L'aumône générale à Toulouse," p. 285.

34. AMT, GG 958, art. XVI, pp. 7–8.

35. ADH-G, Arch. hosp., 2E1, fol. 19.

36. ADH-G, Arch. hosp., 2E1, passim.

the most active artisan groups in the hospital were the brethren shoe-makers, who received a loan from the directors to start up their enter-prise.[37] In the hospital the life of confined paupers was highly regu-lated. They rose at an early specified hour, took meals and worked only with those of their own sex, heard mass every Sunday and holy day, and were taught the Christian doctrine each evening. In public they donned the blue smock that identified them as indigents of the city. Twice yearly they were paraded two by two in a procession through the city, once to the cathedral and then to Saint-Sernin, where they would "thank God for the healthy, good, long and happy life of the King." Here the inhabitants could see the fruits of their alms, proof that the general hospital was working miracles in trans-forming unruly and threatening beggars into obedient and produc-tive Christians.[38]

Such proof was necessary because the directors relied heavily on the charity of the city's inhabitants to keep their hospital solvent. Like other features of the company's plan for poor relief, the method for collecting alms was a rationalization of previous practices. The collec-tion was pyramidal in structure. Prominent inhabitants were selected to direct the collection in their immediate neighborhood. Once week-ly, on a specified day (according to capitoulat), these agents would make the rounds among their neighbors, soliciting money, bread, and other foodstuffs. They were advised to carry a notebook during their solicitations and record the names of those who did not contrib-ute. Once completed on this level, the collection was passed up to the director in each capitoulat, and on Friday all the funds and food were delivered to the general hospital. In this system the person-to-person connection between almsgiver and the poor was severed and re-placed by a bureaucracy of agents who were charged not only to solicit on behalf of the poor but to extract as much as possible on a regular basis. In place of almsgiving, the new system created a de-facto tax on townspeople. It was also a centralized system, designed to eliminate crowds of indigents who gathered around churches, con-vents, and the townhouses of the rich in expectation of handouts. In particular, the regular clergy were instructed not to dispense alms at their doors but to bring their contributions directly to the hospital.[39]

37. Ibid., fols. 59, 68v.
38. AMT, GG 958, arts. xiv, xv, xxxvi, pp. 7, 13; AMT, GG 959, deliberations on May 9 and October 30, 1648.
39. AMT, GG 958, art. xxviii.

Despite its institutional legitimacy, the general hospital was an experiment, one that relied on the energies and commitment of its founders, and one that encountered difficulties and opposition from many quarters. Not surprisingly, the poor were less than enthusiastic about being rounded up and confronted by the choice between confinement or banishment. Violent street fighting broke out between the hospital guards and mendicants, and the capitouls had to insist that those failing to comply with the order would suffer corporal punishment.[40] The same treatment was also threatened against the religious orders, taverns, and other households still harboring and supporting mendicants, for the new system of centralized poor relief struck at long-held urban traditions that fostered ties between the poor and their benefactors.[41] Mendicant orders individually had long served as protectors of the poor, and in addition, it seems as though certain taverns in the faubourgs often took care of day laborers and agricultural workers during periods of slack employment so frequent in the seasonal economy of the Old Regime.

If the mendicants resisted the guards' dragnet outside, inside the hospital they sometimes rioted. At a meeting of the directors on October 7, 1648, the topic of discussion was the "disorders" caused by the women confined in the hospital; at the session of July 9, 1650, the complaint was again against "debauched" women "who reject with obstinacy this confinement and make extraordinary troubles for the house without any hope of conversion."[42] Indeed, prostitutes were a most recalcitrant lot when it came to confinement and the loss of their livelihood. On one occasion they escaped by digging a passageway under the hospital wall; on another they burned down a door; on still another they had their friends invade the premises to accomplish their release.[43] A major point of contention among the directors concerned what course of action they should take with these difficult women, many of whom were suffering from venereal disease. Some directors argued for their expulsion, and, in fact, the toleration of prostitutes in "public" houses represented one more venerable tradition the hospital violated. Other directors insisted that they had a duty to confine and reform these fallen women, and their arguments were supported by the recent edifying example of confined pros-

40. Ibid., art. xxxii, p. 11.
41. AMT, GG 959.
42. Ibid., deliberations of March 21, 1649.
43. ADH-G, Arch. Hosp., 2E1, fols. 97, 161, 228.

titutes who had become nuns.[44] A surgeon was hired to treat the diseased. As an incentive, he was promised the guild mastership if he served three years in the hospital, something that naturally provoked the ire of the leading surgeons of the city, who correctly perceived a threat to their corporate monopoly.[45] The directors' preoccupation with women stricken with venereal disease, evident throughout the records of their weekly meetings, is an indication that the problem was important in the founding of the general hospital. Certainly the disease-carrying potential of the poor in general was one motivation for the dévots to recast charity in a less personal and less spiritual mode. And in particular, as Brian Pullan has suggested, "the infective stench of syphilis could easily drown the odour of sanctity."[46]

The new hospital, then, served as a general place of confinement for the city's poor. It was at once a workhouse, refuge, and reformatory, the forerunner of the modern prison. Indeed, in his influential study *Madness and Civilization*, Michel Foucault stressed the radical nature of what he called the "Great Confinement"—the break from the medieval practice, which persisted into the seventeenth century, of letting the indigent, homeless, and incapacitated wander and beg at large.[47] But the poor had been dealt with harshly in previous times in Toulouse, as had other marginals, especially plague victims and Huguenots. And at least since the early sixteenth century the city as a whole had mobilized on an emergency basis to cope with the burgeoning poor: from time to time special taxes were levied, indigents were put to work, and the city gates barred to foreign mendicants. It was, however, precisely the institutional aspect of the general hospital that distinguished it from these previous efforts at poor relief, for it represented not an ad-hoc or temporary measure, but a serious attempt to reform the poor and eliminate them as a source of crime, corruption, and "disorder" once and for all. Did it, however, serve to cast the poor and other marginals into the category of the "Other," as Foucault also argued? There was, to be sure, much about the poor which transformed them into alien creatures, especially when their indigency took a depraved and violent turn. But though strained by

44. Ibid., July 9 and March 24, 1650.
45. Ibid., March 21, 1649.
46. Brian Pullan, "Catholics and the Poor in Early Modern Europe," *Transactions of the Royal Historical Society*, 5th ser., 26 (1976): 24.
47. Michel Foucault, *Madness and Civilization*, trans. Richard Howard (New York, 1965).

the sheer number of urban poor and mediated by the severe institutional strategy of poor relief devised, the dévots' approach was still infused with sentiments of Christian charity, the belief that the spirit of Christ dwelled among the poor. If the poor were the "Other," they were not thereby banished entirely to another realm. Rather, they were taken on as wards of an extraordinary group of high-born dévots who chose an encounter with this "Other" in their midst.

The creation of Toulouse's poor house in 1647 also allows us to reflect upon the implications of this charitable movement for the larger issue of the nature of seventeenth-century urban society. In a sense, the general hospital, like the other projects of the Messieurs of the Company of the Holy Sacrament, supports Porschnev's view that the seventeenth-century social order was dominated by classes broadly defined, that a "class front" linked the traditional aristocracy and bourgeoisie in the face of the social threat from below. The Company of the Holy Sacrament, one might say, was such a front, uniting as it did municipal officials, magistrates, aristocrats, and high clergymen in enterprises aimed at the control and reform of the poor and lower classes. What bears reiteration, however, is that in this instance "class conflict"—if that is indeed the appropriate term—entailed not distance between the classes but an extraordinary degree of contact, sometimes even care.[48]

Many Toulousains besides the secretive and saintly Messieurs similarly engaged in charitable activities, often as members of lay confraternities, whose statutes usually specified measures of poor relief. This was especially true for the confraternities founded in the seventeenth century. It could be said, in fact, that more people were personally involved then in poor relief than in any other period, either before or after. At the very least, confrères were encouraged to aid the poor, widows, orphans, the sick, or prisoners. Sometimes they were offered spiritual rewards for their charitable efforts, as was the case with the Confraternity of Saint Barbe (founded in 1667), which offered spiritual rewards in the form of indulgences to members who visited the sick and "consoled them in their afflictions."[49] The Con-

48. The relevancy of the Company of the Holy Sacrament to Porschnev's thesis has been pointed out by Kathryn Norberg, *Rich and Poor in Grenoble, 1600–1814* (Berkeley, 1985), p. 62.
49. ADH-G, E 1011, "Indulgence à perpétuité accordée par notre Saint Père le Pape Alexandre VII à la Confrérie de Sainte Barbe . . . 1667."

fraternity of Our Lady of the Dying (*Notre-Dame des Agonisants*), dating from 1668, set aside Friday for visitations and excused confrères who made them from penitential exercises.[50] The dévots belonging to Our Lady of Good News (1637), a socially mixed group of men and women, received a plenary indulgence for visiting the city's prisons and hospitals.[51]

The penitential companies too were active in poor relief, especially in the seventeenth century when they were less the militant associations of ultra-Catholics seen in the religious wars, and more like ordinary, though very large, confraternities. All of the companies' statutes stipulated rather precise charitable measures. The Blacks, for example, called on penitents to aid prisoners, the indigent, and orphans, and in particular to provide for and attend the funerals of the "shameful poor," while the Whites designated two officers to coordinate the company's efforts in behalf of orphans and widows.[52] The charitable activities of the Blues and Blacks expanded considerably in 1688 from the substantial legacy of an Abbé Richard, whose will endowed a program of poor relief. With the money, the two companies founded relief committees (*bureaux des pauvres*) in each parish, although in subsequent years they frequently came into conflict over the use of the abbé's legacy, which in the eighteenth century was rarely applied in accordance with its founder's original intention.[53]

While many confraternities counseled their members to tend to the needs of the poor—emphasizing, in the spirit of the Counter-Reformation, the spiritual rewards attendant upon "good works"—several took the indigent, sick, and wayward as their special concern. The Confraternity of Our Lady of the Annunciation, located in the suburban church of Saint-Pierre de Cuisines, had its statutes renewed by Archbishop Montchal in 1651; it had apparently fallen into inactivity in recent decades. In its new incarnation the Annunciation accepted any resident of the parish, "regardless of sex, age, and condition." Its

50. Julien, *Toulouse chrétienne, Histoire de la paroisse de N.D. de la Dalbade*, pp. 287–89.

51. BMT, MS 208, "Statuts de la dévote Confrairie de Notre-Dame de bonnes nouvelles, érigée en l'église et chapelle royalle St.-Barthélemy, place de Salin, 1637."

52. *Manuel de la dévote Confrérie Sainte-Croix des Pénitens Noirs de Toulouse* (Toulouse, 1667), p. 18; Pecquet, "La Compagnie des Pénitents Blancs de Toulouse," *ADM* 84 (1972): 218.

53. Ousset, "La Confrérie des Pénitents Bleus de Toulouse," *RHT* 13 (1926): 223. On the eighteenth-century disputes over this legacy, see Archives des Jésuites, CA 311, "Registre des délibérations de la dévote et royale Confrérie de Messieurs les Pénitents Bleus de Toulouse, commencé le 4e aoust 1747," p. 24 and passim.

purpose was the care of the parish's indigent, "not in the spirit of general charity but to honor by Imitation . . . the Holy Virgin . . . the mother and nurse of Our Savior Jesus Christ, the chief among the true poor, whom she cherished all her life." To minister to the poor, the Annunciation appointed three "confrèresses," observing as a matter of common knowledge that "women are more suited to care of the sick than men." Though restricted in its activities to its parish, the Annunciation's statutes noted those other "congregations, companies, and particular persons" in the city also engaged in poor relief, and with whom it strove to coordinate its efforts.[54] In all likelihood this was a reference to the Company of the Holy Sacrament, or at least to its more prominent members, for the Annunciation had as its clerical director Arnaud Baric, a Monsieur himself and the clergyman who proposed the creation of the general hospital to the capitouls in 1647. It is thus also likely that the reestablished Confraternity of the Annunciation was a spin-off of the newly established hospital, a kind of ancillary association for poor relief in a suburban parish. This was definitely the case with the Confraternity of Saint Joseph, established in the 1650s, which assembled a number of gentlemen who aided the confined poor in the Hôpital de la Grave. Most of the confrères of Saint Joseph were also members of the Company of the Holy Sacrament, which made the confraternity a sort of public front for the Messieurs' secret brotherhood.[55]

The lay group most explicit in its dedication to poor relief was the Confraternity of Charity, founded in the 1670s under the patronage of the archbishop. According to its statutes, this confraternity was "particularly composed of charitable persons of recognized probity who could, through piety and quality, make succeed the good works to be undertaken." In other words, its confrères were highborn, probably parlementaires and other officers. But the regulations also announced that girls, widows, and "other people of mediocre quality" would be welcome as members to perform certain charitable works, that is, to clean the chambers of the sick and poor.[56] While this attitude—echoed in the statutes of the Confraternity of the Annunciation—was

54. ADH-G, E 1021, "Règlements de la Confraire de Notre-Dame de l'Annonciation dans l'eglise et paroisse de Saint-Pierre de Cuisine de Toulouse, 1651."

55. Ousset, "La Confrérie des Pénitents Bleus à Toulouse," p. 221.

56. Règlemens de la Confrérie de la Charité, dressez par l'ordre de Monseigneur l'illustrissime et révérendissime père en Dieu Joseph de Montpezat de Carbon, archevêque de Toulouse (Toulouse, 1679).

certainly an excuse for burdening women with much difficult and distasteful labor, it should be noted that seventeenth-century Toulouse did produce several legendary models of female service and sacrifice.[57]

Unlike many lay groups, which either condemned or idealized the poor, the Confraternity of Charity took a somewhat comprehensive view of the problem, recognizing "necessity and laziness" as the reasons for peoples' "fall" into destitution.[58] The confraternity was pragmatic and energetic in its approach to poor relief and eschewed the simpleminded, though popular, solutions of either distributing alms or rounding up and confining beggars. For young girls, the Charity attempted to find proper husbands, and it placed boys as apprentices or sent them to the general hospital to learn a trade. As long as they were "honest and hard-working," impoverished artisans were provided loans. In addition, the Confraternity of Charity favored establishing workhouses for the production of textiles in each parish. The superior and his two assistants were specifically charged with informing themselves of the needs of the poor, not only to seek them out and provide for them, but to interrogate others about the poor in their neighborhoods and to consult with those physicians, apothecaries, and surgeons who might know them.[59]

It is clear that in the minds of the founders of the Confraternity of Charity, poor relief entailed information gathering, and also implied surveillance of, and research into, the lives and habits of the poor. Poverty itself was not strictly the problem; the issue, rather, was a fundamental corruption of society and human nature, a corruption typically expressed in terms of disorder or sexual misconduct. The view betrayed a fear that poverty disguised a more profound and troubling disorder in that most fundamental and intimate of human spaces, the family. Workers were warned to observe if brothers and sisters over seven slept in the same bed or with a parent of the opposite sex, and if so, to provide them with extra straw mattresses and covering. To this warning was added the diagnosis that, among the poor, social relations were characterized by "quarrels and contestations" that often ended in violence and death.[60] Despite the

57. ADH-G, E 1021, "Règlements de la Confraire de Notre-Dame de l'Annonciation . . . "; T. Porte, "Esprit social et charité."
58. Règlemens de la Confrérie de la Charité, p. 14.
59. Ibid., p. 34.
60. Ibid., p. 53.

confraternity's apparent solicitude and evident attempt to understand the poor, one cannot escape the underlying message that there
was something savage about the state of poverty. Poverty, then, was
symptomatic of deeper troubles.

The troubles, however, were not limited to the poor alone. For the
Confraternity of Charity, the failure of poor relief reflected also the
greed, profligacy, and parsimony of the city's inhabitants. The program of the confraternity thus had two goals: the salvation and re-
generation of the poor, and the awakening to the Christian obligation
of charity among the more comfortable population. Its call to conscience is worth quoting in full:

> There is not a Worker who cannot save each week a jug of wine . . .
> beyond that is necessary. There is not a Merchant nor others modestly
> accommodated who cannot save a penny a day from their expensive
> ribbons, lace, and other things. As for the rich, there are none who
> cannot at least forsake a bite of stew from their table . . . not to speak of
> their luxuries, clothing, furniture, silver, precious stones, tapestries,
> carriages which perhaps even their fathers never possessed. . . . There
> should not be even a Peasant or a Porter who cannot give a penny or
> two to the poor. And if all the artisans truly wanted to sanctify Sundays
> and Holy Days by abstaining from Gambling and Cabaret on those
> Days principally consecrated to piety, they would find enough to sup-
> port their families, while being able to reserve something in case of
> illness, for the establishment of their children, and even for the poor.[61]

As agencies of poor relief, lay confraternities were easily surpassed
in scale by the general hospital, but their efforts were significant
nevertheless. For unlike the strategy of the "Great Confinement,"
confraternal charity tended to emphasize the personal aspect of poverty and poor relief. Alms were not merely dispensed, nor were the
poor approached indiscriminately. Rather, confraternities exhorted
their members to seek out the poor, to know them and the conditions
of their destitution, and to strive to redeem them in body and soul.
Several confraternities made a point of specializing in the care of
young orphans, "fallen" women, debtors, prisoners, or pilgrims.[62]

Prisoners received particular attention. We have already noted in a
previous chapter the founding by the Jesuits in 1570 of the Confrater-

---

61. Ibid., p. 59.
62. See, for example, ADH-G, E 831 and E 1022, Table de la Miséricorde des pauvres
orphelines du St. Esprit; or ADH-G, E 835, 837, 838, Confrérie de St. Jacques.

nity of Mercy, a brotherhood of the leading officers and clergymen of the city, which during the religious wars undertook periodic visits to the prisons and tended to the spiritual and material needs of the unfortunate inmates. In 1647 these highborn confrères were joined in their labors by the Confraternity of Our Lady of Suffrage, located in the parish church of Notre-Dame du Taur.[63] A product of the Counter-Reformation, this brotherhood bore every sign of the baroque piety of post-Tridentine Catholicism. Like the Confraternity of Mercy, it too encouraged its confrères to visit the city's prisoners and to pray for their salvation; and each year during Holy Week it rescued three incarcerated debtors. But the Confraternity of Our Lady of Suffrage had an otherworldly preoccupation: as much as it cared for those confined in prisons, its primary concern was for those "suffering souls" languishing in purgatory. Protestantism, it will be recalled, denied the existence of purgatory, and the Tridentine response was to assert its reality with even greater fervor and vehemence—and to insist that a Christian could release souls from its clutches through the performance of "good works." Membership in a confraternity dedicated to "suffering souls" was one such "work," and thus, while the confrère of Our Lady of Suffrage aided prisoners, he could be assured that he was also shortening his own time in a prison of another sort. As was so often the case in the Counter-Reformation, to labor was to act symbolically, and to aid the poor and unfortunate was to approach them less as individuals than as holy vessels containing the spirit of Christ. "The poor . . . are the living temples of the Holy Spirit," proclaimed Archbishop Montchal in an ordinance supporting the charitable work of confraternities, "for charity lends perfection to all our actions, and our condemnation or our justification ought to be based on the good that we have done . . . to our neighbors."[64]

A subplot in the story of charity in the Old Regime is the contribution of women, the commitment of many well-to-do ladies to poor relief and their often heroic efforts to turn impoverished young girls, prostitutes, and vagabonds to a life of respectability. This commit-

---

63. *Le confrère charitable aux âmes souffrantes dans le purgatoire pour la dévote et charitable Confrairie de N.D. du Suffrage* (Toulouse, 1650).

64. Simon de Peyronet, *Recueil des ordonnances synodales et autres* (Toulouse, 1669), p. 838.

ment was especially evident during the Counter-Reformation, when service to the poor among ladies of fashion was as much à la mode as the précieuses were to be a generation later. The parallel is indeed correct, for the preponderance of these female servants to the poor were the wives and daughters of officials, just like the précieuses.[65] And like the salon culture, poor relief was an acceptable arena for female activism in a fundamentally patriarchal society where women's participation in public life was largely discouraged.

In Toulouse, several female associations devoted themselves to poor relief. The first, founded at the conclusion of the Wars of Religion, was a Third-Order Dominican group, the Congregation of Saint Catherine of Siena, which gathered spiritually inclined women who wanted to remain "in this world," that is, who were not prepared to take holy orders. The leaders of this congregation were wives of parlementaires or other magistrates. One of them, Germaine de Viguerie, whose husband was a councilor in the sénéchal, extended her care for the poor to transforming her home into a dispensary of clothing and medicine. Others worked with prostitutes confined in the general hospital, and it was largely through their efforts that an order of the Madeleines repenties was founded in the city, an association of "fallen women" turned nuns. In 1621, these Third-Order Dominicans, together with a similar female congregation sponsored by the Jesuits, established an orphan house, which soon proved so successful as a school that even well-to-do families requested to have their daughters educated there alongside the parentless poor.[66] Another group of women, also the wives of parlementaires (Cathelan, DuMay, Camboulas, Roussy), formed the Dames de la Miséricorde, an association dedicated to the care of prisoners.[67] Finally, the secret society of Messieurs had its female counterpart in the Dames du Saint-Sacrement. These ladies, however, did not operate under a veil of secrecy, for their society is mentioned several times in the registers of the Hôpital de la Grave. Mme de Mondonville was a prominent member, as were other wives of magistrates, including Mme de Fieubet, whose husband was a president of the sovereign

65. Carolyn Lougee, Le paradis des Femmes. Women, Salons and Social Stratification in Seventeenth-Century France (Princeton, 1976).

66. On this congregation, see T. Porte, "Esprit social et charité," and Le monastère Sainte-Catherine de Sienne à Toulouse (Toulouse, 1976).

67. Leon-Pierre Raybaud, "Le bureau de la miséricorde de Toulouse aux XVIIe et XVIIIe siècles," in Mélanges Roger Aubenas (Montpellier, 1974), pp. 666–70.

court, and Mme de Caulet, the wife of another parlementaire. These devout women were active on several fronts: they brought bouillon to the sick in their homes, cared for the confined poor in the general hospital, collected alms on their behalf, and, like most female agents of poor relief, strove to protect young girls from the fate of prostitution. They also provided most of the labor in running the female and male Houses for New Converts, an enterprise dear to both Mme de Mondonville and Gabriel de Ciron.[68]

But Mme de Mondonville had other tasks before her. For many years since her first "conversion" in 1653 she had yearned for a calling beyond that of Ciron's helpmate. And indeed, there are signs of some tension between her and her confessor, as well as some hints that their relationship had an amorous tinge. In 1661 her ambitions were fulfilled when she was made the director of the newly established Institut des Filles de l'Enfance de Jésus-Christ, a congregation of girls and young women who felt themselves unsuited for either marriage or a religious vocation, yet who wished to devote their lives to prayer and charity. The institute was not a religious order: the "daughters" were not cloistered, they did not live in community, they wore no special habit, nor did they change their names. That the institute should avoid any sign of being an order was the explicit intent of Ciron, who drew up its regulations. "One cannot persuade oneself," he wrote, "that one can be humble, patient, and disinterested for oneself, while superior, vindictive, and interested in the congregation." The building that housed the institute, purchased with the financial aid of Jean de Garibal, a parlementaire who was a member of the Company of the Holy Sacrament, was devoid of any particular trappings or embellishments that might draw attention: there was no public chapel or belltower, the Holy Sacrament was never exposed there, nor were indulgences offered to outside communicants. Ciron stipulated that the daughters live in private rooms; their quarters should resemble "the houses of good bourgeois, within the limits of Christian simplicity." Although they were not furnished uniforms, the daughters were to dress simply and modestly, without ornaments or embroidery, keeping to smocks of black, gray, brown, and white. In all matters, the goal of the institute was to create the

68. On the Dames du Saint-Sacrement, see Shibano, "Les débuts de la Congrégation," p. 73, and ADH-G, Arch. hosp., 2E1, fols., 181, 187, 210, 214.

conditions for communal piety and charity, while eschewing any external signs of their particular devotion.[69] Such simplicity struck knowledgeable observers as a radical departure from the pomp, finery, and public display that normally marked religious life, and not an entirely innocent departure at that; for the institute mirrored Port-Royal in its implicit critique of both monasticism and the ostentatious religiosity of the day.[70]

From its founding in 1661 to its forced disbanding in 1685, the congregation of the institute enlisted 197 daughters from 149 families. The daughters were divided into three classes: those from noble families, who were given governing roles in the institute; those from "good families," who served as instructors; and those of "low extraction," who worked as servants. Out of the 197 daughters, the social ranks of 101 are known: 48 were in the first, 24 in the second, and 29 in the third.[71] Among the daughters in the first rank were some from the most prominent families of the region; several were the off-spring or nieces of parlementaires: Cathelan, D'Ouvrier, Fieubet (a First President), and Ciron. One was the daughter of a president of the Parlement of Aix; another the daughter of the intendant D'Aguesseau. Initiates with inheritances were asked to endow the institute, while poor girls were accepted without prejudice and indeed were supported at the expense of the foundation. The statutes expressed a preference for poor girls "marked" by piety over more fortunate but less inspired candidates. An entering daughter first served a probationary period, after which she would take a "voeu de stabilité perpétuelle," promising to "live and serve God the rest of her days" in the congregation. Her life would be devoted to prayer, meditation, and service to the poor and ignorant. Ciron wrote into the regulations that in times of "public need" the institute would use its reserves of grain to feed the city's hungry. And it was as servants to the sick and poor that the daughters were known and viewed by the inhabitants of Toulouse. People would see them visiting the Hôpital de la Grave or the other municipal hospitals daily, bringing bouillon to the sick, and mattresses and covering to the needy. In addition, the administration of the institute established

---

69. *HGL*, 13:575.
70. Ibid.
71. A list of the daughters has been compiled by Sister Shibano and is in her possession. I am grateful to her for giving me permission to consult it.

three schools in different neighborhoods of the city, and here young girls were taught by those daughters with some education how to read, write, count, and work at some manual trade.[72]

Among the institute's supporters were the prince and princess of Condé, recently converted to the pious life by Ciron, and friends of the Jansenists. The queen too let it be known that she favored Mme de Mondonville's congregation. In 1662 Pope Alexander VII sent a letter blessing the institute, and the following year it received both the parlement's approbation in the form of a decree and the royal letters patent. In fact, the parlement's decree not only sanctioned the new congregation but also contained an article forbidding any opposition to it. Several bishops of the region lent their support to the institute, including Pierre de Bertier, whose brother had been the First President of the Parlement of Toulouse.[73] Yet despite this impressive roster of supporters and protectors, the institute eventually met with a disastrous demise. It was accused of being the Port-Royal of Toulouse.

Jansenist Toulouse

Before we go searching for explicit evidence of Jansenism among Mme de Mondonville's daughters, or within the devout community of Toulouse as a whole, we should note that as a point of contention between rival theologians and statesmen, clergymen, and dévots, there was little that was precise about the meaning of Jansenism. What passed for religious controversy was in fact often a dispute over politics, power, and state policy, or a disagreement over styles of piety and religious life. To its enemies, Jansenism was everywhere in seventeenth-century France. To oppose the Jesuits and their increasing hegemony over French religious affairs, for example, was to risk incurring the accusation of Jansenism. To express doubts about the

---

72. *HGL*, 13:575. The main sources on the institute are Shibano, "Les débuts de la Congrégation," and "Gabriel de Ciron (1619–1675), Esquisse biographique," *Revue d'Histoire de la Spiritualité* 52 (1976): 89–124; A. Auguste, "Gabriel de Ciron et Madame de Mondonville," *RHT* 5 (1924): 14–25, 129–63, 303–33, and *Les origines du jansénisme dans le diocèse de Toulouse (Notes et documents)* (Paris and Toulouse, 1922); Henry Jaudon, *Port-Royal à Toulouse ou le jansénisme au Parlement* (Toulouse, 1900); Leon Dutil, *Lettres inédites de Mme de Mondonville suivies de fragments de ses mémoires (1655–1697)* (Paris, 1911); *HGL*, 13:574–85.

73. *HGL*, 13:577–78.

Immaculate Conception of the Virgin Mary, to confess dissatisfaction with the way the regime was cynically mixing politics and religion, or to defend the episcopal rights of bishops against the crown was to invite being labeled a dangerous dévot and a partisan of Port-Royal.

Still, the conflict most likely to generate suspicion of Jansensism was opposition to the Jesuits, because the Society of Jesus sponsored a theology of grace that pricked the Augustinian sensibilities of many dévots, Jansenist or not. The Molinist doctrine espoused by the Jesuits was in fact deliberately cast as an alternative to rigorous Augustinianism, with its emphasis on original sin and the uncertainty of salvation. According to the Jesuits, such preoccupations ignored the Christian sacramental promise: Augustinianism, they argued, risked undermining the church's power to offer salvation to all Christians upon performance of the sacraments. The Jesuits not only defined salvation as available to all believers, but also emphasized those actions and sacraments through which it could be secured. Thus it was that the Jansenists and others who shared their Augustinian views reserved their greatest contempt for the Jesuits, both doctrinally and institutionally; indeed, what is often taken for Jansenism was merely a resistance, among certain laymen and clerics alike, to the growing power and prestige of the Society of Jesus.[74]

In Toulouse it was precisely friction between the Jesuits and other religious orders that first indicated that the city harbored sentiments that later would be considered Jansenist. In 1644, the prior of the Dominicans, Père Reginald, published a book attacking the Molinist views expressed in the *Sciencia media*, written by the Jesuits' rector, Père Annat. Already well known as a theological spokesman for his order, Annat would later figure prominently in the Jansenist controversy, first as the target of two of Pascal's *Lettres provinciales* and then as the king's personal confessor at court, where he helped orchestrate the royal attack on Port-Royal. Though not a Jansenist, Reginald's critique of Annat's view of original sin relied heavily on a strict reading of Augustine. What ensued was hardly a theological debate governed by academic protocol, but rather a vicious exchange between the Dominicans and Jesuits and their respective allies entailing calls for censorship, the clandestine printing of pamphlets, personal insults, and denunciatory public placards—everything short of hand-

74. On the disputes between Augustinians and Molinists, see Jean Delumeau, *Le catholicisme entre Luther et Voltaire*, pp. 157–58.

to-hand combat in the streets.[75] The main issue, to be sure, was that of Molinism versus Augustinianism; but behind the theological battle was a mounting resentment against the Jesuits among the professors of the Dominican-dominated university, accumulating ever since the Society of Jesus received royal permission to grant bachelor and master's degrees in 1621.[76] For from the perspective of the Dominicans, whose primacy at the university dated from its founding in the thirteenth century, the Jesuits, with their new, humanistically inclined and antischolastic pedagogy, represented a serious threat to their main institutional base in the city.

But the Dominicans were not alone in feeling threatened by the Jesuits' pretensions. One of Mme de Mondonville and Ciron's most cherished enterprises was the House of New Converts, which took in children from Protestant families, nurtured them, and turned them into good Catholics.[77] In 1664, however, the Jesuits established in the city a Company for the Propagation of the Faith, one of a network of confraternities throughout the realm dedicated to the conversion of Protestants.[78] The Jesuits also sponsored a secret society, founded in 1653—the "AA," which clearly was designed to rival the Company of the Holy Sacrament, tainted as it was by its association with several prominent Jansenists.[79] Perhaps most irritating to the secular clergy was the fact that the Jesuits made a point of wooing communicants away from parish churches and into the confessionals at their own chapel, a clear challenge to the parochial discipline so important to the Jansenists. The Jesuits, in short, were everywhere: they sponsored lay confraternities, educated the young, prepared new priests for their missions, competed for communicants, fostered new religious ceremonies and devotions, and were ubiquitous as preachers

75. On this dispute, see Auguste, *Les origines du jansénisme*, pp. 39–41; L. Vie, "Un incident à l'Université de Toulouse en 1645 à propos de la censure du livre *De Sciencia media*," *Bulletin de la Société Archéologique du Midi* (1912): 303–19, 389–93; H. Bégouen, "A propos de la *Sciencia media*," *Bulletin de la Société archéologique du Midi*, 1913, pp. 73–76.

76. Delattre, *Les établissements des Jésuites*, 4:1289.

77. Shibano, "Les débuts de la Congrégation," p. 72.

78. ADH-G, E 1021, "Statuts de la Compagnie de la Propagation de la Foy, soubs l'invocation et protection de St. François Xavier érigée à Tholose en l'année 1664."

79. On the "AA" see C. Bégouen, *Une société secrète émule de la Compagnie du Saint-Sacrement: L'AA de Toulouse aux XVIIe et XVIIIe siècles* (Toulouse, 1913); Y. Poutet and J. Roubert, *Les "assemblées" secrètes des XVIIe–XVIIIe siècles en relation avec l'AA de Lyon* (Piacenza, 1968); "Congrégations secrètes" in *Dictionnaire de spiritualité*, vol. 2, col. 1505.

during the holy seasons. Clearly the Jesuits were not about to let others monopolize such crucial undertakings. But it is just as clear that their hegemonic efforts created a reservoir of resentment against them.

There were, however, more pronounced Jansenist tendencies in the city than this anti-Jesuit resentment. Several prominent Toulousains had direct ties to Port-Royal. First President Bertier corresponded frequently with Antoine Arnauld; and the hôtels of the magistrates Fieubet and Cathelan, both of whom sent daughters to the institute, were reputedly Jansenist salons. The city's most important Jansenist was, of course, Archbishop Montchal, who compounded his religious nonconformity by opposing Richelieu and his policies. In the region, Montchal was supported by several like-minded prelates, among them Bishops Bertier, Caulet, and Pavillon. In the mid-1660s, Caulet and Pavillon were among the only four bishops in the realm who refused to recognize the five propositions as heretical. Both Bertier and Caulet had relatives in the parlement, while Pavillon, whose archdiocese of Alet was a model of Jansenist discipline, exerted his influence in the city as a preacher at the cathedral and as an officer in both the Black Penitents and the Confraternity of Our Lady of Suffrage.[80] He also had several disciples among Toulouse's younger clergymen, most notably Gabriel de Ciron.[81]

In the 1650s there were several supposed Jansenist nests in Toulouse, lending credence to the growing suspicion that the Catholic capital of the Midi was a breeding ground for the new heresy. The local chapter of the Company of the Holy Sacrament was dominated by Jansenist Messieurs. Because of their discipline, modesty, and fidelity to parochial devotion, the Oratorians of the Dalbade were suspected of Jansenism. In particular, Père Le Jeune, who was also a Monsieur, was considered a partisan of Port-Royal.[82] The Séminaire des Hautes Sciences, established by Ciron to train secular priests, had

---

80. E. Dejean, *Un prélat indépendant au XVIIe siècle: Nicolas Pavillon* (Paris, 1909); G. Doublet, *Un prélat janséniste, F. de Caulet* (Paris and Foix, 1895).

81. On these connections and associations, see Shibano, "Les débuts de la Congrégation," pp. 16, 80, 107; Auguste, *Les origines du jansénsisme*, p. 15 and passim; Dubédat, *Parlement de Toulouse*, 2:161; Henry Jaudon, *Port-Royal à Toulouse ou le jansénisme au Parlement*; and Antoine Dégert, "Les lettres et les moeurs dans la société toulousaine il y a trois cents ans," *RHT* 1 (1914): 385–413.

82. Auguste, *La Compagnie du Saint-Sacrement*, p. 75. See also Ranum, *Paris in an Age of Absolutism*, pp. 117–19.

as its director an outspoken Jansenist, Père Vignaux, who blatantly displayed his partisanship by barring the Molinist preachings of two Capuchins.[83] Vignaux was in addition the confessor to the Maltese Order of Saint-Jean, and his presence there served as a pretext for the persecution of its sisters, who apparently had grown rather independent-minded in theology in recent years. The order had a library stocked with reading material straight from Port-Royal and the nuns brazenly mocked their outraged inquisitors with a barrage of feisty songs and poems.[84] It is likely too that the Company of Black Penitents was a crypto-Jansenist brotherhood, with Mme de Mondonville (whose marriage took place in the company's chapel), Ciron, and Pavillon among its most prominent members.[85] This is made even more likely given the Blacks' singular penchant for "discipline" and their long-standing rivalry with the Blue Penitents, who were under the control of the Jesuits.

Thus by 1661, the year of the founding of Mme de Mondonville's institute, Toulouse had already earned a reputation as a nursery of Jansenism. This was enough to draw suspicion to the new congregation. But the institute did indeed embody several features that smacked of Jansenism. For one, Ciron adopted the contritionist regime of his mentor, Pavillon, and frequently denied or delayed absolution to the daughters (When once he had likewise forbidden Mme de Mondonville to commune, she poignantly confided in her memoirs that his order left her "cruelly starved" for the Holy Eucharist.)[86] For another, the institute deliberately eschewed any appearance of a religious order, a hallmark of a Jansenist congregation: the daughters did not wear a special habit, the building that housed them was preserved as an ordinary domicile, they never assembled in public, nor did they attempt to attract communicants from among the laity. And like the sisters of Port-Royal, they committed themselves to charitable acts and the education of the young. Most incriminating for the institute, perhaps, was Ciron himself. Despite his orthodox avowal that the "five propositions" were heretical, Ciron continued to attract

83. Auguste, *Le Séminaire de Caraman au Faubourg Saint-Etienne à Toulouse* (Paris and Toulouse, 1913), pp. 1, 15, 36, 43, 157–58; C. Tournier, *Histoire des séminaires toulousains* (Toulouse, 1942), pp. 16–19; Auguste, *Les origines de jansénisme*, p. 87.

84. Auguste, "Port-Royal à Toulouse ou le jansénisme des religieuses maltaises sous l'épiscopat de P. de Marca," *RHT* 3 (1920): 161–89.

85. Shibano, "Les débuts de la Congrégation," pp. 16, 80.

86. Ibid., p. 124.

suspicion if only because of his friends and supporters, especially Pavillon. Furthermore, Ciron was an outspoken critic of the regime's war policy and even had the temerity to propound his opinions at court. In 1652 he was asked to preach at Versailles, where he took the opportunity to deliver a passionate tirade in front of the queen herself on "all the miseries of the countryside and all the desolation which the war was causing." The queen was untouched and Ciron quickly removed himself from Paris. Cardinal de Retz in his memoirs lists Ciron as a frondeur; and although there is no other evidence placing him among the rebels, he did only narrowly escape being *embastillé* by Cardinal Mazarin in 1657. Mazarin, to be sure, no connoisseur of fine theological distinctions, had little trouble casting Ciron among the Jansenists.[87]

Whether or not Ciron, Mme de Mondonville, and their institute deserved the Jansenist designation in any theologically precise sense of the term, they were persecuted under the pretext of the heresy nevertheless; and perhaps the real reason was simply that by the 1670s and 1680s their powerful friends and patrons had disappeared, leaving them vulnerable to a regime and an ecclesiastical establishment bent on the elimination of any pocket of unconventional devotion and the imposition of strict religious conformity throughout the realm. In 1666 the Company of the Holy Sacrament was suppressed by the crown, and though we cannot be sure how long the Toulouse Messieurs might have survived the royal ban, there were no signs that the secret society was alive after 1670. In 1683, the intendant D'Aguesseau, who had entrusted his own daughter to the institute, resigned his post. His successor was the notorious Lamoignon de Basville, an ardent supporter of the Jesuits. The main patrons of the institute, the prince and princess of Condé, had both died in the 1670s, and in 1685 the minister Le Tellier, also a strong supporter, passed away. In that same year, the year as well of the Revocation, the institute was abolished, its buildings razed, and, in a scene that presaged the violent destruction of Port-Royal in 1709, the daughters brutally evicted by soldiers of the city. A royal order constrained Mme de Mondonville to spend the rest of her days in exile in Normandy, where she died in 1703.[88]

87. Allier, *La Compagnie de Saint-Sacrement à Toulouse*, pp. 25–27.
88. *HGL*, 13:582–85.

Thus by 1685 the dévot movement had greatly waned in strength. It had begun in the 1640s with the founding of the Company of the Holy Sacrament, and reached the peak of its influence with the reform of municipal poor relief and the establishment of the general hospital, the campaign against the compagnonnages, and the creation of the Institute des Filles de l'Enfance de Jésus-Christ, which enlisted scores of young women in charitable and educational enterprises. The dévot movement drew elites into contact with the poor and ordinary people and involved them in the society around them, a feature, I argue, of public life throughout the sixteenth and seventeenth centuries.

I also suggest a political dimension to religious activism. Whether or not that activism derived its spiritual energy from Jansenism is not clear. Certainly there was a Jansenist presence in Toulouse, in part a result of the influence of several Jansenist bishops, chief among them Charles Montchal, in part a reaction to the Jesuits' growing power over local religious affairs. As has been pointed out by several scholars, Jansenism was first and foremost a clerical movement, and though there were prominent laymen, especially Robe officials, who identified with Port-Royal, the very nature of the sect—its rather esoteric preoccupation with Augustinianism, its concern for the privileges of the parish clergy, the constant sparring with the Jesuits— made its appeal more clerical than laic. The Toulouse dévots who were not Jansenists—as many no doubt were not—at least embodied several tendencies that qualify them as fellow travelers—namely, moral rigor, spiritual refinement, and a displeasure, at the very least, with royal policy on religious, social, or political grounds.

Whether Jansenist or not, the life of a dévot was difficult and demanding; it was only for the pious few. In short, it appealed particularly to elites, giving a religious gloss to their role as governors of society. And this points to its wider political dimension: in exemplary and often heroic lay activism, elites found a means of fulfilling their traditional role in urban society, a role that was increasingly being denied to them by the growth of royal power. As dévots they first effected a transformation in their own persons and characters, having embraced a life of exemplary piety, but this led not to political quiescence or withdrawal.[89] It led rather to social activism and commit-

89. Michel Foucault emphasized that discipline is most often "applied first, with the greatest intensity, in the economically privileged and politically dominant classes." Only then is it turned into an instrument of social control (*The History of Sexuality*, vol. 1: *An Introduction*, trans. Robert Hurley [New York, 1980], p. 120).

ment. It may seem paradoxical that a religious movement of the few should have also maintained this social imperative. But this paradox reflects the fact that those few were at the same time insisting upon their role as legitimate governors of society. They thus embraced a devotional regime that at once steeled them to the exigencies of ruling, managing, and reforming an often restless urban populace while legitimizing their position as an elite spiritually and morally worthy of such power. Like their contemporaries the Puritans, the dévots combined moral rigor with a reforming zeal, and consequently remained, despite their otherworldly concerns, committed to confronting the social realities around them.

7

Spiritual Kinship

Recent work on religious life in early modern society has emphasized its corporate character—how the mass, processions, pilgrimages, and other communal rituals expressed people's belief that salvation was primarily a collective, not an individual, affair. It has shown how holiness, in the preindustrial era, meant concord and peace among Christians as much as it implied a privileged relationship with Christ, Mary, and the saints. To be sure, the corporate character of early modern religiosity was not without exception; in urban settings it prevailed less than in the countryside. And, according to John Bossy, certain forms of collective religious life, especially those based on kinship, were increasingly challenged by the post-Tridentine church.[1]

In some ways, the dévot movement we have just examined embodied the sort of rarefied piety that set the individual apart from the community of faithful, emphasizing the spiritual solitude of the penitent rather than the communal experience of the mass. And in this sense, it represented a break from traditional forms of corporate religiosity. This certainly was the case with Jansenism, which was feared by its critics precisely because of its elitist inclinations. But it should be clear by now that the dévot movement did not preclude

1. John Bossy, "The Counter-Reformation and the People of Catholic Europe," *Past & Present*, no. 47 (1970): 51–70, and *Christianity in the West 1400–1700* (Oxford, 1985); A. N. Galperin, *The Religions of the People in Sixteenth-Century Champagne* (Cambridge, Mass., 1976); Etienne Delaruelle, E. R. Labande, and Paul Ourliac, *L'église au temps de grand schisme et de la crise conciliaire (1378–1449)* (Paris, 1964).

membership in confraternities or contact with the poor and sick, despite its elevated spirituality. Even in a post-Tridentine, urban environment, forms of spiritual kinship were alive and well, and entailed to a surprising degree relationships between people from all classes and stations.

Confraternal Life

Once again, Mme de Mondonville provides us with a window on seventeenth-century religious life. In her memoirs she recounts that as a child she and her brothers would often reenact at home the rituals and ceremonies they had observed at the Saint-Etienne cathedral. On one such occasion they adorned her doll with jewelry and paraded it about their rooms as an image of the Virgin. The original ceremony, she notes, took place on the Day of the Assumption, when the statue of the Virgin "was accompanied with great solemnity and a great gathering of people, with many gentlemen of the Parlement serving as officers, my father one of the most zealous among them."[2]

Her father, those gentlemen, and the other participants in the procession were all members of a devotional brotherhood, the Confraternity of the Assumption of Our Lady, one of the many lay religious groups active in early modern Toulouse. It is understandable that the young Mme de Mondonville should have been so impressed by the ceremonial gathering. For the Confraternity of the Assumption was a mass-based association comprised of several hundred members from throughout the city, the suburbs, and even the countryside, and its confrères included noblemen, magistrates, officers, merchants, and artisans, women as well as men.[3]

The notion of the confraternity is as old as Christianity itself; indeed, it springs from Jesus' enunciation of his mystical presence among all those who gather in his name. The pioneering French sociologist of religion, Gabriel Le Bras, defined the confraternity in terms that highlight its universality and its proximity to fundamental human associations. Confraternities, he wrote, are "artificial families in which all members are united by voluntary fraternity . . . having

2. Shibano, "Les débuts de la Congrégation," p. 4.
3. ADH-G, E 872, "Ensuit les noms et surnoms des Messieurs les Confrères de la Confrairie de l'Assomption Notre-Dame de l'église métropolitaine Saint-Etienne de Toulouse . . . 1643."

for their object the satisfaction, within a narrow context, of the most pressing needs of body and soul."[4] Le Bras's own qualification, "within a narrow context," evokes a distinctive feature of such associations. Throughout their history confraternities have offered a context for religious sociability and devotion parallel to, though smaller than, that of the parish and mass, and thus have often been looked upon with suspicion by the clergy as a threat to the universal church and its unified community of believers.

In Toulouse, however, there does not seem to have been an effort by the clergy to limit the confraternities. On the contrary, large-scale devotional brotherhoods were conceived as a means of uniting the city faithful across parochial and occupational lines at least since the period of the religious wars. If any confraternities were looked upon with official disfavor, they were those craft brotherhoods that predominated in the artisan community, for such associations easily escaped clerical supervision. To the ecclesiastical hierarchy they were little more than drinking societies. An early seventeenth-century text on the Church of the Dalbade mentioned with disdain these "confraternities composed of men of the same trade," "forbidden by the Holy See and prohibited by the king's edicts as a source of debauch and monopolies and the cause of much turmoil and trouble in the Church."[5] Despite this official position, nothing was done to restrict the activities of craft confraternities in the seventeenth century. Craft confraternities, limited to artisans of the same trade, mostly masters, remained strong throughout the Old Regime.[6]

But they did receive some competition from the new confraternities that attempted to gather artisans from several crafts into common association. The parish church of the Dalbade housed a Confraternity of Saint Catherine that united the carpenters, lathe workers, turners, and coopers of the city into a single devotional community. By the end of the seventeenth century, however, the four crafts had parted ways, each establishing its own confraternity in a different church or monastery.[7] The confraternity of Sainte-Barbe, another confraternity of mixed tradesmen, seems to have been more long-lived and pros-

4. Gabriel Le Bras, *Etudes de sociologie religieuse* (Paris, 1956), 2:433.

5. Jean de Chabanel, *De l'estat et police de l'église Nostre-Dame dite la Daurade à Tolose* (Toulouse, 1625), pp. 63–64.

6. A. Du Bourg, "Coup d'oeil historique sur les diverses corporations de Toulouse, *MASIBL* 13 (1883–85): 257–95; 14 (1886–89): 52–91, 240–58.

7. Julien, *Toulouse chrétienne: Histoire de la paroisse N.D. la Dalbade*, p. 95.

perous: a list of members in 1648 shows an assortment of candle merchants, shoemakers, tailors, bakers, pastry makers and inn-keepers; and in 1667 these confrères were granted a perpetual indulgence from Pope Alexander VII.[8] The Confraternity of Sainte-Carbes, founded in 1641 was an even broader-based association of trades;[9] and the Jesuit-sponsored Congregation of Artisans similarly assembled craftsmen from throughout the laboring community.[10] Finally, the White Penitents, though its members came from all levels of society, recruited primarily from the working class and thus was the largest popular, multicraft confraternity in the city.[11] It appears, however, that the recruitment pattern of these confraternities, as appealing as it undoubtedly was to churchmen who exalted the image of an undivided Christian community, proved less than popular among artisans, whose own parochialism inclined them to a more occupational sense of affiliation.

Besides craft brotherhoods, there were two other types of confraternities in the city. One was the lay association that represented a parish as a whole and took responsibility for the secular affairs of the parish church. Perhaps one of the smallest, yet most important, parish confraternities of this sort was the Confraternity of the Work (Confrérie de l'Oeuvre), a committee of four laymen elected by the parishioners of the Dalbade.[12] A similar group was the Confraternity of the Very Holy Sacrament of the Altar, an association of from fifteen to twenty-five parlementaires, lawyers of the court, and merchants who regulated the financial concerns of the Saint-Etienne cathedral.[13] These two confraternities acted somewhat like a board of regents or trustees: they watched over the church's investments, supervised the hiring of clerics and preachers, and occasionally meddled in ecclesiastical and doctrinal affairs. Not surprisingly, conflict between these

8. ADH-G, E 1011, "Indulgence à perpétuité accordée par Notre Saint Père le Pape Alexandre VII à la Confrérie de Sainte-Barbe . . . 1667"; G. A. de Puybusque, "La Confrérie de Sainte-Barbe à Toulouse," *RHT* 3 (1920): 14–16.

9. AMT, GG 816, "Confrérie Sainte-Carbes, Confrérie composée des membres appartenant à toutes les corporations," 1641–1791.

10. Delattre, *Les établissements des Jésuites*, 4:1304.

11. ADH-G, E 929, Pénitents Blancs, 1647; E 932, "Liste des officiers de la Confrérie de Mrs. les Pénitents Blancs pour la présente année 1699 et des confrères députez pour les assemblées par les déliberations des 2 et 17 février 1697. . . ."

12. ADH-G, E 1001, "Confrérie de l'Oeuvre"; Julien, *Toulouse chrétienne*, pp. 82–94.

13. ADH-G, E 849, "Table de Confrérie du Très-Saint-Sacrement, Saint-Etienne," 1642–79.

associations of lay directors and the priests and canons who comprised the church's professional staff was not uncommon. In 1619, the "Workers" of the Dalbade lost a long struggle with the Oratorians and were forced to capitulate to the congregation's bid to take control of both the secular and religious concerns of the church. The Confraternity of the Holy Sacrament was more vigilant in its defense against the pretensions of the cathedral chapter of canons: during a lawsuit in the mid-seventeenth century, it successfully defeated the chapter's attempt, in its words, "to acquire a Despotism" over the affairs of the main altar.[14]

The last type of confraternity in the city was the devotional brotherhood, which gathered people who wished to share with others their affection for a particular saint or a specific religious exercise. Two confraternities, those dedicated to the Saints Roch and Sebastian, had long assembled the faithful in the spiritual combat against plague epidemics.[15] The Confraternity of Saint James, dating from the late Middle Ages, received and cared for the legions of pilgrims who annually converged on Toulouse in the late spring on their way to Compostella. Its statutes, renewed in 1513 and again in 1649, gave members the right to provide burial corteges for their departed confrères while garbed in pilgrim's robes, each bearing a staff and the seashell of Saint James—a privilege that irked the penitential companies, which preferred to think of themselves as the only uniformed lay associations in the city.[16] The Confraternity of the Blessed Sash of Saint Monica, established in the Augustinian convent, accorded members indulgences for participation in processions the fourth Sunday of each month and attendance at special masses. But as the name might indicate, the appeal of this confraternity was to expectant mothers who wished to earn the right to wear the "blessed sash" around their waists during their term of pregnancy.[17] There were many confraternities in the city dedicated to the Virgin, but one, the Confraternity of the Holy Scapular of the Virgin of Mount Carmel, required its brothers and sisters to display their affection for Mary by

14. Julien, pp. 75–85; ADH-G, E 1018, "Réflexions pour le sindic de la Confrairie du Saint-Sacrement contre le chanoine-bayle président de ladite Confrairie," p. 4.

15. Roucaud, *La peste à Toulouse*, pp. 461–64; Rozoi, 4:352.

16. ADH-G, E 835, "Somaire des estatutes de la vénérable Confrairie St. Jacques faicte en l'année mil cinq cent quatorze que ladicte confrairie feust rénouvellée et traduitz de langue vulgaire en françoise en l'an 1649."

17. ADH-G, E 1017, "Instructions pour l'archiconfrérie de la ceinture."

wearing her insignia, the scapular, on one shoulder.[18] Devotional confraternities, attacked by the Protestant Reformers, were sometimes looked upon with suspicion by Catholic clergymen as well, for while they undoubtedly stimulated piety, they also risked promoting a spirit of elitism and separateness among their confrères.[19]

By the latter part of the seventeenth century, there were no less than sixty lay confraternities in Toulouse. This figure excludes the seventy or more craft confraternities, which for the most part will not concern us in this chapter. Many of these confraternities dated from a period of heightened lay piety and activism in the thirteenth and fourteenth centuries; others, as we saw, were founded in the sixteenth century, some during the religious wars. How many were established in the post-Tridentine era, which in Toulouse began in the last decade of the sixteenth century? The question is pertinent because one view has it that the Counter-Reformation church was less than hospitable to confraternal life.

About twenty lay confraternities were founded or reestablished in Toulouse in the seventeenth century (table 3). To these should be added the four penitential companies that underwent substantial overhauling following the religious wars and augmented considerably their influence in the city by constructing their own chapels.[20] Several of these confraternities were devoted to aiding the sick and indigent, such as the Confraternity of Charity and the Confraternity of Our Lady of Suffrage, and thus contributed to the poor-relief movement of the seventeenth century.[21] Some were affiliated with national or even international networks of similar confraternities: the Company for the Propagation of the Faith, established in Toulouse by the Jesuits in 1664, was one of a number of such confraternities dedicated to the conversion of Protestants throughout the realm; and the local Confraternity of Our Lady of the Dying, founded by the Oratorians in 1617, was a member of an archconfraternity based in Rome.[22] At least four confraternities in the city received their impetus

18. ADH-G, E 1011, "Douze Reglés et statutes de la Confrérie du Saint Scapulaire de la vierge du Mont Carmel . . . 1634."

19. Steven Ozment, The Reformation in the Cities (New Haven, 1975), pp. 84–85.

20. On renewal of penitents see Peyronet, Recueil des ordonnances synodales et autres, pp. 826–34.

21. See Chapter 5.

22. ADH-G, E 1021, Compagnie de la Foi, 1664; Exercise de dévotion des personnes

TABLE 3

Lay confraternities founded or renewed, 1590–1700

Confraternity	Sponsor	Date
L'Immaculée Conception	Franciscans	1662
Notre-Dame des Brassiers	Saint-Etienne	1598
Notre-Dame de l'Annonciation	Notre-Dame de Nazareth	1647
Courdon de Saint-Francis	Franciscans	1624
L'Immaculée Conception	Daurade	1662
Notre-Dame de Suffrage	Du Taur	1647
Saint-Sacrement	Daurade	1617
Notre-Dame de l'Agonie	Dalbade	1617
Couronne de Notre Seigneur	Saint-Géraud	1634
Saint Scapulaire de la Vierge du Mont Carmel		1634
Saint Jacques	Saint-Etienne	1649
De la Ceinture	Angustins	1625
Notre-Dame de Bonnes Nouvelles	Saint-Barthélemy	1637
Miséricorde du Saint-Esprit	Saint-Etienne	1699
De la Charité	Archbishop	1679
Notre Dame de l'Annonciation	Saint-Pierre de Cuisine	1651
Propagation de la Foy	Jésuites	1664
Sainte-Barbe	Templiers	1661
Notre-Dame des Agonisants	Dalbade	1668
Saint Joseph	Dalbade	1645
Corpus Christi	Saint-Etienne	1597
Pénitents Bleus		1593
Pénitents Noirs		1593
Pénitents Blancs		1593
Pénitents Gris		1593

from the issuance of papal bulls (Our Lady of Suffrage, the Franciscans' Immaculate Conception, Our Lady of the Annunciation, and the Crown of Our Lord).[23] And several confraternities were refounded in the aftermath of the religious wars. The highly prestigious Confraternity of the Holy Sacrament in the cathedral, for example, reissued its statutes in 1597, noting that in recent years it had been

---

associatées à la Confrérie de Nostre-Dame des Agonisants, érigée dans l'église paroissiale de Nostre-Dame de la Dalbade (Toulouse, 1668).

23. Le confrère charitable aux ames souffrantes dans le purgatoire pour la dévote et charitable Confrairie de Notre-Dame du Suffrage (Toulouse, 1650); ADH-G, E 818, "Noms de dévots confraires enrollés dans la Ste. Confrairie de l'Immaculée Conception de la Ste.

unable even to participate in the Corpus Christi procession, one of the most important religious events on the city's calendar.[24]

Not only were a number of new confraternities founded in the seventeenth century, but confraternal life in general seems to have been notably healthy and active in this period—that is, if the abundance of extant regulation books and other records can be taken as legitimate vital signs. This vitality was clearly an aspect of the Counter-Reformation and the lay piety it fostered. But to link such lay associations with some monolithic movement for Catholic reform would be to overlook the dynamics of religious patronage and competition in the city. Many groups and institutions were imbued with the spirit of Trent; many claimed a role in the religious reconstitution of the diocese and city. And, in the process, many competed for the laity's allegiance. The confraternity was one means for attracting the laity, and thus religious orders and congregations, such as the Jesuits, the Oratorians, the Franciscans, and the Dominicans, all sponsored confraternities, as did the archbishop, the cathedral, important parish chapters, and even groups of dévots. It must not be thus concluded, however, that the laity was merely a passive agent in this process, for it is clear that prominent magistrates and other elites took the lead in founding and directing several confraternities, most notably the penitential companies. Moreover, nearly every confraternity was governed by a committee of officers who were most always laymen.

Perhaps the most distinctive feature of these seventeenth-century confraternities was their size, for they were large in scale, their memberships ranging from several hundred to over a thousand. The Company of Blue Penitents was Toulouse's largest confraternity, with a membership exceeding a thousand.[25] The next largest was the Confraternity of the Cordon of Saint Francis, with 842 confrères and consoeurs, followed by the Confraternity of the Assumption, with 636; the Confraternity of the Immaculate Conception, with 491; the Confraternity of the Annunciation, with 255; the White Penitents with 203; the Gray Penitents, with 195; the Confraternity of Toulousains, with 140; and finally, another Confraternity of the Assumption, with

Vierge . . . établie dans le grand couvent de l'observance St. Françoise de Toulouse par Bulle de N. S. P. le Pape Alexandre VII donnée cette année 1662"; ADH-G, E 833, Confrérie N.D. de l'Annonciation, L'Eglise N.D. de Nazaret; ADH-G, E 1020, "Confrairie de la Couronne de Notre Seigneur, 1642, St. Géraud."

24. ADH-G, E 849, Confrérie du Saint-Sacrement, Saint-Etienne, p. 181.
25. BIC, R MS 40, Livre des Pénitents Bleus.

146 members.[26] These were, in short, mass organizations, not devotional cells.

Not only were these confraternities large, but they also recruited members from throughout the city regardless of parish affiliation. Each of the four penitential companies, as well as three of the largest confraternities, drew people into their ranks from most of the eight city parishes, the suburbs, and even the countryside. The membership list of the Gray Penitents demonstrates this recruitment spread most graphically because it notes the parish of each member (map 5). But we can be sure that other confraternities followed a similar pattern, because, for example, the Blue Penitents included nearly the entire parlement in their association, and the magistrates' domiciles were scattered across several parishes. The same could be said for other confraternities, such as the Confraternity of the Immaculate Conception of the Daurade or the Company for the Propagation of the Faith, both of which assembled the city's ecclesiastical, judicial, and commercial elite. In other words, though many of these confraternities were housed and sponsored by particular parish churches, they recruited members from throughout the city.

The fact that these confraternities depended upon citywide recruitment was not lost on contemporaries; in the eyes of the parish clergy, in fact, it was a particularly troublesome development. To many churchmen and dévots, the rising popularity of this form of Counter-Reformation piety threatened to replace the parish with the confraternity, the church with the chapel.[27] Others, however, saw the confraternity as a helpmate to the church, and indeed, in an era of great demographic growth compounded by clerical neglect, it is not unlikely that confraternities filled the breach where parochial institutions were yet lacking. If we listen to Etienne Molinier's defense of confraternities against the charge that they subverted the parish church, we can detect echoes of this demographic reality. In a chapter entitled, "That the Confraternities do not harm the Church in general, nor Parishes in particular, but are rather beneficial to them," he writes: "As mothers sometimes have need of the help of nursemaids who relieve them in the tasks of feeding and caring for their children,

---

26. ADH-G, E 817; E 872; E 818; E 833; E 929; E 934; *Les privilèges et les règlements de la Confrérie des Tolosains* (Toulouse, 1663), and *Statuts et privilèges de la Confrérie des Tolosains* . . . (Toulouse, 1684); ADH-G, E 820.

27. Bossy, "The Counter-Reformation and the People of Catholic Europe," p. 60.

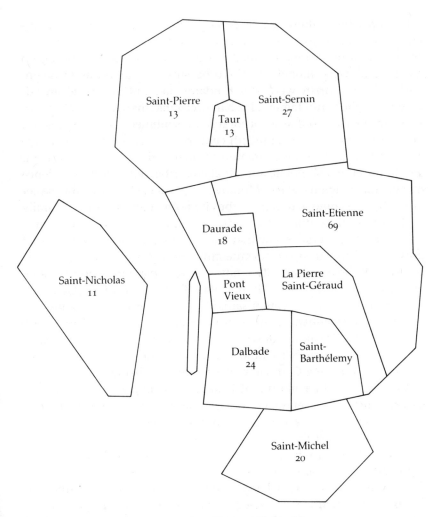

MAP 5. Gray Penitents by parish

a similar necessity is encountered with spiritual mothers, who being happily burdened with so many children with which Heaven has blessed them, are well-advised to call to their aid Religious Orders and secular Confraternities as nursemaids, to relieve them of a part of their concern."[28]

28. Molinier, *Des confraires pénitents* (Toulouse, 1625), pp. 29, 33.

Perhaps, then, there was a demographic basis for the confraternities' citywide recruitment pattern. In addition, it simply may have been that for many inhabitants the city as a whole had now become a meaningful associational space. To be sure, the divisions of neighborhood and parish were still fundamental. But alongside an adherence to these fundamental urban divisions, there was also a rising sense of the city itself as a corporation, a sentiment given expression in the sixteenth and seventeenth centuries in various municipal legends and symbols, public ceremonies such as the general procession, and in the citywide mobilization that characterized collective violence during the religious wars. Moreover, the magistrates of the parlement, having come to dominate the city both politically and culturally in the sixteenth century, clearly did not limit their vistas to parochial boundaries. It would seem that the large-scale confraternities that proved so popular in the seventeenth century were yet another expression of the corporate city—how else to explain the popular name of the Confraternity of the Immaculate Conception in the Daurade, "The Confraternity of Toulousains?"[29] Natalie Davis has written of the way Protestantism in sixteenth-century Lyons served to "open up" the city, breaking down the particular structures of neighborhood and parish.[30] I would suggest that in the large-scale confraternity we have a Catholic variation on this theme.

As noted, another important feature of seventeenth-century confraternal life was a tendency to assemble people from a mixture of professions and trades, classes and orders (table 4). To be sure, not all confraternities cast their recruitment nets so widely, and perhaps a majority adhered to the prevailing pattern of social and occupational segregation. But the examples of mixed confraternities are notable. The Confraternity of Our Lady of the Assumption in the cathedral, for example, included a near-equal number of elites, mostly magistrates and nobles, and artisans; artisans also made up a full one-third of the otherwise well-born confrères of Our Lady of the Annunciation. In another, much smaller confraternity, the Table of Our Lady of the Assumption, artisans were not merely members but also shared in decision making as regents and intendants alongside lawyers, officers, and merchants.[31]

29. Les privilèges et les règlements de la Confrérie des Tolosains (Toulouse, 1663).

30. Natalie Zemon Davis, "The Sacred and the Body Politic in Sixteenth-Century Lyons," Past & Present, no. 90 (1981): 40–70.

31. ADH-G, E 833, "Registre des noms des confraires . . . de la dévote Confrairie de

TABLE 4
Occupations of confraternity members

Confraternity	Nobles and parlementaires	Low officials and professionals	Merchants	Artisans	No profession listed	Other[a]
Assumption, Saint-Etienne (1643)[b]	151	83	50	127	62	163
Annunciation, Notre-Dame de Nazareth (1648)[c]	22	47	25	60	73	28
Immaculate Conception (1662)[d]	93	58	187	56	0	97
Gray Penitents (late 17th century)[e]	0	4	10	101	75	7
White Penitents (1642)[f]	3	26	33	49	91	1

[a]Includes clergy, students, soldiers, musicians, writers, artists.
[b]ADH-G, E 872.
[c]ADH-G, E 833, "Registre des noms et surnoms des confraires et confrairesses de la dévote Confraire de Nostre-Dame de l'Annonciation establie en l'eglise Nostre-Dame de Nazareth."
[d]"Noms des dévots confraires enrollés dans la Ste. Confrairie de l'Immaculée Conception de la Ste. Vierge Mère de Jesus Christ concevée sans péchée originel N.S. Pere le Pape Alexandre VII dans cette année . . . 1662," ADH-G, E 818.
[e]ADH-G, E 934, "Répertoire des Pénitents Gris," n.d.
[f]ADH-G, E 929.

The mere fact of such social mixing remains meaningless without an understanding of what was implied by membership in a confraternity. Did confrères of different stations interact in any meaningful way? Undoubtedly one implication for prospective members in joining was the promise of aid and company in sickness and some provisions for burial, for the confraternity was traditionally a mutual-aid society and was looked upon as a kind of insurance policy against absolute helplessness and solitude in times of personal hardship. Members of the Confraternity of the Five Wounds of Our Lord were entitled to financial assistance in case of illness, though the regulations are careful to specify repayment upon recovery.[32] Like many devotional societies, the Confraternity of the Holy Scapular appointed two or three members to look after sick confrères and offered indulgences to those who attended burials or otherwise aided sufferers.[33] Most confraternities maintained themselves on members' dues and an occasional legacy, so it is unlikely that after the expenses of supporting a priest, subsidizing masses, and keeping a chapel, there was much left over for in-house charity. But people probably sought personal solace and moral support from their confrères, rather than financial assistance. Especially in a large city, the confraternity could serve as a surrogate kin group or community network, and it is in this sense that membership implied charity for those who joined for whatever other reasons. For example, there is nothing in the regulations of the Confraternity of the Cordon of Saint Francis that distinguishes it from other large confraternities, yet over the years there seems to have been a process of self-selection, borne out by the fact that by the mid-seventeenth century over two-thirds of the enrollees were women, a large majority of whom were specifically identified as widows. Whatever the original intentions of its founders, this confraternity had clearly become a de facto refuge for widows and a haven for women otherwise alone and lonely.[34]

The confraternity offered charity and aid to its members, but it also obliged them to act charitably and peaceably toward their confrères, an ideal expressed in an article of the Confraternity of Our Lady of Good News, whose members were urged "to behave among them-

---

Nostre Dame de l'Annonciation," 1648; E 820, "Livre de la Table de Notre Dame de la Sumption de l'eglise de la Daurade," 1668–84.

32. ADH-G, E 1020, Confrérie des Cinq Playes de Nostre Seigneur J.C., 1638.

33. ADH-G, E 1011, Confrérie du Saint Scapulaire, art. 11.

34. ADH-G, E 817, Confrérie du Courdon Saint-François.

selves with a true and cordial affection and to love each other as children and servants of the Mother of delight, without permitting that there be among them any enmity . . . [and] while striving to avoid any occasion for disorder, however it may arise. And to help each other mutually and charitably in all their necessities, whether spiritual or corporeal, as much in life as in death."[35]

One finds such sentiments expressed in most confraternity documents, and they make sense as more than gratuitously sentimental statements when placed against the background of a society chronically blighted by turmoil and conflict. The Black Penitents did not insist on genuine affection, but they did stipulate that disputes between members be kept *en famille*, so to speak, and not immediately turned over to civil authorities: "any trial or difference between confrères will respectively be put to the Rector, and to his said Counsel, with the consent of the parties; not otherwise, without the involvement of Justice, but amiably with as much as can be known and determined about it."[36]

The message was clear: confrères were not to fight, certainly not in public, where their behavior, like that of good brothers and sisters, was to be at all times above reproach. All prospective members were expected to lead an "honest life," free from excesses such as dancing, drinking, swearing, and sexual misconduct. A typical initiation into a confraternity involved a general confession of one's sins to the priest attached to the association; in one case the confession was to be delivered before the general assembly, a practice that bound members together with a sort of trust based upon the sharing of incriminating information. Some confraternities, however, put little store in mere trust and were quite forthright in serving notice that to be a member was to submit to a certain degree of surveillance and policing. Several required a "research" into the conduct and morals of proposed members before initiation proceedings could begin. The Confraternity of Our Lady of the Annunciation in the parish church of Saint-Pierre de Cuisine accepted all inhabitants of the community "without regard to sex, age, and condition." The regulations go on to state, however, that "those persons of bad character, scandalous and

35. BMT, MS 708, "Statuts de la dévote Confrairie de Notre-Dame de bonnes nouvelles . . . 1637."

36. *Manuel de la dévote Confrérie Sainte-Croix des Pénitents Noirs de Toulouse* (Toulouse, 1667), p. 81.

defamed, such as it is with gamblers, drunks, blasphemers, concubines, and others, will be absolutely excluded." Suspicion of misconduct would be followed by three or four warnings from "Monsieur l'Intendant," beyond which the confrère would be judged "incorrigible," expelled from the ranks, and denounced before the community.[37] This procedure was quite typical, even mild compared with that of the Black Penitents, who designated special officers to monitor their members' conduct and morals:

> The Censors . . . will be charged to inform themselves continually and diligently on the life and conversation of the said confrères, and to remonstrate with them in detail and fraternally about their sins and imperfections which, if they are unwilling to correct, will denounce them to the Rector who will prescribe the correction or punishment, . . . whether it be with fasts, orations, discipline, and other manner of Penitence, up to the point of being driven out of the Confraternity, if need be.[38]

One can detect in the new confraternities a desire on the part of churchmen and lay dévots to create a new elite, one not necessarily political or social, but moral and devout, recruited, if possible, from a cross section of society. Unlike the "number of unbridled and intolerable societies . . . instruments and motives of debauchery, gluttony, and drunkenness"—Archbishop Joyeuse's words of condemnation for the purely craft associations—the confraternities of the Counter-Reformation were to involve elites and ordinary people alike in activities that were spiritually elevating, morally edifying, and socially constructive.[39]

But what sort of activities were these? On the first plane were the devotional exercises and pious prescriptions—the masses, processions, prayers, fasts, disciplines, and meditations—that were to stamp a confrère as a dévot. All confrères were in principle first and foremost members of their parish church, but in practice their confraternal exercises often separated them from their fellow parishioners, or even their curé. Instructions to members of the Confraternity of the Holy Sacrament advised that "a Mass celebrated even by a wicked Priest" deserved their full devotion and participa-

37. ADH-G, E 1021, "Règlemants de la Confrairie de Notre Dame de l'Annonciation dans l'église et paroisse de Saint-Pierre de Cuisine de Toulouse," 1651.
38. *Manuel de la dévote Confrérie . . . des Pénitents Noirs*, p. 81.
39. Peyronet, *Statuts synodaux*, chap. 15.

tion, and that in confession one should speak to the priest "as if talking to Jesus Christ hidden in him."[40] The undertone of such instructions is that some of the clergy, or even the visible church itself, might prove spiritually inadequate for pious confrères, unless they prepared themselves spiritually. Indeed, before the reform of the clergy by the Counter-Reformation, the church was riddled with curates who were clergymen in name only, who were ill trained and even illiterate, who abused their charges, kept concubines and were absent from their parishes for months at a time. Some confraternities, therefore, prescribed a series of preparations for the mass, communion, and confession, such as those contained in a pamphlet issued to the "brothers and sisters" of the Holy Scapular of the Virgin Mary, which details a routine of orations, meditations and prayers whose goal was summed up in a chapter called, "Remedies against Spiritual Barrenness."[41] Some such guides suggested devotional measures to be practiced in solitude: members of Our Lady of Suffrage were prompted to fast frequently, mortify their flesh, or practice other "acts of humility," such as kissing the ground several times, with arms crossed. They were also required to carry on their person a "Crown of the Holy Virgin," blessed by a clergymen and containing diverse prayers.[42] Most confraternities emphasized collective exercises, such as the article from the statutes of the White Penitents which counseled members to join with other penitents each evening "in a corner of their house before a statue of either Our Lord or the Virgin Mary to pray, confess, and examine their conscience."[43]

Above all, membership in a confraternity bound one to participate in public processions. The procession was the one religious exercise entirely in the hands of the lay membership. When a confraternity held masses or prescribed "discipline," priestly supervision was almost always required. When confrères took to the streets, however, though clergymen might join them, they did so as any other member, and the confraternity appeared as an undifferentiated body. In the procession a confrère was fully active in his devotion. To onlookers,

40. *Instructions, constitutions et exercises de piété pour la direction des confrères de la Confrairie du Très-Saint-Sacrement, établie en l'église paroisselle Notre-Dame du Taur en Tolose, par Simon de Peyronet, prestre, docteur en théologie et recteur de ladite église* (Toulouse, 1665).
41. R. P. Collonques, *La pratique spirituelle de l'âme dévote* (Toulouse, 1633).
42. *Le confrère charitable . . .* , p. 193, and statute 3.
43. Pecquet, "La Compagnie des Pénitents Blancs," p. 218.

the processing confraternity was a unit, distinguished as a group of people who, regardless of their worldly vocations, shared an identity and preoccupation on a higher devotional plane. The procession revived the drama of the church as a growing, living community. Writing in 1625, Etienne de Molinier described the procession as an evocative emblem of both the primitive and militant church. When the people came to listen to Jesus, they came in procession, wrote Molinier. When he entered Jerusalem, he entered in procession. His way to the cross was marked by a procession; after his resurrection it was in procession that he walked with his disciples. But the procession could also serve as a weapon of conquest—Molinier cites Joshua's seige of Jericho—before which "Demons take flight, impiety groans, heresy sighs, and the wicked become confused. Were not these processions shadows and figures of those that we undertake to thank God for favors received, or to ask for new ones?"[44]

The procession was a great instrument for the Counter-Reformation—the church militant, unified, numerous, and purified. And as well, in taking to the streets such confraternities as those dedicated to the Holy Sacrament or to the Immaculate Conception of the Virgin Mary could promote new types of devotion in keeping with the spirit of the Counter-Reformation. Contrary to the scores of craft confraternities, each patronized by a saint, each emerging several times yearly parading its saints' banners, images, and relics before the townsfolk, the new confraternities publicly championed a more sophisticated and abstract type of piety, and thus implicitly challenged the cult of the saints in the streets. In this context it is interesting to note the Gray Penitents' manner of devotional promotion. In seventeenth-century France, Christo-centric piety—a meditative approach to Christ as the absolute center of one's personal spiritual universe—was associated with the mystic and father of the Catholic Renaissance, Pierre Bérulle; and in Toulouse, Bérulle's teachings were especially dear to the Company of Gray Penitents.[45] During the Octave of Saint-Jean each year, these barefoot, shrouded penitents crisscrossed the city in solemn procession, stopping at the major churches, monasteries, and chapels, and at each station they would intone a prayer glorifying a different aspect of Christ's majesty. At the Grays' own chapel, Jesus was the Father; at the Basilica of Saint-Sernin, he

44. Molinier, *Des confraires pénitents*, pp. 469–79.
45. Brémond, *A Literary History of Religious Thought in France*, 3:133 and passim.

was the Priest; at the Blue Penitents', he was the King; then he was, at successive stops on the route, Redeemer, Brother, Provider, Doctor, Physician, Husband, Pastor, Lawyer, and finally Judge.[46] Few people had ever heard of Bérulle, who wrote for the pious elite, but in the procession of the Gray Penitents we see how his spiritual vision of Christ was dramatized, allowing ordinary people to share the rather sophisticated insight that one deity might have many faces and powers.

Most confraternities staged formal processions at least twice a year, and almost all provided burial corteges for deceased members. In 1644 a visitor from Strasbourg expressed his shock upon viewing the White Penitents escorting a body draped in a blue cloth, its face exposed "in the fashion of the pagans and Italians."[47] But the procession was also a vehicle by which the confraternity could express interests that were not strictly religious and which transcended the preoccupations of church and churchmen. The Confraternity of the Immaculate Conception joined with the capitouls on the occasion of a royal or princely birth and culminated their processional ceremonies with a gigantic fireworks display in the Daurade plaza.[48] The Company of Blue Penitents acted as a sort of permanent processional corps for the crown, especially in times of war. For the entire siege of La Rochelle, in 1628–29, the Blues marched to the accompaniment of music every three days; and they repeated this routine during Louis XIV's numerous military campaigns as well. It was not for nothing that the Blues were known as the Royal Penitents.[49]

As strange as it may seem, confraternities were also tiny islands of republicanism in a society which, if anything, was growing even less consultative politically. Nearly every confraternity held annual elections to choose its officials. The procedures governing these elections varied widely from association to association: some carefully screened and preselected nominees for office, others left the complete election process open to the entire membership. For example, the Confraternity of the Holy Sacrament of the parish church of Du Taur annually

46. *Prieurs pour les processions annuelles et autres exercises de la dévote Confrérie des Pénitents Gris de Toulouse* (Toulouse, 1679).

47. André Laurent, "Ce qu'on a dit de Toulouse: Elie Brackenhoffer, strasbourgeois," *L'Auta* 41 (May 1931): 69.

48. *Les privilèges et les règlements de la Confrérie des Toulousains*, p. 64.

49. Thouron, *Histoire de la Royale Compagnie des Messieurs les Pénitens Bleus*, pp. 300, 420, 490.

elected nine committeemen to "regulate the riches and revenues of the Confraternity." But the elections were limited by having the outgoing officials select a list of nominees as their potential successors.[50] In the case of the penitential companies, on the other hand, members simply named their rectors and four bailles through a plurality of voices at a general assembly the first Sunday of Advent.[51] The Company for the Propagation of the Faith had a more elaborate election process, both for accepting new members and selecting officers. For each proposed member or nominee for office, the confrères placed dyed grains—white for acceptance, black for rejection—in a box passed among them by the secretary, with the results determined by a two-thirds majority.[52]

Voting in church institutions was not entirely unprecedented; in fact it was long-standing practice in some parishes, especially rural ones, for parishioners to choose their curates in a popular manner. Elections were not new, but what was somewhat unusual was the context in which they took place: broad-based associations where a natural consensus was not determined by a common professional or social inclination. In the large confraternities in particular, with their varied memberships, elections were a challenge to the values and skills of cooperation and harmonious sociability preached by these associations. They are also further evidence that confraternities were cells of activism in a society that was supposedly moving toward a state of paralysis engendered by absolutism. To be sure, other corporations and groups of functionaries in the Old Regime also enfranchised their members to vote and govern themselves, but these involved people of the same social standing or profession.

Moreover, while corporations of craftsmen and officials fit into a hierarchy of orders into which the Old Regime ceremonially and juridically divided itself, the social composition of many confraternities seemed to challenge this hierarchy, or at least placed its supposed all-pervasiveness in doubt. For how rigorous and universal could it have been if people readily ignored or violated the prevailing social code and joined with those of other stations in these socioreligious clubs? How seriously can we take the view of Roland

50. *Instructions, constitutions et exercises de piété pour la direction des confrères de la Confrairie du Très-Saint-Sacrement*, statute v.

51. Pecquet, "La Compagnie des Pénitents Blancs," p. 217.

52. ADH-G, E 1021.

Mousnier that these orders were fundamental to both the ideology and comportment of life in the Old Regime when we see evidence of, for example, artisans, merchants, and noblemen democratically regulating the affairs of their confraternities, following the principle of "one man, one vote"? In short, the confraternity is one more argument against portraying the Old Regime as a society of sharply defined orders, without acknowledging the legitimacy and importance of other forms of social interaction and association.

The problem can be posed in slightly different terms. The confusion over the precise nature of the social order of the Old Regime might result not only from a peculiarly modern assumption that beneath the phenomena of various social interactions one should be able to discover the noumenal cast of a primordial social structure. It is also likely that the extraordinary social and religious changes that France underwent in the sixteenth and seventeenth centuries— changes only inadequately expressed by the descriptions of state-making, civil war, and religious reform—occasioned social arrangements that did not conform to either the categories of orders or classes. In waging civil war, imposing order, caring for the poor, creating new cultural and religious forms, resisting the political order, or seeking a place in the rising regime, elites were prompted to address the social elements beneath them in a variety of ways. And in the process they created new forms of association not classifiable in customary terms. Elites viewed the common people as allies, victims, clients, paupers, and even confrères; and their dealings with them cut across juridical, social, and economic boundaries so that what we see is not so much a fixed social structure or hierarchy but an assortment of social interactions fostered by the exigencies of urban life in the sixteenth and seventeenth centuries.

If Mousnier's "society of orders" finds little confirmation in the socially mixed memberships of many lay confraternities, the same could be said for Porschnev's class analysis of early modern society. For here is one context where social intermingling, while not the rule, still was not merely an exception. To be sure, social and professional differences did not somehow dissolve in the midst of confraternal sociability, and there is every indication that elites dominated and controlled those confraternities in which they were enrolled. But they were not primarily class-based associations, and on this count, at least, Mousnier's insight into the "verticality" of social relations in the Old Regime seems correct. For reasons that were complex and varied, elites found that interactions with those socially beneath them were both meaningful and useful.

Godparenting

Another routine form of interaction involved a different sort of spiritual kinship. Like Catholics everywhere, parents in early modern Toulouse chose godparents to accompany their newborn to the baptismal font for christening. The custom of selecting godparents created multiple ties—between godparents and parents, between godparents and child, and among godparents as well. Like the confraternity, godparenting partook of two worlds. It fell largely under the control and supervision of the clergy and was endowed with specifically religious meanings; but it also belonged to a tradition of popular practices which saw in important life passages an occasion to declare formal friendships, create fictive kinships, and affirm social solidarities.[53]

Godparenting was a more personal form of sociability than the confraternity; it implied the mutual recognition of parents and sponsors, and it also created ties across generations that promised tutelage, support, and protection. Godparenting could foster surrogate kinship where biological or marriage connections were absent or weak. It thus offered a range of choices and opportunities to parents. Would a father choose a godparent for his child from among his friends, colleagues, or neighbors, or would he prefer to select a kinsman if one were available? Would he decide to solicit his employer, a powerful patron, or perhaps a wealthy customer to honor his family by standing as the godfather of his child? Or would he rather choose an underling or a dependent, in that case confer honor rather than receive it? As might be expected, for the most part the choice of godparents fell within the boundaries of a father's immedi-

---

53. On godparenting in general, see John Bossy, "Blood and Baptism: Kinship, Community and Christianity in Western Europe from the Fourteenth to the Seventeenth Centuries," in *Sanctity and Secularity: The Church and the World*, ed. D. Baker (Oxford, 1973); Abbé Berthet, "Un réactif social: Le parrainage du XVIe siècle à la Révolution," *Annales: ESC* 2 (1946): 43–50; Sidney Mintz and Eric Wolf, "An Analysis of Ritual Co-Parenthood (Compadrazgo)," *Southwestern Journal of Anthropology* 6 (1950): 341–68; George M. Forster, "Cofradía and Compadrazgo in Spain and Spanish America," *Southwestern Journal of Anthropology* 9 (1953): 1–28.

ate milieu, within the limits of family, neighborhood, and work. Yet often parents and godparents were of a distinct and different social standing—indeed, at times from different worlds—and it is primarily these instances that will interest us here.

In the eyes of the post-Tridentine church, the godparent's role was strictly that of a child's sponsor as he or she entered into the faith. It was the godparent who would guarantee the child's orthodox upbringing. The church had an interest in limiting the number of godparents for each child, for according to church doctrine each sponsor entered into a sacred relationship with his or her godchild, a relationship that, of course, precluded marriage between them. In a peasant society with a small marriage pool, the selection of multiple godparents risked creating the prospect of people mating with their spiritual kin, something the church regarded as incestuous. Thus, at the twenty-fourth session of the Council of Trent, sponsors at baptism were limited to "one person only, whether man or woman, or at most one man and one woman . . . and spiritual relationships shall be contracted between these only and the one baptized and his father and mother, and also between the one baptizing and the one baptized and the father and mother of the one baptized."[54] In particular, by stipulating that those who might "touch the one being baptized . . . shall not in any way contract a spiritual relationship, any constitutions asserting the contrary notwithstanding," the decree forbade the participation of additional sponsors.[55] But Toulouse was not a village, and it was in any case a common practice among people of Catholic Europe to include a whole group or an assembly of friends as sponsors at baptism. In Toulouse, many artisan corporations, as well as the capitouls, routinely stood collectively as godparents for their colleagues' newborn children.

In 1630 Archbishop Montchal of Toulouse issued ordinances governing the choice of godparents that were even stricter and more detailed than those decided upon at Trent. Godparents had to be at least fourteen years of age, themselves baptized, and recognized as good, practicing Christians of the Roman faith. A godparent also had to be of the same sex as the child, a rather surprising restriction, since it clearly denied natural parentage as a model, but understandable in

54. *Canons and Decrees of the Council of Trent*, ed. and trans. H. J. Schoreder (London, 1940), p. 185.
55. Ibid., p. 186.

terms of the church's fear of anything more than a spiritual liaison between child and sponsor. Godparents and their godchildren were forbidden to marry. Parents could not stand as godparents for their own children, nor could other close relatives, and theoretically this interdiction extended to the seventh degree of kinship within which marriage was forbidden. The ordinance goes on to forbid "très-expressément" the giving of gifts on the part of godparents, so as to "avoid that by an artifice of the Devil someone could be provoked to present himself to the said Sacrament to obtain something temporal, rather than for receiving the spiritual grace it confers."[56] In practice, most of these restrictions were flagrantly violated. Cousins, grandparents, aunts and uncles, even brothers and sisters often served as godparents, although the coincidence of kin and sponsors is found mostly among the upper classes. Godparents as well almost always came in pairs, one male and one female. And the ritual of baptism was an occasion for festivities, both within and outside the church; gifts were exchanged and the godparents were expected to defray the expenses of the ceremony.[57]

Despite Tridentine churchmen's attempts to emphasize the sacramental aspect of godparenting—its ancillary relationship to baptism—and thus its uniqueness, godparent relationships should not be viewed in isolation, for they belonged to an array of associations that modeled themselves on kinship. Confraternities, youth groups, corporations, even whole villages strove to imitate and appropriate the affective ties inherent in family relationships. A godparent was a surrogate parent. Therefore, to be ushered into an association by a "godparent"—the commonly used term for initiates' sponsors into scholastic groups, corporations, and academies—was to acknowledge that the ties that bound the group together were kinlike. Further, it is clear that despite the fact that what we see in parish registers (and what the church prescribed) were godparent relationships between individuals, the likelihood in most cases is that the partici-

---

56. Peyronet, *Recueil des ordonnances synodales et autres*, pp. 813–16.

57. There is one document left by a nobleman who noted his expenses from the baptism of a sister-in-law's son in 1785 at which he stood as the godfather and his wife as godmother. The total, which came to over 323 livres, included a robe for the new mother, a bonnet for the godmother, a kerchief for the infant, candy and bouquets for all assembled, plus payments to servants, candlemakers, florists, porters, the carilloneur, and the attending clergy (Jean Lestrade, "Frais d'un baptême à Toulouse en 1785," *RHT* 3 [1920]: 134–35).

pants viewed these as binding groups of people together. In other words, the godparent relationships we shall examine in Toulouse suggest the existence of larger, more corporate or collective associations among kin, friends, and coworkers.

In seventeenth-century Toulouse, the dominant pattern of godparenting was horizontal but extensive; that is, people most often chose godparents from their own social class or milieu, but usually went outside their particular trade, craft, or profession. In tables 5 and 6 we see evidence of this pattern drawn from the baptismal entries in Saint-Etienne for four years. What these figures represent are the godparent choices of petty tradesmen, craftsmen, laborers, and domestics: in a majority of these choices godparents were recruited among people in trades and occupations different from those of the parents.

How often did people restrict their choice of godparents to professional peers and coworkers; that is, how frequently were godparent ties horizontal and exclusive? How often, for example, did shoemakers or bakers select sponsors for their children from among their colleagues in their particular trade or corporation? From the same sample we see that spiritual kinship conformed to corporate and trade affiliations only in a minority of cases. In 1640, among the laborers who restricted their choice of sponsors to their own class, only 24 percent of their choices for godparents came from their coworkers. In the course of the seventeenth century this figure declined, which may be an indication of a decline in guild solidarity. In 1700, only 16.7 percent of godparents for the children of the laboring class in this sample came from coworkers.

TABLE 5
Status of godparents of craftsmen and laborers, parish of Saint-Etienne

	Total no. of godparents	Godparents from laboring class		Godparents from coworkers	
		(number)	(percent)	(number)	(percent)
1640	558	350	62.7	86	24.6
1660	244	140	57.4	43	17.6
1680	451	276	61.2	68	15.0
1700	478	367	76.7	80	16.7

Source: AMT, GG 207 (1640), 210 (1660), 251 and 252 (1680), 277 (1700), birth registers, Saint-Etienne.

TABLE 6

Status of godparents among coworkers, parish of Saint-Etienne

	Same status		Unequal status		Fathers are higher status	Fathers are lower status
	(number)	(percent)	(number)	(percent)	(percent)	(percent)
1640	72.0	62	28.0	24	12.0	16.0
1660	86.0	37	14.0	6	7.0	7.0
1680	85.0	58	15.0	10	9.0	6.0
1700	92.5	74	7.5	6	5.0	2.5

Source: AMT, GG 207 (1640), 210 (1660), 251 and 252 (1680), 277 (1700), birth registers, Saint-Etienne.

Though by far the predominant pattern of godparenting was horizontal, a significant number of parents did cross class lines to secure sponsors for their children at baptism. In fact, throughout the seventeenth century, the elite of Toulouse—the nobility, magistrates, and other officers of the city—exhibited a willingness to enter into personal relationships with the *menu peuple*—craftsmen, laborers, petty tradesmen, and domestics—by standing as their childrens' godparents with remarkable regularity (tables 7, 8, 9). As is evident in Figures 2, 3, and 4, up to 25 percent of all godparents for children of the commonfolk were recruited among the elite—and this was the case for all three parishes examined. Moreover, merchants were also a popular choice as godparents for children of the laboring classes. Taken together, the merchant community, the judicial elite, and the

TABLE 7

Elites serving as godparents for laboring class, parish of Dalbade

	Parlementaires	Officers and lawyers of the court	Capitouls (old and new)
1630 and 1635	4	18	0
1640 and 1645	7	23	0
1650 and 1655	4	16	0
1660 and 1665	5	17	1
1670 and 1675	8	22	4
1680 and 1685	8	13	5
1690 and 1695	3	5	4
1700 and 1705	0	4	3
1710 and 1715	0	15	0
1720 and 1725	8	1	0

Source: AMT, GG 13, 14, 15, 16, 39, 43, 44, 45, 46, 47, 49, 50, 51, 52, 53, 55, 56, baptismal registers, Dalbade.

TABLE 8
Elites serving as godparents for laboring class, parish of Saint-Etienne

	Parlementaires	Officers and lawyers of the court	Capitouls (old and new)
1630	3	10	0
1640	12	36	0
1650	14	24	0
1660	11	14	0
1670	16	21	0
1680	8	12	11
1690	4	26	3
1700	4	12	0
1710	5	7	3
1720	6	8	5
1730	4	12	0
1740	2	13	1

Source: AMT, GG 205, 207, 209, 210, 245, 246, 251, 252, 266, 277, 286, 287, 297, 298, baptismal registers, Saint-Etienne.

nobility of Toulouse account for from a quarter to a third of the godparents for their social inferiors during much of the seventeenth century. Thus, a significant number of godparent relationships proceeded in a vertical direction, with craftsmen and laborers willing and able to secure either merchants or officers—people richer and more powerful than they—as their spiritual kin. By the first decades of the eighteenth century, this pattern begins to change notably—a change we shall examine in a future chapter in the context of other changes in urban sociability.

One can readily understand the incentive for laborers and craftsmen to have elites stand as sponsors at baptism for their children. But what motivated a nobleman or parlementaire to offer himself as a godfather of a common laborer's child? Take the case of Jean-Baptiste de Ciron, *président à mortier* and one of the most powerful men in the entire province. A glance at the parish register of baptisms for 1650 in the cathedral shows that he stood as godfather for the children of a baker, a simple artisan, a master shoemaker, and a tailor—all in one year.[58] Table 10, which enumerates the godchildren of several presidents of the parlement in the course of a couple of decades (again, in only one parish), also illustrates the propensity of elites to serve as spiritual kin to lower-class townspeople. So too does table 11, listing

58. AMT, GG 209, Saint-Etienne, 1650.

TABLE 9
Occupations of godparents of children of tailors, parish of Saint-Etienne

	1630	1640	1650	1660	1670	1680	1690	1700	1710	1720
Tailors	4	8	10	5	8	4	4	15	9	11
Artisans and laborers	8	13	14	4	7	19	13	19	10	1
Merchants	2	10	10	5	8	6	7	0	0	3
Nobles, magistrates, high officials	2	7	6	4	4	5	4	1	0	1
Low officers and lawmen	5	5	10	5	16	7	1	2	3	1
Clergy	1	1	4	0	3	0	1	0	0	0
Students	0	0	0	0	2	1	4	0	0	0
Free professions	0	1	2	0	2	2	1	1	0	1

Sources: AMT, GG 205, 207, 209, 210, 245, 246, 251, 252, 266, 277, 286, 287, 297, 298, baptismal registers, Saint-Etienne.

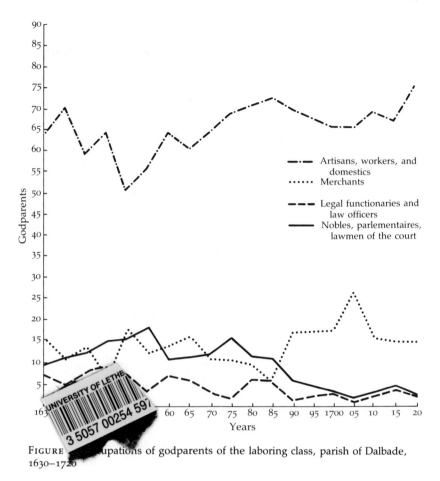

FIGURE ... upations of godparents of the laboring class, parish of Dalbade, 1630–1720

the godchildren of the Bertiers, a clan of magistrates and high church-men. What did these associations entail and how did they come to be made? One obvious explanation is that they were simply ties growing out of routine economic and business transactions related to the sup-ply and management of these elites' townhouses, country estates, and extensive entourages of family, friends, and servants. To main-tain congenial relations with producers was an important considera-tion for a noble household. In the economy of the Old Regime cash could not always bring forth desired commodities; shortages in essen-tial items were common and inventories rarely kept. Thus, con-sumers would find it in their interests to flatter producers with the

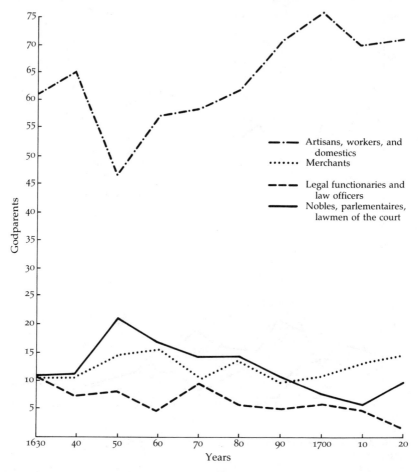

FIGURE 3. Occupations of godparents of the laboring class, parish of Saint-Etienne, 1630–1720

honor of their patronage, expressed not merely in monetary terms but in the moral currency of spiritual kinship. Further, while noblemen like Ciron were quite rich, their wealth was in property, lands, and offices; they were often short of liquid funds and thus routinely contracted debts with tradesmen, workers, and producers. To serve as the godfather to a creditor's son was to grant a sort of personal or moral interest on a debt whose payment might then be postponed if not canceled.

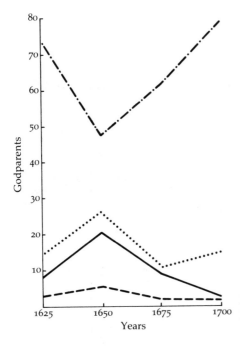

FIGURE 4. Occupations of godparents of the laboring class, parish
of Daurade, 1625–1700

In addition, officers like President Ciron were usually involved in church and civic enterprises that depended upon the services and good graces of artisans, laborers, and craftsmen. A group of noble members of the Confraternity of the Blessed Bread was charged with the supply of several hundred "petits pains" for each Sunday mass at the cathedral; several other lay confraternities took on the task of reconstructing the city's chapels and churches following the devastation and neglect of the religious wars; the Messieurs of the Company of the Holy Sacrament routinely proselytized within the artisan community and among the poor. In short, many of the activities spawned by the Counter-Reformation had the effect of drawing the elite into contact with the *menu peuple*, often as confrères of the same lay associations. Moreover, the ties of spiritual kinship went beyond the world of confrères and clients, extending even to the poor and infidel. In the death notices of 1653, for example, we find that on July 16, one "Jean George, native of Turkey and godson of Monsieur le Président Gragnaque died at the age of fifty at the home of the said president

TABLE 10

Occupations of parents of godchildren of several presidents of parlement, parish of Saint-Etienne, 1640–1670

	Ciron	Bertier	Donneville	Terrasse	Fieubet	Caulet	D'Auscaut
Noble and high officers	6	7	10	2	2	4	1
Law and low officers	1	3	2	1	4	0	3
Merchants	2	0	0	1	0	1	1
Artisans	4	10	7	1	4	4	6
Domestics	1	1	1	0	0	0	1
Free professions	1	2	1	1	0	0	2
Functionaries	0	2	0	3	2	0	2
No occupation listed	0	2	1	1	3	0	1
Total	15	27	22	10	15	9	17

Source: AMT, GG 207–11.

TABLE 11
Occupations of parents of godchildren of Bertier
clan, parish of Saint-Etienne, 1630–1660

Parents of godchildren	Number
Nobles and high officers	42
Law and low officers	24
Merchants	12
Functionaires	4
Free professions	2
Artisans and laborers	25
Domestics	2
No occupation given	2
Total	113

Source: AMT, GG 205–10.

and was buried in the church of Saint-Jacques."[59] As for the poor, they were themselves sometimes chosen by Toulousains for godparents. A survey of the baptism records from the parish of Saint-Etienne from 1640 to 1670 reveals that fifty-four parents chose "poor of the hospital," "poor beggars," "two poor infants," or the like, as godparents to their children. What we have in cases such as these, it seems, is an extension of the new effort of poor relief into the realm of spiritual kinship. To choose an indigent as the godparent to one's child was to invite him into one's circle of kin; it also amounted to a public declaration of one's care and solicitude, not only toward that particular impoverished individual but toward the poor in general. And, in an urban society blighted by poverty and the "disorder" it frequently entailed, the multiplication of such ceremonial ties across the class divide separating the well-to-do from the poor would ideally culminate in some understanding of a social truce.

One might object that such small numbers can reveal nothing of significance. In response it must be stressed that the cases of poor people serving as godparents are drawn from only one of the city's eight parishes. Furthermore, in the eighteenth century such ceremonial solicitude toward the poor entirely disappeared, which makes the examples of spiritual kinship between respectable Toulousains in the seventeenth century all the more noteworthy. More important,

59. AMT, GG 240, Saint-Etienne.

perhaps, these admittedly unusual examples of spiritual kinship must be placed in the wider context not only of other godparenting ties but of the patronage routinely exercised by such elites as high magistrates. Historians of seventeenth-century France have begun to appreciate the role of patronage in the political functioning of society, but most of their attentions have been focused on the transmission of power and spoils from Parisian kings and ministers to local officials and magnates.[60] It is clear, however, that the line of transmission continued down to the lowest levels of society and that local elites used such rituals as godparenting to symbolize their patronage.

The early modern city was dense with vertical associations between people of different classes and social ranks, associations arising out of a variety of experiences and enterprises, from the mass mobilization of the religious wars to new efforts at poor relief, from civic ceremonies to lay confraternities, from the desire on the part of some elites to seek support and legitimacy among the people to the need on the part of others to contain and placate a sometimes restless urban populace. Despite the fact that corporate and class divisions were pronounced in the Old Regime and were insisted upon both juridically and ceremonially with great regularity, there were also forms of sociability which routinely cut across these divisions, forms of association which drew elites and ordinary people into contact with one another, sometimes with a surprising degree of intimacy.

In sum, these social connections must be placed in the context of a public life that promoted the social and local commitments of ruling elites, which served as an expressive vehicle for legitimizing their role as the managers and governors of society. Clearly, however, this role was open to question, and increasingly so at the end of the seventeenth century when the crown turned its imperious attentions on the realm's municipalities and profoundly altered the nature of city government. In the next section we shall turn to this and other challenges to traditional elites' authority and privileges and attempt to relate these challenges to the city's changing public life. But absolutism had varied implications, some of them cultural. It is to the cultural reorientation of one of Toulouse's most cherished institutions that we turn first.

60. See especially Sharon Kettering, *Patrons, Brokers, and Clients in Seventeenth-Century France* (New York, 1986).

PART FOUR

The Emerging Cosmopolitan City

8

Cultural Absolutism

In Antoine Furetière's *Dictionnaire universel*, first published in 1685, a "provincial" is defined as "someone who does not have the air or manners of the court, who lacks polish, who does not know how to conduct himself, and who has never moved in society."[1] We can only guess how literate provincials might have reacted to Furetière's definition, but we can be sure that in the last decades of the century those of Toulouse tried to prove him wrong. For during those years many upper-class Toulousains busied themselves creating institutions in their provincial capital that would embody a "society" in the sense that Furetière meant—a milieu composed exclusively of the highborn and literate, where what was prized most was *politesse*, correct French, elegance, poise, and wit. Barely a generation earlier the atmosphere in Toulouse had been heavy with religious concerns, with the controversy over Jansenism taking center stage. In the 1690s, controversy is again the order of the day, although of a more genteel sort: now it entails competition between two groups of elites with literary and cultural pretensions, each soliciting royal approval for its academy. Something had changed in Toulouse's cultural life, for the most conspicuous activities of its leading citizens had turned away from local concerns, and specifically those related to the religious and social reform of society, and were focused instead on language, manners, the ways of Paris, and, most important, on royal approval for their own cultural endeavors.

1. Antoine Furetière, *Dictionnaire universel, contenant généralement tous les mots françois tant vieux que modernes* . . . (1685; Rotterdam, 1690), 3:348; quoted in David Maland, *Culture and Society in Seventeenth-Century France* (New York, 1970), p. 278.

In other words, efforts were being made to bring the best of Paris to the capital of the Midi. Lately, in fact, the ways of Paris had become familiar to the reading public of Toulouse, for by the end of the century several newspapers were circulating in the realm, providing provincials with a glimpse of high life at Versailles and in the capital's leading salons. Beginning in 1673, Jean and Jean-Jacques Boude, *imprimeurs du roi* in Toulouse, reprinted Theophraste Renaudot's *Gazette de France*, which continued to circulate until 1746. And in 1694 the Boudes similarly took charge of republishing *Le Mercure Galant*. These early newspapers—among the earliest in the history of the European press—emanated from Paris and featured the lives of "les grands" there. Part propaganda organs, part gossip sheets, they gave prominence to France's military and diplomatic fortunes and thus broadcast to the literate public an image of Paris as the center of the supreme European power. While the *Gazette* would lighten its pages with bizarre and amusing anecdotes—that, for example, a stricken European monarch was bled seven times in one day, or that a foppish prince arrived in Paris with eight changes of attire for his week-long visit—the *Mercure* treated its readers with more elevated reading fare, such as news of the disputes at the Académie Française. In 1695 a third Parisian periodical, the *Journal des Savants*, began to appear in Toulouse. A more serious publication than either the *Mercure* or the *Gazette*, it reported on contemporary scientific discoveries and literary controversies throughout Europe; the *Journal des Savants*, in fact, was influenced by a European-wide trend that was fostering greater communication among intellectuals at the end of the seventeenth century, a trend that Pierre Bayle viewed favorably as creating a genuine "Republic of Letters," and whose own publication, the *Nouvelles de la République des Lettres*, inaugurated in 1684, had many readers in Toulouse.[2]

Increasingly aware of the intellectual and social fashions of the Parisian elite, the leading inhabitants of Toulouse must have experienced some discomfort and envy when they turned their eyes on the dismal cultural life of their own city. For the truth is that Toulouse, for centuries the cultural capital of the Midi, had experienced a decline in past years. And recent attempts to revive the arts and sciences had

2. M. T. Blanc-Rouquette, *La presse et l'information à Toulouse* (Toulouse, 1967), pp. 96–100, 115; L. Charlet, J. Godechot, R. Ranc, and L. Trenard, *Histoire de la presse française* (Paris, 1969), 1:83–114.

foundered, largely because the political and religious controversies of the day subverted any intellectual consensus that might have served as a basis for the city's cultural renewal. Indeed, until the 1680s it was Jansenism, more than anything else, which captured the intellectual energies of the literate community. Toulouse did have its salons, but they were conventicles for Jansenists rather than gathering spots for budding literati, amateur scientists, and aspiring academicians. Perhaps it was to efface Toulouse's reputation as a breeding ground for Jansenism that many of the city's leading inhabitants campaigned for royal recognition of a local academy in the last decade of the seventeenth century. No doubt the creation of provincial academies throughout the realm in recent years, especially in the rival city of Montauban, also spurred civic-minded Toulousains to join the academic vogue. And no doubt increased awareness of the matters that engaged and occupied the Parisian elite was a factor as well. In short, motivated by a complex of political, social, and cultural factors, late-seventeenth-century elites virtually fell over themselves demonstrating their conformity to Parisian ways, their loyalty to the crown, and their desire to rise above local tradition and enter the "century of Louis the Great."

Ancients Versus Moderns

In the 1690s two groups of savants competed for the honor of recognition as Toulouse's royal academy. The first was the Society of Floral Games, the most venerable literary institution in the Midi, perhaps in all of France, and a source of much local pride and popular affection. Though the Floral Games had lost much of their luster as a forum for poetic excellence, especially for poetry in Occitan, they still attracted entrants from far and wide and were still celebrated with great fanfare and popular enthusiasm. The competitions each May remained an occasion for citywide celebration; the legendary patroness of the games, Clémence Isaure, was still venerated by the populace as a sort of municipal saint. And though most of the poetry was declaimed in French, each year some entrants maintained the tradition of verse-making in Occitan. If the Floral Games had become decidedly unfashionable in the eyes of more sophisticated Toulousains, now attuned to the ways of Paris and Versailles, the local festival was as entrenched as ever in the city's civic culture.

In the mid-seventeenth century there emerged a rival to the Society of Floral Games. Perhaps reacting to a decline in the literary standards of the games, perhaps also in response to the recent establishment of the Académie Française, a group of local scholars and officers founded the Société des Lanternistes in 1640.[3] The name they gave themselves, the Lanternistes, followed the fashion set by the intellectual conventicles of the late Italian Renaissance and announced their intention to bring the light of wisdom and knowledge to the city. It is also likely that their name referred to the secrecy that surrounded their early meetings and the lantern that presumably guided members to their evening seances. If so, they might have run into another group of gentlemen likewise acting under the cloak of secrecy, for the year after the Lanternistes' first meeting, the local Company of the Holy Sacrament was founded. Indeed, at least one magistrate in the parlement, Gabriel de Malapeire, divided his energies between the two secret societies. By 1645, however, the Lanternistes ceased to meet, a victim, it seems, of the social and spiritual concerns that claimed the attentions of the city's elite.

In 1667 the Lanternistes were resurrected under the leadership of Géraud de Donneville, first president of the parlement. The membership was fixed at twenty, and it included the bishop of Comminges, a councilor in the présidial, a parlementaire, a trésorier général, an abbot renowned as a Latin poet, and a scholar who was both an amateur scientist and a historian. In 1670 they were joined by François Bayle, brother of Pierre Bayle, the famed Protestant savant, and himself a professor of medicine at the university. Other newcomers included a Cartesian philosopher who later would be appointed to the Parisian Académie des Sciences, a Minime astronomer, an abbot who was also a physicist of optics, and a Jesuit scholar. Despite this impressive roster of serious savants, by 1676 the society's vitality waned and it disappeared from view until 1680, when the Society of Lanternistes was reestablished under the patronage of President Fieubet. Fieubet's ties with the capitouls (whom he appointed) as-

---

3. On the Lanternistes, see Desbarreaux-Bernard, *Les Lanternistes, essai sur les réunions littéraires et scientifiques qui ont précédé à Toulouse l'établissement de l'Académie des Sciences* (Paris, 1858); Armieux, "Etat des membres de l'Académie des Sciences, Inscriptions et Belles-Lettres," *MASIBL*, 7th ser., 8 (1876): 255–99; *Mémoriaux annuels des Lanternistes* (Toulouse, 1795).

sured an official source of support, but interest still flagged. One problem was that leading local savants found the pull to Paris irresistible, and many abandoned the society for the more lively and lucrative capital. In 1690, however, the Lanternistes were again reborn. Led by the three Carrière brothers—a lawyer, a theologian, and an amateur scientist—the society finally found a firm footing, due in no small part to the support of the intendant Lamoignon de Basville. The Lanternistes were now in a position to challenge the Society of Floral Games for the cultural leadership of the city.

From its very start, the Society of Lanternistes demonstrated a preference for the natural sciences and the "new learning" of Bacon and Descartes. But despite the scientific interests of its members, it seems as though the young society deliberately cultivated the image of a literary academy, of a company of literati who could serve as the counterparts of the Parisian academicians in the provincial outpost. Once a semisecret society, the Lanternistes went public in the last decade of the seventeenth century, and in their sessions literary matters took precedence over the study of natural history, physics, and medicine. Like their rival, the Society of Floral Games, the Lanternistes also began to sponsor contests to attract the public's attention, contests that demonstrated their concern for correct language, eloquence, and felicitous speech. One of these made use of a popular game of the day called "bout-rimes," or end rhymes. In this game the contestants were given the last word for each line of a sonnet; their task was to construct a poem utilizing these words, thereby displaying their skill at turning light phrases within the limitations imposed by the given end words. To call the results poetry would be like calling painting by number art. Even prizewinning sonnets were contrived and frankly ridiculous. But the constraints of the bout-rimes produced verses that were regular in their rhyming scheme and predictable in form, and this conformed to the canons of contemporary classicism—the quasi-official art style of the realm. By encouraging the production of such poetry, the Lanternistes were identifying themselves with Parisian classicism and embracing the principle that, in language and art, correct form was paramount. Conformity in art was matched by political obsequiousness: although the subject of the sonnet was ostensibly left to the contestant's discretion, the society did avow that it would look with more favor on "verses made in praise of the king." Such was the theme of these rather typical lines which won the Lanternistes' prize for one chevalier de Dupont de Castelsarrasi in 1694:

Grand Roy, dont jadis Rome eut adoré le *Buste*.
Tu scais, malgré l'horreur des frimats des *Glacons*.
Hâter des tes lauriers les fertiles *Moissons*,
Mars ne parut jamais si fier ni si *Robuste*.

Tout tremble, tous se rend à ton aspect *Auguste*.
Ton exemple fournit d'héroïques *Leçons*.
Peut-on assez vanter, par de nobles *Chansons*,
Un vainqueur comme toi, sage, intrepide, *Juste?*
Au comble de la gloire on te vois sans *Orqueil;*
A l'air majestueux tu joins un doix *Accueil*,
Tes progrez ont toujours ta clémence pour *Dique*.

De cent peuples unis tu romps tous les *Ressorts*,
Et ton coeur, attendri du sang qui se *Prodique*,
Sacrifié à la paix ses plus vaillans *Transports*.[4]

The Lanternistes' desire to be noticed at Versailles for their exemplary loyalty went even further. Each year they offered prizes for the best discourses on different aspects of the "glory of Louis the Great." In 1694, for example, the subject was the "moderation of the King, who is ready to sacrifice his own glory for the tranquility of Europe by offers of Peace made to his Enemies even while his conquests and his victories promise yet more glorious progress to his arms." A priest at the cathedral won a first-prize medal by proclaiming that "Louis the peacemaker" deserved even more admiration than "Louis the vanquisher" because while a conqueror needs the help of others, in granting peace Louis acts alone.[5] The second-prize winner, a lawyer in the présidial at Nîmes, painted the portrait of a devastated Europe, the regrettable result of France's victories. Such a sight truly saddens Louis, he wrote, but he is not to blame, for it is his enemies who "have lit the flames that have consumed you."[6] A third prize was

---

4. M. Lapierre, "Les bout-rimes des Lanternistes," *MASIBL*, 8th ser., 9 (1887): 273. Tallemant des Réaux notes that the bout-rime games were the rage in mid-seventeenth-century polite society, having been introduced by the poet Dulot, "ce fou poète royal et archiépiscopal" (*Histoirettes*, ed. A. Adam, 2 vols. [Paris, 1960], 1:306). See also Molière's *Les femmes savantes*, in which Vadius says to Trissotin, "Et dans les bout-rimes je trouve adorable" (act 3, scene 3).
5. *Recueil de plusieurs pièces d'éloquence, présentées à Messieurs des conférences académiques de Toulouse* (Toulouse, 1694), p. 17.
6. Ibid., p. 30.

awarded to a Jesuit of Toulouse who mocked France's enemies for foolishly thinking they could thwart Louis's might: "Have you, ungrateful Dutch, fearful Spanish, proud Germans, and you poorly counseled inhabitants of the Alps, have you any refuge against our soldiers?"[7] Finally, an anonymous woman proved worthy of a fourth prize in the judgment of the Lanternistes for addressing Europe in these terms: "Enemies of my King! For the last time, you must understand: Peace is the only way to stop this conqueror; the victory he brings over his passions is more advantageous to you than all your efforts, and this Prince will grant you more Cities in a moment through negotiation than all that your bravest Generals could gain in the course of many years."[8]

Lest we conclude that these were empty political exercises, that the Lanternistes were merely currying favor from the crown with such obsequious pap, we should note that 1694, the year of the competition, was a time of acute crisis, both for the people of Toulouse, with dearth and grain riots their nearly daily fare, and for the realm as a whole, which was faced with the dual disasters of fiscal insolvency and military stalemate. Behind the facade of hyperbolic patriotism one can surmise a note of genuine desperation, and thus I suggest we take the content of these literary efforts quite seriously, not as the result of forced conformity but as genuine expressions—formulaic and artless ones to be sure—of a concern both for the state of France and for the authors' city in the terrible last decade of the century.

Above all, however, the stated goal of the Lanternistes was "the growth of Belles Lettres and the perfection of Eloquence," which, they noted, "had languished of late in the second city of the realm, while they flourish in other less considerable cities."[9] They were, in other words, convinced that Toulouse was in need of a cultural and literary renaissance, one that, in their opinion, could not be accomplished by the venerable but eviscerated Society of Floral Games.

The creation of a royal academy had long been contemplated by Toulouse's leading literati. From the founding of the society, the Lanternistes saw themselves as the progressives and cosmopolitans among the city's elite, as a group of "moderns" worthy of academic

7. Ibid., pp. 52–53.
8. Ibid., p. 78.
9. Ibid., p. 2.

status. There were some followers of the Floral Games, however, who realized that they would have to break out of their provincialism and time-honored customs if they were to survive with favor in the new atmosphere of cultural absolutism in Louis XIV's France. In 1684 Jean de Palaprat, a mainteneur of the Floral Games and a well-known playwright, proposed a reform of the games, one that would transform them into a royal academy. Palaprat's arguments were clear: the capital of Languedoc has been left behind; it "remains idle" while everywhere else preparations for a "happy and beautiful reign of the mind" are in progress. "We are in the most refined and most polite century there has ever been since the beginning of the world," he proclaimed. "Would not it be a shame if we [of Toulouse] failed to make our contribution in this age and under the reign of the greatest king who ever was?" What Palaprat proposed is that the Floral Games cease entertaining frivolous love verses, obtuse allegories, and eulogies to Clémence Isaure. Rather, the literary voices of the city must join in the realm's chorus of praise to the almighty king. "A single one of his campaigns would provide the themes for many poems greater than the *Iliad*," Palaprat concluded. "The world will end before such a subject is exhausted. It is thus the glory of the king which is the primary motive which animates us, so that his praises will be sung until the end of time."[10]

For the moment, Palaprat's plea went unheeded: the devotees of the Floral Games were far from eager to transform their cherished literary society into a royal academy and thereby dissolve three hundred years of local tradition. The Lanternistes thus stepped into the breach. In 1692, one Martel, a secretary to the society and a lawyer in the parlement, published two pamphlets urging the establishment of a royal academy in Toulouse, arguing that the Lanternistes, not the Floral Games, deserved the honor.[11] Martel echoed Palaprat's concern that Toulouse was absent among those cities singing the king's praises. The very nature of a man of letters, he asserted, "is to interest himself solely in the glory of his King and his Country. . . . It would appear that in these times when the victories of Our Invincible

10. Palaprat's pamphlet is largely reproduced in *HGL*, 13:656–57; see also Gelis, *Histoire critique des Jeux Floraux*, pp. 148–50.

11. Martel, *Factum pour l'établissement fixe d'une Académie de Belles-Lettres dans la ville de Tolose* (Montauban, 1692), and *Réponse à des mémoires qui ont paru contre l'établissement d'une Académie de Belles-Lettres dans la ville de Toulouse* (Montauban, 1692).

Monarch furnish more ample material for *Eloges*, Toulousains should show more zeal for their Prince through continual demonstrations in Eloquent French."[12]

Beyond producing a steady stream of homage to the Sun King, Martel thought, an academy might educate the elite of Toulouse. Martel strongly argued what Palaprat only hinted: Toulouse not only lagged behind her sister cities by not having an academy, it was behind the times more generally—insufficiently modern, uncivilized, and mired in its outdated, provincial ways. "Because it is situated in a Province far removed from the Capital of the realm and because one hardly finds the means of self-perfection in Eloquent French, there reigns a kind of barbarism in the Language of the Inhabitants."[13]

One needs to recall that for centuries Toulousains had prided themselves on their literary talents, on their hospitality to the *belle muse*, and on the vitality and charm of their native tongue—*la lenga mondina* —to appreciate what a rude turnabout Martel's criticism represents. Martel was not interested in poetry or charm: in him we meet the quintessential "modern," the savant who views language as an instrument of state, the classicist who values correct form above all else. He bemoans, for example, the fact that the lawyers and magistrates of Toulouse cannot find "critics" capable of judging their texts. Rather, the province is brimming with pedants, "and although Toulouse produces some true geniuses, born for any kind of literature, it can be observed that if they are well conceived, they are nurtured poorly, and their best works never have that clarity, that force and refinement that one admires in the learned works of many academicians."[14]

What was to blame for Toulouse's cultural mediocrity and backwardness? In Martel's view the fault lay squarely with the Floral Games. "Who could prefer," he asked, "the poverty of such grotesque poetry to all the charm of that which has the approbation of the court and the Académie Française?"[15] Martel attacked the Floral Games for awarding prizes equally for verses in French, Gascon, and Provençal; for honoring contestants according to their birth and rank and not for their literary talents; for being merely a contest and not a serious-minded society.[16] His most revealing criticism, however,

12. Martel, *Réponse à des mémoires*, p. 58.
13. Ibid., p. 23.
14. Ibid., p. 24.
15. Ibid., p. 12.
16. Ibid., p. 19.

struck at the popular aspect of the games. "They are mere spectacles," he sneered, "which serve for the amusement of the lower people. . . . Perhaps schoolboys and children or the common people would be quite saddened by their elimination, but People who are somewhat enlightened and reasonable, far from feeling the loss, would passionately hope for such a serious reform so glorious for the City."[17] Thus in Martel's view, what is popular and what is intellectually worthy are mutually exclusive. There is more than condescension and scorn in his tone; there is an outright critique that draws the line between popular and elite cultures. A royal academy led by the Lanternistes would rescue cultural life from the realm of spectacle; it would create a context where elites would meet for "exercises in which the most rude will become polite and the most polite still improve."[18] It would, Martel suggested, finally allow Toulouse to gain entry into the "Century of Louis the Great."[19]

We must step back from Martel's attack on the Floral Games in order to appreciate the wider context of his polemic. While the immediate issue was the establishment of a royal academy in Toulouse, his arguments contained echoes of a larger debate that was raging in France at the time—the debate between "ancients" and "moderns."[20] Seventeenth-century French culture, like the culture of Europe in general, was still governed by the principles and values of Renaissance humanism, insofar as the art, literature, and philosophy of the Greeks and Romans were still considered the summit of human achievement. Those who remained faithful to this notion, who considered, for example, Euripidean tragedy or Seneca's prose the models of perfection upon which one could not hope to improve, became known as the "ancients." In France, Nicolas Boileau and Racine were their most prominent spokesmen. Those who, on the other hand, sought to free culture from the paradigms of antique forms and who believed, moreover, that the contemporary era was possessed of a genuis all its own, called themselves the "moderns." Charles Perrault and Desmarets led this group. Superficially, then, the debate be-

17. Ibid., p. 22.
18. Martel, *Factum pour l'établissement*, p. 16.
19. Martel, *Réponse à des mémoires*, p. 12.
20. For a concise summary of the quarrel between the ancients and moderns, see Antoine Adam, "Anciens et Modernes," in *La France au temps de Louis XIV*, ed. Jacques Goimard (Paris, 1965), pp. 215–41.

tween ancients and moderns had to do with style and the canons of taste, but on a more profound level it evoked divergent views on the course of history. The ancients, convinced that antiquity was a golden age, a state of perfection and purity, tended to view the later centuries as a period of decadence and confusion; and while they believed that the restoration of classical letters in the Renaissance had rescued European culture from absolute corruption, they still could not admit that their own achievements were more than pale reflections of antique ideals. The partisans of the ancients, in short, had a sense of inferiority with relation to antiquity. From the modern position emerged the notion of progress in history, for the moderns insisted that, as inheritors of ancient culture, and indeed of all the accumulated wisdom and experience of the past, they were in a position to improve upon their classical forebears. Rather than view the course of history as a decline, they saw it as a growth from infancy to maturity where they, the elders, could look back upon the Greeks and Romans with affection, perhaps, but without any sense of inferiority or envy. Moreover, some moderns, rather than idealizing antiquity, turned a critical eye on the morals and tastes of the ancient world, and concluded that such violence and excess both in art and life reflected barbarism, not civilization.

There was a political dimension to the ancient and modern positions, as might be expected in Louis XIV's France, where the interests of state loomed so imperiously, especially in the cultural realm. The moderns were prepared to argue that the achievements of their king were in themselves sufficiently grand to match the standards of antiquity. Under the Sun King, they claimed, the glory and brilliance of France had inaugurated a new reign, one surpassing even Periclean Athens or Augustus's Rome. Given these sentiments, it is not surprising that the modern position was embraced by the court, the academies, and much of the public as well. Those who sided with the ancients, on the other hand, were for the most part drawn from the great aristocracy and the high magistracy, dévots and others who had reason to look upon the regime with less than hyperbolic enthusiasm. But the exigencies of state prevented the lines from being drawn between the two camps in such a clear-cut, political fashion. As Marc Soriano has persuasively argued, the politics of culture in seventeenth-century France could not risk a debate among savants that might foster contention and thus divide their ranks. Too much was at stake for the crown. The struggle against Calvinism and popular superstition, the creation of a technocratic elite, the elevation of French to a national language, Louis's European-wide propaganda campaign, the erection of an artistic and cultural facade for the state—all of these enterprises required the services of intellectuals, writers, and artists. Cooperation among them, however, presupposed tacit agreement on what Soriano calls a "common doctrine," and in seventeenth-century France, given the classical, largely humanist education dispensed at collège and university alike, that doctrine could only be one based on the "cult of the ancients." Thus, the crown's official position on the debate between the ancients and moderns, despite its own sentiments, was to consider it a secondary issue, if not a dangerous one insofar as it risked fomenting dissension within the nation's elite of savants.[21]

Returning to Toulouse, it is clear that the ancients and moderns each had their partisans in the provincial capital. The Lanternistes, a product of the seventeenth century and originally inclined toward the sciences, were Toulouse's moderns, while the followers of the Floral Games, whose literary tastes ran to Greek idylls and classical forms, were the local ancients. How was the crown to decide between these two groups? The Lanternistes had powerful patrons, the most important of whom was the intendant Basville. The Floral Games had tradition on its side, as well as an identification with classical culture. Perhaps it was this association with the ancients that was decisive, or perhaps it was the fact that both the magistrates of the parlement and the capitouls maintained close ties with the Floral Games. In any event, in September 1694 the Society of Floral Games received the royal letters patent transforming it into an academy of belles lettres. If the royal sanction was intended to put an end to the skirmishing between Toulouse's rival groups of literati, it did nothing of the kind. In one of the first sessions of the new Academy of Floral Games, D'Auterive, a parlementaire, delivered a vicious broadside against the Lanternistes and their allies, denouncing them as "people seized with a vain nobility by which they hope to gain approval for their laziness and their ignorance and their gawdy riches . . . who painfully suffer because there are other means of distinguishing oneself than by birth and riches."[22]

21. Marc Soriano, *Les contes de Perrault: Culture savante et traditions populaires* (Paris, 1968), pp. 300–305.
22. Quoted by J. de Lahondès, "Simon de Laboubère," *Revue des Pyrénées* 7 (1895): 358.

The Royal Academy of Toulouse

The Academy of Floral Games resembled the old society, which it superseded, only slightly. The royal edict augmented the membership from seven to thirty-five mainteneurs, the additional academicians appointed by the crown. They included five presidents and five magistrates of the parlement, five high clergymen (including two bishops), three lawyers, two trésoriers de France, one former capitoul, one physician, one playwright, a member of the Académie Française, and the mayor of Toulouse. Once again, magistrates of the court dominated a local association. The king placed the academy under the protection of the chancellor of France, Sieur Boucherat, a man of Versailles, not Toulouse. The king further required the city to furnish the academy 1,400 livres annually—300 livres to cover the expenses of its meeting, and the balance of 1,100 livres for the four prizes awarded each May.[23] As in the past, prizewinners were awarded floral bouquets along with their monetary awards, only now the ranking of the flowers was rearranged slightly. The royal edict demoted the violet, the traditional flower of the Gay Savoir, to the second prize, while the amaranth took its place as the most coveted honor.[24] This was, to be sure, a petty point, but it is of interest to us as an indication of the level of detail to which the crown was willing to attend in order to leave its mark on a time-honored custom. A more serious reform related to the kind of poetry entertained at the Floral Games. The chant royal was abandoned as a "form of poetry too cumbersome" in favor of an ode delivered for the first-prize amaranth. The violet would go to a poem of between 60 and 100 alexandrine verses "whose subject should be heroic, such as an Elegy on Friendship or a description of a virtuous act or a great military exploit." The marigold could be won with an elegy, ecologue, or idyll. In all cases, only poems that were "regular, having nothing burlesque, or satirical, or indecent, or against Religion, or contrary to decent morals" would be considered. The letters patent also created a new category for entrants. Once a poetry prize, the dog-rose bouquet

23. "Lettres patentes du roy portant érection des Jeux Floraux de Toulouse en une Académie de Belles-Lettres, avec le Brevet de Nomination d'un chancelier de ces jeux, et de trente-cinq académiciens ordinaires" (1695), in Lafaille, Annales, 2:107–9. Also printed in Gelis, Histoire des Jeux Floraux, pp. 361–65.
24. "Statutes pour les Jeux Floraux de Toulouse," in Gelis, Histoire des Jeux Floraux, pp. 365–89, statute III.

would now go to the writer of a prose work "in order to stimulate the study of eloquence." The mainteneurs would announce the subject for this prose discourse, and the royal edict also specified that every five years the subject could be a translation from an ancient work, such as an oration of Cicero or Demosthenes.[25]

The crown dictated the standards for poetic and literary excellence at the new academy: no more would prizes be dispensed indiscriminately to magistrates and officers without regard to the merits of their offerings. Rather, prizes would go only to works "of great beauty and few faults," and the judges would pay particular attention to meaning, style, and language. In all cases, the emphasis fell on form and style, on the correctness and probity of language:

> The beauty of meaning and of character shall be considered first, then the nobility, daring, neatness and other qualities of style, and finally the purity of language. Nevertheless, the language could be so full of barbarisms and solecisms that they would justly degrade the beauty of the meaning and that of the style. And likewise the style could be so common or so stiff or in general so little suited to the subject, that the work, while otherwise sensible and of a pure language, becomes despicable because of it.[26]

The new academy was to function as a forum where provincials could be indoctrinated in the canons of classicism, where they could perfect their French and purge their regional literary culture of the excess and indiscipline that had marked the baroque Occitan. It would have little to do with the populace, with the popular festivities that had been the centerpiece of the Floral Games for centuries. The prize bouquets were still retrieved from the altar of the Daurade church and taken in procession to the Hôtel de Ville each May 3, but only three mainteneurs were to participate in the ceremony. Clearly, the intent of the royal edict was to limit the public aspect of the games while still acknowledging tradition. Even Germain de Lafaille, who was made the permanent secretary of the new academy, was forced to admit that "our city has lost, by this novelty and the seriousness of the academy, that wonderful festive day which we celebrated in earlier times with so much joy."[27] The new statutes did allow for a mainteneur to deliver a eulogy to Clémence Isaure, the legendary

25. Statutes VI and XVII.
26. Statute XI.
27. AMT, BB 267, Testament de Lafaille, p. 70.

patroness of the Floral Games, but specified that this should be done "in few words."[28] By the second decade of the eighteenth century, the city had disavowed the patronage of Dame Clémence, asserting that her contribution to the support of the games was "merely a fable."[29]

The most telling commentary on the new Floral Games came from none other than Jean de Palaprat, the man who in 1684 had first proposed the creation of a royal academy in Toulouse. The fact is that Palaprat was sorely disappointed in the new academy, and his testimony is a fitting summary of the transformation in public life that its creation symbolized. Palaprat bemoaned the loss of precisely that characteristic of the games that Martel had been so eager to expunge—its popular appeal. "I would have wished," he wrote, "that in dressing this new academy in all its majesty, we had not completely stripped it of joy. . . . Our fathers knew what they were doing: they were not content with their pleasures if they could not share them with the people. They understood how important it was to associate with them. . . . The works that are crowned today in our Academy of Toulouse can only charm minds of the first order; the people hearing nothing in them."[30] "I would have thought that what is suitable on the banks of the Seine is not equally appropriate on the shores of the Garonne," added Palaprat. Let the Académie Française occupy itself with the serious task of judging eloquent French and the like. Since their founding, the Floral Games have always had a dual purpose: to challenge clever minds and to entertain the people. And Palaprat ended his polemic in words that belie in unmistakable terms the split that had developed between learned and popular culture:

> Poor people, that all those who should love you would love you as I do. . . . I do not blush at having popular sympathies. And I swear that if I had been able to elevate our games into an academy, I would have overlooked nothing in order to attract poets from throughout the realm, but I would have never consented to do it at the expense of the public festival; and as much as I would have sought glory, I would have found it too expensive if it had diminished the mirth of my fellow citizens.[31]

28. Statute XXIII.
29. Rozoi, 4:37.
30. Alexandre du Mège, *Histoire des institutions religieuses, politiques, judiciares et littéraires de la ville de Toulouse*, 4 vols. (Toulouse, 1864), 1:108–9.
31. Ibid.

The dilemma Palaprat expressed was not his own; it was a reflection of the cultural, social, and political developments that had cast the interests of the elite into a realm far removed from the concerns of "the people." For generations the Floral Games had served as a common forum for both the literati and the populace. Now that forum had been radically transformed.

In fact, the Floral Games themselves were only a minor part of the activities of the new academy. The statutes stipulated that each week during the year the mainteneurs would meet for "Assemblées de Littérature" devoted to the study, "in the original Greek and Latin," of the kinds of works they would be called upon to judge at the annual games. At these meetings, "they will search for good taste, among the odes of Horace, for example . . . and attempt to discover what has caused them to be considered models for so many centuries." The study of French writers and poets was not ignored, but now it meant comparing them with the ancient Greeks and Romans, "not for the sake of elevating the one over the other but to discover the beauty in both." In any case, the academy was prohibited from taking up the study of any work of a living author, "even if that author desires it." A mainteneur was to be "a man of merit, sociable, and a lover of Letters." Still, he was forbidden to discuss contemporary literary matters in a company of his esteemed peers.[32]

Though defeated in their attempt to rise to the level of a royal academy, the Lanternistes did not disappear from the scene after 1694. In 1698, in fact, they welcomed Mlle L'Heritier to Toulouse with great fanfare. A Parisian writer, she was also the cousin of Charles Perrault, himself the leader of the "modern" party. In the discourse greeting her, Arnaud Laborie, the secretary of the Lanternistes, was lavish in his praise: "How could one draw an adequate portrait of the clarity and the politeness of your style, of the vividness of your expression, of the beauty of your thoughts, always new, of your profound and broad erudition, of that extraordinary facility you have to write well, or that exquisite taste and that natural felicity which lends to your writing all the attractiveness and delicacy possible."[33]

Mlle L'Heritier was made an honorary member of the Society of

32. Statutes xxi and xxii.
33. "Lettre de réception pour Mlle L'Heritier," *Mercure Galant,* May 1698, pp. 203–4.

Lanternistes, and her reception is an indication that the skirmishing between ancients and moderns had not come to an end at Toulouse. As we have noted, the new statutes of the Academy of Floral Games forbade the members of that body from discussing the works of contemporary authors. Here we see their rivals not only discussing one such literati's works, but welcoming her into their midst as well. Moreover, in treating with such deference and seriousness a female writer, the Lanternistes were allying themselves with the précieuses, another wing of the modern camp. Again, they were taking issue with the Toulouse academicians who, though formally open to the participation of women in their annual competition, stipulated that "they could no longer hope to win a prize," and, "because of the modesty of their sex," barred them from becoming members of the royal body.[34]

The rivalry between the Academy of Floral Games and the Lanternistes was not to continue indefinitely. In a sense, the competition between ancients and moderns—a controversy essentially involving literati—ultimately resolved itself by each party taking refuge in a different intellectual domain. Thus, the ancients of Toulouse, the academicians of the Floral Games, remained the official guardians of belles lettres, while the Lanternistes, the moderns, returned to their original interest in the natural sciences, becoming in 1729 the Société des Sciences de Toulouse. By the mid-eighteenth century there were several academies in Toulouse, and indeed, a whole network of associations now reserved exclusively for the literate elite. Public life in the Age of Enlightenment would thus take on a very different cast, reflecting both a growing spirit of cosmopolitanism and the city's changed social and political conditions.

Student Culture Revisited: Classical Theater in the Collèges

When last encountered, the students of Toulouse were noted for their irreverent and fractious ways. University life often entailed years of hardship for these young men: relative poverty and privation, routine violence, itinerancy—even, for some, long stretches of study. It is unlikely that students' mores improved in the seventeenth cen-

34. Statute VIII.

tury, but there were forces operating on the university community that gradually served to discipline their behavior and impose order on the various foundations for higher learning. The Counter-Reformation was one of these forces; as in the city at large, it succeeded in involving many students in the activities of the church, especially by recruiting them into lay confraternities (in particular, the Blue Penitents). Another was the reform of the university, instituted in the late 1670s, which increased the number of professors, eliminated some antiquated endowments, and generally improved upon the institution's ability to carry out its mission.[35] Perhaps the most innovating force was represented by the appearance of two teaching orders in the city, the Society of Jesus and the Fathers of the Christian Doctrine. By the seventeenth century their collèges together enrolled several hundred younger students, and some older ones as well, for the Jesuits were granted the privilege to award advanced degrees. With their exemplary discipline and humanistically inclined pedagogy, these teaching fathers embodied a higher educational standard than had previously prevailed within Toulouse's university community. Furthermore, they brought to the city's public life a new kind of theater, one which, like the exercises of the new academicians, combined a stream of homage to the king with classical forms and themes.[36]

The collèges' plays, ballets, and recitations were performed and written by the students themselves.[37] The first was probably presented in the 1670s (if the surviving texts are any indication), and they continued to be mounted on a yearly basis; some years saw several performances, usually for the enjoyment of the officialdom of Toulouse, the capitouls, the magistrates of the parlement, and other royal officers, whose sons and nephews were among the actors. From 1675 to 1698 twenty-five such theatrical works were staged, seven at the collège of the Doctrinaires, the balance at the Jesuit collège. The occasion most years was the annual granting of degrees and prizes, but special events, such as the king's recovery from illness or the birth of the duke of Burgundy, were also celebrated with theatrical offerings.

Indeed, a preoccupation with affairs of state—with the health and well-being of the monarch, with France's diplomatic and military for-

<hr>

35. On this reform, see *HGL*, 14:997–1030.

36. For more on the theatrical tradition of the Jesuits, see Pierre Peyronnet, "Le théâtre d'éducation des Jésuites," *Dix-Huitième Siècle*, no. 8 (1976): 107–20; and R. Po-chia Hsia, *Society and Religion in Munster, 1535–1618* (New Haven, 1984), pp. 171–76.

37. The texts of these plays are to be found in BMT, Res. C. xvii, 50.

tunes—runs throughout the schoolboys' dramatic efforts. *La paix de retour*, which the Jesuit students presented to the magistrates of the parlement in 1678, extolled with dance, verse, and song "the Peace which the King has just accorded his people."[38] Four years later, in *Le triomphe de la joye*, the encomium to Louis took the form of an extended dispute among the gods over who would have the honor of elevating the king into their ranks.[39] Rome's conquest of the Corinthians served as the historical allegory for the Doctrinaires' tragedy *Corinthe*, mounted in 1684, which was introduced in the following terms: "Holland on its knees before the King, forced to seek peace, is an agreeable enough spectacle to offer a comparison with those Republics humiliated by the Greeks and Romans."[40] Another conquest, this the crusaders' sack of Constantinople in 1203, in which French troops played a prominent role, was acted by the Doctrinaire students in 1689. The occasion for the play, however, was a less than glorious one: the humiliating aftermath of Louis's doomed alliance with the last of the Stuarts, which the text's prologue referred to in the hopeful terms of France ("Religion and Loyalty") one day prevailing over the Dutch usurpers of the English throne ("Perfidy and Discord").[41]

But the schoolboys learned more than patriotism and xenophobia through their dramatic exercises. Some were instructive in the virtues of friendship, honor, courage, piety, and the like. For example, in 1675 the Jesuit students presented a twin bill of edifying tableaux. The first translated to the stage Cicero's tale of Damon and Phintias, whose heroic friendship managed to melt the heart of the notorious tyrant, Dionysius II.[42] This play, subtitled *Les véritables amis*, was coupled with a lighter though still instructive drama, *Les faux amis*, which depicted a pair of double-dealers whose profuse expressions of affection, pronounced only to cloak their perfidious deeds, ultimately lead to their mutual undoing.[43] The themes of friendship and loyalty, combining age-old chivalric ideals with the emerging concept of *honnêteté*, were prominent on the seventeenth-century Parisian stage; here they found an echo in the dramatic fare which the Jesuits presented to the elite of provincial Toulouse. So too did the new stan-

38. *La paix de retour* (Toulouse, 1678).
39. *Le triomphe de la joye* (Toulouse, 1682).
40. *Corinthe* (Toulouse, 1684).
41. *Alexis, ou Le rétablissement d'Ysac* (Toulouse, 1689).
42. *Damon et Pythias, ou Les véritables amis* (Toulouse, 1675).
43. *Les faux amis* (Toulouse, 1675).

dards for polite conduct now expected of the true French *gentilhomme*, for the schoolboy thespians were tutored in a full range of theatrical skills, including oratory, music, dance, and correct articulation, as well as in the contemporary principles of French classical theater. Ballet, de rigueur on the Parisian stage, accompanied each Toulouse production. But, of course, these skills had more than theatrical relevance; theater always instructs as well as entertains. In demonstrating their students' dramatic accomplishments, the Jesuits and Doctrinaires also provided their audience, those ladies and gentlemen of Toulouse striving to shed their provincial ways and assimilate the culture of Paris and the court, with living models of the new refinement.

As with French high culture at the time, this refinement was cloaked largely in classical guise. Some of the dramatic personnae were figures from the medieval past or the biblical era, especially those such as the Macabees, whose heroic exploits in service of the faith could be used as a foil for France's military adventures.[44] But most were personages, both mythical and historical, who inhabited the classical world. "You are among the gods," Bossuet told his king.[45] On stage, at least, so were the schoolboys of Toulouse, who, costumed as Jupitor, Juno, Neptune, Mars, Apollo, Mercury, Minerva, and other deities, brought to life the mythological cosmos of the Romans.[46] In the collèges, the culture of the "ancients" prevailed uncontested. The most compelling productions were derived from the Greek and Roman tragic traditions, all stories recounting the passions and conflicting loyalties among the royalty of the ancient world, all lessons in the travails of statecraft, all illustrations of the terrible sacrifice rulership entailed. In only one play, *Constantin Porphyrogenite*, the story of the Byzantine emperor's competition for power with his ruthlessly deceptive mother, was any reference made to Toulouse: during a balletic interlude, Pallas, goddess of the arts and sciences, is invoked as the special protector of Toulouse.[47]

This exception, in a sense, proves the rule: the dramatic fare offered up by the teaching fathers' students had cultural meanings that tran-

---

44. *Matathias* (Toulouse, 1685).

45. On Bossuet's declaration, see Jean-Marie Apostolidès, *Le roi-machine: Spectacle et politique au temps de Louis XIV* (Paris, 1981), p. 83.

46. See *Triomphe de la joye, La règne d'Auguste* (Toulouse, 1685), and *Mars guéri* (Toulouse, 1687).

47. *Constantin Porphyrogenite* (Toulouse, 1688).

scended the city and local concerns. The plays themselves were performed before an elite audience, within the enclosed collèges, insulated from the ruder, more public aspects of city life. Although the
Jesuits' and Doctrinaires' students were only a part of the university
community, one might compare their cultural exercises with those of
their sixteenth-century counterparts. For then, as we noted, student
life was intimately involved with the city's popular culture, both linguistically and socially. To be sure, many students in the seventeenth
century continued to lead a pell-mell existence, little affected by either
the reforming efforts of the Counter-Reformation church or the teaching fathers' exemplary discipline. But the establishment of an enclave
of student culture removed from the promiscuous world of street and
populace marked a departure from the mores that had prevailed in
the university community—a departure parallel to the transformation
of the Floral Games into the royal academy of Toulouse. This withdrawal from the dangerous vicissitudes of city life was noted by the
teaching fathers themselves who, in a prologue to one of their plays
staged in 1694 (a year, as we shall see, of widespread rioting in
Toulouse), noted that the cultivation of belles letters was the surest
means of keeping their students from that "idleness which is the
unhappy source of disorder in even the best governed cities, and the
fatal stumbling block of youth."[48] In the eighteenth century, such
"disorder" mounted steadily, and its impact on public life would be
significant.

48. *Thieste* (Toulouse, 1694).

9

Elites between Versailles and the People

The year 1685 should have been a great one for the faithful of Toulouse, as presumably it was for most Catholics of the realm. After all, the revocation of the Edict of Nantes had long been in the prayers of such dévots as the Messieurs of the Company of the Holy Sacrament, who indeed had lobbied for the cause of ending even partial toleration for the Protestants of France. But that year also saw the violent destruction of the Institut des Filles de l'Enfance, the exile of Mme de Mondonville to Brittany, and the forced confinement of many of her "daughters" in the general hospital. Not since the sixteenth century had a local religious issue been settled with such violence, and rarely before in Toulouse's history had the arm of royal authority intruded so brutally into the city's life. The destruction of the reputedly Jansenist institute was a lesson in the cost of religious deviation; it also helped usher in an era of conformity to the ways of Paris and Versailles in several domains. This chapter will set the stage for this cosmopolitan movement, which increasingly defined the character of the city's public life in the eighteenth century. It was not that Toulouse lapsed into political quiescence; quite the contrary, for if anything, the parlement's opposition to royal demands mounted as the century progressed. But if absolutism did not always promote obedience, it did direct the attention of urban elites to vistas that transcended the city, to Paris, Versailles, and the French nation as a whole.

Versailles and Toulouse

Royal intrusion into the affairs of the city was not unprecedented at the end of the seventeenth century. Since the early sixteenth century, the city had been forced from time to time to loan the crown various sums, usually as a condition for the preservation of its traditional privileges; and since the ministry of Richelieu, the crown had been careful to cultivate a royalist faction of parlementaires which promoted its interests within both the sovereign court and the city at large. Perhaps the most flagrant form of royal intrusion, in the eyes of the parlement, was the violation of the customary selection process of the sovereign court's First President, the most important single position in the city. As recently as 1686 the king passed over the parlement's own nominees and designated the intendant of Provence, Thomas de Morant, for the office. But for the city as a whole the most troubling form of royal intrusion was the crown's assault on municipal government, a campaign that would persist for the balance of the Old Regime.

The assault commenced as early as the mid-1650s and was managed by the First President, Gaspard de Fieubet, a royal appointee with connections, through his brother, at court. Fieubet began by insinuating his agents into the Hôtel de Ville. He had Germain de Lafaille named syndic of the city, and this loyal underling, whose municipal service eventually spanned fifty-five years and who at the age of ninety-six penned his "Testament syndical" documenting the deterioration of Toulouse's government, served as the First President's spy in the corridors of city hall. Fieubet also arranged the marriage between his valet and the daughter of the Hôtel de Ville's concierge, thus providing him with another source of information on the inner workings of municipal government. Then in 1659, through the good graces of his brother, who was the queen's Secrétaire des Commandements, Fieubet secured the king's approval of a list of his friends and clients to be capitouls. Two years later the king empowered Fieubet to name the municipal council permanently. In one stroke, therefore, the city was denied a privilege it had exercised, with some exceptions to be sure, since the capitoulat's creation in the twelfth century.[1] Following Fieubet's resignation in 1683, this task was inherited by the new intendant, Basville.

1. AMT, BB 267, "Le testament syndical de M. de Lafaille" (manuscript), pp. 14–18.

A word must be said about this particular intendant. Appointed in 1685, Lamoignon de Basville was the quintessential royal servant–efficient, incorruptible, talented, and, when necessary, ruthless. Son of the First President of the Parlement of Paris, he had already served as intendant in Pau, Montauban, and Poitiers before his assignment to Languedoc. He was, in other words, a career royal agent. Basville was closely connected to the inner circle at Versailles: he was a *créature* of Louvois, a confidant of Mme de Maintenon, and a friend of the influential Jesuit Père La Chaise. His ties to the Jesuits, in fact, were a factor in his being sent to Languedoc, for the crown wanted an agent who, unlike his predecessor Henry d'Aguesseau, would prove immune to Jansenism. Indeed, Basville did play an important part in the destruction of Mme de Mondonville's institute. But it is as the persecutor of the Huguenots that Basville gained notoriety, for it was he who was responsible for carrying out the revocation of the Edict of Nantes in the Midi, and it was he who unleashed the infamous drag-onnades upon the beleaguered Calvinists of the Cévennes. Religious fanaticism, however, entered little into his actions; Basville was the perfect bureaucrat, combining unswerving loyalty to royal policy with an expert knowledge of the province and its inhabitants. His tenure as intendant of Languedoc was an unprecedented thirty-four years, during which he came to dominate the provincial elite.[2] Saint-Simon dubbed him the "king of Languedoc." He might also be called the boss of Toulouse.

For Basville not only appointed the capitouls, he also controlled the city's treasury. In 1683 a royal edict placed the control of municipal finances into the hands of intendants throughout the realm, and in 1688 we see this edict being put into effect in Toulouse. In June of that year Basville arrived in town, and his fifteen-day stay produced something of a municipal revolution, or rather a peaceful *coup de ville*. Ensconced in a chamber in the Hôtel de Ville, he assembled the capitouls for daily conferences and proceeded to dictate a new course of municipal government. He scrutinized the tax rolls and ordered documentary proof for those who claimed fiscal exemptions. He for-bade the capitouls to appropriate more than 100 livres—mere pocket money—without his permission. He demanded to examine the re-

2. On Basville, see Henri Monin, *Essai sur l'histoire administrative du Languedoc pendant l'intendance de Basville* (Toulouse, 1884); Beik, *Absolutism and Society*, pp. 115–16; and Charles Tilly, *The Contentious French* (Cambridge, Mass., 1986), pp. 164–76.

ceipts of the *octrois* every month and appointed his own subdelegate Mariotte to serve as treasurer of the city. He prohibited the capitouls from appointing their own commissioners to attend to the city's business and made sure to enjoin them not to send delegates to Versailles to lobby for their interests at court. Finally, he denied them permission to convene official assemblies without the presence of a royal officer, meaning either himself or his subdelegate.[3]

Basville had established himself and his subdelegate as the effective rulers of Toulouse, and he had stripped the capitouls of their most fundamental powers. A man did not seek a place on the town council primarily to become powerful, though, but rather to become a nobleman, for the position of capitoul traditionally conferred full noble status. In 1691, however, even this most precious of privileges was challenged when the crown imposed a tax on the *noblesse de cloche* of the realm. In Toulouse, all families ennobled through the capitoulat since 1600 were declared subject to the tax; moreover, the sitting capitouls themselves were charged with the difficult and onerous genealogical task of assembling a list of their predecessors' descendants for Basville. As might have been expected, the outcry from the capitouls was immense, and they turned in desperation to the powerful archbishop and First President to press their case at Versailles. During the months of negotiation there was even talk of physical resistance. But the capitouls were ultimately saved from such desperate measures and from the tax itself, for the crown was up to its old trick of manipulating privilege in exchange for revenue, of looking for the quick fiscal fix rather than securing regular sources of taxation. In short, the crown was probably never serious about taxing the capitouls but simply wanted to extort the largest possible sum in return for the guarantee of their nobility—and their fiscal immunity. This is precisely what happened. Basville let it be known that the king, owing to his "great need," would look with particular favor and gratitude on the capitouls if a "voluntary" amount were forthcoming from the city. The capitouls quickly responded with a "gift" of 250,000 livres. Three months later the king declared that it had never

3. This and the next few paragraphs are assembled from the following sources: AMT, BB 267, Testament de Lafaille, and BB 282; *HGL*, 13:603–6. 630–43; Rozoi, *Annales*, 4:583–84, 593–98; H. Roques, *L'administration municipale à Toulouse de 1693 à 1694* (Toulouse, 1908). For a fuller treatment of this period in Toulouse's municipal history, see Robert A. Schneider, "Crown and Capitoulat: Municipal Government in Toulouse, 1500–1789," in Benedict, *Cities and Social Change in Early Modern France*.

been his intention to include the capitouls of Toulouse in the royal levy on the *noblesse de cloche*, and assured them that "their children and descendants (would) enjoy in the future as in the past, the same prerogatives and all the other advantages which nobles of extraction and family enjoy."[4]

The capitouls could congratulate themselves for having rescued, at a cost, their nobility and the fiscal privilege it entailed, but they were not able to savor their victory for long. In August 1692 the crown launched another assault on the structure of municipal government, this time by imposing the office of mayor on the realm's cities. Only Paris and Lyons were spared this humiliating innovation. Like other royal offices, that of town mayor was venal, and in addition it ennobled the possessor and his descendants. In Toulouse, the office went to Jean Daspe, a councilor in the parlement, who purchased it for 100,000 livres. As the new mayor, Daspe enjoyed privileges and honors that effectively demoted the capitouls in the city's social hierarchy and piqued their collective pride as well. Although his authority was largely ceremonial—in all substantive matters he was obliged to defer to the intendant—Daspe was intent on milking his office for the maximum *éclat*. He marched ahead of the capitouls in all public processions, and he led the city's delegation to the provincial estates. His name figured first on all municipal ordinances and placards; his personal retinue included four city archers, a sergeant, and a valet, and he was also furnished lodgings in the Hôtel de Ville. To the capitouls, who had just witnessed a drastic erosion of their own authority and prestige, the elevation of Daspe to such honorific heights was insult added to injury.

But they did not have to suffer this indignity for long, for in 1700 the king allowed the city to buy back and retire the office of mayor, and thus the crown was remunerated twice in the transaction, in both the purchase and the repurchase. Like the capitouls' struggle with the crown over their fiscal exemptions, their tug-of-war with Versailles over the office of mayor ended with a costly return to the status quo ante. The crown got the funds it needed; the city was restored in its privileges. But such struggles were bitter object lessons for municipal notables in the ways of Versailles. They were forced to learn that the legitimacy of their offices depended upon royal favor and that the fiscal demands of the state could destroy time-honored customs and privileges in a single stroke.

4. *HGL*, 13:630–34; Rozoi, 4:593–98.

Subsequent lessons followed quickly, for the city was next subjected to a battery of unprecedented taxes, the most notorious being
the *capitation*, levied in 1695, a head tax on all inhabitants, regardless
of their privileges.[5] But the city's resources were squeezed as well
through a variety of other techniques, several applied directly to the
Hôtel de Ville. On two occasions the capitouls were coerced into
purchasing shares in royal trading companies, first in the Compagnie
des Indes, for which the sum of 120,000 livres was demanded, and
then in the Compagnie du Nord, where the loan was bullied out of
the town councilors with the threat of a new tax as the alternative.
The most usual form of royal extortion, however, was the creation
and sale of offices, from which virtually no corporation or segment of
society was spared. In the 1680s and 1690s royal offices were forced
upon each of the city's craft guilds for the total sum of 250,000 livres;
upon the Hôtel de Ville, which saw itself saddled with a *procureur du
roy*, but which it managed to buy off for a "mere" 300,000 livres; upon
the town merchants, whose compliance was ensured under pain of
the confiscation of their property; upon the town officers, whose own
tax collectors were summarily dismissed and replaced with twelve
new assessors, each having purchased his office for 6,000 livres; upon
the city millers, who financed the new office with a new tax; and
upon the militia, now graced, against its will, with a royal lieutenant
of police. The cumulative yield of these burdens was somewhere in
the area of two million livres, lending credibility to Lafaille's complaint that it all amounted to a conspiracy "to strip us down to our
nightshirts." As if these financial sacrifices were not enough, moaned
Lafaille, "there came yet another mortification": in 1692 the crown
deprived the city of its artillery and canons, a move that not only
symbolically denied Toulouse's right of self-defense, but also removed its capacity for celebrating festivals and entries with sufficient
éclat.[6]

These late-seventeenth-century innovations and impositions were
merely the first round in what was an ongoing royal policy of admin-
istratively monitoring the city and fiscally exploiting its resources. But
this first assault on the municipality's privileges and powers had
more than political implications. Let us recall that the movement for
royal recognition of a Toulouse academy, described in the preceding
chapter, emerged in the 1690s, in the wake of the crown's reform of

5. *HGL*, 13:673–75.
6. AMT, BB 267, pp. 73–74.

city government, its unprecedented intrusion into local affairs. A direct link between the academic vogue and this royal assault is difficult to establish with precision. But it seems likely that the political atmosphere in the city, charged as it was with meddling from Versailles on nearly every front, prompted elites to refashion their cultural institutions in a royally sanctioned mode. Political and cultural absolutism were linked.

In the eighteenth century, municipal offices continued to be taxed and offered for sale: in 1737 the capitouls calculated that recent fiscal charges on offices amounted to 2,017,000 livres.[7] And the intendant or his subdelegate became fixtures on the municipal scene. Little could be done without these royal agents' approval—from architectural repairs and improvements to the prosecution of gamblers. Indeed, the royal officers frequently took the initiative in those enterprises when the capitouls' enthusiasm flagged.[8]

The royal assault on the capitoulat continued in the eighteenth century as well and eventually promoted rather fundamental alterations in Toulouse's age-old municipal government. In 1734 a royal edict mandated a change in the very structure of the town council: four capitouls were to be selected by the king, and the remaining four places, called "commissioned" capitouls, offered for purchase. Payments under the table had long been practiced as the means of gaining access to the Hôtel de Ville, but now such payment was an explicit prerequisite.[9] In 1746 the composition of the town council was again altered by royal decree: there were to be eight permanent *titulaire* capitouls, each having purchased the office, but only two of whom would serve at any given time along with the six "elected" capitouls.[10] The ostensible purpose of this reform was to ensure the continuity of municipal government by stipulating a rotation of eight men as councilors, each having accumulated experience in city affairs and each to serve once every four years. But in reality, those who purchased the office were usually less than scrupulous in the exercise of their duties. In 1737 the capitouls complained that only the "elect-

7. AMT, BB 283, p. 379.
8. On the intendant and subdelegate in the eighteenth century, see AMT, BB 283 and BB 284, passim; M. F. Buchalet, *L'assistance publique à Toulouse au dix-huitième siècle* (Toulouse, 1904).
9. Rozoi, 4:70–72.
10. Ibid., p. 99.

ed" among them actually served in the Hôtel de Ville, and the next year it was claimed that six months into his term one commissioned capitoul had not yet set foot in town.[11] As with the reforms at the end of the seventeenth century, the real purpose seems to have been to regularize the capitoulat's function as a source of revenue for the crown through venality.

In the second half of the century the crown's reforming campaign took yet another turn, for royal officials were increasingly concerned that municipal governments had lost their capacity to administer the realm's cities. In the 1760s the crown imposed the so-called Laverdy reforms on most cities, the aim of which was to restore to town councils the responsibilities and powers they had once enjoyed.[12] In Toulouse, these reforms were stalled by the efforts of the parlement, which resented the idea of a revived city government. But in 1778 the royal plan could not be put off any longer. Four features marked this reform. First was the elimination of the custom whereby the capitouls represented separate municipal districts. Second was the creation of the position of *chef de consistoire*, appointed by the king, an officer entrusted with ultimate authority in the Hôtel de Ville. The most controversial innovation called for the selection of the capitouls from three "classes": noblemen (two), former capitouls (two), and city notables (four). Finally, the entire structure of municipal government was recast into several overlapping councils, each recruited from the lay and ecclesiastical notables of the city. In addition, service on the capitoulat was extended to two years, and only those men who had been members of the Conseil général—the central governing council under this new regime—would be eligible for election to the capitoulat.[13]

These reforms, of course, barely had a chance. Proposed in 1778, they were not enacted until 1783, owing to the parlement's opposition, thus leaving a mere seven years before the Revolution radically changed the nature of urban politics. What can they tell us about the nature of local government in the eighteenth century? On the one hand, these reforms further demonstrate the crown's tendency to

11. Ibid., pp. 72, 80.
12. On the Laverdy reforms, see Maurice Bordes, *L'administration provinciale et municipale en France au XVIIIᵉ siecle* (Paris, 1972), pp. 254–326.
13. ADH-G, C 284, "Mémoire sur la nécessité de la réformation de l'administration municipale de la ville de Toulouse et sur la manière la plus efficace d'y procéder" (1775); L. Dutil, "La réforme du capitoulat toulousain," *ADM* 19 (1907): 305–63.

interfere virtually unimpeded in municipal affairs. They were imposed upon Toulouse and flouted local political traditions in almost every respect. But on the other, the very nature of these reforms—as well as the substantial body of public opinion which welcomed them—served as an indictment of the administration of municipal government in decades past. Even the crown, it seems, was forced to acknowledge that years of undermining the autonomy of the Hôtel de Ville for fiscal purposes had created a situation that thwarted effective government. Thus at the heart of the reforms of 1778 was an attempt to attract men of standing—mostly noblemen and other notables— who had heretofore been alienated from the town council. This alienation, it would seem, was a feature of elites' relationship to their city ever since the late seventeenth century. It was, as Alexis de Tocqueville argued, one result of absolutism.

If by the eighteenth century Toulouse's town council had largely become a plaything of royal policy, the fate of the parlement could not have been more different. As was the case with the other sovereign courts of the realm, the Parlement of Toulouse engaged in a near-permanent struggle with the crown over a range of fiscal and religious issues, especially in the middle decades of the eighteenth century, which were the high point of parlementary resistance. To review these issues would require a summary of much of the political history of eighteenth-century France, clearly not our purpose here. But one feature of the parlements' various campaigns against the crown that has lately been emphasized by historians of the Old Regime does have a place in our account: the way parlementary opposition increasingly entailed both unprecedented cooperation among the realm's sovereign courts and the articulation of their grievances, not in local or strictly corporate terms, but in a language that spoke to the interests of the entire nation. In other words, individual parlements—as well as other corporate institutions—were more and more regarding themselves as belonging to a single body, one, moreover, that had a legitimate claim to represent the French nation.[14]

14. On this theme, see Jean Egret, *Louis XV et l'opposition parlementaire* (Paris, 1970), pp. 72–76; Franklin Ford, *Robe and Sword: The Regrouping of the French Aristocracy after Louis XIV* (New York, 1965), chap. 10; Dale Van Kley, *The Jansenists and the Expulsion of the Jesuits from France* (New Haven, 1975). For the move toward national cooperation among other corporations, see David D. Bien, "The *secrétaires du roi*: Absolutism, *Corps*, and Privilege under the Ancien Régime," in *Vom Ancien Régime zu französischen Revolu-*

Parlementary opposition in the eighteenth century thus approached a national movement, whereas even during the Fronde the Toulouse court's grievances were expressed mostly in a provincial context and in alliance with regional powers. Two eighteenth-century issues revealed the growing national character of the parlement's action and its close association with the other courts. The first was the court's participation in the campaign against the Jesuits, culminating in their expulsion from the realm in 1762–63. Here coordination was essential, for the Parlement of Paris alone could not hope to root out the Jesuits, since so many of their collèges and other properties lay outside its jurisdiction. The magistrates of Toulouse were eager to participate in the campaign, in part because many identified themselves as Jansenists—at least according to an inquiry from earlier in the century.[15] The spirit of revenge was at work as well, for the Jesuits had assisted in the assault on the Institut des Filles de l'Enfance, whose destruction still stuck in the minds of many Toulousains, especially those magistrates with Jansenist leanings. But they were also motivated by the conviction, shared by their counterparts in the other sovereign courts, that the Jesuits, by their very constitution, contravened the principles of the Gallican church and thus were a standing threat to the nation's integrity. It was such a high-minded position that brought the various parlements, which in past years had rarely achieved unanimity or even cooperation on any issue, to form a common front against the Society and its supporters. In 1756 the Parlement of Paris made its famous declaration that the realm's sovereign courts "were diverse classes of a single and unique Parlement, the diverse members of a single and unique body, animated by the same spirit, nourished on the same principles, concerned with the same object."[16] And the Parlement of Toulouse, in a letter to the Parisian court concerning the exchange of some documents relevant to the campaign against the Jesuits, echoed these sentiments, insisting upon the "intimate fraternity which will never cease to unite us with you for the well-being of religion, service

---

tion: Forschungen und Perspektiven/ De l'Ancien Régime à la Révolution française: Recherches et perspectives, ed. Albert Cremer (Göttingen, 1978), pp. 153–68; and Gail Bossenga, "From Corps to Citizenship: The Bureaux des Finances before the French Revolution," Journal of Modern History 58 (1986): 610–42.

15. Maurice Virieux, "Une enquête sur le Parlement de Toulouse en 1718," ADM 87 (1975): 37–65.

16. Quoted in Egret, "Le procès des Jésuites devant les Parlements de France," Revue Historique, nos. 203–204, July–September 1950, pp. 1–27.

to the king, and the interest of the State."[17] These expressions were more than mere verbiage, for during their deliberations against the Jesuits the Toulouse magistrates remained in constant contact with the Parisian architects of the campaign. This contact was particularly crucial, since there was a significant pro-Jesuit faction in the court, led by First President Bastard, and thus those magistrates willing to prosecute the society needed all the help and guidance their Parisian counterparts could provide.[18]

The second controversy that revealed the widening range of parlementary cooperation followed quickly on the heels of the campaign against the Jesuits. This was the parlements' opposition to the proposed tripling of the *vingtième* in 1763. This tax, a 5 percent levy on income, especially landed income, had first been introduced in 1749, when it aroused only a flurry of parlementary opposition. Most of the objections then came from the clergy and the provincial estates. The doubling of the vingtième in 1757 and another levy in 1760 set off a more serious round of opposition, which, however, was appeased with promises from the crown that these would be the last impositions of their kind. When in 1763 a tripled vingtième was announced by royal edict, without the excuse of the fiscal urgencies of wartime, and imposed upon the Parlement of Paris in a *lit de justice*, trouble broke out in the provinces.[19]

In Toulouse the magistrates resolutely voted not to register the tax. Their action was met with what was then a rather novel (though not unprecedented) royal response: the occupation of Toulouse by troops led by the duc de Fitz-James and the house arrest of the magistrates themselves. Although released after the tax edict was modified, the magistrates were not mollified: they attempted to arrest Fitz-James and did not cease their protestations until the duke had quit the province.[20] Throughout all this the magistrates of Toulouse were not alone. Other sovereign courts waged their own campaigns against the vingtième and had to deal with the crown's heavy-handed strategy as well. The various parlements coordinated their opposition, a

17. *HGL*, 13:1173.

18. On the participation of the Toulouse parlement in this campaign, see *HGL*, 13:1173–80; Dubédat, *Histoire du Parlement de Toulouse*, 2:431–56; Van Kley, *The Jansenists*, pp. 190–91.

19. David Hudson, "The Parlementary Crisis of 1763 in France and Its Consequences," *Canadian Journal of History* 7 (1972): 97–117; Egret, *Louis XV*.

20. On this episode, see *HGL*, 13:1180–85; Dubédat, *Histoire du Parlement*, 2:457–90.

strategy that emboldened them to persist in their campaign. The aggrieved parlements exchanged letters of support, and the Toulouse magistrates received expressions of solidarity from the courts of Grenoble, Besançon, Dijon, Pau, Bordeaux, Aix, and Rennes.[21] That from the magistrates of Pau, written in February 1764, was typical: "United with you by the same wishes, we have vowed always to share your troubles and your successes. Linked by the same duties, we are forever linked as well by our love for the sacred person of the king, by our efforts to protect and execute his laws, by our zeal for the splendor and happiness of the State. We remain, Messieurs, your very dear brothers and your good friends."[22]

The emerging unity among France's parlements was clearly a factor in the formation of a national movement opposing royal policy in the years leading up to the Revolution—however ephemeral that concerted movement proved to be. Out of this parlementary front emerged a concept of national politics which held that certain judicial and administrative corporations, and not only the monarchy, could represent and ultimately did embody the French nation. For our purposes, the parlement's participation in such a movement shows that the dynamics of opposition in the eighteenth century entailed, at least for the magistrates, integration in a form of politics transcending the city and province, one that serves as a backdrop to the cosmopolitanism that then began to characterize the city's public life.

To review the relationships between the crown, on the one hand, and the parlement and capitouls, on the other, is to view the politics of absolutism at its most contentious. But these interactions do not describe the entire scope of the monarchy's relationship to the city and its officialdom. To draw local elites into line with the wishes of Versailles, the crown used a carrot as well as a stick. William Beik has amply documented how provincial elites had much to gain materially from absolutism, and nothing exemplifies better the benevolent, beneficent face of Louis XIV's rule in Languedoc than the construction of the Canal du Midi.[23]

21. *HGL*, 14:2276–80, "Lettres des parlements de France au Parlement de Toulouse concernant l'affaire du duc de Fitz-James."
22. Ibid., p. 2280.
23. Beik, *Absolutism and Society*, pt. 4. The following discussion relies primarily on the account in Georges Frêche, *Toulouse et la région Midi-Pyrénées au siècle des lumières (vers 1670–1789)* (Paris, 1974), pp. 579–611.

A canal connecting the Atlantic Ocean with the Mediterranean had long been contemplated, perhaps as early as Roman times. Serious discussion about the venture began in the sixteenth century, when various individuals approached the crown with a scheme to utilize the waters of the Ariège River to create a canal running from the Garonne to a Mediterranean port. There were, however, many technical obstacles to this scheme, obstacles that might have doomed the project forever if it were not for the fact that in the seventeenth century landowners and notables in Languedoc began to look upon its economic possibilities with greater interest. For with the spread of American corn in the region as a basic food source, there was now a surplus of wheat but little means for export. Lower Languedoc, chronically grain-starved, was one potential market, but landowners and merchants set their sights on the whole Mediterranean basin as well.

It took the resources, knowhow, and energy of Pierre-Paul Riquet, a wealthy tax farmer from Béziers, to bring the plan to fruition. Intimately acquainted with the province's geography, Riquet realized that there were enough streams, rivulets, and springs in the Black Mountain region to create two reservoirs that could serve as the canal's water source, thus obviating the expensive and technically unfeasible task of tapping the Garonne, Aude, and Ariège rivers. By 1662, Riquet had won the support of the archbishop of Toulouse, who introduced him to Colbert, who in turn looked favorably on the canal both commercially, as an outlet for the province's grain, and militarily, as an easy water route between the Atlantic and Mediterranean which would avoid the enemy sea-lanes around the Iberian peninsula.

Work began on the canal in 1662; it opened for navigation in 1682. Formally named the Canal Royal des Deux Mers, the enterprise was not solely or even for the most part a royal undertaking, for it was financed mostly with resources drawn from the region. As the intendant D'Aguesseau revealed in his report of 1684, over half of the funding was supplied by the estates of Languedoc, and 12 percent was contributed by Riquet himself. Riquet's contribution did not originate from his personal fortune, however; he borrowed extensively, and the identities of his backers give us a better appreciation of the province's role in the undertaking. Among Riquet's largest investors were three financiers of Languedoc, a magistrate in the Parlement of Toulouse, and a former capitoul. The rest were also from the region.

In addition, the members of the royal commission appointed to study the project in the 1680s were all regional notables, including the archbishop of Toulouse and the eight capitouls. As Georges Frêche has shown in his illuminating study of the Canal du Midi, the officials who participated most eagerly in its planning and financing were those drawn primarily from the Toulouse region, for it was western upper Languedoc, the Ukraine of France, that stood to gain most from its realization.

Provincial elites were not always so willing to cooperate with Colbert in his efforts to improve France's commercial capabilities. As Frederic C. Lane showed in a classic article on the wine trade of Bordeaux, merchants and notables often had to be coerced into funding new enterprises, in this case a shipping company that could compete with Dutch traders.[24] And, as has been noted, on two occasions the capitouls of Toulouse were bullied into contributing to royal companies. The example of the Canal du Midi, however, presents us with a case of regional notables voluntarily cooperating with the crown, and among themselves, in a venture designed to bring prosperity to their province. Even with the advent of absolutism, royal power could appear benevolent and salutary to provincial elites, many of whom in other contexts found themselves stripped of their traditional privileges.

Not only did the creation of the Canal du Midi provide an occasion for local elites to cooperate in a royal enterprise serving their region; the grain trade it fostered also turned their interests toward national vistas. Not only did mercantilism serve landowners by opening up wider markets for their goods; over the years it also worked to change the thinking of certain authorities, in particular the parlementaires, about the nature of trade and their duties toward the local populace. For generations local grain policy had been governed by the principle of protection. By the second half of the eighteenth century, however, an important change had set in: the magistrates of the parlement, in part encouraged by royal ministers, in part motivated by their own economic interests, turned away from this principle, embracing rather a policy of free trade, thus contradicting both the municipal mercantilism of the capitouls and the sentiments of an often hungry populace.

---

24. Frederic C. Lane, "Colbert and the Commerce of Bordeaux," in *Venice and History* (Baltimore, 1966), pp. 311–30.

In order to appreciate the dimensions of this shift, we need to remind ourselves how entrenched the tradition of protection was in both the practices of local authorities and the expectations of the populace. Perhaps there was no greater obligation facing the authorities in the Old Regime than that of ensuring an adequate grain supply in times of dearth. The concern was not, of course, for the virtue of charity but for the necessity of public order. Indeed, increasingly in the eighteenth century, it was the protective measures and emergency provisioning of civic authorities which took the place of old-style Christian charity. When grain shortage threatened, officials traditionally relied upon a battery of policing actions. In 1720, for example, the capitouls forbade the transport and sale of grain anywhere but in the city or its banlieue.[25] And in 1734 they mustered the city militia to ensure that local stores of grain were transported directly to the central market, La Pierre, and "not to the Canal."[26] On other occasions their ordinances were directed at the so-called monopolists, the hoarders of grain whose nefarious dealings were always suspect in times of dearth.[27] One man's monopolist, of course, was another's good businessman; and what was considered pernicious hoarding in days of want was merely normal stockpiling in times of plenty. The capitouls, however, as well as the populace, had a more dogmatic view of things. For them, shortages and price rises were willful, explained by the unnatural, even unholy actions of the monopolists, those veritable enemies of humanity. The "Annales" noted in 1736: "Avarice and greed for gain are such dangerous passions and so serious that they strip those who are possessed by them of their humanity. They lead to famine because of the monopolies which these people create in order to make usurious profits from the necessities of life."[28] Pierre Barthès, a master tutor of Latin whose eigh-

---

25. Jack Thomas, "Economie politique des marchés: L'Ancien Régime," a chapter of his thesis, "La vie des foires et des marchés dans le Midi toulousain, 1750–1914" (Université de Toulouse-Mirail, 1989), p. 17. On the grain trade in the eighteenth century, see Charles Tilly, "Food Supply and Public Order in Modern Europe," in *The Formation of National States in Western Europe* (Princeton, 1975), pp. 380–455, and *The Contentious French*, chap. 4; Louise Tilly, "The Food Riot as a Form of Political Conflict in France," *Journal of Interdisciplinary History* 2 (1971): 23–57; Steven L. Kaplan, *Bread, Politics and Political Economy in the Reign of Louis XV*, 2 vols. (The Hague, 1976), and *Provisioning Paris* (Ithaca, 1984).

26. Thomas, "Economie politique," p. 40.

27. Ibid., p. 30.

28. AMT, BB 283, p. 366.

teenth-century diary is a primary source on the city's public life, echoed the popular view that such "monopoleurs"—"public blood suckers," he called them—were always to blame for grain shortages.[29] Accordingly, the capitouls made sure to police the city markets, requiring that only licenced vendors dealt in grain; they increased their surveillance over the guild of official weighers; they sometimes forcibly prevented grain from leaving the city; often they took direct action against the monopolists and speculators who attempted to profit from grain shortages. Ultimately their obligations extended to scouring the region for available food supplies in order to provision a hungry urban populace. In short, their actions, often encouraged by a riotous crowd, aimed to prevent the free flow of grain.

Ideally, these actions were backed by the authority of parlement; and indeed, on several occasions right down to the Revolution, the royal magistrates found themselves squarely on the side of protectionism and such municipal mercantilist policies. But in the 1760s their views on the grain trade took a decided turn away from traditional municipal policy and popular expectations. Several factors stand behind this shift in mentality. For one, there was the spread of physiocratic ideas, which vaunted the principle of free trade in opposition to the time-honored notions of protectionism and controlled markets. And as some of the more intellectually cosmopolitan individuals in the region, the parlementaires were particularly receptive to such advanced, enlightened views. For another, there was a change in royal policy itself, first the declaration of May 25, 1763, which guaranteed the free circulation of grain throughout the realm, and then the rise to ministerial power of Turgot and the physiocrats. Finally, and perhaps most important, there were the material interests of the parlementaires themselves, who to a person were large landowners deep in the grain trade. How else to explain the fact that the parlementary magistrates of Toulouse were among the most vocal partisans for the principle of free trade in all of France?

But such a stance often placed the parlement in direct opposition to the capitouls. In 1766, for example, the capitouls ruled to limit the number of vendors of grain who could operate in La Pierre, aiming by this regulation to prevent the invasion of the city's market by export brokers. The parlement immediately countermanded this ruling, not

29. BMT, MS 704, p. 66.

only asserting that the capitouls lacked the authority to regulate trade in such a fashion, but more significant, backing their position with a principled defense of free trade. "Commerce," they declared, "is the source of public happiness." And by "commerce" they meant that of an unfettered kind. On another occasion, the sovereign court's stance led it to contravene the actions of the sénéchal of Rodez, which in 1770 had attempted to regulate the amount of grain stockpiled by individual vendors. Again the parlement broke this time-honored, local ordinance, and again it based its ruling not only on the principle of free trade but also on the royal declaration of 1763. A year later, however, the court found itself at odds with a now-reversed royal policy, for with the ascendancy of Terray to ministerial power, the crown had once again embraced protectionist measures. The Parlement of Toulouse refused to register the royal letters patent ordering a return to the status quo with regard to the grain trade, and it was joined in its refusal by the courts of Bordeaux, Aix-en-Provence, and Dauphiné.[30]

Although in subsequent years the sovereign court of Toulouse was forced to back down from its free-trade stance, its fundamental orientation had been made clear on a number of occasions. In the face of tradition, popular pressures, municipal policy, and royal edicts, the parlementaires embraced a rather advanced and certainly unpopular position of free trade for the most essential commodity that the province of Languedoc produced. For our purposes, their position signaled a shift in the social orientation of these elites in two respects. First, like their opposition to the crown over religious and fiscal issues, the parlementaires' free-trade position placed them in concert with other elements in the realm whose vistas were national, not primarily local. Second, the parlement's new policy meant a severing of the moral ties that traditionally bound urban authorities to the populace, especially in times of dearth. In both respects, the shift contributed to the emerging cosmopolitanism taking hold over Toulouse's public life in the eighteenth century.

An Indigent Populace

If the orientation of Toulouse's elite was shifting in response to royal challenges and new economic opportunities, there also emerged social

---

30. Thomas, pp. 70–73; Kaplan, *Bread, Politics, and Political Economy*, 2:586–90. Kaplan also notes the important disagreements among the parlements on this issue (1:155.)

forces that contributed to a parallel development—an increasingly divided city in the eighteenth century. This development was more than a matter of landowning elites, particularly magistrates, turning away from the traditional protectionism that favored a hungry populace. It entailed a whole range of factors that in the eighteenth century conspired to create the conditions of increased rootlessness, vagabondage, poverty, and social protest sometimes leading to large-scale rioting. The poor were a ubiquitous presence on the urban scene throughout the Old Regime, as I have noted several times, but in the century before the Revolution social conditions degenerated markedly, creating an increased subpopulace of both indigent migrants and resident poor. Although urban society was as factionalized as ever along professional and corporate lines, it was the division between the poor and the well provisioned that more and more defined the nature of the social order.[31]

Several factors contributed to the rise in social misery. Probably the most important was the price inflation that set in at the end of the seventeenth century and continued until the eve of the Revolution. From about 1650 to 1690 grain in the Toulouse region remained relatively cheap, between four and five livres for a *setier* of wheat. These depressed prices, combined with the absence of plague since the epidemic of 1653, allowed the people of Toulouse to avoid the "crisis of the seventeenth century," at least for a few decades. But between 1690 and 1692 the price of grain doubled; and in the space of a few months in 1694 prices rose to three times their 1690 level. Again, in 1709–10, prices shot up to three times what they had been in the first half of 1709. After a period of relative price stability (still not at the level of 1689–90), wheat regained the prohibitively high cost it had attained in 1709. Within a little more than twenty years Toulouse had experienced three abrupt and brutal price increases affecting not only wheat but also other grains and vitals.[32] At mid-century, grain prices again shot up precipitously: between 1746 and 1747 the increase was more than twofold, setting the stage for some of the worst rioting in the city's history. And similar price rises continued to afflict the

---

31. On the problem of poverty in eighteenth-century France, see Jean-Pierre Gutton, *La société et les pauvres: L'exemple de la généralité de Lyon* (Paris, 1971); Olwen Hufton, *The Poor of Eighteenth-Century France, 1750–1789* (Oxford, 1974); Cissie Fairchilds, *Poverty and Charity in Aix-en-Provence* (Baltimore, 1976); and Kathyrn Norberg, *Rich and Poor in Grenoble, 1600–1814* (Berkeley, 1985).

32. Frêche, pp. 99–107; Wolff, pp. 305–9.

Toulouse region for the balance of the Old Regime, especially in the 1770s and on the eve of the Revolution.[33]

The immediate explanation for these price increases was a series of crop failures due to the "seasons being out of joint," or so people and authorities alike assumed. One year it was the incessant rains, flooding, and hail storms; another, it was the excessive heat. Accordingly, the city staged processions imploring God to curb his ire and return the seasons to their normal course. But although the climate of Languedoc certainly had an adverse effect on local harvests, another, man-made factor contributed to the province's lack of grain: the Canal du Midi. While providing landowners and merchants with wider markets, the canal also drained grain from the region, beyond the reach of ordinary people. Moreover, the pace of grain exportation was driven by the free-trade sentiments of royal and parlementary officials, who argued that, since grain was the major, almost sole, source of Languedoc's wealth, its export must continue even in times of dearth.[34]

This policy explains why Toulouse was the scene of grain riots even as grain was being stockpiled in the provincial capital. There was an abundance of grain, but it was grain waiting to be shipped out on the Canal du Midi. To the authorities, this influx of grain into Toulouse argued against the legitimacy of the crowd's complaint. "In fact," noted one official in a report to the crown following a series of riots in the late seventeenth century, "there is lack neither of wheat nor of bread. Wheat constantly passes through the suburbs of Toulouse on the canal; it is quite expensive, but a little less than in the vicinity, and it is not the dearth that causes the uprisings."[35] What authorities either failed or refused to understand is that even though the supply of grain was relatively plentiful in Toulouse as compared with the countryside, prices were controlled and constantly pushed upward by the demands of a national market. As Georges Frêche has shown, by the end of the seventeenth century, prices in Toulouse were escalating in tempo with those of Paris. And after 1740 the local price rise even outpaced that experienced in the capital.[36]

33. Frêche, pp. 692–93.
34. AN, G7 295 (Mémoire pour la sortie des graines avec franchises, 1673); Frêche, p. 758; Le Roy Ladurie, The Peasants of Languedoc, p. 448.
35. AN, G7, 302, Letter of Abrancout to the crown, 5 May 1694.
36. Frêche, pp. 692–93. See also Louise Tilly, "The Food Riot as a Form of Political Conflict in France," p. 47.

But despite this dangerous inflationary trend, the populace proved less vulnerable to the crisis mortalities that had so often afflicted it in previous times of dearth. The last "Old-Regime crisis" was in 1751, when, in accordance with this well-documented pattern, the rise in prices was matched by an equally precipitous increase in deaths.[37] Subsequent crises were of a new type, where dramatic increases in grain prices created misery, vagabondage, and deep discontent, but not widespread mortality. By the mid-eighteenth century, in short, the Malthusian cycle had been broken: population now increased because food supply was more plentiful, or at least increasingly available, owing to improved transportation, distribution, and more effective emergency provisioning.[38]

For the city of Toulouse, however, the end to the Malthusian cycle had somewhat complicated results. It did not directly lead to a dramatic increase in population; deaths continued to surpass births on the order of 22,000 for the century between 1695 and 1789.[39] The city did experience a modest demographic rise in the course of the century, however, owing to migration. One local historian has calculated that 37,000 migrants made their way to Toulouse during this period.[40] Some were craftsmen drawn to the provincial capital by the booming luxury and building trades, others were simple laborers recruited to work on various public projects such as the Canal de Brienne or the construction of new quays, esplanades, and plazas. Most, it seems, were rural indigents seeking sustenance. And it is these impoverished migrants who most troubled the resident populace, disturbed the public peace, and fostered by their collective presence a new level of intolerance for the wandering poor.

Legions of peasants became migrants and vagabonds, not simply because of price inflation, but also because of changes in the coun-

37. Wolff, *Histoire*, pp. 339–40; Jean Rives, "L'évolution démographique de Toulouse au XVIIIᵉ siècle," *Bullétin d'Histoire Économique et Sociale de la Révolution Française*, 1968, pp. 119–120. On this subject, see the classic works of Goubert, *Beauvais et les beauvaisis*; Le Roy Ladurie, *Les paysans de Languedoc*; and Jean Meuvret, *Le problème des subsistances à l'époque de Louis XIV*, 2 vols. (Paris, 1977).

38. Rives, p. 120. On eighteenth-century demography and agriculture, see F. Braudel and C. E. Labrousse, eds., *Histoire économique et sociale de la France aux XVIIᵉ et XVIIIᵉ siècles* (Paris, 1970); Michel Morineau, "Y a-t-il une révolution agricole en France au XVIIIᵉ siècle?" *Revue Historique*, no. 237 (1967): 299–326. For a model demographic study of an eighteenth-century urban center, see Jean-Pierre Bardet, *Rouen aux XVIIᵉ et XVIIIᵉ siècles*, 2 vols. (Paris, 1983).

39. Coppolani, *Toulouse*, p. 102.

40. Ibid., p. 103.

tryside, which squeezed the basis of their subsistence and sometimes dispossessed them of their lands. Commercial agriculture, in short, was reshaping the rural economy. The opportunities of an increasingly lucrative market economy, especially in grain, prompted landlords to run their farms more efficiently. Economic efficiency, however, usually spelled hardship for tenants. Landowners enclosed once-open fields, eliminated common grazing rights, extended their ownership over marginal lands, and often foreclosed on indebted tenants.[41] And in all of this they were backed by the Parlement of Toulouse, which in a series of rulings affirmed landowners' absolute right to private property.[42] Though peasants sometimes contested these moves toward "agrarian individualism," more often than not they were forced to adapt to the new regime and increasingly turned to wage labor for their livelihood. But here too there was hardship, for the rise in population depressed wages in the course of the century. And while many small landowners attempted to adapt to the market economy by turning their plots to viticulture, their strategy ultimately fell victim to overproduction and a fall in the price of wine. Finally, in addition to these economic forces, natural disasters took their toll in misery and uprootedness. In the 1770s, for example, the region was hit by animal distemper, which decimated the peasantry's livestock. A series of bad winters in the last three decades of the Old Regime caused the loss of many crops and destroyed large numbers of olive groves. These and other factors transformed many peasants into the wandering poor.[43]

Immigrants normally made up the majority of confined paupers in the Hôpital de la Grave, and thus an increase in their numbers is one indication of the rise of the influx of poor into Toulouse. In 1736 there were 593 inmates in La Grave; in 1759, there were 1,400; in 1778, 2,219; and in 1782, 2,600.[44] The registers of the hospital for the sick, the Hôtel-Dieu, also give evidence of this high rate of immigration. Between 1752 and 1790, over two-thirds of those who died in the hospital were from outside the city, and half of them were from

---

41. Tilly, *The Contentious French*, pp. 195–200; Jean Bastier, *La féodalité au siècle des lumières dans la région de Toulouse* (Paris, 1975), pp. 290–93.

42. Colin Jones, *Charity and Bienfaisance: The Treatment of the Poor in the Montpellier Region, 1740–1815* (Cambridge, 1982), p. 31. For a skeptical view of the success of agrarian individualism in the eighteenth century, see Hilton Root, *Peasants and King in Burgundy* (Berkeley, 1987).

43. Jones, p. 34; *Affiches et annonces de Toulouse pour l'année 1775*, pp. 2–3, 38.

44. Rives, p. 131; Buchalet, *L'assistance publique*, p. 52.

beyond the diocese of Toulouse.[45] A local researcher has calculated
with some precision that economic hard times and the influx of the
rural poor were indeed closely linked. For years of crisis—when
prices were high and grain in short supply—the deaths of foreigners
to Toulouse in the Hôtel-Dieu accounted for 75 percent of those registered; by contrast, in "good" years the share was markedly lower, 60
percent.[46] With the arrival of rural indigents came an increase in
abandoned infants, for one cause of such migration was the flight to
the city of unwed pregnant peasant girls. Here again, the increase
was dramatic. While in the first half of the century the percentage of
births with "mother and father unknown" hovered around 10 percent of those registered in the city, after 1750 the figure rose to 17
percent, reaching 25 percent in the years leading up to the Revolution. In the lower-class suburban parish of Saint-Pierre de Cuisine
nearly 40 percent of all children born between 1750 and 1792 were
abandoned.[47] Even the wealthy parish of Saint-Etienne was not
spared this scourge: while in 1725 and 1750 the rate of infants born to
unknown parents was 6.3 and 7.5 percent, respectively, in 1775 the
figure shot up to 17.7 percent.[48]

People in difficult straits flocked to the big city for various reasons.
There village girls could escape the shame of unwed motherhood and
dispose of their babies in the hope that they would be cared for as
foundlings; there poor relief was available in the Hôpital de la Grave
and other institutions; and there rural beggars could escape the dragnet of the maréchaussée, which in 1768, under a royal order, began to
round up the itinerant poor.[49] But once in the city, life was hardly
pleasant for these desperate immigrants: unwed mothers who abandoned their infants were subject to arrest; confined paupers were put
to a strict regime of hard labor, short rations, and heavy-handed
Christian indoctrination; and periodically the Watch would forcibly
empty the city of the homeless poor. The resident poor had it little
better than their immigrant counterparts. Urban crowding grew more
severe in the eighteenth century. In the Cité the density of urban
settlement increased 22.7 percent between 1695 and the Revolution;
in the Bourg the increase was 36 percent; and in the popular quarter

45. Rives, p. 132.
46. Rives, p. 133.
47. Wolff, Histoire, p. 339.
48. AMT, GG 302, 327, 752.
49. AMT, BB 284, p. 106. See also Hufton, The Poor, pp. 219–244.

of Saint-Cyprien on the Garonne's left bank, it was 34.6 percent in the same period.[50] It was not uncommon to find eight families plus a tradesman's shop crammed into a three-story house.[51] And, according to Barthès, the shortage of wood in winter was so serious that many artisans were forced to burn their furniture for heat.[52] In difficult times, then, all sorts of people, not only poor immigrants, found themselves forced to resort to extraordinary means to sustain themselves—public relief, crime, rioting, or begging. It was the last that proved the most burdensome to the populace on a daily basis. An anonymous report in 1778 attacked the growing hordes of vagrants as "public enemies against which any government has the right to defend itself with rigor":

> Toulouse is one of the cities most infected by this vermin; one sees them in the streets, in public squares, in churches and houses. One cannot leave without being surrounded and harassed from every side. One is struck by their cries, by groups of them wailing in passageways, especially at certain times. They present a hideous, disgusting spectacle to citizens, insufferable because of their importunity . . . worthy of compassion if they are truly poor but only indignation if they beg out of laziness and without need.[53]

Barthès echoed the insecurity shared by his neighbors, decrying the "mass of tricksters and vagabonds who, under the pretext of asking for alms, manage to enter houses in broad daylight, and, pistol at one's throat, extort from the timid and even people of distinction."[54] An increase in crime was indeed one result of the rise in indigency, and so too, as we shall see, was the periodic rioting that plagued Toulouse in the eighteenth century.

The eighteenth-century city, in short, was increasingly polarized between the well-provided and the crowds of poor and hungry, and perceptions of the urban social order began to reflect this polarization. I am suggesting that this sharply defined social division—often fraught with fear and violence—was one factor in the transformation of public life in the last century of the Old Regime. Other factors were

50. Coppolani, p. 99.
51. Castan, Les criminels de Languedoc (Toulouse, 1980), p. 261.
52. BMT, MS 701, p. 156.
53. Quoted in Jacques Vedel, "La consommation dans le Haut-Languedoc aux XVIIᵉ siècles" (Thèse de doctorat, 3ᵉ cycle, Université de Toulouse-Mirail, 1973), p. 378.
54. BMT, MS 703, p. 182.

at play: the increasing intrusiveness of royal power in municipal government, the emergence of a parlementary opposition conscious of its
place on the national scene, an awareness of the advantages absolutist policies could bear, and a more market-oriented perspective on
the part of landed elites who thus in effect broke with any allegiance
to the notion of a moral economy. These transformations ultimately
recast Toulouse's public life in the eighteenth century, a recasting that
will become apparent in the following chapters. But can these transformations be understood as a coherent whole, or are they merely a
grab bag of changes often found in the course of social and political
development? Indeed, to borrow from Charles Tilly's conceptualiza-
tion of the twin forces behind modern development in France and
elsewhere, these transformations fall into either the process of state
making or the changes inherent in nascent capitalism.[55] The imposition of royal control over Toulouse's city government and the dialec-
tics of the parlement's resistance to absolutist authority were different
aspects of state making in late seventeenth- and eighteenth-century
France. The creation of the Canal du Midi was a prime example of
mercantilism, another feature of state making. And both the broaden-
ing of landed elites' economic horizons and the social pressures creating increased vagrancy and poverty were part and parcel of the pro-
cesses of commercial development in a capitalist mode. These fundamental, large-scale social and political transformations also contributed to a breakdown in traditional associational patterns, a decline in
local culture, and a general recasting of public life.

55. Tilly, *The Contentious French.*

10

A Divided City

One of the enduring myths in social science is that formulated by the late-nineteenth-century German sociologist Ferdinand Tönnies, who put forth the notion that as society becomes "modern" it experiences a breakdown of community, the disintegration of the communal ties found in families, villages, and guilds, and develops rather in the direction of a larger, impersonal agglomeration of atomistic individuals. Hence the Gemeinschaft-Gesellschaft formulation. It is a myth not because it lacks foundation—indeed, clearly it captures something essential about historical development, thus its enduring appeal—but because it disguises the complex and varied trends that combined to form modern societies. Moreover, it posits a terminus a quo and a terminus ad quem that are misleading caricatures of social realities: premodern societies were rarely cohesive, strifeless communities, whereas modern life is hardly bereft of communal ties emerging from the contexts of family, work, neighborhood, and the like. Whatever the validity of Tönnies's view, however, much of contemporary historical research has in some way been engaged in the investigation of society's evolution along the lines he suggested. And much of what we have learned about the early modern period, at least, has revealed social dissolution on several levels. For example, starting in the sixteenth century, village society became increasingly fragmented between landless laborers and more prosperous peasants. The spread of literacy, religious reform, and other acculturating forces created a cultural divide in many communities. And patron-client relationships between great noblemen and lesser elites tended

to break down as the state imposed its monopoly over the mecha-
nisms of legal and administrative authority.[1]

As might be expected, the early modern city was even more prone
to social and cultural fragmentation than rural society; indeed, a
range of fundamental divisions would seem to characterize urban life
by its very nature. But in late-fifteenth- and early-sixteenth-century
Toulouse there emerged a new elite of royal magistrates and wealthy
merchants that further complicated the city's social structure, creating
an urban order now dominated socially and culturally by an imposing
upper class. The appearance of this elite, however, did not put an end
to meaningful ties and associations between the upper and lower
classes, nor did it entail an upper-class withdrawal from local affairs.
Much of this book has been devoted to proving the validity of this last
statement.

Like the sixteenth, the eighteenth century was an era of heightened
elite self-consciousness, but in the latter century the interests and
behavior of urban elites turned largely away from their city and its
populace. The next chapter documents elements of the cosmopolitan
culture which emerged in the century before the Revolution. For now
we must examine a parallel development: the weakening of those
enterprises that heretofore had fostered vertical social contact, compounded by the mounting social conflict and violence that increasingly characterized class relations. The cosmopolitan city, in short,
was also a divided one.

Urban Sociability: The Breakdown of Vertical Ties

A range of activities, many of them religious in nature, traditionally
involved people from different classes and professions. In public ceremonies everyone from artisans to royal magistrates and ecclesiastical
hierarchs had a role as essential and honored participants. Many lay

---

1. To pursue the theme of social and cultural breakdown in the early modern period,
see, for example, Le Roy Ladurie, *Les paysans de Languedoc*, and K. Wrightson and D.
Levine, *Poverty and Piety in an English Village* (New York, 1979), on the division of
peasant society between the prosperous and the poor; Robert Muchembled, *Culture
populaire et culture des élites dans la France moderne* (Paris, 1978), and Peter Burke, *Popular
Culture in Early Modern Europe* (New York, 1978), on the formation of two cultures; and
Robert Harding, *Anatomy of a Provincial Elite* (New Haven, 1978), and Jonathan Dewald,
Pont-St.-Pierre (Berkeley, 1988), on the diminishing ties between nobles and their
clients.

confraternities recruited members from across the social spectrum and thus transformed the lowborn and upperclass alike into confrères. It was not uncommon for the rich and powerful to offer themselves as the godparents of the children of craftsmen; and some elite Toulousains even selected paupers of the hospital as godparents for their own children. Poor relief as well was an enterprise that drew upon the charitable energies of upper-class dévots, bringing them into contact, sometimes quite intimate contact, with the poor, especially during the Counter-Reformation. The eighteenth century, however, witnessed a diminished effectiveness of these activities in fostering association and solidarity across the social spectrum.

General Processions

Until about the mid-eighteenth century, citywide processions were the most important and largest of Toulouse's public ceremonies. They massed thousands of its inhabitants in the streets—representatives from every level of society—and attracted thousands more as spectators, many from the surrounding countryside.[2] The general procession was mounted for holy days, the births and deaths of monarchs, France's victories on the battlefield, and during times of natural emergencies. The greatest of these gatherings was on May 17, to commemorate the massacre of Toulouse's Huguenots in 1562 and the so-called deliverance of the city. It was this ceremony Voltaire dubbed "the procession to thank God for four thousand murders."[3]

Even for this most important event on the city ceremonial calendar, the eighteenth century saw a turn away from participation in the procession on the part of various groups. As early as 1703, the parlement had to issue a decree against four religious orders for failing to occupy their rank and carry their assigned holy relics in the ceremony.[4] In the seventeenth century, one local historian has noted, such reprimands were rare; in the eighteenth century they became routine.[5] In 1736 it was the locksmiths, carpenters, and glaziers who

---

2. In the eighteenth century the Fête-Dieu processions attracted 40,000 spectators and visitors (Castan, *Les criminels de Languedoc* [Toulouse, 1980], p. 263).

3. Quoted in Greengrass, "The Anatomy of a Religious Riot in Toulouse in May 1562," p. 367, and in Christie, *Dolet*, p. 52.

4. AMT, GG 789, "Arrêt du Parlement de Toulouse portant injonction à tous les ordres religieux de la ville de se rendre à l'église abbatiale de S. Sernin le 17 et le jour de la Pentcôte de chaque année pour assister aux processions. . . ."

5. Cassan, "La fête à Toulouse," p. 228.

were prosecuted by the capitouls for failing in their obligation to carry the busts of several saints.[6] Two years later, a royal order noted that the general procession of August 15 had been neglected by the city.[7] In 1741, several artisan guilds again refused to carry the city's relics.[8] In 1743 the parlement had to order municipal officials to assemble for the processions on holy days.[9] In 1762 the city's surgeons and apothecaries petitioned for an exemption from the ceremony.[10] Such examples could be multiplied. In 1765 a few magistrates apparently even considered abolishing the public ritual because, in their view, it revived religious passions better forgotten.[11] Barthès, always an avid booster of civic and religious ceremonies, sadly admitted in 1771 that the procession of May 17 no longer attracted the legions of rural visitors it had in years past.[12] After 1782 the city cut its expenditures in half for the procession, and the next year the Confraternity of Holy Bodies balked at fulfilling its traditional task of providing the relics of Saint-Sernin for the annual procession.[13] Although Toulouse's eighteenth-century calendar was still punctuated by a variety of processions, it seems clear that there was an erosion of support for that ceremonial display that had long symbolized the urban community.

Confraternities

Like elsewhere in urban France, lay confraternities experienced a decline in popularity in eighteenth-century Toulouse.[14] As previously noted, a number of different confraternities were founded in the course of the Wars of Religion and the Counter-Reformation, and the

6. ADH-G, C 309; AMT, BB 283, p. 367.

7. Cassan, p. 232.

8. Ibid.

9. GG 789; Cassan, p. 228.

10. Pierre Barranguet-Loustalot, "La pratique et le sentiment religieux dans le diocèse de Toulouse au milieu et à la fin du XVIIIe siècle" (Mémoire maîtrise, Université de Toulouse, 1953), p. 70.

11. Ibid., p. 134.

12. BMT, MS 704, pp. 155–56; MS 705, p. 100; Bien, The Calas Affair (Princeton, 1960), p. 174.

13. Bien, Calas; AMT, C 309.

14. On the general decline of confraternities, see Bossy, "The Counter-Reformation and the People of Catholic Europe"; Agulhon, Pénitents et francs-maçons; John McManners, French Ecclesiastical Society under the Ancien Régime: A Study of Angers in the Eighteenth Century (Manchester, 1960), p. 124. On the vitality of confraternities in some eighteenth-century settings, see Timothy Tackett, Priest and Parish in Eighteenth-Century France (Princeton, 1977), pp. 194–202.

sociability and activities they fostered marked public life for much of the early modern period. In the eighteenth century no new confraternities were established. Other associations, such as learned academies and Freemason lodges, claimed the allegiance of the city's elite. Pierre Deyon observed how elites in Amiens began to withdraw from confraternities, thus contributing to their weakening and decline.[15] This is something already apparent in late-seventeenth-century Toulouse. For example, before the Confraternity of the Annunciation in the Church of Nazareth was reconstituted in the early seventeenth century, it had exclusively served a group of textile workers and their masters. In the following decades this craft association was taken over by an assortment of parlementaires, officers, professionals, and merchants. By the latter part of the century, however, the rolls of the confraternity once again revealed a predominance of clothworkers, the more socially prominent confrères having withdrawn.[16] In the case of the Confraternity of the Assumption, the process was reversed. Here the association went from a rather mixed membership, with artisans making up over 30 percent in the mid-seventeenth century, to one that exhibited a rather feeble participation of the lower classes, and this despite a high number of enrollees in the 1690s.[17]

Other confraternities demonstrated a decline in vitality during the eighteenth century. The Confraternity of Saint James, the brotherhood of pilgrims to Compostella and one of the oldest in the city, underwent a reform in mid-century that effectively excluded the membership from directing the confraternity, placing its control in the hands of a new council of fourteen confrères and limiting the number of general assemblies.[18] The records of several venerable confraternities exhibit a decline in either membership or annual receipts, most the result of confrères' dues (fig. 5). The Confraternity of the Blessed Bread, for example, went from 862 members in the latter part of the seventeenth century to 309 in the mid-eighteenth.[19] In the Church of the Dalbade the Confraternity of the Holy Sacrament, another brotherhood with a long history, suffered such declining enroll-

---

15. Pierre Deyon, *Amiens: Capitale provinciale* (Paris, 1967), p. 379.

16. ADH-G, E 833, Confraternity of Our Lady of the Annunciation.

17. ADH-G, E 820, "Libre de table Notre-Dame de la Sumption de l'Eglise de la Daurade."

18. ADH-G, E 836, "Registre des délibérations de la Confrairie St. Jacques commencé le viii aoust 1756."

19. ADH-G, E 870.

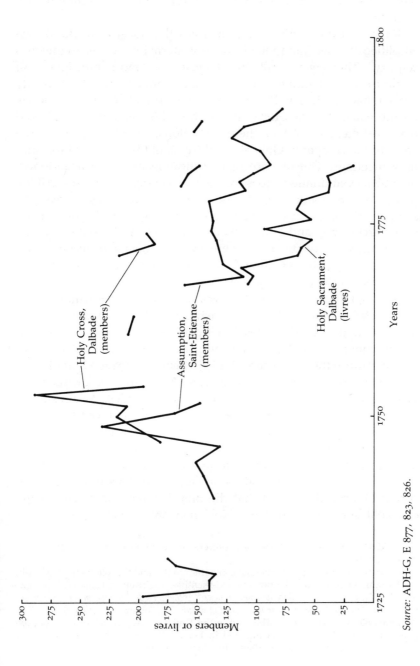

Source: ADH-G, E 877, 823, 826.

FIGURE 5. Decline of three confraternities in eighteenth-century Toulouse

ments that in 1782 it was forced to merge with the Confraternity of
Saint Joseph.[20]

But it was the penitential companies that most dramatically exemplified the declining vitality of confraternal life in the eighteenth
century. They were still the largest and most prestigious of
Toulouse's lay confraternities and had a prominent role in nearly
every religious display. But the fervor they tried to evoke was clearly
on the wane. In 1722, for example, the Blue Penitents complained
that most members, "even the most zealous," had forgotten the true
spirit of the company. Only about thirty could be mustered for ordinary meetings. The practice of mortification had been abandoned;
members even donned shoes for their processional exercises. All the
penitential companies took to introducing secular music played by
symphonic orchestras at their festive gatherings, which drew the ire
of the archbishop and other devout observers. And it seems that by
mid-century many penitents were even indulging in alcoholic re-
freshments—"boissons rafraichissantes"—during their processional
excursions in the countryside.[21]

Most significant, membership was down in the companies. Once
an association of more than 1,000 members, the Blues had declined to
half that number by the 1770s. The financial problems of all the penitential companies reflected this drop in membership. In the eighteenth century they were chronically in debt: by 1778 the Blues had to
borrow 4,500 livres to cover expenses. Not only was membership
down, but many penitents refused to pay their dues. As a result, in
order to increase their treasuries, the companies reduced their standards in accepting new confrères, which only contributed to the decline in penitential zeal. Perhaps the most direct testimony of the
decline of the penitents comes to us by way of the observations of
Mrs. Cradock, an English lady who stopped in Toulouse in the late
spring of 1785. She noted that the Blue Penitents were one of the
city's oldest religious "orders." Noblemen and often kings were once

20. ADH-G, E 826, "Catalogue des confrères et confrèresses du Très-Saint-Sacrement, La Dalbade."
21. On the decline of the penitential companies in this and the following paragraph,
see Barranguet-Loustalot, "La pratique et le sentiment religieux à Toulouse," pp. 82–
85; ADH-G, E 926, *Ordonnance de Monseigneur l'Archevêque de Toulouse portant règlement
pour les processions des pénitens de ladite ville et du diocèse* (Toulouse, 1749); Ousset, "Les
Pénitents Bleus de Toulouse." The shift in the Toulouse lawyers' allegiance from the
penitents to the Masons is documented in Lenard R. Berlanstein, *The Barristers of
Toulouse in the Eighteenth Century* (Baltimore, 1975), pp. 127–30.

members, "but," she observed, "their composition is no longer the same. Now their processions are comprised mostly of commoners." To her horror, Mrs. Cradock spied her cook, who had just returned from a penitential procession, frolicking with her other servants and sprinkling them "with the same censor and the remains of the holy incense used to bless the Holy Sacrament."[22]

Now it might be said that the decline both in confraternal life and processional participation resulted primarily from the waning faith of many Toulousains under the influence of the Enlightenment, not from any such sociological factor as a breakdown of traditional forms of public life. After all, these two enterprises were largely religious in nature, and thus a growth in secularism presumably would have undermined their vitality. To be sure, the academic and Masonic vogues that swept many elites into their ranks also signaled a general turn toward Enlightenment culture, if not necessarily thought. Was there something, to simplify somewhat, about the enlightened mentality that prompted people to turn away not only from certain religious practices but especially from those involving contact with the general community of believers? Certain research on de-Christianization in the eighteenth century has suggested that it was indeed a disenchantment with collective, particularly ostentatious rituals, rather than a loss of faith, that accounted for demonstrable changes in religious attitudes and practices.[23] In other words, faith was not necessarily on the wane but, among some people, simply becoming more private. Such refined religiosity, it should be pointed out, did not originate with the Enlightenment; it was a product of humanism and its critique of many popular Christian traditions that were seen as vulgar, spiritually distracting, and unbiblical. The Enlightenment, of course, was confronted with a somewhat different Catholicity than were the sixteenth-century humanists: the Counter-Reformation, "baroque" piety that the philosophes denounced as exercises in poor taste and superstition. The question comes down to whether withdrawal by elites from collective devotional exercises, such as confraternal life and processions, can be explained exclusively in terms of

22. *La vie française à la veille de la Révolution. Journal inédit de Madame Cradock: Voyage en France (1783–1786)*, trans. O. Delphin-Balleyquier (Paris, 1911), p. 193.
23. See especially Michel Vovelle, *Piété baroque et déchristianisation en Provence au XVIIIᵉ siècle* (Paris, 1973).

a shift in mentality. The perspective offered here is that while refined, elite forms of culture and religion had long been available to upper-class Toulousains, at least since the Renaissance, it required a shift in political and social conditions, not simply a shift in mentality, to alter the contours of public life. And it was in the eighteenth century that this shift became apparent.

Godparenting

The most striking evidence supporting the breakdown of vertical sociability in the eighteenth century is the change in patterns of godparenting. As I noted for the seventeenth century, most godparenting relations were struck between people of the same social class, if not the same profession, occupation, or family. But a significant number of such ties were created across class lines—up to a third in the seventeenth century—and this I have taken to be added proof of the vertical sociability then common. In the eighteenth century, however, this sort of cross-class godparenting vanished (table 12). Moreover, the willingness seen in the seventeenth century of some elites to select the poor as godparents of their infants also disappeared in the eighteenth.

Poor Relief

The area of poor relief presents a less clear-cut case of a breakdown of vertical ties than these other experiences. On the one hand, the

TABLE 12

Godparents of children of artisans, domestics, and workers in the parishes of Saint-Etienne and Dalbade, 1750 and 1775

	Saint-Etienne		Dalbade
	1750	1775	1775
Artisans, domestics, and workers	106	60	18
Merchants	11	11	3
Lawmen, low officers, students, medical men	11	6	3
High officers and nobles	1	1	0

Note: The low figures for 1775 are a result of a lack of notation for godparents in most of the entries.
Source: AMT, GG 61, 327, 352.

confinement of the poor continued in the Hôpital de la Grave throughout the eighteenth century, and the number of inmates there increased
notably toward the end of the century. Also in the years before the
Revolution, attempts were made to reform the methods of poor relief.
Bureaux de charité were established, which aided impoverished families in their homes by providing them food in times of need. Workshops were set up in various sections of the city. And other sources of
charity, most notably the penitential companies, continued to serve
the poor in the course of the eighteenth century.[24] But on the other, the
traditional poor-relief institutions—those established in the seventeenth century under the influence of the Counter-Reformation—
clearly underwent a crisis. This was most apparent with the general
hospital itself. The crisis began in the last years of the seventeenth
century, when the number of poor migrants to Toulouse increased
dramatically. In 1698 the directors of La Grave refused to accept any
more poor. From 1706 to 1718 the city stopped payment of its annual
pension to the hospital. When the municipal subsidy was continued in
1718, it was only half its original amount. By the end of the second
decade of the century, the institution had accumulated 10,000 livres in
debts. During that period, although many poor were being fed from its
resources, only about 50 were confined at La Grave. Toward the
middle of the century the hospital again attempted to effect the confinement of vagabonds and mendicants: in 1752 there were 2,400
inmates; in 1759, a year of great misery, 1,400. It was this wave of
confinements that ultimately strained the resources of the general
hospital to the breaking point. In 1765, La Grave declared a bankruptcy, and its creditors managed to secure a liquidation of its possessions. In the pamphlet campaign that led up to its failure, one group of
creditors expressed the opinion that "justice must take precedence
over charity."[25]

Although the general hospital managed to recover from its financial
crisis and serve Toulouse as a depository for the poor for the rest of
the Old Regime, it clearly had severe troubles. Moreover, even when
it remained solvent and functioned adequately, it relied primarily

24. On the various instruments of poor relief in the eighteenth century, see M. F.
Buchalet, L'assistance publique à Toulouse au dix-huitième siècle (Toulouse, 1904); Barranguet-Loustalot, "La pratique et le sentiment religieux," pp. 86–91; AMT, BB 284, p.
278, on the ateliers de charité; ADH-G, E 924, 925, 941, 942, 947, 950, 951, 958, on
penitential charity.
25. ADH-G, E 966; Buchalet, L'assistance publique, pp. 74–78.

upon municipal, provincial, and royal subsidies, *rentes*, income from properties, and work by its inmates rather than individual legacies and alms. Throughout the eighteenth century, the portion of the general hospital's annual receipts from gifts and charity remained about 10 percent, rarely going higher, sometimes much less. Most important, starting in 1765, the hospital was subsidized by an annual royal grant of 60,000 livres, a sum representing almost half of its normal expenditures.[26] Financially, then, by the last decades of the Old Regime this major institution was clearly a royally sponsored enterprise.

In any case, there are other reasons for concluding that poor relief then demanded less from townspeople. First, the sorts of confraternities which in the seventeenth century had called upon its members to undertake charitable acts were less widespread in the eighteenth. Second, the general hospital was now largely under the control of the intendant, not lay directors or the city. Third, it was the actual founding of the general hospital, the greatest monument of Counter-Reformation lay activism, that drew upon the commitments of a whole range of elites. Once its founding was accomplished, the subsequent history of La Grave was institutional: it was henceforth in the hands of various authorities—municipal, provincial, and royal—and did not depend upon the extraordinary efforts of lay people. Finally, the hospital itself was staffed in the eighteenth century with orders of nuns who specialized in charity, with professionals, so to speak. In the seventeenth century, by contrast, it was lay groups like the Dames du Saint-Sacrement, the Confraternity of Saint Joseph, or Mme de Mondonville's institute that provided the day-to-day care for the indigent inmates. In short, although poor relief increasingly required additional resources to manage the rising number of poor, it did not require the personal commitment of the laity. Nor did it call forth the heroic sacrifices of lay dévots. Rather, in times of need, the city officials relied mostly upon emergency provisioning as a means of keeping indigency in check.[27]

Crime, Collective Violence, and the Police City

To these examples of the breakdown of social solidarity and cross-class sociability in the eighteenth century, we must add other forms

26. ADH-G, HG 785.
27. BMT, MS 704, p. 204.

of interaction, these, however, of a negative sort. One was a rise of criminality, a phenomenon that has been observed for all of France in the last decades of the Old Regime, especially in larger towns and cities.[28] Although crimes of violence actually declined in the period, the overall number of crimes and particularly crimes against property by the lower classes took a dramatic turn upward, thus contributing to the feelings of insecurity and fear which increasingly set in among the upper classes. What caused this eighteenth-century crime wave takes us back to the social and economic changes that created the conditions of aggravated misery for much of the populace: the mass migration to the city of rural indigents, many of whom had been dispossessed of their lands; the breakdown, under the pressure of new trends in commercial agriculture, of the structures of agrarian communities, and thus the commensurate disintegration of the constraints and supports that had traditionally kept people within the bounds of legality; the steady rise in grain prices, which after 1740 rose at an even greater rate than in Paris, and the periodic subsistence crises that followed in the wake of the most precipitous of these upturns; and the rise in Toulouse's population and the consequent urban crowding, social pressures and tensions. To these we must add the weakening of those forms of vertical interaction and social solidarity that characterized urban sociability for much of the sixteenth and seventeenth centuries. For crime is not only the result of poverty and misery; it is a function also of the collapse of those social patterns and constraints—whether they be understood in terms of deference, charity, clientage, or community—that can deter or inhibit delinquent behavior. And in the eighteenth century many of these patterns and constraints had lost their effectiveness.

That crime was indeed on the rise in eighteenth-century Toulouse has been amply documented by Nicole Castan, the historian of criminality in pre-revolutionary Languedoc. Her research demonstrates that particularly after 1760 crime rose faster in the city than in the countryside. For the province as a whole, the number of crimes doubled between 1760 and 1789.[29] In Toulouse, crimes against property

28. On eighteenth-century criminality in France, see A. Abbiateci, *Crimes et criminalité en France aux XVIIe et XVIIIe siècles* (Paris, 1971); Pierre Deyon, *Le temps des prisons* (Paris, 1975); Nicole Castan, *Les criminels de Languedoc* (Toulouse, 1980), and *Justice et repression en Languedoc à l'époque des lumières* (Paris, 1980); Hufton, *The Poor*, pt. 3; Norberg, *Rich and Poor*, chap. 9.

29. Castan claims that 13.7 percent of thefts can be classified as banditry, (*Les criminels*, p. 237). In Toulouse, criminal decisions issued by the parlement doubled between 1730 and 1786 (Castan, *Justice et repression*, pp. 133–34).

predominated in cases brought before the capitouls; and among those accused of theft, the vast majority were workers, journeymen, servants, and seasonal laborers. One of her most significant findings relates to the numbers of crimes committed in the city by immigrants: among those accused of theft, 57 percent were such outsiders; and in the last years of the Old Regime the figure reached 85 percent.[30] In short, eighteenth-century Toulouse was increasingly burdened by legions of impoverished migrants, many reduced to begging and vagrancy, many too who resorted to theft as a means of subsistence. Official commentary reflected the mounting anxiety about this crime wave. In 1726, the "Annales" resorted to mixed metaphors to express the city's difficulty in coping with crime, likening it to "the hydra of the fable—as soon as its head is struck a crowd of others reemerges from its ashes."[31] The capitouls sat in judgment for crimes committed in the city, but at mid-century they began to despair at both the number of cases brought before them and the depraved nature of the accused. In 1754 they complained that it was nigh impossible to "discern the facts about such illiterate, ill-mannered people."[32] The language of class is striking in the pages of the "Annales" in the eighteenth century, when references to the unruly mob, the myriad crimes committed by the lower classes, and the insecurity of the better sort in the face of rising crime abound.[33] In 1787 it was noted that the great increase in "bad and idle people" would require "more surveillance."[34] From Barthès one gets the sense that the city prisons were bursting at the seams, teeming with rebellious convicts, many of whom indeed managed to escape with the cooperation of corrupt guards. Though a fierce partisan of law and order and the iron fist— he describes with undisguised approval, even glee, the nearly 300 executions and other public punishments meted out to convicts in Toulouse during the forty-three years he kept his journal—Barthès at least acknowledged the connection between the populace's misery and its apparent propensity toward lawlessness.

It is possible, of course, that both these sentiments and the figures on the increase in criminality merely reflect a combination of height-

30. Ibid., p. 9.
31. Ibid., p. 290.
32. AMT, BB 283, p. 196.
33. Ibid., BB 284, p. 316.
34. BMT, MS 703, p. 182.

ened sensitivity to crime and more effective policing measures. As ever, crime is a social fact that results in part, at least, from public perceptions and legal definitions of deviant behavior, and such perceptions and definitions are subject to change. It is quite possible that the eighteenth century witnessed such a change when, in the face of increased vagrancy and poverty, established opinion took a sterner, more fearful view of "disorder" and when the authorities responded to it with more decisive legal measures. Still, it is certain that, whatever the role public opinion and administrative responsiveness played in the perceived increase in crime, disorder did escalate in the eighteenth century, especially collective violence.

This returns us to the issue of the relationship between ruling elites and the crowd, a theme sounded several times in past chapters. Frequently in the sixteenth and seventeenth centuries, episodes of religious riot or collective protest entailed the joint participation of elites and ordinary people. Certainly this was the case during the Wars of Religion; and in the seventeenth century there were also moments when ruling elites were prepared to take up popular grievances against the crown, although they were growing increasingly wary of the wayward potential of the crowd. But even when elites faced a hostile populace, their attitude was likely to be somewhat ambivalent as to their proper role, for the issue that most often prompted popular protest, that of the crushing royal tax burden, was one that touched them too. Through much of the seventeenth century, urban authorities were caught in a Janus-like position, turned in one direction toward a monarchy that could threaten them in a variety of persuasive ways and from which their formal legitimacy ultimately derived, and in another toward a populace that demanded their protection and from which they derived legitimacy of a different sort. Moreover, what was striking about social conflict in the seventeenth century was its relative infrequency: despite the desperate straits of much of the populace, Toulouse was only rarely the scene of popular riots. Beginning in the last decade of the seventeenth century and continuing through the eighteenth, however, we get an entirely different picture of urban social conflict. For it was then that grain riots and other types of collective action increasingly pitted elites against an angry, often desperate urban populace. Let us look at three episodes of such conflict as an illustration of the violence and contention that characterized public life in the last century of the Old Regime, at least at street level.

In May of 1694, increases in grain prices and the demands of the city's bakers prompted authorities to authorize a rise in the maximum price for bread. At this, crowds of hungry women, artisans, and poor invaded the bakers' shops and made away with the available stores of flour. An angry crowd then appeared before the townhouse of the mayor Daspe who noted his surprise that the distribution of alms "did not end their cries."[35] Daspe found himself the target of the crowd's anger not only because of his official capacity as mayor but also because he was widely suspected of hoarding grain. The next day the crowd had grown to over 1,500 persons, a majority of them women, many carrying stones in their skirts, and a number of artisans armed with sticks and knives. The protestors meant business, for they threatened to burn down Daspe's house and seize the Hôtel de Ville. Daspe and several municipal and parlementary officials met at the city hospital to discuss the crisis, but a large crowd sought them out, forcing them to flee. Chased across the Pont Neuf, Daspe's carriage was attacked by a "multitude of rioters who insulted me with a thousand imprecations, crying that they did not want a Mayor and regarding me as the author of their Misery." Daspe escaped unharmed, though two of his servants and two soldiers were wounded in the rock-throwing assault. Two days later, the parlement met to hear Daspe's report on the situation, but again a crowd assembled around the palace, forcing Daspe to retire in the company of three presidents and the court's doyen. This time a further attack on Daspe and the magistrates was met with gunfire, followed by swift and severe parlementary justice. Several women, the presumed leaders of the uprising, were banished from the city and had their property confiscated; another was publicly whipped until "the effusion of blood" and then exiled; one woman was whipped, strangled, and hanged. All of the women accused of crimes during the events of 1694 were wives of laborers.[36]

The riots of 1694 were not isolated incidents. The first price increases in August of the previous year also set off two days of rioting and the pillaging of bakers' supplies. And at the turn of the century the pace of social unrest continued to increase: not since the Wars of Religion had Toulouse been the scene of such popular violence. In

35. AN, G7, 302, Report of Daspe, May 5, 1694.
36. Ibid., "Extrait des régistres de la Cour de Messieurs les Maire et Capitouls de la Ville de Toulouse," 1694.

1700 it was the "lackeys" and other "men of no station" who rioted.[37] When in 1707 the intendant encountered some difficulties in collecting the capitation, thus necessitating the arrival of royal troops, there appeared placards in the street warning First President Riquet to recall that "President Duranty [sic] was killed in Toulouse because he had too zealously supported the king."[38] And again in 1715 it was a new tax on flour that incited the people to violent protest.[39]

After 1740, the price of grain again took a precipitous turn upward, thus throwing large segments of the populace into a state of want. It was this new price rise that set the stage for the rioting and pillaging of 1747, the worst in the city's history since the religious wars. In March of that year the city's tavernkeepers and innkeepers protested the imposition of a new tax on their trade. But it was the events of that winter that brought turmoil to the city. On the last day of November a group of women stretched chains across a main thoroughfare, forcibly halted a cart loaded with wheat as it was passing through the city, and made off with its cargo. They then commandeered a barge stopped on the canal. Soon a vast crowd gathered and, encouraged by the women's actions, proceeded to pillage the stores of a local grain dealer. In an attempt to placate the crowd, the capitouls arrested two suspected speculators, only moments before the rioters would have torn them limb from limb and burnt their houses to the ground. Barthès claimed that between two thousand and three thousand setiers of wheat had been confiscated by the populace, many of whom were injured in the melee. The rioting and pillaging of grain stores continued into the next evening, in part encouraged by the widespread assumption that the arrest of the two grain dealers was tantamount to official endorsement of such popular action.[40] Even after the rioting was put down by the City Watch, the populace continued to seethe with discontent, especially when several of the participants were executed the following month. Then popular sentiment took a millenarial turn. It was said that the sky turned colors over the spot where the cadavers of the executed were displayed, that their "unhappy souls" cried out at night. Crowds began to gather in vigils around the remains of these "martyrs" and people took to possessing bits of their clothing and even skin as sorts of holy

37. AMT, BB 282, p. 283.
38. AN, G7, 309, January 27, 1707.
39. HGL, 13:905.
40. On the riots of 1747, see BMT, MS 699, pp. 252–55; AMT, BB 283, pp. 519–21.

relics. Although the bodies of executed criminals normally remained on display until they rotted, the capitouls decided that it would be wiser to break with tradition and inter them without more delay.[41]

In 1778 the city was again the scene of a large-scale disturbance, this time occasioned not by grain shortages—at least not directly— but by the forced conscription of artisans into the city guard. It appears that one June evening a shoemaker refused to fulfill his obligation to participate in the nightly patrol, claiming fatigue and the misery of his family; his refusal encouraged a strike among his fellow conscripts, who also resented the burden of this "corvée." An angry crowd gathered, only to be met with a parlementary decree forbidding any congregating in public places. The next day, the last of Pentecost, a crowd of strollers got mixed up with the City Watch; a confused movement of people was perceived, cries of alarm were heard, and the panicky militia men charged the gathering. A massacre ensued, with the soldiers firing upon people as they fled down back streets and alleys. "A quantity of people were killed," in this "horrible butchery," which Barthès, not normally given to criticizing the authorities, likened to the "worst sort of despotism." If nothing else, this episode illustrates the jittery state of an urban community where the social divide between the upper and lower classes was compounded by misery and distrust.[42]

The general hardship of the times also engendered increased strife within the laboring classes. The master hatmakers reported the existence of "syndicates and monopolies of journeymen" who used the convents of friendly religious orders to organize their strikes; the carpenters' guild likewise complained of actions of the *compagnonnage* leading to violence and even murder.[43] Table 13 is a summary of the incidents of collective violence and protest in Toulouse during the century between 1690 and 1789. Although grain riots were not the most numerous among these violent events, they were the most serious and entailed the largest crowds, many dominated by women. The grain rioters of 1778 were menacing enough to keep the frightened capitouls barricaded inside the Hôtel de Ville.[44] The restlessness

41. BMT, MS 699, pp. 265–67.
42. An account of the events of 1778 can be found in BMT, MS 705, pp. 158–62.
43. Du Bourg, "Les diverses corporations de Toulouse," *MASIBL* 13 (1883–85): 245; 14 (1886–89): 69.
44. Tilly, *The Contentious French*, p. 189.

TABLE 13

Collective violence in Toulouse, 1690–1789

Date	Type of riot
1690	artisans
1691	tax
1693	grain
1694	grain
1698	tax
1713	lackeys
1713	grain
1717	lackeys
1721	students
1724	lackeys
1737	students
1739	students
1739	lackeys
1739	charivari
1740	students
1742	grain
1747	grain (several)
1750	students
1758	prisoners
1766	prisoners
1771	prisoners
1773	grain
1776	grain
1778	grain
1782	artisans
1782	grain
1789	grain

Sources: AMT, 282, 283, 284; AN, G7, 302–25; BMT, MSS 699–706, "Les heures perdues de Pierre Barthès"; Rozoi, 4; Charles Tilly, The Contentious French (Cambridge, Mass., 1985), chap. 6; F. Dumas, "Une émeute d'étudiants à Toulouse en 1740," Revue des Pyrénées 19 (1907): 23–43; Marc Miguet, Les fourches patibulaires de la salade et la justice à Toulouse aux XVIII siècle (Toulouse, n.d.); Jack Thomas, "Economie politique des marchés: L'Ancien régime"; Inventaire sommaire (Montpellier, 1865), 5:349; Kaplan, Bread, Politics, and Political Economy, 2:565.

of the lackeys—those young men who served noblemen as errand boys and servants—is also worth noting. Here, as Cissie Fairchilds has pointed out, the eighteenth century witnessed a general shift away from affective ties between masters and servants to more contractual, cash-based relationships. And in the latter case there was more often occasion for conflict, betrayal, and harshness.[45] In 1754 the city's servants were the objects of a special municipal ordinance ordering them to remain in service with their masters—so restless and footloose had they apparently become in recent years.[46] If domestics were conforming less to the image of the faithful servants they presumably once were, the same could be said for the common people as a whole. It was in the aftermath of the grain riots of 1747 that the "Annales" began to use the terms *habitants* and *bas peuple* to distinguish two distinct classes of city dwellers. Following the execution of the riot's leaders, the "Annales" proclaimed that "all those who go by the name *habitant* of this city are most satisfied to see these exemplary punishments carried out, while the *bas peuple* have barely begun to exhibit their submission and repentance." The annalists continued: "The conduct of the *bas peuple* has disqualified them from being considered *habitants*. It is misery, more than anything else, which has brought them to such excesses, but it was the *habitants* who were the victims of their faults."[47]

How did the city respond to this troubling situation? Assuming that in generations past the vertical ties and other forms of social solidarity described earlier played some part in keeping the urban populace in order, in mitigating the class divisions that were still fundamental to early modern society, how then was this task met in the eighteenth century? One answer, of course, is that it was not met at all or insufficiently, as the numerous riots, social disturbances, and crimes would seem to testify. Another is that justice became more severe, and there are grounds for considering this: in 1759, for example, the notorious *fourches patibulaires*—the scaffold structure designed for the display of the rotting corpses of executed criminals— was refurbished, in the hopes, noted the "Annales," that "the spectacle would be capable of inspiring terror in the hearts of evildoers."[48] More realistically, in the last decades of the Old Regime it was armed militias, either municipally controlled or royal, that increasingly bore the burden of imposing civil tranquility.

45. Cissie Fairchilds, "Masters and Servants in Eighteenth-Century Toulouse," *Journal of Social History* 12 (1978): 368–93.
46. Rozoi, 4:132.
47. AMT, BB 283, pp. 523–25.
48. AMT, BB 283, p. 685; Miguet, *Les fourches patibulaires de la salade et la justice à Toulouse*.

Like most early modern cities, Toulouse had a police force, the Famille de Guet (or City Watch), which, as noted in an earlier chapter, was placed on a permanent footing in the early sixteenth century. And, as also suggested then, the creation of this municipal guard was one indication of the vitality of municipal government in that earlier period; it reflected the practical side of civic humanism. Until the end of the seventeenth century, the Watch was composed of not more than 40 men, armed only with pikes and batons. Then a series of reforms followed. In 1690, at the urging of the intendant, the city augmented the Watch by 20 men and outfitted all the guards with new uniforms. In 1733, it added 10 more men. In 1743, the Watch was put on a "military footing," that is, it was endowed with firepower. In 1750 and again in 1766, the Watch was increased, bringing its total strength to over 100 men. During that period the military capacity of the guards was enhanced as well, each now equipped with a carbine and bayonet. The reform of 1771 was the most ambitious to date: not only was the size of the Watch increased to 123 men, but it was also deployed round-the-clock and divided into specialized brigades.[49] The account of this reform in the "Annales" reflected the anxiety it was meant to quell: "This public force will give us sufficient authority at all times and places. . . . Protected by these patrols, our citizens will walk without danger and will live without fear."[50] But by the 1780s an investigation by the intendant concluded that "the Company of Guet of Toulouse is insufficient to assure good order and public tranquility in that city."[51] Consequently, the Watch was again augmented and reorganized into three divisions, bringing the total force to 210.[52]

It would be difficult to determine how effective these reforms were in promoting a better-policed city. But one thing is clear: in the eighteenth century the authorities displayed a willingness to encroach upon marginal space and brand activities illicit that previously had

49. On these reforms of the Guet, see AMT, BB 283, p. 475, and BB 284, pp. 72, 146, 170; ADH-G, C 314-15, "Ordonnance du Roi du 13 décembre contenant règlement pour la Compagnie du Guet"; "Ordonnance de Messieurs les capitouls de Toulouse concernant la discipline de la Compagnie du Guet"; Lamouzèle, *Essai sur l'organisation et les fonctions de la Compagnie du Guet*, pp. 118-142.
50. AMT, BB 284, p. 146.
51. ADH-G, C 314.
52. Ibid. On the strengthening of the Parisian police force, see Daniel Roche, *Le peuple de Paris* (Paris, 1981), pp. 278-84; and A. Farge, *Vivre dans la rue à Paris au XVIIIe siècle* (Paris, 1979), pp. 163-243.

been left unmolested. Two examples illustrate this new official intru-
siveness. "La Campa" was an age-old rite in which gangs of youths,
armed with slingshots, would engage in pitched battles, usually on
Rogations Day but at other times of the year as well. According to
Catel and other local antiquaries, the origin of the ritual combat dates
to the period of the Albigensians, when the city's two divisions—
Bourg and Cité—conformed to two different parties in the crusade.
Thus, the two youthful gangs would shout out, "Down with the
Bourg!" or "Down with the Cité!" as they fought.[53] There is no record
of this ritual being prosecuted by the authorities, that is, not until the
eighteenth century when the capitouls declared it a source of public
disorder and danger and unleashed the Watch to prevent its occurrence. Barthès as well, always ready to condemn any breach in public
order, decried the custom many times in his journal. To be sure, the
ritual could prove deadly; at least one youthful combatant in La Campa was killed. But it is unlikely that it had grown deadlier than in past
centuries, yet it was in the eighteenth century that the authorities felt
compelled to repress the popular ritual.[54] This was also the case with
the city's various gambling dens. Starting in mid-century, a concern
for the vice of card playing and other games of chance became a
perennial refrain in the pages of the municipal "Annales." The capitouls fulminated against the "secret academies," "perverse assemblies," and the cabarets and inns that provided refuge to an apparent
army of professional gamblers who reputedly duped strangers, corrupted the sons of good families, and seduced students with their
nefarious tricks. On several occasions the attempt to root out these
denizens of vice ended in rioting, and once the gamblers themselves
put up armed resistance. The municipal authorities, however, remained vigilant, although it seems that their efforts were largely the
result of the intendant's proddings. In 1770 the capitouls announced
their success in "penetrating these obscure retreats where the vilest
sort of people wallow pell-mell and most shamefully. And we have
dispersed far from us these disgusting objects," they boasted.[55]

Despite the fact that a concern for the powers of the police was

53. On La Campa, see Catel, *Mémoires*, pp. 137–38; C. Barrière-Flavy, "Un sport
dangereux à Toulouse au XVIIIᵉ siècle," *RHT* 12 (1925): 188–92; "Toulouse jadis,"
Revue des Pyrénées 2 (1890): 847–48.
54. AMT, BB 283, pp. 392, 534; BMT, MS 699–706, passim.
55. On gambling and the campaign against it, AMT, BB 283, pp. 581, 601, 667, and
BB 284, pp. 32–33, 66, 133; Feugère, "Le capitoul David"; Castan, *Les criminels*, p. 266.

widespread in eighteenth-century France, it is well known that the realm remained notoriously underpoliced. This too was the case for the city of Toulouse, for even the augmented and reorganized Watch proved in need of a supplementary armed force in the course of the century, especially with the ever-increasing threat of rioting. This force came in the form of royal troops. Such troops had been imposed upon Toulouse a couple of times early in the century to persuade the populace to pay a new royal tax. But it was in 1747, following the tumultuous grain riots, that they became an important factor in the pacification of the urban populace. Eight companies of troops were lodged in Toulouse that year.[56] In 1749, two batallions of the Bourbon regiment were placed on guard in the city's major squares and thoroughfares.[57] In 1755, the First Batallion of the regiment of the Sarre arrived in town.[58] And in succeeding years other regiments came and went with regularity; some stayed as long as sixteen months.[59] During the epidemic of animal distemper which struck the region in 1775, hundreds of troops poured into the city, ostensibly to set up a barrier against the movement of livestock in the province, but also as a demonstration of royal might.[60] These troops were more than just billeted in the city; they patrolled the streets and added a martial flavor to Toulouse's public life. Townspeople were treated to a range of novel displays, from the firing squads staged all too frequently to execute deserters, to the "petits guerres," maneuvers, and military parades that attracted thousands of delighted spectators. But the inhabitants were not always so pleased with their military guests, for the soldiers naturally attracted an army of prostitutes in their wake and on occasion they helped themselves to the city's daughters. Until the city made arrangements to house the regiments in collèges and newly constructed barracks, many were billeted in inhabitants' homes— something "unheard of," noted Barthès.[61] Although municipal officials were forced to admit the need for such reinforcements to police their city, they also expressed discomfort at what was formally "a challenge to our privileges," for Toulouse was traditionally exempt from the billeting of troops. "But," noted the capitouls in 1749, "far

56. AMT, BB 283, p. 522.
57. Ibid., p. 544.
58. BMT, MS 699, p. 294.
59. Ibid., MS 702, pp. 82, 112–13.
60. *Affiches et annonces de Toulouse pour l'année 1775*, pp. 6, 38.
61. BMT, MS 699, p. 257.

be it for us to want to undo the designs of the king. It is sufficient to know that they are guided by wisdom and reason."[62]

The *habitants* under siege by the *bas peuple*, the city polarized between rich and poor, a hungry populace perpetually on the verge of revolt, traditional forms of solidarity and interclass association breaking down—does not all this tend to exaggerate the social divisions present in eighteenth-century Toulouse? And does not such a portrait suffer from a teleological preoccupation with the Revolution, when contention and violence, compounded by ideological passions, reached epoch-making proportions? Surely the city was just as divided during the Wars of Religion. Indeed, there never was a time in the early modern period when the urban populace was not profoundly divided between rich and poor, officials and ordinary people; when religious or political controversy did not risk degenerating into open class conflict; or when the city was not perceived as a dangerous place, haunted by thieves and murderers. Moreover, a case could be made for viewing the eighteenth century as a time when traditional activities still performed the function of fostering interclass solidarity. Witness the many religious displays that managed regularly, despite the growing influence of the Enlightenment, to arouse the populace; or city officials' periodic efforts, grandiose and usually symbolic at best, at public charity. Perhaps the best evidence against the view of eighteenth-century social interaction offered in this book is the case of the parlement's triumphant return from exile after Maupeou's fall from power. If ever one wanted proof of the people's affection for the royal magistrates, of the ties between ruling elites and the people they governed, it would have to be in the exuberant celebrations that greeted the parlementaires upon their return to Toulouse in 1775.[63] But were the people really greeting the return of their "fathers and protectors" or, rather, the wealthy gentlemen whose lavish expenditures kept many of them employed?

In any case, the point is not to argue that Toulouse was entirely transformed in the eighteenth century, that the last century of the Old Regime experienced a radical break with traditional forms of social interaction, but rather to specify a trend in the evolution of

62. AMT, BB 283, p. 544.
63. On the return of the parlement and the festivities that greeted it, see *Affiches*, 1775.

public life in the decades leading up to the Revolution. The break-down of traditional patterns of cross-class sociability, an increase in crime, and the rising threat of social revolt are only some of the elements that contributed to this trend. Others were the corrosive effect of absolutist policy on local government and its rather different effect on parlementary magistrates, who increasingly saw themselves as part of a national front of Robe officials opposed to the crown. And there were others as well, especially the economic interests of land-owning elites, whose deepening involvement in the grain trade made them reluctant to acknowledge local needs and traditions. There were, finally, cultural and intellectual forces, many originating from beyond the city, many linked to the Enlightenment, which added a new element of cosmopolitanism to public life. Toulouse in the eighteenth century was a less provincial city but also a less distinctive one than ever before in its history.

11

The Cosmopolitan City

History remembers Toulouse primarily for two events. The first was the Albigensian crusade of the early thirteenth century, a military campaign against the Cathar heresy that proved disastrous for the city and its much cherished autonomy. Even today, Toulousains will assume that a historian visiting the city is there to research that long-ago event, for if they know nothing else about their city's past they can at least recite the names Simon de Montfort and Count Raymond of Toulouse. But another name evokes a later well-known episode: Jean Calas, the unfortunate Huguenot accused of murdering his son, whose trial and execution in 1762 made the city a byword for fanaticism.[1] As we have seen, however, those same royal magistrates who convicted Calas in 1762 also participated in the national campaign to expel the Society of Jesus—the very embodiment of militant, uncompromising Catholicism—from the realm that same year. Also in that year the Academy of Floral Games, now a royal literary society, began to take an interest in some controversial matters, suggesting a turn toward enlightened sentiments among its elite members, a majority of whom were parlementaires. In many respects, eighteenth-century Toulouse was still a conservative, Counter-Reformation city, still dominated by haughty magistrates and ecclesiastical bigwigs, an urban society relatively untouched by the commercial revival that was reshaping many other French cities. Nevertheless, change was working its way in this quintessential Old Regime city, and a definite strain of cosmopolitanism was the result.

1. On Calas see David D. Bien, *The Calas Affair* (Princeton, 1960).

Enlightened Toulouse

The change was even apparent in the proceedings of the Floral Games. Though now rivaled by several other academies, the new Academy of Floral Games maintained its preeminence among Toulouse's learned societies throughout the eighteenth century. Its forty *mainteneurs*, elected for life, were a mix of parlementary magistrates and other officers, lawmen, church officials, noblemen, and professors.[2] Until the latter part of the century their literary activities inclined toward poetry, mythology, mild theological discussions, and other harmless topics. Then in 1762, a note of Enlightenment began to creep into the proceedings. That year the prizewinning poem on Charles IX contained a diatribe against religious fanaticism. In 1767 a subject for discussion among the mainteneurs was "To determine the advantages for the state to be enlightened in the pursuit of its policies." In 1769 a "Eulogy to President Duranti," the slain leader of the politique Catholics during the Wars of Religion, served as an occasion for a denunciation of the excesses of the church, as did the following year a similar "Eulogy to Raymond VII," the last count of Toulouse before the Albigensian crusade. Such critical, enlightened discussion did not go uncontested. The intendant found the discourse on Count Raymond "full of reprehensible things." And when in 1772 the mainteneurs proposed a "Eulogy to Pierre Bayle," they met with opposition from the crown and the archbishop. Bayle was replaced by Saint-Exupère (whose remains were in the crypts of Saint-Sernin) for the Toulouse academicians' homage, but the choice of the Protestant philosopher was successfully defended the following year. And in 1780 the eulogy went to Voltaire—despite the fact that less than twenty years earlier, in the aftermath of the Calas trial and execution, he had branded Toulouse as an outpost of intolerance. The Enlightenment had won partisans within the highest echelons of Toulouse society, something Voltaire himself was forced to admit in 1768. "There has occurred such an extraordinary change in the Parlement of Toulouse," exclaimed Calas's defender. "Half [of the parlementaires] have become philosophes and the old heads, infested with the ringworm of barbarism, will soon die."[3]

2. Ibid., p. 161; Axel Duboul, *Les deux siècles de l'Académie des Jeux Floraux* (Toulouse, 1901), vol. 2.
3. Wolff, *Histoire*, p. 367. On the spread of Enlightenment in the Floral Games academy, see Bien, *Calas*, pp. 161–62; F. de Gelis, "Les philosophes du dix-huitième

Though preeminent, the Floral Games academy was not institutionally unrivaled among the city's learned inhabitants. The Lanternistes had reemerged in 1729 with royal sanction as the Société des Sciences, and in 1746 received the letters patent as the Académie des Sciences, Inscriptions et Belles-Lettres. At its founding, its members came from a range of disciplines: there were three each from the fields of geometry, astronomy, mechanics, anatomy, chemistry, and botany, and fifteen from the general category of inscriptions and belles-lettres. Each year the academy offered a 500-livre prize for the best submission in one of three alternating categories: physics-math, medicine-physics, or belles lettres. Though less controversial in the range of its inquiries, the new Academy of Sciences was even more cosmopolitan in its membership than the Floral Games academy, which recruited primarily from among the regional elite. Like the older academy, it enlisted a cross section of the city's leading inhabitants, from parlementaires, high officers, and other administrators to churchmen, professors, physicians, lawyers, military men, and aristocrats. But it also attracted 111 corresponding members between 1758 and 1790, most from other cities in France, but some from Spain, England, Germany, the Low Countries, and other lands.[4]

A third royal academy was founded in 1748. Since 1726 the capitouls had maintained a school in the Hôtel de Ville for students of painting and architecture, largely as a matter of encouraging work that would aid in the artistic aspects of civic culture—the embellishment of municipal buildings, the orchestration of public festivities, and the like. In 1738 Guillaume Cammas, the architect responsible for remodeling the Capitole, took control of this informal academy, which in 1748 became the Académie Royal de Peinture, Sculpture et Architecture. From 1751 to 1791, the academy sponsored an annual exposition of paintings and sculptures in the Hôtel de Ville; like that held in Paris, it lasted eight days and commenced on August 25.[5]

siècle et les Jeux Floraux," *MASIBL* 11th ser., 8 (1920): 15–56; ADH-G, C 2813; ADH, C 6855 in *Inventaire sommaire* (Montpellier, 1865), 5:348.

4. On the Academy of Sciences, see Rozoi, *Annales*, 4:100; Michel Taillefer, *Une académie interprète les lumières: L'Académie royale des sciences, inscriptions et belles-lettres de Toulouse au XVIIIᵉ siècle* (Paris, 1984). The membership list is from Louis Armieux, "Etat des membres de l'Académie des Sciences, Inscriptions et Belles-Lettres de Toulouse, aux diverses époques de son histoire (1640–1875)," *MASIBL*, 7th ser., 8 (1876): 255–99.

5. Rozoi, 4:117; Baron Desazars de Montgailhard, "Les salons de peinture au XVIIIᵉ siècle," *MASIBL*, 10th ser., 2 (1902): 265–94; M. E. Saint-Raymond, "Les débuts de l'école publique de dessin à Toulouse," *MASIBL*, 10th ser., 12 (1912): 171–202; Robert

Although patronized by the capitouls in the amount of 400 livres a year, the budding academy soon found itself short of funds. Also, two painters, who were resentful of Cammas's near monopoly on artistic activities in the city, waged a campaign against it and especially against its leader. The new academy might have expired altogether had it not been for the labors of a leading local supporter of the arts, Louis de Mondran, who appealed to his friends and patrons in Paris to petition the king for direct intervention. Mondran's campaign was successful and in 1751 he was able to present the rather surprised capitouls with a new set of statutes, which placed the artistic academy on a firm footing and ordered the city's continued support.[6]

Although the capitouls appeared unwilling to support the new academy of art, its annual expositions were enthusiastically welcomed by the public and attracted many local patrons. Over 450 individuals contributed works of art during the forty years between 1751 and 1791. Of the contributors, most were noblemen or high officers, with members of the parlement predominating, although a number of artisans also lent their cherished possessions for the expositions (table 14). Most of the latter, however, were wealthy, highly skilled craftsmen, such as goldsmiths, gilders, and tapestrymakers.

Despite this demonstration of local support, the sponsors of the exposition were vocal in their concern that many individuals were withholding their artistic possessions, thus denying the public the benefit of viewing important treasures. More than the other two learned societies, the academy of art had a mission to educate and edify the public. Its prologues to the annual exposition catalogues read as exhortations to the cause of art and its presumed ability to dispel ignorance, provincialism, and that greatest of evils in the eighteenth century, bad taste. The academicians likened themselves to France's bravest generals and soldiers—so formidable did they see their task in the provincial outpost. Indeed, apparently many critics saw their enterprise as a losing cause—"Cynics claiming that the arts are wasted on men who are aggressive, savage, and brutish." "Oh

---

Mésuret, *Les expositions de l'Académie royale de Toulouse de 1751 à 1791* (Toulouse, 1972). The catalogues for these expositions are in the Bibliothèque Municipale de Toulouse (Res. D XVIII 383) and the Musée Paul Dupuy, Toulouse (D 49-1-9); they are also reproduced in Mésuret, *Les expositions.*

6. AMT, GG 926, "Fragment du journal de l'Académie tenu par Mondran" (1760–76).

TABLE 14

Contributors to the annual exposition of
the Royal Academy of Painting, Sculpture,
and Architecture of Toulouse, 1751–1791

Noblemen	50
High officers	77
Academicians, artists	25
Women	51
Churchmen	21
Low officers, city and royal functionaries	17
Capitouls	16
Artisans	23
Merchants	14
Engineers and medical men	7
Total identified	301

Source: Mésuret, Les expositions.

my country! Oh public, Oh fellow citizens!" pleaded the academicians. "Love, cherish, take to your breasts this Society of zealous
citizens, who, after having planted in your hearts a felicitous taste for
talent, still takes infinite care and trouble each year to nourish this
flame." Your houses and cities, they warned, "would be nothing but
dreadful caves if the thick clouds of ignorance which cover these
unhappy places prevented the light of Art from reaching you."[7]

Some of these same academicians belonged to other associations
dedicated to serving humanity and dispelling the clouds of ignorance, although in a less public fashion. These were the 600 members
of the twelve Masonic lodges active in Toulouse after 1740. The
Toulouse orders were imports from Ireland and Scotland. All of the
lodges were socially segregated and nearly all enlisted men from the
upper and middling levels of society, although one, the Loge En-
cyclopédique, founded in 1787, had a significant contingent of shopkeepers and artisans. The Freemasons were not hostile to the church
and, indeed, included many clergymen in their ranks. One had to be
a baptized Catholic to join. Many lodges participated in religious
festivals and Masons usually attended mass before their festive ban-

7. Catalogue des ouvrages exposés au Salon de l'Hôtel de Ville par l'Académie Royale de
Peinture, Sculpture et Architecture . . . (Toulouse, 1774).

quets.[8] They were, as Maurice Agulhon noted, the successors to the lay confraternities, especially the penitential companies, founded in the sixteenth and seventeenth centuries, and performed many of the same functions, including mutual aid.[9] But the differences between the Masons and the penitents were pronounced. Despite their public avowal of the principle of equality, the Masons, unlike the penitents, allowed for very little social mixing. And their charitable exercises were mostly for the benefit of the Masons themselves; they did not engage in large-scale poor relief, like the penitents and other lay confraternities. Most important, the Freemasons were conventicles of enlightened thought, espousing the religion of humanity and rejecting religious intolerance. But their social respectability was not impeached by such views. Even Barthès, a spokesman for the established order and a fierce critic of the philosophes, expressed his outrage that the "ignorant and credulous" should dare attack the Masons for their views and practices.[10]

Toulouse's embrace of Enlightenment culture was virtually complete by the last decades of the Old Regime, a rather impressive fact in light of the ecclesiastical establishment's local power and a still strong tradition of religious intolerance, most recently displayed in the Calas trial. There were perhaps more learned academies in Toulouse than in any other provincial city, and, after Lyons and Paris, it had more local subscribers to the Encyclopédie as well.[11] How the Enlightenment managed to prevail in this bastion of Counter-Reformation Catholicism and parlementary conservativism is difficult to explain, although clearly a range of forces, some cultural, some political and social, prompted local elites to identify with Parisian fashion and cosmopolitan notions. But beyond the preconditions of enlightenment, it is worth considering its local consequences. What did it mean for the city to harbor these conventicles of the new sensibility?

8. On Freemasonry in Toulouse, see Wolff, Histoire, pp. 367–68; Bien, Calas, pp. 174–76; J. Gros, "Les loges maçonniques de Toulouse," La Révolution française 40 (1901): 234–70, 297–318; and especially Taillefer, La Franc-maçonnerie toulousaine: 1741–99 (Paris, 1984).
9. Maurice Agulhon, Pénitents et francs-maçons dans l'ancienne Provence (Paris, 1968).
10. BMT, MS 699, p. 172.
11. Robert Darnton, The Business of Enlightenment (Cambridge, Mass., 1979), pp. 591, 595.

Central to the Enlightenment was the spirit of improvement, and among the academicians of Toulouse were several intent on improving the conditions of life in their city. The most active were those who spearheaded the movement for the physical amelioration of Toulouse, a movement to be discussed shortly. But there were others as well. The Royal Academy of Art, convinced that artistic appreciation could foster good citizenship, clearly had a mission to expose the general public to works of aesthetic value. It also sponsored a school for budding artists recruited among the city's youth. One academician saw in this school nothing less than a moral crusade for the rescue of the young from a life of depravity and brute labor—"a life less human than that among orangoutans." "Our children would have languished disgracefully," he had their parents say. "But they have found adoptive fathers."[12] After decades of mostly abstract and rather theoretical discussions, the Academy of Sciences also turned its attentions to the practical task of improving local society. In the 1780s its sessions took up such topics as the improvement of the region's commerce and agriculture; and it also provided expert advice to the capitouls on matters relating to the municipality's well-being.[13] In short, while the Toulouse academicians proved generally unconcerned with practical issues—certainly this remained the case with the Academy of Floral Games—it dawned on some that there was usefulness in enlightenment.

But this spirit of improvement was matched by a critical view of much that was distinctively Toulousain. We have already seen how the creation of a royal academy in the late seventeenth century involved abandoning age-old popular traditions associated with the Floral Games. For some late eighteenth-century literati, the debunking of local historical myths and legends was indeed a mark of enlightenment. In 1771 a minor philosophe, Barnabé-Farmien du Rozoi, published a four-volume history of Toulouse, Annales de la ville de Toulouse, which so pleased the capitouls that they made him an honorary citizen of the city.[14] Rozoi's history, despite its scholarly pretensions and archivally based research, was an Enlightenment morality tale, a narrative recounting the errors of superstition and the crimes

12. "Discours prononcé dans l'assemblée de l'Académie des Arts de Toulouse, le dimanche 31 janvier 1773," in Rozoi, 4:104–5.

13. Taillefer, Une académie, p. 135.

14. Bien, Calas, p. 165.

of Christianity. But he also turned his critical method on some oft-repeated founding legends of Toulouse, especially those from the pre-Christian era when the city was both a great capital of the Tectosages and an important Roman outpost. For example, Rozoi found nothing to support the belief, shared by every historian of Toulouse since the sixteenth century, that the city was once the site of two pagan temples, those of Apollo and Minerva.[15] As for the most cherished of the city's myths, that of the "Gold of Toulouse," he was skeptical at best. He found no trace of either the lake or swamp in which the treasure supposedly had been secreted. And although he did not entirely dismiss the legend, he saw its persistence across the centuries as evidence of unenlightened chroniclers' willingness to succumb to "chimerical terrors" and to submit to "false prognostications." "History," he declared, "must be entirely purged of prejudice and superstition." In Rozoi's hands, this enlightened dictum meant demystifying Toulouse's history, or at least denying one traditional source of its civic pride.[16]

If the Enlightenment could be at once serviceable to local society and critical of its traditions, it also created a social milieu out of its followers. With the Enlightenment, in short, we have the emergence of a public. The dimensions of this eighteenth-century public were varied. On one level it included members of learned academies, Freemasons, and habitués of cultivated salons, largely people of the upper classes. In this sense the sociability fostered by the Enlightenment was restricted in comparison with the social mixing that often characterized associational life under the Counter-Reformation. But one should not thereby exaggerate the exclusiveness of enlightened society, for the ranks of the Freemasons and academicians included a range of men, from merchants and tradesmen to rich financiers and parlementaires. Moreover, the spirit of *fraternité* sometimes prevailed in these associations, especially the Freemason lodges, which styled themselves as true brotherhoods.

15. Rozoi, 1:19–20.
16. Ibid., pp. 24–29. It is interesting to compare the account of this legend by two other historians, contemporaries of Rozoi. The Benedictines, C. Devic and J. Vaissette, wrote their magisterial *Histoire générale de Languedoc* in the latter part of the eighteenth century. Although their history, based on prodigious research, is still a valid source, their uncritical respect for the legendary past, including the myth of the gold of Toulouse, distinguishes it from Rozoi's more "enlightened" account. See *HGL*, 1:32, 82, 185.

The Enlightenment's public had another dimension, a broader con-
stituency than the relatively few who declared their cultural partisanship by joining learned academies or Freemason lodges. For
these new associations also reached out to a wider audience of
Toulousains. This appeal was implicit in the academy of art's annual
salons, which directly addressed the public. "It is for the enlightened
Public to appreciate our efforts," the artists declared in their brochure
of 1776.[17] The founding of the *Musée* in 1784, a society that sponsored
a range of activities, from musical performances and genteel literary
discussions to sessions devoted to the public consideration of ways to
improve the local economy, also targeted a wider audience.[18] Such a
public, of course, did not embrace the entire populace but merely
those with pretensions to cultivation and learning. Here again one
can draw both a contrast and similarity with the Counter-Reformation
church and its appeal to the laity. On the one hand, the Enlightenment's limited appeal clearly contrasts with the church's ideal of a
sacramental community, a gathering of all the faithful. But like the
tendency within the Counter-Reformation to create a spiritual elite of
dévots and confrères, the Enlightenment too appealed to a limited
public, those with cosmopolitan tastes and interests, and those who
could read.[19]

It was this literate public that supported a local press in the last two
decades of the Old Regime. The *Affiches et annonces de Toulouse* began
publishing in 1775 and continued, with one hiatus, into the Revolution. Its first publisher was Jean-Florent Baour, a sort of Théophraste
Renaudot of eighteenth-century Toulouse, who was also the editor
and director of the annual *Almanach historique de la ville de Toulouse.*[20]

17. Mésuret, *Les expositions.*
18. On the Musée, see *Affiches, 1784,* pp. 122–23; Bien, *Calas,* p. 165.
19. A survey of marriage contracts indicates a clear and not surprising difference
between the ability of people from different classes to sign their names—one indication
of literacy. In 1749, only 6 percent of nobles and 30 percent of bourgeois could not sign
their names; among artisans the figures were 47 percent for men and 80 percent for
women. People in the lowest classes were the least likely to know how to sign their
names: 79 percent of men and 96 percent of women (Wolff, *Histoire,* p. 363).
20. The extant *Affiches* of Toulouse are bound in volumes by year and deposited in
the Bibliothèque Municipale de Toulouse (Res. XVIII 130) for the years 1775, 1776, 1781,
1782, 1783, 1784; and the Bibliothèque de l'Arsénal, Université de Toulouse (Res. 93111)
for the years 1774, 1777, and 1789. Missing are the years 1778, 1779, 1780, 1785, 1786,
1787, and 1788. On the *Affiches* and Baour, see M. T. Blanc-Rouquette, *La presse et
l'information à Toulouse, des origines à 1789* (Toulouse, 1965), pp. 129–85, and "Un im-

Baour's model was indeed Renaudot's *Bureau d'adresse*, for one of his stated purposes in founding the weekly was to provide a clearinghouse for the purchase and sale of all sorts of commodities, properties, and services. Thus, on the weekly's first pages one could find notices for everything from music lessons and domestics for hire to the offer of a *metarie* or the sale of royal offices. Printed as well was a listing of grain prices and a summary of the region's weather. Baour's other purpose was to provide the public with a literary and intellectual forum, including accounts of the activities of Toulouse's learned academies, notices of recently published books, and excerpts from scientific and belletristic writings. But the twenty or so weekly pages contained a potpourri of information and commentary—fabulous stories, political reportage, news from various military fronts, Chinese parables, letters to the editor, medical cures, moral anecdotes, gossip from Versailles, and the like. For several issues running in 1777 the *Affiches* contained an extended, lurid account documenting the dangers of "precipitous burials."[21]

The newspaper was a vehicle for the Enlightenment. In 1777 it proclaimed, "The Powers of a well-ordered Nation are those that are the most enlightened."[22] Homages to the leading philosophes were frequent. On Voltaire's birthday in 1781, the *Affiches* printed a panegyric poem to the late sage of Ferney written by a ten-year-old girl.[23] Several issues in 1782 contained long excerpts from Rousseau's *Les rêveries du promeneur solitaire*, and the weekly of January 7, 1784, reprinted Condorcet's "Eulogy to d'Alembert."[24] New advances in science were eagerly followed. The *Affiches* of that year faithfully recounted every launching of the Montgolfiers' balloons, including several local experiments in hot-air aviation.[25] Mesmerism also received a critical, somewhat skeptical hearing in the weekly's pages.[26] Although the *Affiches* normally treated religious affairs and ceremonies with restrained respect, the editor occasionally let slip his real

---

primeur toulousain au XVIIIᵉ: Jean-Florent Baour," *Revue Française d'Histoire du Livre*, no. 27 (1980); and P. Wolff, ed., *Les toulousains dans l'histoire* (Toulouse, 1984), p. 223.

21. *Affiches*, 1777, pp. 23, 68. On the widespread fear in France of "precipitous burials," see John McManners, *Death and the Enlightenment* (Oxford, 1985), pp. 48–49, 70.

22. *Affiches*, 1777, pp. 1–2.

23. *Affiches*, 1781, p. 24.

24. *Affiches*, 1782, p. 110; 1784, p. 2.

25. *Affiches*, 1784, passim.

26. *Affiches*, 1784, p. 212.

sentiments, as, for example, when he declared "laughable" a particular procession of Gray Penitents (which, it must be said, included a
stumbling gaggle of children outfitted as saints and popes).[27] But the
editor attempted, or perhaps felt it prudent, to maintain a balanced
view toward religion. In 1781 he reprinted the text of a long condemnation of the works of Rousseau delivered by the archbishop of
Vienne.[28] And the paper's account of the first communion of a converted Jew, a rabbi named David Wormo, demonstrates a still palpa-
ble affection for the Christian mysteries: "His sighs, his tears, and his
eyes fixed on the Supreme Being to whom he was now attached by
this first religious act, offered a very tender spectacle."[29]

Perhaps the best indication of the intellectual outlook of the *Affiches*
comes by way of its listings of recently published books. Each week
the editor cited several titles, either of books available in Toulouse or
those published elsewhere. Sometimes he provided summaries or
reviews; there does not seem to have been any method to his process
of selection. For the seven years of *Affiches* examined, there are 236
titles mentioned (table 15). They are what one might expect as the sort
of reading fare of a late-eighteenth-century literate public. Only a
minority of books are religious in nature, while works on law and
politics, history, literature, and science predominate. Titles from the
philosophes are rare. By far the most important category includes
writings of a practical bent—encyclopedias and almanacs, manuals
for raising children, guides on home economics and agriculture,
home remedies for treating venereal disease, gout, and the like. Occasionally the editor offered his opinion on certain books, and once he
boldly introduced a work that "among all the books composed since
the invention of printing, none has been more promising of greater
success than the one we are announcing." Its title was *The Art of
Rendering Women Faithful*.[30]

The *Affiches*, in short, though enlightened, did not aggressively
flout conventional thought and established institutions, especially the
church. Rather, the paper entertained a range of opinions, skewed, to
be sure, toward Enlightenment but well within the bounds of acceptable thinking in late-eighteenth-century France. And yet, after only
two years of publication, Baour was confronted with such opposition

27. *Affiches, 1782*, p. 108.
28. *Affiches, 1781*, p. 154.
29. *Affiches, 1782*, p. 3.
30. *Affiches, 1783*, pp. 125–26.

TABLE 15
Books announced in the Toulouse *Affiches*
in seven years, 1775–1784

Religion	27
History and biography	34
Science and medicine	23
Practical works (education, agriculture, economics, encyclopedias and almanacs)	47
Geography	9
Literary works	34
Philosophy	19
Law and politics	35
Other	8
Total	236

Source: *Affiches et annonces de Toulouse* (1775, 1776, 1777, 1781, 1782, 1783, 1784).

that he was forced to relinquish control of the paper, which did not reappear until four years later. The nature of this opposition tells us something about what was at stake at the end of the Old Regime, what ignited men's passions and drove them to take public action. In this case it was not the Enlightenment. It entailed, rather, a perceived infringement on corporate privilege. Briefly, the fracas began when the *Affiches*, in the course of a discussion of the return of the parlement, touched upon the Basoche, the confraternity of law clerks. Soon, Baour was hit with a lawsuit initiated by the Basoche, charging him with sowing the seeds of dissension in their confraternity. The next year, after an article appeared on municipal reform, it was the procureurs turn to claim offense and take Baour to court. In each case the plaintiffs vehemently asserted that the paper had violated corporate privileges by exposing essentially private matters to public view.[31] At stake was indeed the issue of a free press, but, significantly, the issue was joined not because offending views had been expressed but because traditional rights had been violated. The issue, in short, pitted a relatively new concept, that of the public, against the corporatism that was at the heart of the Old Regime. Although Baour successfully defended himself in the courts, the cost of litiga-

31. *Affiches*, 1776, pp. 153–58; Blanc-Rouquette, *La presse*, pp. 146–48; Desazars de Montgailhard, "Les débuts du journal à Toulouse," *MASIBL*, 10th ser., 11 (1911): 137–76.

tion forced him to abandon the *Affiches*, and at the end of 1776 he bade farewell to his readers, likening himself to those "philosophers who have had the pen ripped from their hands by persecution, while striving to enlighten their century and posterity."[32]

Elite Sociability

Beyond new cultural associations, eighteenth-century Toulouse developed other novel contexts exclusively for the entertainment and edification of the elite. The most conspicuous of these was the Théâtre du Capitole, constructed in the Hôtel de Ville in 1740. Dramatic presentations of various sorts had long been a feature of public life, from the mystery plays mounted during religious festivals to the comedies periodically presented for the enjoyment of the common people. We have already noted the theatrical tradition initiated by the Jesuits and the Fathers of the Christian Doctrine, who used their students as actors. And the outdoor dramatics sponsored by such aristocratic grands as Montmorency and Ventadour in the early seventeenth century have also been discussed. From time to time in the mid-seventeenth century the theatrical troops patronized by the duke of Orléans or Epernon would pass through Toulouse; on one of these visits Molière was reputed to be among the actors, and legend has it that he once met with Godolin.[33] All of these dramatic productions were either religious in nature or played to a socially mixed audience. The new Théâtre du Capitole was different in both respects, presenting the latest plays, operas, and ballets to an audience of the well-to-do. A good seat for the season cost 144 livres. The theater premises were impressive, with several stages, loges, galeries, mezzanines; and so was the dramatic offering, which included plays by Racine, Corneille, Molière, Voltaire, Beaumarchais, Diderot, and Marivaux, as well as scores of lesser playwrights.[34] Of the better known, those by Molière were by far the most frequently produced. (In 1751, a capitoul, outraged at the moral implications of *L'avare*, demanded to know who wrote it. Informed by the theater manager, he replied, "Is

---

32. *Affiches*, 1776, p. 223.
33. Jean Dubois, "Molière à Toulouse le 8 août 1650," *RHT* 9 (1922): 149–52.
34. On the Toulouse theater, see Forster, *The Nobility of Toulouse*, pp. 158–59; Mésuret, *Evocation de vieux Toulouse*, pp. 315–19.

this Molière here? I will teach him to have morals and to respect them." Assured that the playwright was long dead, he remarked, "So much the better. But, my dear man. . . . Can you only perform the plays of obscure authors?")[35] Jean-Jacques Rousseau's operas were staged, as were several by Gluck. Fielding's Tom Jones had two incarnations, once as a musical in three acts, another time as Tom Jones à Londres, a five-act play in verse. The theater contained several halls, and the dramatic fare was divided among comedies, tragedies, operas and operettas, and ballets, pantomimes, and other dances. A document has survived listing the offerings for the 1786–87 season. The list is remarkable if only for the number and variety of presentations. In all, 694 stagings were mounted; most plays were in repertoire, some presented ten or more times during the season. They included 225 comedies, 78 tragedies, 233 operas, and 158 ballets. Some of the ballets were coupled with operas, in the French fashion.[36] If the 1786–87 season is representative of other years, the cultivated Toulousain had at his disposal the full range of French classical theater and more. He could not expect to do better in Paris.

This same document lists a series of grand bals for January and February, private parties held in the Capitole for patrons of the theater. Such exclusive entertainments became popular in the eighteenth century, as the elite sought ways of socializing at a distance from the urban crowd. Exclusive balls and dinner parties were now in fashion, especially on occasions of citywide celebration, when the populace was given over to general merriment in the streets. In 1763, for example, during the celebrations for the peace concluded with England and Portugal, First President Bastard and his wife hosted a party in their town house to which all ladies and gentlemen "of condition" were invited. It was an opulent affair, with the hôtel's interior entirely redecorated with tents, balconies, tapestries, and special illuminations. Nearly 200 diners gathered, the women served by the men. Dancing afterward continued until seven the next morning. The following day another dinner dance was presented in the Hôtel de Ville in honor of Madame la Présidente. Barthès remarked on "the good taste of the feast, the grace with which it was served, the quantity and

35. P. Casteras, La société toulousaine à la fin de l'Ancien Régime (Toulouse, 1891), pp. 44–45, quoted in Forster, The Nobility, p. 159.
36. AMT, GG 943, "Catalogue de comédies, tragédies, opéras, drames et autres pièces en tout genre qui ont été jouées . . . 1786."

delicacy of the meats, the beauty of the illuminations, the splendid concert that took place during the meal, and finally the variety and quality of the wines and liquors served." Again there was dancing in a ballroom opulently done over for the occasion. This time, the dancers held out only until dawn. The following day the same celebrants regrouped at the Cordeliers' convent for the performance of a symphony, a musical form new to the eighteenth century.[37] Two years later, the visit of a princess was the occasion for another exclusive gathering. The lavish banquet was followed by a symphony, which "merited the approbation of everyone, and that of the Madame la Princesse in particular, who acknowledged her satisfaction." Then the guests retired to another room for an assortment of card games and other contests of chance, including whist, brelan, and piquet. The party, noted the "Annales," was one of the most brilliant and successful ever, largely because "of the precaution of not letting anyone attend who did not have an invitation."[38]

These sorts of lavish, novel, and rather exclusive entertainments were mounted with some frequency in the course of the century;[39] and I would suggest that they are emblematic of the urban elite's desire to cultivate its own forms of refined sociability—to create a haut monde well insulated from the crowd. There were other manifestations of this sentiment. One was the appearance of a salon culture within the city. Some aristocratic salons were merely gathering spots for inveterate gamblers and other well-heeled profligates. The most notorious of these, the townhouse of Mme de Fontenilles, attracted some of the region's best-known libertines, and was even raided by the City Watch in 1769.[40] Others were conventicles of enlightenment. The wife of President Maniban offered her country house as a place of refuge for the beleaguered Rousseau in 1766.[41] The hôtel of First President de Cambon had a reputation for cultivation and elegance. Cambon even kept a "philosopher" as a part of his household at the cost of 300 livres a year.[42] Other magistrates—or

---

37. BMT, MS 703, p. 132.
38. AMT, BB 284, p. 48.
39. See BMT, MS 699, p. 115; and F. Galabert, "Feux d'artifices et collations capitulaires (1770)," *Bullétin de la Société Archéologique du Midi de la France* 40 (1909): 109–23.
40. A. Feugère, "Le capitoul David et les jeux défendus," *ADM* 44 (1932–33): 305–6.
41. Lenard R. Berlanstein, *The Barristers of Toulouse in the Eighteenth Century (1740–1793)* (Baltimore, 1975), p. 95.
42. Forster, *The Nobility*, p. 166.

rather their wives—also maintained salons in which the learned and pretentious could gather. That of Mme du Bourg, wife of a president in the parlement, was probably the most Parisian in tone. Mme la Présidente was a lady of some intellectual accomplishment and an avid follower of new trends. She used the *Emile* as a guide to raising one of her twenty children and was conversant in the ideas of the leading philosophes. In the 1780s, her salon became a center for mesmerism in Toulouse, and Mesmer himself paid it a visit in March of 1786.[43] The philosophe Saint-Martin, who also stopped at the Du Bourgs' hôtel on two occasions, was a confidant of the First President. "When the door is wide open," he wrote Du Bourg regarding his philosophy, "the riff-raff can enter like the *honnêtes gens*, if we are not careful to post strong and intelligent sentinels who let in only those people of good society. . . . Thus I keep this idea for myself and for those who are capable of hearing it."[44]

If cultivation and learning were now the calling cards of some elites, an eagerness to appear fashionable and well heeled was characteristic of many more. Like elsewhere in Western Europe, wealthy Toulousains in the eighteenth century had access to comforts and luxuries unavailable to their ancestors—and unaffordable to the vast majority of their contemporaries.[45] No season would be complete without a visit to the warm springs of Bagnères de Luchon, where fashionable Toulousains hobnobbed with their French and English counterparts.[46] And by the beginning of the eighteenth century, no self-respecting upper-class Toulousain had to suffer the indignity of rubbing shoulders with the common sort, for the sedan chair bore him down the crowded thoroughfares in style.[47] Parisian fashion was available to all who could afford it. The *Affiches* kept its readers abreast of the many luxuries and consumables now on sale in the provincial capital. There were fine alcoholic beverages from Nancy "in English bottles," a range of fruit brandies and cream liquors on sale "chez Mlle Cenac, mer-

---

43. Bien, *Calas*, pp. 170; Clement Tournier, *Le mesmerisme à Toulouse, suivi de lettres inédites sur le XVIIIe, d'après les archives de l'Hôtel du Bourg* (Toulouse, 1911).

44. Ibid.

45. On the growth of luxury markets in eighteenth-century cities, see Daniel Roche, *Le peuple de Paris* (Paris, 1982), pt. 2; Perrot, *Genèse d'une ville moderne*, pp. 916–17; and N. McKendrick, J. Brewer, and J. H. Plumb, *The Birth of a Consumer Society* (Bloomington, Ind., 1982).

46. Forster, *The Nobility*, p. 157.

47. The occupation of *porteur de chaise* first makes its appearance in the parish registers in the late seventeenth century in Toulouse.

chande mercier, vis-à-vis Hôtel de Prince." A Sieur Bosquet, just arrived from Paris, offered his services as "Coiffeur des Dames." Another Parisian merchant announced the opening of his boutique displaying paintings, trophies, artificial flowers, jewelry, watches, and other expensive items. Women's couture, of course, was de rigueur in society. One "marchande de modes de Paris," assured readers that she sold only the "latest fashions."[48] The local ladies apparently availed themselves of her wares, for in 1785 Mrs. Cradock noted with surprise that many women of Toulouse dressed "more elegantly than I had seen in Paris."[49]

Clearly then, the tone of eighteenth-century Toulouse had changed in the last decades of the Old Regime. In part it was more aristocratic than before; in part upper-class life had become more refined and cultivated; and in part the change was the result of more wealth, greater conspicuous consumption, even a proclivity toward decadence among certain city dwellers. One source of the elevated tone of upper-class living was the presence of new groups of well-to-do outsiders, each adding something distinctive to the city's haut monde, each bearing elements of cosmopolitanism to the provincial capital. The region's traditional aristocracy, for example, long content to remain ensconced in their country estates where they could indulge their endless passion for the hunt and other rustic pleasures, began to take an interest in the more refined pastimes offered by city life.[50] Many of them took up residence in Toulouse and participated in the upper-class's whirlwind "season" of balls, dinner parties, and other festivities. It was the hôtels of these aristocrats, it seems, that provided a haven for the city's burgeoning gambling devotees. Though not aristocrats, the so-called "americains," those Toulousains who had returned from making their fortunes on the sugar plantations of Santo-Domingo, also introduced a degree of opulence, certainly worldliness, to life in the city.[51] Since the 1680s, Toulouse had hosted a substantial community of Jacobites, members of an underrecognized diaspora that disseminated British families of wealth and distinction throughout Catholic Europe, especially France. Two

48. *Affiches*, 1777, p. 17; 1784, pp. 130, 154.
49. *Journal inédit de Madame Cradock*, p. 173.
50. Forster, *The Nobility*; see also Dewald, *Pont-St.-Pierre*, pp. 114; Sharon Kettering, *Judicial Politics and Urban Revolt in Seventeenth-Century France: The Parlement of Aix, 1629–1659* (Princeton, 1978), p. 28.
51. Wolff, *Histoire*, p. 351.

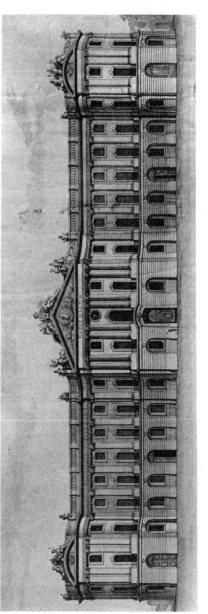

Two facades for the Capitole (Archives Municipales de Toulouse)

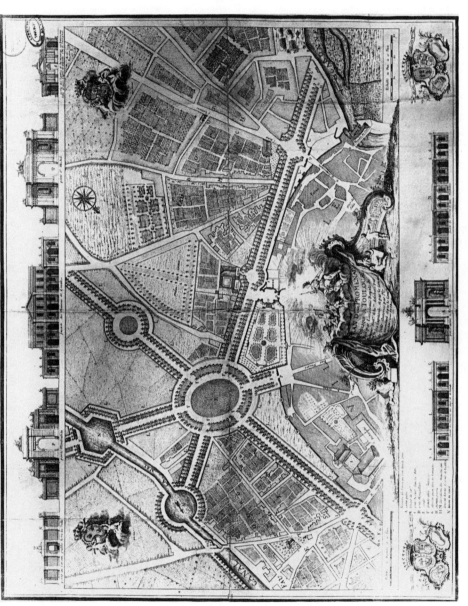

Plan for the new promenade of Toulouse (Archives Municipales de Toulouse)

scions of local Jacobite families, Henri de Nesmond and Arthur Dillon, rose to become archbishops of Toulouse, while the latter also left his mark on the city by sponsoring the construction of the promenades by the Garonne that bear his name.[52] Another, the comte de MacCarthy, gained a reputation throughout Europe for his extensive collection of fine books.[53] The presence of the Jacobites was one reason Toulouse was so receptive to Freemasonry, for several lodges were Scottish in origin. Along with these religious exiles from across the Channel, Toulouse apparently had a colony of English expatriates, enough at least to make the finicky Laurence Sterne feel somewhat at home during his visit to the city in the 1760s.[54] Finally, the tone, if not the morality, of upper-class society was elevated considerably upon the arrival of one of France's most notorious bon vivants, Jean-Baptiste Du Barry, who, along with his brother and two sisters, chose Toulouse as their place of exile after the death of Louis XV. Popularly known as "the Roué," this promoter-pimp and one-time lover of the king's famous mistress built himself a luxurious townhouse on the Place Saint-Sernin and furnished it in a manner befitting his reputation. The Hôtel Du Barry, its three floors and gardens crammed with statues, frescoes, mirrors, furniture, and tapestries from the best workshops in Europe and paintings by Rembrandt, Rubens, Mignard, Boucher, Greuze, and Fragonard, was a monument to the *douceur de vie*—or wasteful opulence—of the last days of the Old Regime. Such tourists as Arthur Young and Mrs. Cradock came to gawk in amazement at its bizarre splendor, while young Toulousain aristocrats found there a well-appointed refuge for their sporting pastimes.[55]

The Du Barry clan, swollen with spoils and pensions from their years as courtiers at Versailles, was responsible for constructing or

52. Ibid., p. 345; On the Jacobite diaspora, see Guy Chaussinand-Nogaret, "De l'exil religieux aux affaires: Les jacobites aux XVIIIe siècle," *Annales: ESC* 28 (1973): 1097–1122.

53. Forster, *The Nobility*, p. 168.

54. Henri Dumeril, "Un humoriste anglais en Languedoc au XVIIIe siècle," *Revue des Pyrénées* 7 (1895): 9–21.

55. On the Du Barrys and their installation in Toulouse, see Wolff, *Histoire*, p. 374; Forster, *The Nobility*, p. 174; M. L. Santi, "Madame Du Barry-Cères," *MASIBL*, 11th ser., 5 (1917): 21–70; Mésuret, *Evocation du vieux Toulouse*, pp. 496–98; Lamouzèle, "Inventaire du mobilier de l'hôtel de Jean Du Barry, à Toulouse, 1794," *Bulletin de la Société Archéologique du Midi de la France*, 2d ser., no. 30 (1902): 197–208; *Journal Inédit de Madame Cradock*, pp. 181–84.

refurbishing three large hôtels in Toulouse, town houses that set new standards in size and lavishness for domiciles of the provincial rich. But they were not the only aristocrats to leave an architectural mark on the city. The eighteenth century saw the greatest wave of private construction since the Renaissance; and like those constructed during the sixteenth century, these new hôtels provided a domestic haven for the elite.[56] That constructed by the count d'Espie (but quickly liquidated when his fortunes collapsed with the Lisbon earthquake) contained thirteen rooms on the first floor alone behind a deceptively modest facade.[57] An architectural detail that appeared on many eighteenth-century hôtels adds to the image of the Toulouse elite increasingly removed from the urban populace. This was the metal balcony that allowed well-to-do city dwellers to observe and enjoy street life below—popular festivities, religious processions, the boisterous crowd—without mingling with the ruder sort.[58] The construction of similar balconies has also been noted by James Amelang in his study of the aristocracy of early modern Barcelona, and he too sees them as emblematic of an elite increasingly self-conscious of its privileges and sensitive to its sometimes threatening surroundings.[59]

Eighteenth-Century Urbanism: Refashioning the City

Beyond these private hôtels, Toulouse itself underwent some structural changes that made the city a more agreeable environment for its genteel inhabitants. Until the eighteenth century there was very little in the way of open spaces in the city—a plaza here and there, a few urban gardens, and of course the many cemeteries. Toulouse was a crowded city—unsalubrious and poorly lit, with narrow, nearly impassable streets and few promenades, its main thoroughfares usually choked with carriages, people, and markets. It was also fundamentally still a medieval city. Despite the considerable construction that had taken place since the sixteenth century, the overall shape and outlines of the city remained the same, confined to its ramparts, constricted by centuries-old configurations of streets and neighborhoods. And centuries of neglect had taken their toll on many

56. Wolff, *Histoire*, p. 373–76; Mésuret, *Evocation du vieux Toulouse*, passim.
57. Wolff, *Histoire*, p. 373.
58. Ibid.
59. James Amelang, *Honored Citizens of Barcelona* (Princeton, 1986), pp. 208–10.

public buildings and sections. In the eighteenth century, however, the cityscape began to change, although the alterations were not as pronounced as those effected in Nantes, Bordeaux, Caen, Nîmes, Montpellier, and other provincial cities.[60]

This change came about largely as the result of a movement of architects, artists, intellectuals, and royal officials, a sort of lobby group for the cause of local urban renewal. Though interested in improving the physical state of their city, the capitouls had little to do with animating this movement, in part because of the inertia of municipal government in the eighteenth century, in part because of lack of funds. But whatever interest they had was also frustrated by the parlement, which balked at any undertaking even remotely likely to reflect well on their governmental rivals, the town councilors. The initiative, rather, rested with men only marginally involved in local politics. The troika of such partisans of urbanism included two powerful archbishops of Toulouse, Arthur Dillon and Lominie de Brienne, who drew upon the support of the estates of Languedoc, which they headed; the intendants and governors of the province; and a group of artists, architects, and engineers, most of whom were linked to the Toulouse academy of art. It was this local academy, in fact, that served as a kind of pressure group for the cause of urban renovation.[61]

The most articulate among this last group, and the most farseeing and forceful proponent of urbanism, was Louis de Mondran, the same Toulousain with well-placed connections in Paris whose attentions rescued the art academy from the capitouls' neglect. Indeed, Mondran spoke on behalf of the academic artists and architects in his pamphlets; he was also related by marriage to François-Philippe Garipuy, the director of public works for Toulouse, himself a pam-

60. On the transformation of French cities in the eighteenth century, see P. Lavedan, *Histoire de l'urbanisme*, vol. 2, *Renaissance et temps modernes* (Paris, 1953); Le Roy Ladurie et al., *Histoire de la France urbaine*, vol. 3, *La ville classique de la renaissance aux révolutions* (Paris, 1981), pp. 439–82; J.-C. Perrot, *Genèse d'une ville moderne: Caen au XVIIIᵉ siècle* (Paris and La Haye, 1975); Henri Michel, "Urbanisme et société à Montpellier sous l'Ancien Régime," *ADM* 86 (1974): 21–43; Line Teisseyre-Sallmann, "Urbanisme et société: L'exemple de Nîmes aux XVIIᵉ et XVIIIᵉ siècles," *Annales: ESC* 35 (1980): 965–86.

61. On these urbanists, see Georges Costa, *Les plans d'urbanisme pour Toulouse au milieu du XVIIIᵉ siècle* (Toulouse, 1953), and "Un projet d'urbanisme toulousain au second quart du XVIIIᵉ siècle," *Bulletin de la Section de Géographie*, 1953, pp. 79–98; Saint-Raymond, "Les travaux d'utilité publique de l'Académie Royale des Beaux Arts," *MASIBL*, 11th ser., 2 (1914): 117–40, 349–83.

phleteer for the cause of urbanism, who subsequently executed many of the projects for urban renovation. In Mondran we have a spokesman for a genuine campaign. Mondran was a man of many hats—economist, architect, engineer, artist, statesman, and philosopher; in short, he fit the mold of the enlightened man of learning, eager to apply the spirit of improvement and reason to every human domain. He was also an indefatigable booster of a number of worthy local projects, and his writings reflect a deep impatience with the institutional and intellectual barriers to the forces of progress.[62] Mondran wrote two pamphlets outlining his vision for the physical transformation of Toulouse. The first, published in 1754 but probably written and privately circulated many years earlier, was a *Plan général pour l'embellissement de la ville de Toulouse*, constructed as a dialogue between a Toulousain partisan of urbanism, exasperated by the lack of local receptivity to his plans, and his sympathetic Parisian interlocutor.[63] The second, also published in 1754, was a *Projet pour le commerce le pour les embellissements de Toulouse*, an ambitious architectural scheme for the city's rehabilitation that, if realized, would have promoted Toulouse into the ranks of such refashioned eighteenth-century cities as Nîmes and Bordeaux.[64]

Mondran's plan was global in scope. It called for a massive program of urban clearance, renewal, and reconstruction, entailing the creation of a network of gardens, promenades, plazas, city gates, avenues, and embankments. He even urged the construction of a new canal. His designs were both commercial and aesthetic in purpose; indeed, these two concerns were linked in his mind, for he was convinced that Toulouse's economic languor was rooted in the same lack of civic pride evident in its dilapidated physical state. Perhaps the most emblematic of his proposals was for the building of a large oval garden radiating spokes of alleys in the southeast of the city. The royal garden, as it was to be called, and the six promenades were designed to provide a spacious and agreeable environment for strollers and an opening to the countryside. Here Toulousains would

62. Costa, "Louis de Mondran, économiste et urbaniste (1699–1792)," *Urbanisme et habitation*, 1955, pp. 33–78.

63. *Plan général pour l'embellissement de la ville de Toulouse mis en dialogue entre un parisien et un toulousain* (Toulouse, 1754).

64. *Projet pour le commerce et pour les embellissements de Toulouse* (Toulouse, 1754). Both these projects were published anonymously, but Mondran's authorship is not in doubt.

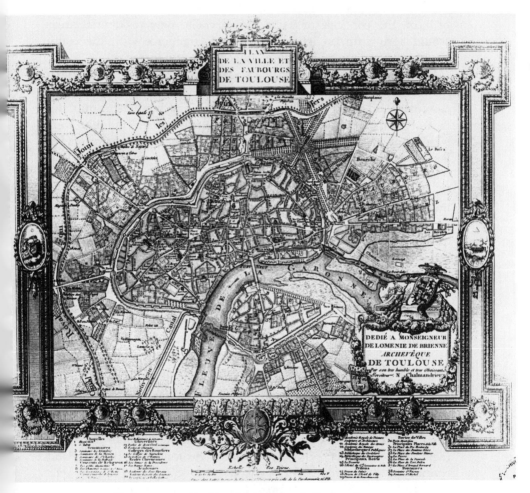

Toulouse, 1774 (Archives Municipales de Toulouse)

discover the pleasures of a more genteel sociability than that available in the crowded inner city, where intermingling was often rude and promiscuous. But along with such pleasures, Mondran hoped that the Ovale would provide a means of opening up the city, connecting the Garonne, the canal, the faubourgs, and the countryside in a manner that would both symbolically and commercially invigorate urban life. With these new constructions, he reasoned, the city would finally burst the confines of its medieval walls, new residential areas would spring up on its outskirts, and commerce with the countryside, the source of Toulouse's wealth, would increase.

Mondran's Ovale was eventually realized, although in a somewhat modified form. Several of his other proposals proved too ambitious—too costly and too disruptive of the city's architectural status quo. But in all, the results of eighteenth-century urbanism in Toulouse were significant. Even before Mondran and his friends and supporters began their campaign, there were projects afoot to refurbish various landmarks. In the late seventeenth century a proposal to create a Place Royal in front of the Hôtel de Ville found favor in the eyes of the intendant and capitouls, and by the mid-eighteenth century this large square was largely completed. Other city squares, including the Place Saint-Georges, damaged by a fire in 1724, were also enlarged and refurbished. The Hôtel de Ville itself received a new facade according to the neoclassical design drawn up by Guillaume Cammas, the city's official artist and main figure in the founding of the art academy. The Garonne was graced with promenades and quays on both its banks—those on the right bank thanks to the combined efforts of Archbishop Brienne, the intendant, the province's governor, Richelieu, and the estates of Languedoc. Brienne also presided over the opening of a new canal, which bore his name, providing a more effective link to the Garonne River than the Canal du Midi. Many wells and crosses, vestiges of the medieval city, were dismantled, especially in busy intersections where they hindered free circulation. Some streets were even paved. In 1762 the intendant attempted to promote the alignment of city streets, whose irregularity he found "ridiculous and contrary to good order."[65] His success was only partial. But in 1782 the city finally managed to provide its main thoroughfares with oil lampposts and accordingly ordered the whitewashing of those houses along the route in order to maximize the lighting effect. Thus,

65. Coppolani, p. 90; HGL, 14:2207–13.

among other things, eighteenth-century urbanism meant effacing, in part, Toulouse's red hue, for centuries one of the city's most distinctive features.[66]

What was the impetus behind this movement of urbanism? Students of more modern schemes for urban renovation, especially those undertaken in nineteenth-century Paris and New York, have debated the ideological, political, and economic determinants for the recasting of urban life. Some contend that the need for policing the city in an era of social unrest lay behind such plans. Others argue rather that they were inspired by a revived spirit of civic republicanism. Still others are convinced that they reflected new middle-class cultural demands for a more spacious, genteel urban setting insulated from the growing neighborhoods of workers and immigrants.[67] In eighteenth-century Toulouse, where the conditions obviously differed from those of the late-nineteenth-century city, the forces promoting urbanism were just as complex. Civic pride and public mindedness certainly animated such urbanists as Mondran and his colleagues— values, they were quick to point out, notably absent in the capitouls, parlementaires, and other "particulars." Not only individuals but corporate entities like cities possessed a strong sense of honor in the Old Regime, and the eighteenth-century urbanists felt they were upholding that of Toulouse.[68] A sense of pride and honor, although more individual, was also evident in the actions of Brienne and the intendants, who bristled at being outdone in these ventures by their counterparts in rival cities, especially Bordeaux. As men of the Enlightenment, the Toulouse urbanists naturally abhorred the "gothic" irregularity and confusion that prevailed in the city and aimed to create a more orderly, rational urban environment. But many of them were artists as well, and thus their Cartesian quest for order was matched by a desire to beautify their city, especially to make it more attractive to visitors: witness the emphasis on transforming the city gates into impressive monuments. Again, a strong sense of civic

66. On the transformations actually accomplished in the eighteenth century, see Coppolani, pp. 88–93; and *Toulouse: La ville au XVIIIe siècle*, Catalogue de l'exposition, Ecole d'Architecture de Toulouse (Toulouse, n.d.).

67. For views of urban renewal in the nineteenth century; see, for example, David Pinkney, *Napoleon III and the Rebuilding of Paris*, (Princeton, 1958), and T. J. Clarke, *The Painting of Modern Life* (Princeton, 1984). I have benefited from conversations with my colleague David Scobey on this subject.

68. On this theme, see Mervyn James, "Ritual, Drama, and Social Body in the Late Medieval English Town," *Past & Present*, no. 98 (1983): 3–29.

pride served to spur their reforms. Finally, all proponents of urban renovation shared a concern for improving the health and safety of urban living: more open space was considered more salubrious, and the river quays were designed to prevent flooding, a chronic problem on the banks of the Garonne.

Beyond these concerns and interests, the eighteenth-century urbanists seemed to be inspired by two other impulses. The first, evident both in Mondran's pamphlets and the creation of the Canal Brienne, was a desire to invigorate commerce. Mondran's reasoning, although obviously influenced by physiocratic principles, was novel. The problem with Toulouse's commercial life, he argued, lay not with the capitoulat, which generations of critics blamed for causing merchants to abandon their businesses, nor with the parlement, but rather with the languor, even laziness of the people of Toulouse. Their "deplorable inactivity," however, was not innate. It was caused by the low price of essential commodities. "People in Cities where essentials are expensive are industrious and hard-working," he observed.[69] Thus, the cost of living must be raised by encouraging the circulation of goods, and such would be the result of opening up the city to more trade and to a greater influx of laborers and tourists. Mondran translated the principle of free trade into structural terms: open spaces, an absence of barriers, and a more economically congenial urban environment were necessary to foster commerce and promote a hard-working populace.

Although not every urbanist shared Mondran's particular physiocratic ideas, an eagerness to stimulate commerce was clearly widespread among these modernizing elites. Another, more diffuse sentiment can be detected behind the urbanist enterprise. This one is difficult to characterize. Perhaps it was merely a case of disappointed civic pride; a more blunt characterization would be that of shamefulness. For the Toulouse partisans of urban renovation, especially Mondran, made no pretense of disguising their shame for the shabby state of their hometown, especially when compared with other French cities. Indeed, shame figures prominently in their arguments. This sentiment was voiced not only by the urbanists. It emerged with some regularity whenever partisans of progress and change argued against the supposedly benighted traditions of their city. For example, when in the late seventeenth century Martel attacked the popular

69. *Projet pour le commerce*, p. ii.

side of the Floral Games festivities, he spoke in terms of being ashamed of his city's customs.[70] When the academy of art complained of a lack of municipal support, it too noted how shameful it was that works of beauty were so little appreciated in the provincial capital. The *Affiches* also occasionally denigrated Toulouse's intellectual life. And, in the aftermath of the Calas trial, some local partisans of the Enlightenment, especially those sensitive to Voltaire's withering attacks on their city, spoke of a hopeful turn away from intolerance in tones that belied a shamefulness in what had been committed in their name.[71] When the *Affiches* of 1783 celebrated some of the improvements recently wrought in the city, the editor noted the previous generations of neglect, "to the shame of our ancestors."[72] Finally, Mondran's shame is evident throughout his writings. His mock dialogue is constructed to convey both the Toulousain's shame and disappointment in his city and the Parisian's air of solicitude and condescension. Mondran's shame extended to the past: "Let us avoid having our Descendants think of us as we think of our Predecessors."[73] Whatever pride eighteenth-century Toulousains might have had in their city's legacy was not shared by this man of progress.

Essential to the Enlightenment was the so-called "critical spirit." But what do we call criticism when it departs from the realm of the intellect, is turned on one's native culture and traditions, and is invested with the emotion of shame? Robert Muchembled has suggested that the process of acculturation in the era of religious reform entailed a dawning sense of shame on the part of villagers as they were forced to confront their past complicity in practices now forbidden by the Tridentine clergy.[74] And it is not hard to detect a sense of shame in the views of many eighteenth-century French philosophes and statesmen, especially when they compared their government's inept ways with the English system, or contemplated their recent military losses to Austria and Prussia, supposedly backward coun-

70. See above, Chapter 8.
71. Bien, *Calas*, p. 154.
72. *Affiches*, *1783*, p. 10.
73. *Project pour le commerce*, p. xvii. See also the remarks of Garipuy, who also disparaged the "laziness and chicanery" of Toulousains: ADH-G, C 331, "Mémoire addressé à l'intendant ou Garipuy se plaint de l'opposition d'une partie du Conseil de bourgeoisie de Toulouse. . . ."
74. Robert Muchembled, "The Witches of the Cambrésis: The Acculturation of the Rural World in the Sixteenth and Seventeenth Centuries," in James Obelkevich, ed., *Religion and the People, 800–1700* (Chapel Hill, N.C., 1979), p. 221–76.

tries and second-rate powers.[75] The spread of enlightenment in the last decades of the Old Regime is well documented, but very little has been proposed to explain the motivations behind provincials' embrace of the new sensibility. As noted, a rejection of local traditions and customs usually went hand-in-hand with enlightened thinking, and I would suggest that such a rejection sometimes entailed a sense of shame as well. It certainly was present among the urbanists of eighteenth-century Toulouse.

Whatever forces animated the movement of urbanism, it clearly set Toulouse on a new course of development, although the changes effected during the eighteenth century were in fact modest. The Revolution interrupted some projects, and it was not until the late nineteenth century that, under the pressures of industrialization and dramatic population growth, the city emerged refashioned as a sprawling metropolis. But even in the eighteenth century, Toulouse had begun its turn outward, beyond the city walls that had confined it for centuries. The construction of two canals, the Canal du Midi and the Canal Brienne, provided a commercial opening for the landlocked provincial capital. Urban expansion followed the creation of these canals, which encircled the periphery of the city, thus drawing urban activities into the faubourgs. As a result, Toulouse had a significant permanent urban settlement outside its city walls for the first time in its history. The construction and improvement of roads and avenues radiating toward the exterior complemented this residential and commercial expansion. By the Revolution, Toulouse was a vastly more accessible city.[76] And its push toward the exterior was matched by cultural influences—Parisian fashion, learned academies, a salon society, an enlightened press—that went a long way toward transforming the provincial outpost into a cosmopolitan city.

The Festive City

What of the rest of the populace? The spirit of cosmopolitanism was surely irrelevant to the vast majority of Toulousains. The eighteenth century did bring change to them as well, although change of a some-

75. On this theme see George Armstrong Kelly, *Mortal Politics in Eighteenth-Century France* (Waterloo, Ontario, 1986), chap. 7.
76. Coppolani, pp. 92–93. See also Guy Arbellot, "La grande mutation des routes au milieu du XVIIIe siècle," *Annales: ESC* 27 (1973): 765–91.

what brutal sort—increased poverty, social conflict, and a beefed-up repressive apparatus. But if royal troops and an augmented police force were novelties to eighteenth-century urban life, so was a new scale of citywide festivities and public entertainments. Of course, the city had always been a stage for great ceremony, mostly of a religious and civic sort. The great religious procession, still mounted with regularity, was the most emblematic of such ceremonies. But the new festivities of the eighteenth century represented a departure from previous ceremonial forms in several important respects. For one, they were larger in scale and more lavish than earlier celebrations and public rituals. In addition, they usually promoted the interests of the monarchy and the state. Finally, while in other rituals, most notably the general processions, many of the townspeople had a role as participants, in the eighteenth-century festival people were relegated to mere spectators.

Perhaps the most visible feature of festive life in the eighteenth century, as opposed to previous times, was the ceremonial reliance on fireworks. To be sure, fireworks were not unknown in the past; the art of mounting such displays in France was perfected at Louis XIV's Versailles, and in Toulouse the bonfire gave way to fireworks as the appropriate manner for ending citywide celebrations sometime in the seventeenth century. But the eighteenth-century fireworks were greater in scale than earlier ones—they were both more costly, more elaborate, and entailed far more firepower. For example, in 1643, fireworks for the occasion of the feast of Saint-Etienne, the patron of the cathedral, cost 75 livres; in 1770 the expenditures for a pyrotechnic display in honor of the new First President exceeded 2,000 livres.[77] The scale of these eighteenth-century spectacles was so immense—usually entailing a massive scaffolding and hundreds of rounds of various artifices—that a misfiring in 1754 injured more than a hundred people.[78] Moreover, there were fireworks for virtually every occasion: royal birthdays and marriages, military victories, saints' days and other religious occasions, public fêtes, the entries of officials, and the like. Barthès describes scores of them.

Most were mounted to celebrate the military victories of France's armies. Celebration of the monarch's military conquests was begun

77. J. Lestrade, "Le feu d'artifice de Saint-Etienne," *RHT* 2 (1915–19): 168; F. Galabert, "Feux d'artifices et collations capitulaires (1770)," *Bulletin de la Société Archéologique du Midi de la France* 40 (1909): 109–23.
78. BMT, MS 702, pp. 21–22.

during the reign of Louis XIV, but again, in the eighteenth century this custom took on a greater prominence in the city's ceremonial life. From 1680 to 1788 there were 108 large-scale festivals celebrated in the city: 58 were on the occasion of a royal victory; 27 celebrated a marriage or birth in the royal family; 10 were in honor of the king; 8 followed a declaration of peace; and only 5 had to do with the city itself.[79] Such celebrations even began to rival religious rituals in their frequency. Moreover, they took on the character of true celebrations, not simply propagandistic displays—that is, they always entailed fireworks and other illuminations, as well as public balls and the like. Clearly the public life of provincial Toulouse—an eight-day journey from Versailles—was increasingly marked by the fortunes of the monarchy's war policy; and clearly the populace was enticed to identify with these fortunes.

Other evidence suggests that entertainment characterized public life more and more. In July 1765, for example, a group of Englishmen living in Toulouse mounted a horse race just outside the city gates—a spectacle never witnessed before, noted Barthès. He called it a new kind of circus. The spectacle attracted 30,000 spectators, who were regaled with food and drink served under large tents.[80] In May 1761 the students of the university sponsored another novel exhibition, this an elaborate mock naval combat between two barges and their respective crews, one dressed up as French sailors, the other as English.[81] In 1771 the Garonne was again the site of a new display: this time the fisherman of the city staged a boat race and a demonstration of their naval skills.[82] Other entertainments appeared in the eighteenth century, especially the public dances sponsored by the city for the populace's enjoyment. In 1768 a troupe of French and Italian acrobats performed in the streets, not an entirely novel event, except for the fact that they were accompanied by an elephant, which, commented the subdelegate, "attracted an infinite crowd."[83] The presence of animals in the streets was not uncommon. During her short stay in Toulouse in 1785, Mrs. Cradock came upon several animal acts as she strolled through the city, one featuring a dancing bear and six costumed monkeys. "What lighthearted people," she thought to her-

79. Cassan, *La fête à Toulouse*, p. 11.
80. BMT, MS 703, pp. 194–95.
81. Ibid., p. 41.
82. Ibid., MS 704, p. 163.
83. ADH-G, C 6855, *Inventaire sommaire*, 5:348.

self. "How easily you are amused!"[84] To celebrate France's naval victory at Port Mahon in 1765, the people were offered a variety of circuslike spectacles. First they were treated to a "bloody combat of a bull," followed by other animal-baiting contests, including a fight between a large wolf and several dogs. Then a double fireworks display was staged, designed to imitate the successful siege of the British fortress in Majorca. Finally, amid the smoke and flame, a dog was lofted into the air by means of hot air and parachute.[85]

Not only animals were launched into the skies. Less than a year after they demonstrated the aeronautic potential of their hot-air balloon in Paris, the Montgolfier brothers exhibited their invention in Toulouse. In January 1784 more than 20,000 Toulousains anxiously watched as the balloon ascended over their city and crossed over the canal, only to burst into flames moments later.[86] The year 1784, in fact, witnessed a veritable outbreak of balloon launchings. The city was the scene of at least nine such early experiments in aviation, probably more, each the occasion of much fanfare and public discussion. Usually the city staged firework displays to celebrate the launchings, which drew thousands of spectators.[87] Nearly every issue of the *Affiches* in 1784 was devoted to the "globistes": some articles offered technical discussions of the design and workings of balloons, others were more whimsical reflections on the poetry of flight. One contributor mused, apropos of a failed launching, "Is it bad? Is it good? Following the logic of Doctor Pangloss, I would say that it is something from which all Globistes can learn, in order to avoid a similar accident, which seems to be the stumbling-block of the Toulouse balloons."[88] Balloons were the rage, even in the world of fashion: the women of Toulouse apparently took to coiffing themselves "en Globe"—whatever that might have been.[89] Late in the summer an entrepreneur and adventurer named Duvernai proposed a manned expedition, with himself as the voyager. To cover the finances of his enterprise, Duvernai sought local contributors to provide his ex-

84. *Journal inédit de Madame Cradock*, pp. 179, 185.

85. ADH-G, J 477.

86. ADH-G, C 2090; Christian Cau, "Toulouse terre d'envol," *Lo Reveih D'Oc* 53 (1984): 3.

87. Ibid., p. 18; *Affiches, 1784*, p. 11.

88. Ibid., p. 16.

89. Ibid., p. 20. Medical experiments in inoculation apparently inspired Parisian ladies to style their hair "à l'inoculation." See McManners, *Death and the Enlightenment*, p. 47.

penses of 700 livres. More than 100 Toulousains subscribed, including the archbishop, leading members of the parlement, the whole séné-chal, as well as other officers and professional and military men. His first attempt barely made it off the ground. But on August 30 his balloon took flight and soared over 300 meters above the city, only to sink to the earth as it developed a tear. Duvernai saved himself by jumping onto the roof of a house.[90]

The most spectacular of these new spectacles was what the city itself called the "Fête de la Ville." Barthès describes five of these in a forty-year period. Each was occasioned by a royal event—the recovery from illness of Louis XV, the ascension of Louis XVI, and the like. And thus each was a moment when the populace was forced to acknowledge the importance of royalty and royal power. These were, to be sure, political festivities with political meanings. But their scale and nature also marked them as entertainments of gargantuan proportions. That of September 1744, celebrating the recovery from illness of Louis XV, was typical. Like other such celebrations, the festival lasted several days. Not only were there illuminations and fireworks throughout the city, not only were there Te Deums sung in every church and processions everywhere, not only was the Hôtel de Ville festooned with inscriptions, garlands, fleurs-de-lys and various edifying tableaux, but the city fathers also had constructed in the central square fountains sprouting forth hundreds of gallons of wine—day and night for several days—which gathered in open vats so that, noted Barthès, "quantities of that charming liquor was drunk by everyone at his pleasure."[91] (As for the soothing properties of wine on a miserable populace, the authorities were only too aware. "It is a blessing," commented the subdelegate in 1781 regarding the abundance of cheap wine, "because the drink allows the people to forget the weight of misery that burdens them from all sides.")[92] The festivities of 1763, celebrating a peace concluded with Portugal and England, also lasted several days and again featured spectacular illuminations, large quantities of wine, and novel displays. This time as well there was a dinner and ball to which "people of condition"—meaning the upper classes—were invited. But the common people were not to be denied: while the haut monde danced within, they frolicked without, for a *bal populaire* was permitted for their plea-

90. ADH-G, 309; *Affiches, 1784*, p. 146.
91. BMT, MS 699, pp. 165–74.
92. Quoted by Buchalet, *L'assistance publique*, pp. 26–27.

sure.[93] In 1775 the Fête de la Ville was for the ascension of Louis XVI. Along with other displays and entertainments, the capitouls constructed an outdoor theater in the main square, where an orchestra played while the people danced. On another stage were marionettes and actors; on a third, according to Barthès, performers of a high-wire act "amused everyone with their dexterity and suppleness."[94]

The eighteenth century witnessed the transformation of public life in Toulouse. A network of privileged arenas—academies, salons, Freemason lodges, private parties, and the like—emerged for the upper classes, while a sort of mass culture exemplified by the Fête de la Ville preoccupied the rest of the populace. Ties that were apparent in earlier centuries no longer connected the upper and lower classes, and this lack was aggravated by social conflict brought on by deepening class differences. Increasingly, the authorities relied upon armed might to keep the populace pacified. The eighteenth-century city was thus two cities. One was cosmopolitan, in which flourished an Enlightenment culture and a glittering haut monde. But beyond the salon windows and Masonic lodges was another city—impoverished, restless, and less integrated into the municipality's official public life than it had been in generations past. The Revolution is beyond the purview of this study, but if the transformation of public life in the eighteenth century was as dramatic as I have suggested, then the fact that the breakdown of the Old Regime led to such ferocious social conflict should be seen in a clearer light.

93. BMT, MS 703, pp. 133–34.
94. Ibid., MS 705, pp. 52–55. In his interesting reconstruction of several new forms of entertainment in eighteenth-century Paris, Robert Isherwood argues against the view put forth by Burke and others that a clear split emerged in the early modern period between popular and elite culture (*Farce and Fantasy: Popular Entertainment in Eighteenth-Century Paris* [New York, 1986]). His critique could also be applied to my interpretation of the new festivals in eighteenth-century Toulouse, for it is clear that these were frequented by all classes. I plan to investigate this question further in the context of Toulouse in a book based upon Pierre Barthès's diary. Here I would emphasize three elements of eighteenth-century festive life that marked a departure from that of earlier times. First was the fact that, unlike, for example, the general procession, people were relegated to the role of spectators, not participants; the new festivals were primarily entertainments. Second, there is virtually nothing local about the Fête de la Ville, whereas earlier ceremonies and rituals (most obviously the Floral Games) often embodied local traditions and bore local meanings. Finally, while eighteenth-century festivals attracted a range of spectators from all classes, restricted dinners, dances, and other entertainments marked the existence of a more segregated cultural milieu. For an elaboration on these and similar themes, see my "The Ceremonial City: Toulouse Observed 1737–1780" (paper presented at the Annual Conference of the Western Society for French History, Los Angeles, November 1988).

Conclusion

Despite the fashion "histoire immobile," all history is ultimately about both continuity and change. Public life in an early modern city such as Toulouse was both static and changing. In large part, I have been describing a structure of public life. Throughout much of the sixteenth and seventeenth centuries, Toulouse was characterized by multiple vertical associations and by political and ceremonial expressions of the local community—despite the fact that urban society was increasingly beset by profound social and economic differences and by corporate rivalries on various levels. The determinants of this structure of public life were varied: tradition and a prevailing sense of localism rooted in city government; civic humanism and its vaunting of the city as a municipal republic; popular and elite aspects of Catholicism fostering a commitment to social concerns; the exigencies of confessional strife and the need to create new associational forms to mobilize the masses; the social conditions of urban society, especially the ever-present problem of the poor; and even intercorporate rivalry between governing elites, which often provoked them to seek support among the urban populace.

Although these determinants were varied and complex, the relationship of urban elites to their community before the eighteenth century can be seen in two successive movements, each associated with a different period. In the sixteenth century the notion of the city as an integral community was still strong, associated as it was in many minds with the idea of a municipal republic. Behavior and attitudes were conditioned by allegiance to this community and by a need to defend it from various threats, whether political, religious, or social. Even the extraordinary mobilization that occurred during the religious wars was as much a defense of the spiritual integrity of the urban community as it was a confrontation between confessionally rival parties. But in the seventeenth century the relationship of elites to the urban populace found a somewhat different footing. Gone was the myth of the municipal republic, and in its stead there emerged a movement for Catholic renewal and reform that simultaneously served political and social ends. In the new lay piety and activism, urban elites found a vehicle for confronting at once the social exigencies of governing a restless populace and the growing intrusion of royal authority. Through that religious revival they found the basis for their legitimacy as elites. In sum, it appears that the rise of a self-conscious urban officialdom, a true elite in its cultural inclinations and social orientations, did not preclude ties between the classes or upper-class affinity for the local community. In spite of what others have argued, much of what I have presented suggests a rather durable structure of public life that perpetuated precisely such ties and affinities, at least through most of the seventeenth century.

In the late seventeenth century, however, this structure of public life began to break down. And this suggests that the last century of the Old Regime was indeed a new era. It was then that various associational patterns and municipal traditions were dramatically transformed, and for several reasons. The crown, attacking the traditions and privileges of city government, was one. Another was the economic conditions that aggravated class differences and led to chronic unrest and riots. Many elites, especially royal magistrates, began to see themselves as actors on the national, rather than local, political stage, and royal patronage of the local academic movement reinforced this trend. Increasingly the ideal life of the elite was fashioned after the ways of Paris. These and other changes created the conditions for the cosmopolitan city that emerged in the eighteenth century, a city marked by a combination of greater refinement, an expanded festive life, and armed surveillance.

It was a city where the culture of the Enlightenment was at home, and thus we can return to where we began, with a consideration of Jean-Jacques Rousseau's view of public life in the eighteenth century. One might conclude from a reading of his *Lettre à M. d'Alembert* that Rousseau's prescription for rectifying the ills of his century was to turn back the clock to a simpler time, when city life in particular was less frantic and smaller in scale, and when human pursuits were not so guided by self-love, fame, and ambition. There is, to be sure, a strain of nostalgia, even primitivism in his writing, which has often caused readers to assume that he had little to offer in the way of constructive commentary. But Rousseau did indeed have a political theory that went beyond mere condemnation of contemporary manners and morals and a yearning for some idealized past. As several commentators have argued, his ideas of true community reflected a political kinship with the tradition of civic republicanism, modified somewhat by Rousseau's own sensibility, his demanding political and moral goals, and the circumstances in Old Regime France, where such a tradition was weak.[1] His theory of community was expressed not only in *The Social Contract*, but in various other writings as well, such as the *Discourses*, *Emile*, and his commentaries on the governments of Corsica and Poland. The problem he posed was how to transform individual self-love and self-interest into an unforced, authentic acceptance of the good of the community, that is, the general will. His solution was complex, even tortured in its logic, and it combined moral and psychological arguments with a dash of mysticism. No one would confuse his path to the general will with a policy proposal. But in the course of *The Social Contract*, he did argue for different forms of association as a means of creating citizens, endowed with a sense of the general good, out of self-interested individuals. "By new associations," he wrote, "let us correct, if possible, the lack of a general association."[2]

Now one might argue that, given this particular prescription, Rousseau should have been encouraged by some of the associational developments apparent in eighteenth-century France, associations that struck at the heart of the Enlightenment. Take two new kinds of associations we have observed in eighteenth-century Toulouse: the various royal academies and the Masonic lodges. Were not these associations wide-ranging in their recruitment (though shunning the lower classes), high-minded and purposeful, imbued with a sense of public service and a mission to improve mankind? They were indeed, but not in a way that could please Rousseau. For his condemnation of

1. Judith Shklar, *Men and Citizens* (Cambridge, 1969); J. G. A. Pocock, *The Machiavellian Moment: Florentine Political Thought and the Atlantic Republican Tradition* (Princeton, 1975), p. 504.
2. Jean-Jacques Rousseau, *Du contract social*, in *Oeuvres complètes*, 3:288–89; quoted in Nannerl O. Keohane, *Philosophy and the State in France* (Princeton, 1980), p. 437.

eighteenth-century civic life was wholesale and struck particularly at the literate, academic culture that proved so hospitable to many of his fellow philosophes. Why he found this milieu so unpalatable can, of course, be explained largely by his own psychological makeup, a disposition sometimes bordering on paranoia. But there was an objective basis for his judgment and, in a sense, a case for that position has been provided here.

My purpose is not to justify Rousseau's outrage and disgust with his society but rather to suggest that, given his political ideals, there was in fact some basis for his reactions. Interestingly, his reading of contemporary society and culture later received support from an unlikely source. One can hardly imagine two thinkers more temperamentally and ideologically opposed than Rousseau and Alexis de Tocqueville, and yet the radical philosophe and the aristocratic conservative shared a similar critique of public life in the Old Regime. Like Rousseau, Tocqueville bemoaned the fact that pre-revolutionary France lacked proper arenas for the exercise of civic virtue. Instead, there was merely the "group individualism" he so carefully anatomized in *The Old Regime and the French Revolution*, the endless competition between rival classes and institutions that thwarted concerted political action. Whereas Rousseau condemned the self-interest of individuals and blamed this in part on human nature and in part on civilization, the arts, and science, Tocqueville, a shrewder political analyst, took aim at the never-ending scramble for privilege, another sort of self-interest, although corporately expressed, which blighted the Old Regime. The most important difference between the two thinkers, however, was that Tocqueville laid the blame for this group individualism on the crown and its policy of steadily undermining society's traditional bases of authority and political participation.

A more analytical version of Rousseau's disgust with contemporary society is thus to be found in the pages of Tocqueville. The culture of the Enlightenment could not fulfill the goals of civic virtue and disinterested public service because the social and political conditions for these qualities had been destroyed by a century of royal policy. No culture could compensate for the rending of social bonds and the destruction of traditional forms of political participation. Indeed, in Tocqueville's view, the Enlightenment itself represented an estranged form of thinking, detached from political practice, which gained a hold on public opinion only because the aristocracy had forfeited or been denied (or both) its traditional leadership role in society, especially local society.

Rousseau's outrage at the cosmopolitanism of his day and his disgust with an urban culture that transformed the whole city into the theater he despised suggest that this transformation was a recent occurrence. Having surveyed public life in Toulouse across three centuries, we are in a position to conclude how recent this transformation really was. And it is in comparison with the centuries preceding it that the eighteenth century stands out as an era of fundamental change. But if Rousseau gives us a sense of the originality of eighteenth-century public life, Tocqueville opens the way for understanding the basis for the transformation then apparent. Although his perspective is perhaps exaggerated because he focuses exclusively on the actions of the crown, there can be little doubt that the political relationship of local elites with their communities was profoundly altered in the course of the eighteenth century and that absolutism shares a large responsibility for that alteration. Indeed, it is this Tocquevillian theme that I have tried to echo and elaborate upon in this book. But absolutism cannot be made to bear the whole weight of such a transformation. Rather, a range of additional factors must be appreciated, from the evolution of culture and the waning appeal of collective religious rituals to the changing nature of social conflict and the widening vistas of local elites' political horizons.

A possible conclusion one could draw from this study is that the violence and hatred directed toward the upper classes during the Revolution should be understood in the context of the breakdown of interclass ties and associations in the generations preceding it. But the Revolution itself offers examples of the reforging of such vertical ties, suggesting that such a breakdown was far from definitive. To cite an example that relates to some of the evidence I have presented in an earlier chapter, during the local debate over the Civil Constitution of the Clergy there ensued a lively pamphlet campaign between the two factions, and most of these polemical writings were not only pitched to the general populace but were, accordingly, written in Occitan.[3] In the nineteenth century too, in the era of the Restoration, one sees in Toulouse a conscious attempt on the part of ultra-Royalists and conservatives to reconstitute a Catholic, paternalistic urban order that

3. See, for example, *Cansou cantado per habitans de' Sent-Genies a l'arribado d'el Pero Sermet* (Toulouse, 1791), and other such texts in BMT, D xvIII 248. Also, Timothy Jenkins, "Le père Sermet entre Godolin et l'abbé Grégoire," in Anatole, *Pèire Godolin*, pp. 315–23.

would serve to reinforce a reestablished traditional regime.[4] The lesson here is that history does not travel in one direction, neither generally nor in the case of the evolution of public life I have tried to reconstruct. Although I have used the concept of "breakdown" to describe what transpired in the eighteenth century, I do not mean to imply that what prevailed before then was somehow primordial or timeless. Indeed, I have taken pains to avoid the suggestion that certain forms of public life were "natural" or "organic," conversely giving way to others that were inauthentic and unnatural. Just as tradition can be "reinvented," so can forms of association and various cultural allegiances. Still, one wonders whether in the realm of social interaction and the parameters of people's communal interests a certain threshold was not passed in the eighteenth century, and whether that passage can ever be reversed.

4. David Higgs, *Ultraroyalism in Toulouse* (Baltimore, 1973). See also Ronald Aminzade, *Class, Politics, and Early Industrial Capitalism: A Study of Mid-Nineteenth-Century Toulouse, France* (Albany, 1981).

Selected Bibliography

Manuscript Sources

ARCHIVES MUNICIPALES DE TOULOUSE

AA 301–12: ordinances and privileges of the city.

BB 10, 12, 14, 17, 20, 30, 32, 34, 42, 43, 45, 49, 51: various deliberations of municipal councils (sixteenth through eighteenth centuries).

BB 65: "Table des déliberations, Gondet et Montels" (1659–1791).

BB 267: "Le testament syndical de Monsieur de Lafaille, ancien syndic et doyen des anciens capitouls de Toulouse."

BB 274–84: "Annales manuscrites de la ville" (1539–1787).

CC 14, 21, 48, 76, 77: cadastres for capitoulat of the Daurade (1478, 1555, 1571, 1678).

GG 13, 14, 15, 16, 39, 43, 44, 45, 46, 47, 50, 51, 52, 53, 55, 56, 61: parish registers, the Dalbade (seventeenth and eighteenth centuries).

GG 93, 97, 128, 133: parish registers, the Daurade (seventeenth and eighteenth centuries).

GG 205, 207, 209, 210, 245, 246, 251, 252, 266, 277, 286, 287, 297, 307, 317, 327, 352: parish registers, Saint-Etienne (seventeenth and eighteenth centuries).

GG 709: processions.

GG 788: Confraternity of the Holy Bodies of Saint-Sernin.

GG 812: Confraternity of Our Lady of the Daurade (1562–1600).

GG 828: Holy League.

GG 926: "Fragment du journal de l'Académie tenu par Mondran" (1760–76).

GG 943: "Catalogue de comédies, tragédies, opéras, drames et autres pièces en tout genre qui ont été jouées" (1786).

GG 949, 959: Hôpital de la Grave, deliberations.

GG 958: "Règlemens sur l'establissement d'un hôpital . . ." (1647).

365

BIBLIOTHÈQUE MUNICIPALE DE TOULOUSE

MS 208: Confraternity of Our Lady of the Good News.
MSS 699–706: "Les heures perdues de Pierre Barthès" (1737–80).
MS 1178: Confraternity of the Holy Sacrament, Saint-Etienne.

ARCHIVES DÉPARTEMENTALES, HAUTE-GARONNE

Archives hospitaliers, 2E1: Hôpital de la Grave.
C 287: intendant.
C 309: processions.
C 314–15: Compagnie du Guet.
C 331: "Mémoire de Mrs. de Sagets et Dufours, au sujet du plan de la ville de Toulouse."
E 816: Confraternity of Saint-Carbes.
E 817: Confraternity of the Cordon of Saint Francis.
E 818: Confraternity of the Immaculate Conception of the Virgin.
E 820: Confraternity of the Assumption, Daurade.
E 823: Confraternity of the Holy Cross, Dalbade.
E 826: Confraternity of the Holy Sacrament, Dalbade.
E 831: Table for the Mercy of Poor Orphans.
E 833: Confraternity of Our Lady of the Annunciation.
E 835–38: Confraternity of Saint-Jacques.
E 849: Confraternity of the Holy Sacrament, Saint-Etienne.
E 861: Confraternity of Saints Roch, Fabian and Sebastian.
E 863: Confraternity of the Five Wounds of Jesus Christ, Augustins.
E 870: Confraternity of Our Lady of the Blessed Bread.
E 872, 877: Confraternity of the Assumption of Our Lady, Saint-Etienne.
E 920, 923: Blue Penitents.
E 926: penitents.
E 929, 932: White Penitents.
E 934, 940: Gray Penitents.
E 942, 951: Black Penitents.
E 997: Confraternity of Saint-Germiers; Confraternity of Saint Joseph.
E 1001: Confraternity of the Work.
E 1011: Confraternity of Sainte-Barbe; Confraternity of the Holy Scapular of the Virgin.
E 1017: Confraternity of Our Lady of Pity; Archconfraternity of the Sash.
E 1020: Confraternity of the Crown of Our Lord; Confraternity of the Five Wounds of Our Lord Jesus Christ.
E 1021: Confraternity of Our Lady of the Annunciation; Company of the Faith.
E 1022: Table of Purgatory, Saint-Agne.
E 1037: Table of Purgatory, Saint-Etienne.

HG 225, 229, 230, 243, 745, 748, 750, 756, 757, 778, 780, 785, 786, 787, 793, 796, 797, 799, 805: accounts, Hôpital de la Grave (eighteenth century).
MSS 147–49: "Mémoires, collections et remarques du palais," Malenfant.

BIBLIOTHÈQUE DE L'INSTITUT CATHOLIQUE DE TOULOUSE
R MS 40: "Livre des Pénitents Bleus, registre des inscriptions depuis 1577."
R MS 61: "Livre des statutz de la Compagnie de St. Hierosme" (1572).

ARCHIVES DE JÉSUITES

CA 311: "Registre des déliberations de la dévote et royale Confrérie de Messieurs les Pénitents Bleus de Toulouse, commencé le 4e aoust 1747."

ARCHIVES NATIONALES

G7, 294–336: correspondence of intendant of Languedoc with contrôleur général (1669–1739).

Published Sources

L'advertissement particulier et véritable de tout ce qui s'est passé en la ville de Tholose, depuis le massacre & assassinat commis en la personne des princes catholiques touchant l'emprisonnement & mort du premier président & avocat du roy d'icelle Paris. Paris, 1589.
Affiches, annonces, avis divers de Toulouse et du Haut-Languedoc pour l'année. . . . Toulouse, 1775–77, 1781–84.
Alexis ou le retablissement d'Ysac. Toulouse, 1689.
Amilhat, Barthélemy. *Tableu de la bida del parfait Crestia.* Toulouse, 1673.
[Argenson, René de Voyer d'.] *Annales de la Compagnie du St.-Sacrement par le comte René de Voyer d'Argenson.* Ed. H. Beauchet-Filleau. Marseille, 1900.
"L'aumône générale. Les désordres que causent les pauvres dans Tholose." Reprinted by Abbé Jean Lestrade as "L'aumône générale à Toulouse au dix-septième siècle." In *Mélanges Léonce Coutre: Etudes d'histoire méridionale.* Toulouse, 1902.
Baro, Balthasar. *Le Cléosandre ou sont rapportez tous les passe-temps du Carneval de Toulouse.* Toulouse, 1624.
Berry, André, ed. *Anthologie de la poésie occitane.* Paris, 1961.
Bertrandi, Nicolas. *Les gestes des Tolosains et d'autres nations de l'environ.* Trans. Guillaume de la Perrière. Toulouse, 1555.
[Bosquet, M. G.] *Mémoire de M. G. Bosquet sur les troubles advenu en la ville de Tolose l'an 1562.* Toulouse, 1595.
Catel, Guillaume. *Mémoires de l'histoire du Languedoc.* Toulouse, 1633.
Cayla, J. M., and Paul Cleobule, eds. and trans. *Oeuvres Complettes de Pierre Godolin.* Toulouse, 1843.

Chabanel, Jean de. *De l'état et police de l'église Nostre-Dame dite la Daurade à Tolose.* Toulouse, 1625.

Collonques, R. P. *La pratique spirituelle de l'âme dévote.* Toulouse, 1633.

Le confrère charitable aux âmes souffrantes dans le purgatoire pour la dévote et charitable Confrairie de N.D. du Souffrage. Toulouse, 1650.

Constantin Porphyrogenite. Toulouse, 1688.

Corinthe. Toulouse, 1684.

Damon et Pythias, ou Les véritables amis. Toulouse, 1675.

Dayde, Raymond. *L'histoire de St. Sernin, ou L'incomparable trésor de son église abbatiale de Tolose,* Toulouse, 1661.

Depping, Georges Bernard, ed. *Correspondance administrative sons le règne de Louis XIV.* 4 vols. Paris, 1850–55.

La doctrino crestiano meso en rimos, per poude estre cantado sur diberses ayres. Toulouse, 1641.

Doujat, Jean. *Le dicciounari moundi. Dictionnaire de la langue toulousaine.* Toulouse, 1638.

Ducedre, Pierre. *Las ordenansas et coustumas de libre blanc.* Ed. J. B. Noulet. Toulouse, 1555; Paris, 1878.

Dutil, Léon, ed. *Lettres inédites de Mme de Mondonville suivies de fragments de ses mémoires (1655–1697).* Paris, 1911.

L'esprit de l'institut de la Congrégation des Pénitents Bleus. Toulouse, 1727.

Los estatutz de la tresque devote, nobla, antiqua Confrayria de la grada conception de Nostra Dama mayre de Nostre Senhor Dieu Jhesu Chryst, fundada en la devota et antiquissima gleys de la Daurada de Tholosa. Toulouse, 1515.

Exercise de dévotion pour les personnes associatées à la Confrérie de Nostre-Dame des Agonisants, érigée dans l'église paroissiale de Nostre-Dame de la Dalbade. Toulouse, 1668.

Les faux amis. Toulouse, 1675.

Gadave, René. *Les documents sur l'histoire de l'Université de Toulouse.* Toulouse, 1910.

Gardy, Philippe, ed. *Pèire Godolin: Le Ramelet mondin et autres oeuvres.* Aix-en-Provence, 1984.

Graham, V. E., and W. M. Johnson. *The Royal Tour of France by Charles IX and Catherine de Medici: Festivals and Entries.* Toronto, 1979.

Lafaille, Germain de. *Annales de la ville de Toulouse depuis la réunion du comté à la couronne.* 2 vols. Toulouse, 1687.

Lafont, Robert, trans. and ed. *Anthologie des baroques occitanes.* Paris, 1976.

Lamouzèle, E. *Toulouse au XVIIIe siècle d'après les "Heures perdues" de Pierre Barthès.* 1914. Reprint. Marseille, 1981.

La Roche-Flavin. *Treize livres sur les parlements de France.* Toulouse, 1621.

Lettre d'excommunication de l'archevêque Montchal. Toulouse, 1639.

Loutchitsky, Jean, ed. *Documents inédits pour servir à l'histoire de la réforme et de la lique.* Kiev, 1875.

Loyseau, Charles. *Traité des ordres.* Paris, 1610.

Lublinskya, A. D., ed. *Lettres et mémoires adressés au chancelier Séquier, 1633–1649.* Moscow and Leningrad, 1966.

[Maillard, Olivier]. *La confession generala de fraire Olivier Maillart en lengatage de Tholosa.* Toulouse, 1502.

Manuel de la dévote Confrérie Saint Croix des Pénitens Noirs de Toulouse. Toulouse, 1667.

Mars guéri. Toulouse, 1687.

Martel. *Factum pour l'établissement fixe d'une Académie de Belles-Lettres dans la ville de Toulouse.* Montauban, 1692.

————. *Réponse à des mémoires qui ont paru contre l'éstablissement d'une Académie de Belles-Lettres dans la ville de Toulouse.* Montauban, 1692.

Matathias. Toulouse, 1685.

Mémoire sur la nécessité de la réformation de l'administration municipale de la ville de Toulouse et sur la manière la plus efficace d'y procéder. Toulouse, 1775.

Mémoriaux annuels des Lanternistes. Toulouse, 1795.

Mesnard, Pierre, ed. *Oeuvres philosophiques de Jean Bodin.* Paris, 1971.

Mésuret, Robert, ed. *Les expositions de l'Académie Royale de Toulouse de 1751 à 1791.* Toulouse, 1972.

Minuit, Gabriel de. *De la beauté avec la Paule-Graphie ou descriptions des beautez d'une dame tholosaine nommée la Belle Paule.* Lyons, 1587.

Molinier, Etienne. *Des confraires pénitents; ou, Il est traicté de leur institution, reigles et exercises.* Toulouse, 1625.

————. *A Mirrour for Christian States.* Trans. W. Lyrwhirt. London, 1635.

[Mondran, Louis de.] *Plan général pour l'embellissement de la ville de Toulouse mis en dialogue entre un parisian et un toulousain.* Toulouse, 1754.

[————.] *Project pour le commerce et pour les embellissemens de Toulouse.* Toulouse, 1754.

[Montchal, Charles de.] *Mémoires de Mr. de Montchal, archevêque de Toulouse contenant des particularitez de la vie du ministère du cardinal de Richelieu.* Rotterdam, 1718.

Montluc, Adrien de. *L'infortune des filles de joye.* Paris, 1624.

————. *Les jeux de l'Inconnu.* Rouen, 1630.

Mouflard, Marie-Madeleine, ed. *Liber nationis provinciae provinciarum: Journal des étudiants provenciaux à l'Université de Toulouse (1558–1630).* 2 vols. La Roche-sur-Yon, 1965.

Mousnier, Roland, ed. *Lettres et mémoires adressés au chancelier Séguier.* 2 vols. Paris, 1964.

Noguier, Antoine. *Histoire tolosaine.* Toulouse, 1556.

Noulet, J. B., ed. *Oeuvres de Pierre Goudelin.* Toulouse, 1887.

Noyer, Madame de. *Lettres historiques et galantes de deux dames de condition.* Amsterdam, 1738.

Odde de Triors, Claude. *Les joyeuses recherches de la langue tolosaine.* Toulouse, 1578; Paris, 1847.

Ordonnance de Monseigneur l'archevêque de Toulouse portant règlement pour les processions des pénitens de ladite ville et du diocèse. Toulouse, 1749.

La paix de retour. Toulouse, 1678.

Perrière, Guillaume de la. *Le mirroir politique.* Lyons, 1555.

[Peyronet, Simon de.] *Instructions, constitutions et exercises de piété pour la direction des confrères de la Confrairie du Très-Saint-Sacrement, établie en l'église paroisselle Notre Dame du Taur en Tolose, par Simon de Peyronet, prestre, docteur en theologie et recteur de ladite église.* Toulouse, 1665.

Peyronet, Simon de. *Recueil des ordonnances synodales et autres.* 2 vols. Toulouse, 1665.

———. *Statuts synodaux de la cité et diocèse de Tholoze.* Toulouse, 1597.

Platter, Thomas. *Journal of a Younger Brother.* Trans. S. Jennet. London, 1963.

Pradel, Charles, ed. *Lettres de Coras, celles de sa femmes, de son fils et de ses amis.* Albi, 1880.

Prières pour les processions annuelles et autres exercises de la dévote Confrérie des Pénitens Gris de Toulouse sous l'invocation de S. Jean-Baptiste. Toulouse, 1679.

Les privilèges et règlements de la Confrérie des Toulousains. Toulouse, 1663.

Recueil de plusieurs pièces d'eloquence, présentée á Messieurs des conferences académiques de Toulouse. Toulouse, 1694.

Règlements de la Confrérie de la Charité, dressez par l'ordre de Monseigneur l'illustrissme et révérendissime père en Dieu Joseph de Montpezata de Carbon, archevêque de Toulouse. Toulouse, 1679.

Règles, coutumes et prières de la Congrégation des Messieurs érigée à Toulouse dans la Maison professe des Pères de la Compagnie de Jésus. Avignon, 1760.

Rousseau, Jean-Jacques. *Politics and the Arts: Letter to M. d'Alembert on the Theatre.* Trans. Alan Bloom. Ithaca, 1968.

La règne d'Auguste. Toulouse, 1685.

Roussel, François. *Le dialogue du mardy gras de Carneval, avec le mardy maigre de Caresme, aux masquez curieux de nouvelles masquées.* [Toulouse ?], n.d.

Rousselot, M. X., ed. *Oeuvres philosophiques de Vanini.* Paris, 1842.

Rozoi, Barnabé-Farmien de. *Annales de la ville de Toulouse.* 4 vols. Paris, 1771–76.

Salvat, Joseph ed. *Oeuvres de Péire Godolin.* Toulouse, n.d.

Schroeder, H. J., ed. and trans. *Canons and Decrees of the Council of Trent.* London, 1940.

Statuts de la Confrérie de l'Assomption Nostre-Dame, Vierge, mère de Jésus-Christ, instituée en l'église métropolitaine Saint-Estienne en Tolose. Toulouse, 1553.

Statuts de la Confrérie de la Miséricorde, établie à Toulouse pour le soulagement des pauvres prisonniers, l'an 1570. Toulouse, 1808.

Statuts et privileges de la Confrérie des Tolosains. Toulouse, 1684.

Les statutz, ordonances et establissements de la saincte et très dévote Confrérie de dieu à l'honneur de la sacrée conception de la glorieuse Vierge Marie fondée an la saincte et anticque Esglise de la Daurade de Tholose ensemble la teneu de lau ctozisation et confirmation dy ceulx. Toulouse, 1523.

Tallemant des Réaux, G. *Historiettes.* Ed. A. Adam. 2 vols. Paris, 1960.

Thieste. Toulouse, 1694.

Thouron, Jean-François. *Histoire de la Royale Compagnie de Messieurs les Pénitens Bleus de Toulouse.* Toulouse, 1688.

Tournier, Antoine. *Reiglement et ordre des affaires de la maison de la ville et cité de Toulouse.* Toulouse, 1558.

Tournier, Clément. *Le mesmerisme à Toulouse, suivi de lettres inédites sur le XVIIIe siècle, d'après les archives de l'Hôtel du Bourg.* Toulouse, 1911.

Le triomphe de la joye. Toulouse, 1689.

Vachet, J. A. *L'artisan chrétien; ou, La vie du bon Henry.* Paris, 1670.

La vie française à la veille de la Révolution. Journal inédit de Madame Cradock: Voyage en France (1783–1786). Trans. O. Delphin-Balleyquier. Paris, 1896.

Wolff, Philippe, ed. *Documents de l'histoire du Languedoc.* Toulouse, 1669.

Secondary Sources

Abbiateci, A., et al. *Crimes et criminalité en France aux XVIIᵉ et XVIIIᵉ siècles.* Paris, 1971.

Adam, Antoine. *Histoire de la littérature française au XVIIᵉ siècle.* 5 vols. Paris, 1948–56.

Agulhon, Maurice. *Pénitents et francs-maçons dans l'ancienne Provence.* Paris, 1968.

_____. "La sociabilité, la sociologie et l'histoire." *L'Arc,* no. 65 (1976): 76–84.

Allen, Don Cameron. *Doubt's Boundless Sea.* Baltimore, 1964.

Allier, Raoul. *La Compagnie du Saint-Sacrement de l'Autel: La cabale des dévots.* Paris, 1902.

_____. *La Compagnie du Saint-Sacrement à Toulouse.* Toulouse, 1914.

Amelang, James. *Honored Citizens of Barcelona: Patrician Culture and Class Relations, 1490–1714.* Princeton, 1986.

Aminzade, Ronald. *Class, Politics, and Early Industrial Capitalism: A Study of Mid-Nineteenth-Century Toulouse, France.* Albany, N.Y., 1981.

Anatole, Christian. "Echo des poésies de Pey de Garros au XVIᵉ siècle." *Revue des Langues Romanes* 82 (1976): 119–27.

_____, ed. *Pèire Godolin, 1580–1649.* Actes du Colloque International, Université de Toulouse-Mirail. Toulouse, 1980.

Anglade, Joseph. *Origines du gai savoir, receuil de l'Académie des Jeux Floraux.* Toulouse, 1919.

Armieux, Louis. "Etat des membres de l'Académie des Sciences, Inscriptions et Belles-Lettres." *MASIBL,* 7th ser., 8 (1876): 255–99.

Aston, Trevor, ed. *Crisis in Europe, 1560–1660.* New York, 1965.

Astre, F. *Essai sur l'histoire et les attributions de l'ancienne bourse de Toulouse.* Toulouse, 1934.

_____. "Introduction à l'histoire du Parlement de Toulouse." *MASIBL,* 7th ser., 4 (1872): 285–305.

Atkinson, James B. "Naïveté and Modernity: The French Renaissance Battle for the Literary Vernacular." *Journal of the History of Ideas* 35 (1974): 179–98.

Auguste, Alphonse, *La Compagnie du Saint-Sacrement à Toulouse: Notes et documents.* Paris and Toulouse, 1913.

_____. "Gabriel de Ciron et Madame de Mondonville." *RHT* 1 (1914): 14–25, 129–63, 303–33; 2 (1915–19): 20–69.

_____. *Les origines du jansénisme dans le diocèse de Toulouse: Notes et documents.* Paris and Toulouse, 1922.

_____. "Port-Royal à Toulouse ou le jansénisme des religieuses maltaises sous l'épiscopat de P. de Marca." *RHT* 3 (1920): 161–89.

_____. *Le Séminaire de Caramen au Faubourg Saint-Etienne à Toulouse.* Paris and Toulouse, 1913.

Baccrabère, Georges. "La pratique religieuse dans le diocèse de Toulouse aux XVIe et XVIIe siècles." *ADM* 74 (1962).

Bardet, Jean-Pierre. *Rouen aux XVIIe et XVIIIe siècles.* 2 vols. Paris, 1983.

Barnavi, Elie. *Le parti de Dieu: Etude sociale et politique des chefs de la Ligue parisienne, 1585–1594.* Brussels and Louvain, 1980.

Barnes, Andrew. "*De poenitentibus civitatis massaliae:* The Counter-Reformation, Religious Change, and the Confraternities of Penitents of Marseille, 1499–1792." Ph.D. diss., Princeton University, 1983.

Barranguet-Loustalot, Pierre. "La pratique et le sentiment religieux dans le diocèse de Toulouse au milieu et à la fin du XVIIIe siècle." Mémoire maîtrise, Université de Toulouse, 1953.

Barrière-Flavy, C. *La chronique criminelle d'une grande province sous Louis XIV.* Paris, 1926.

_____. "Les prisons de la conciergerie du palais à Toulouse aux XVIIe et XVIIIe siècles." *RHT* 10 (1923): 161–68.

_____. "Un sport dangereux à Toulouse au XVIIIe siècle." *RHT* 12 (1925): 188–92.

Bastide, M. "Un exemple de reconstruction urbaine: Toulouse après l'incendie de 1463." *ADM* 80 (1968): 7–26.

Baudouin, Adolphe. *Histoire critique de Jules-César Vanini, dit Lucilio.* Toulouse, 1903.

Baudrillart, Henri. *Histoire du luxe.* 3 vols. Paris, 1880.

Beauroy, J., J. Bertrand and E. Gargan. *The Wolf and the Lamb: Popular Culture in France.* Stanford French and Italian Studies 3. Stanford, 1977.

Beckerman-Davis, Barbara. "Poverty and Poor Relief in Toulouse, 1474–1560." Manuscript. 1985.

Begouen, H. "A propos de la *Sciencia media.*" *Bulletin de la Société Archéologique du Midi de la France.* 1913, pp. 73–76.

_____. "Les pèlerinages de pénitents à Notre-Dame de Garrison." *L'Auta* 41 (May 1931): 120–23.

_____. *Une société secrète émule de la Compagnie du Saint-Sacrement: L'AA de Toulouse aux XVIIe et XVIIIe siècles.* Toulouse, 1930.

Beik, William. *Absolutism and Society in Seventeenth-Century France: State Power and Provincial Aristocracy in Languedoc.* Cambridge. 1985.

_____. "Magistrates and Popular Uprisings in France before the Fronde: The Case of Toulouse." *Journal of Modern History* 46 (1974): 585–608.

_____. "Two Intendants Face a Popular Revolt: Social Unrest and the Structure of Absolutism in 1645." *Canadian Journal of History* 9 (1974): 243–62.

Bellas, Jacqueline. "Adrien de Monluc." In *Actes de Journées Internationales d'Etude de Baroque, 1966.* Montauban, 1967.

Benedict, Philip. *Rouen during the Wars of Religion.* Cambridge, 1981.

_____, ed. *Cities and Social Change in Early Modern France.* London, 1989.

Bercé, Yves-Marie. "De la criminalité aux troubles sociaux: La noblesse rurale du sud-ouest de la France sous Louis XIII." *ADM* 76 (1964): 41–59.

_____. *Fête et révolte: Des mentalités populaires de XVIᵉ au XVIIIᵉ siècle.* Paris, 1976.

_____. *Histoire des Croquants.* 2 vols. Paris, 1974.

Berlenstein, Lenard R. *The Barristers of Toulouse in the Eighteenth Century.* Baltimore, 1975.

Berry, André. "Les psaumes de Pey de Garros." *Bulletin de la Société Archéologique du Gers,* 1965, pp. 319–51, 499–525.

Bien, David D. *The Calas Affair: Persecution, Toleration, and Heresy in Eighteenth-Century Toulouse.* Princeton, 1960.

_____. "The *secrétaires du roy:* Absolutism, *Corps,* and Privilege under the Ancien Régime." In *Vom Ancien Régime zu französischen Revolution: Forschungen und perspektiven/ De l'Ancien Régime à la Révolution française: Recherches et perspectives,* ed. Albert Cremer. Göttingen, 1978.

Biraben, J. N. *Les hommes et la peste en France et dans les pays européens et méditerranéens.* 2 vols. Paris, 1976.

Bitton, Davis. *The French Nobility in Crisis, 1560–1640.* Stanford, 1969.

Blanc-Rouquette, M. T. *La presse et l'information à Toulouse.* Toulouse, 1967.

Blickle, Peter. *The Revolution of 1525.* Trans. T. Brady and E. Midelfort. Baltimore, 1981.

Bois, Guy. *Crise du féodalisme.* Paris, 1976.

Bonnery, Bernard. "L'évolution démographique toulousaine de 1650 à 1700." Mémoire maîtrise, Université de Toulouse-Mirail, 1967.

Bonney, Richard. *Political Change in France under Richelieu and Mazarin, 1624–1661.* Oxford, 1978.

Bordes, Maurice. *L'administration provinciale et municipale en France au XVIIIᵉ siècle.* Paris, 1972.

Bossenga, Gail. "From *Corps* to Citizenship: The *Bureaux des Finances* before the French Revolution." *Journal of Modern History* 58 (1986): 610–42.

Bossy, John. "Blood and Baptism: Kinship, Community and Christianity in Western Europe from the Fourteenth to the Seventeenth Centuries." In *Sanctity and Secularity: The Church and the World,* ed. Derek Baker. Oxford, 1973.

_____. *Christianity in the West, 1400–1700.* Oxford, 1985.

_____. "The Counter-Reformation and the People of Catholic Europe." *Past & Present,* no. 47 (1970): 51–70.

Bourciez, Edouard. "Le réalisme et la fantaisie dans Goudelin." *Revue des Pyrénées* 8 (1896): 258–75.

Braudel, Fernand. *Capitalism and Material Life, 1400–1800.* Trans. M. Kochan. New York, 1975.

_____. *The Mediterranean and the Mediterranean World in the Age of Philip II.* 2 vols. Trans. Sian Reynolds. New York, 1972.

Braudel, Fernand, and C. E. Labrousse, eds. *Histoire économique et sociale de la France aux XVIIᵉ et XVIIIᵉ siècles.* Paris, 1970.

Brémond, Alphonse. *Histoire de toutes les saintes reliques conservées dans l'insigne Basilique le Saint-Saturnin.* Toulouse, n.d.

Brémond, Henri. *A Literary History of Religious Thought in France.* Vol. 3. Trans. K. L. Montgomery. London, 1936.

Brenac, Madeleine. "Toulouse, centre de lutte contre le protestantisme au XVIIe siècle." *ADM* 77 (1965): 31–45.

Brown, Irene Q. "Politics and Renaissance Educational Reform: Toulouse and the Founding of Its Municipal College." Ph.D. diss., Harvard University, 1969.

Brown, John L. *The "Methodus ad facilem historiarum congnitionem" of Jean Bodin: A Critical Study.* Washington, D.C., 1939.

Brun, C. *Recherches historiques sur l'introduction du français dans les provinces du Midi.* Paris, 1923.

Buchalet, M. F. *L'assistance publique à Toulouse au dix-huitième siècle.* Toulouse, 1904.

Burke, Peter. *Popular Culture in Early Modern Europe.* New York, 1978.

Cabos, Alban, *Guy du Faur de Pibrac.* Paris, 1922.

Cassan, Michel. "La fête à Toulouse au dix-huitième siècle." Thèse de doctorat, 3e cycle, Université de Toulouse-Mirail, 1980.

Castan, Felix. "Une épopée baroque de 1610 et le sens de la première renaissance littéraire occitane." *Actes des Journées Internationales du Baroque, 1964.* Montauban, 1965.

Castan, Nicole. *Les criminels de Languedoc. Les exigences d'ordre et les voies du ressentiment dans une société pré-révolutionnaire (1750–1790).* Toulouse, 1980.

———. *Justice et répression en Languedoc à l'époque des lumières.* Paris, 1980.

Castan, Yves. *Honnêteté et relations sociales en Languedoc (1715–1780).* Paris, 1974.

Caster, Gilles. *Le commerce du pastel et de l'épicerie à Toulouse, 1450–1561.* Toulouse, 1962.

Casteras, P. *La société toulousaine à la fin de l'Ancien Régime.* Toulouse, 1891.

Cau, Christian. "Toulouse terre d'envoi." *Lo Reveih d'Oc* 53 (1984): 1–5.

Caussette, T. R. *Notice sur Notre-Dame la Daurade à Toulouse.* Toulouse, 1874.

Cayre, Abbé. *Histoire des évêques et archevêques de Toulouse.* Toulouse, 1873.

Chabaneau, Camille, ed. *Origine et établissement de l'Académie des Jeux Floraux.* Toulouse, 1885.

Chalande, Jules. *Histoire des rues de Toulouse.* 3 vols. Toulouse, 1920–29.

———. "La maison publique aux XVe et XVIe siècles à Toulouse." *MASIBL,* 10th ser., 11 (1911): 65–86.

Chartier, R., G. Chaussinand-Nogaret, H. Neveux, and E. Le Roy Ladurie, *Histoire de la France urbaine.* Vol. 3: *La ville classique de la renaissance aux révolutions.* Paris, 1981.

Chaussinand-Nogaret, Guy. "De l'exil religieux aux affaires: Les jacobites aux XVIIIe siècle." *Annales: ESC,* 28 (1973): 1097–1122.

———. *Les financiers de Languedoc au XVIIIe siècle.* Paris, 1970.

Chevalier, Bernard. *Les bonnes villes de France du XIVe au XVIe siècle.* Paris, 1982.

Chill, Emanuel. "The Company of the Holy Sacrament: Social Aspects of the Counter-Reformation." Ph.D. diss., Columbia University, 1961.

Christian, William A., Jr., *Local Religion in Sixteenth-Century Spain.* Princeton, 1981.

Christie, Richard C. *Etienne Dolet: The Martyr of the Renaissance.* London, 1880.

Cibiel, M. E. "Les arrêts somptuaires du Parlement de Toulouse." *MASIBL*, 7th ser., 2 (1878): 248–66.

Contrasty, J. "Les prédicateurs du XVIᵉ siècle à Sainte-Marie de la Dalbade à Toulouse." *RHT* 34 (1947).

Coornaert, Emile. *Les compagnonnages en France du moven âge à nos jours*. Paris, 1966.

Coppolani, Jean. *Toulouse: Etude de géographie urbaine*. Toulouse, 1954.

Corraze, Raymond. "Le collège de l'Esquille." *MASIBL*, 12th serv., 14 (1941): 213–38.

———. "Le collège de l'Esquille au XVIᵉ siècle." *MASIBL*, 8th ser., 3 (1936): 67–92.

Costa, Georges. "Louis de Mondran: Economiste et urbaniste (1699–1792)." *Urbanisme et Habitation*, 1955, pp. 33–78.

———. *Les plans d'urbanisme pour Toulouse au milieu du XVIIIᵉ siècle*. Toulouse, 1953.

———. "Un projet d'urbanisme toulousain au second quart du XVIIIᵉ siècle." *Bullétin de la Section de Géographie*, 1953, pp. 79–98.

Coveney, P. J., ed. *France in Crisis, 1620–1675*. Totowa, N.J., 1977.

Crouzet, Denis, "Recherches sur les processions blanches—1583–1584." *Histoire, économie et société* 4 (1982): 511–63.

Darnton, Robert. *The Business of Enlightenment*. Cambridge, Mass., 1979.

Davies, Joan. "Persecution and Protestantism: Toulouse, 1562–1575." *Historical Journal* 22 (1979): 31–51.

Davis, Natalie Zemon. "Protestantism and the Printing workers of Lyons: A Study in the Problem of Religion and Social Class during the Reformation." Ph.D. diss., University of Michigan, 1959.

———. *The Return of Martin Guerre*. Cambridge, Mass., 1983.

———. "The Sacred and the Body Politic in Sixteenth-Century Lyon". *Past & Present*, no. 90 (1981): 40–70.

———. *Society and Culture in Early Modern France*. Sanford, 1975.

Dawson, John. *Toulouse in the Renaissance*. New York, 1921.

Dégert, Antoine. "Les lettres et les moeurs dans la société toulousaine il y a trois cents ans." *RHT* 1 (1914): 385–413.

Delaruelle, L. "Un président au Parlement de Toulouse, Jacques Minut (+ 1536)." *ADM* (1923): 137–53.

Delattre, Pierre, ed. *Les établissements des Jésuites en France depuis quatre siècles*. 5 vols. Enghien, 1949–57.

Delumeau, Jean. *Le catholicisme entre Luther et Voltaire*. Paris, 1971.

Deroo, André. *Saint Charles Borromée, cardinal réformateur, docteur de la pastorale, 1538–1584*. Paris, 1964.

Desbarreaux-Bernard. *Les Lanternistes: Essai sur les réunions littéraires et scientifiques qui ont précédé à Toulouse l'établissement de l'Académie des Sciences*. Paris, 1858.

Descimon, Robert. *Qui étaient les Seize? Mythes et réalités de la Ligue parisienne (1585–1594)*. Paris, 1983.

Dewald, Jonathan. *The Formation of a Provincial Nobility: The Magistrates of Rouen, 1499–1610*. Princeton, 1980.

——. *Pont-St.-Pierre, 1398–1789: Lordship, Community and Capitalism in Early Modern France*. Berkeley, 1987.

Deyon, Pierre. *Amiens, capitale provinciale*. Paris, 1967.

——. *Le temps des prisons*. Paris, 1975.

Diefendorf, Barbara B. *Paris City Councillors in the Sixteenth Century: The Politics of Patrimony*. Princeton, 1983.

——. "Recent Literature on the Religious Conflicts in Sixteenth-Century France." *Religious Studies Review* 10 (1984): 362–67.

Douais, S. G. *Documents sur l'ancienne province de Languedoc*. 2 vols. Paris and Toulouse, 1904.

——. *La visitation de Toulouse: Etudes, souvenirs et documents*. Paris, 1905.

Doublet, G. "Un seigneur languedocien: Compositeur de comédies sous Louis XIII." *Revue des Pyrénées* 8 (1896): 457–69.

Drouot, Henri. *Mayenne et la Bourgogne: Etude sur la Ligue en Bourgogne, 1587–1596*. 2 vols. Paris, 1937.

Dubédat, Jean-Baptiste. *Histoire du Parlement de Toulouse*. 2 vols. Paris, 1885.

Dubois, Jean. "Molière à Toulouse le 8 août 1650." *RHT* 9 (1922): 149–52.

Duboul, Axel, *Les deux siècles de l'Académie des Jeux Floraux*. 2 vols. Toulouse, 1901.

Dubrat, Clémence-Paul. "L'influence espagnole sur le décor des hôtels toulousains de la renaissance." *ADM* 66 (1954: 129–42.

Du Mege, Alexandre. *Histoire des institutions religieuses, politiques, judiciares et littéraires de la ville de Toulouse*. 4 vols. Toulouse, 1864.

Dumeril, Henri. "Un humoriste anglais en Languedoc au XVIIIe siècle." *Revue des Pyrénées* 7 (1895): 9–21.

Dutil, Léon. "Philosophie ou religion: Lomenie de Brienne, archevêque de Toulouse.: *ADM* 61 (1948): 33–70.

——. "La réforme du capitoul toulousain." *ADM* 19 (1907): 305–63.

Egret, Jean. *Louis XV et l'opposition parlementaire*. Paris, 1970.

——. "Le procès des Jésuites devant les parlements de France." *Revue Historique*, nos. 203–204 (1950): 1–27.

Elias, Norbert. *The Civilizing Process*. Trans. E. Jephcott. New York, 1978.

Estèbe, Janine, "La bourgeoisie marchande et la terre à Toulouse au seizième siècle." *ADM* 76 (1964): 458–67.

——. *Tocsin pour un massacre: La saison des Saint-Barthélemy*. Paris, 1968.

Fabry, Michel. "Carte des propriétés ecclésiastiques de Toulouse à la fin du XVIIe siècle." Mémoire maîtrise, Université de Toulouse-Mirail, 1963.

Fairchilds, Cissie. "Masters and Servants in Eighteenth-Century Toulouse." *Journal of Social History* 12 (1978): 368–93.

——. *Poverty and Charity in Aix-en-Provence*. Baltimore, 1976.

Farge, Arlette. *Vivre dans la rue à Paris au XVIIIe siècle*. Paris, 1979.

Feugère, A. "Le capitoul David et les jeux défendus." *ADM* 44 (1932): 296–331.

Fons, M. V. "Coutumes religieuses de l'Hôtel de Ville de Toulouse." *Mémoires de la Société Archéologique du Midi de la France* 11 (1874): 82–107.

____. "L'organisation municipale à Toulouse du temps des capitouls." *Recueil de l'Académie de Législation de Toulouse.* 26 (1877–78): 19–84.

____. "Le Parlement de Toulouse en temps de l'épidémie." *MASIBL*, 7th ser., 10 (1878): 39–51.

Ford, Franklin. *Robe and Sword: The Regrouping of the French Aristocracy after Louis XIV.* New York, 1965.

Forster, George. "Cofradia and Compadrazgo in Spain and Spanish America." *Southwestern Journal of Anthropology* 9 (1953): 1–28.

Forster, Robert. *The Nobility of Toulouse in the Eighteenth Century.* Baltimore, 1960.

Foucault, Michel. *A History of Sexuality.* Vol. 1. *An Introduction.* Trans. Robert Hurley. New York, 1981.

____. *Madness and Civilization.* Trans. Richard Howard. New York, 1965.

Franklin, Julian H. *Jean Bodin and the Sixteenth-Century Revolution in the Methodology of Law and History.* New York, 1963.

Frêche, Georges. *Toulouse et la région Midi-Pyrénées au siècle des lumières (vers 1670–1789).* Paris, 1974.

Fremy, Eduard. *Un ambassadeur libéral sous Charles IX et Henry III: Ambassade à Venise d'Arnaud du Ferrier.* Paris, 1880.

Galabert, F. "Feux d'artifices et collations capitulaires (1770)." *Bulletin de la Société Archéologique du Midi de la France* 40 (1909): 109–23.

Galperin, A. N. *Religions of the People in Sixteenth-Century Champagne.* Cambridge, Mass., 1976.

Garrioch, David. *Neighborhood and Community in Paris, 1740–1790.* Cambridge, 1986.

Gatien-Arnoult, M. "Note pour servir à une étude sur Vanini." *MASIBL*, 6th ser., 5 (1867): 281–94.

Gelis, François de. *Histoire critique des Jeux Floraux.* Toulouse, 1912.

____. "Les Jeux Floraux pendant la renaissance." *MASIBL*, 11th ser., 6 (1918): 141–61.

____. "Les philosophes du dix-huitième siècle et les Jeux Floraux." *MASIBL*, 11th ser., 8 (1920): 15–56.

____. "Les poètes humanistes des Jeux Floraux." *MASIBL*, 11th ser., 7 (1919): 45–68.

____. "Quelques poètes des Jeux Floraux." *MASIBL*, 12th ser., 12 (1924): 21–46.

Geremek, B. "La popolazione marginale tra il medievo e l'erà moderna." *Studi Storici*, 1968, pp. 623–40.

Giesey, Ralph. "State-Building in Early Modern France: The Role of Royal Officialdom." *Journal of Modern History* 55 (1983): 191–207.

Gilmore, Myron. *Arguments from Roman Law in Political Thought, 1200–1600.* Cambridge, Mass., 1941.

Ginzburg, Carlo. *The Cheese and the Worms.* Trans. J. and A. Tedeschi. Baltimore, 1980.

Godechot, Jacques, and Suzanne Moncassin. "Structures et relations sociales à

Toulouse en 1749 et en 1785." *Annales historiques de la Révolution française* 37 (1965): 129–67.

Goimard, Jacques, ed. *La France au temps de Louis XIV.* Paris, 1965.

Goldmann, Lucien. *The Hidden God.* Trans. P. Thody. New York, 1964.

Gorsse, Pierre de. "Toulouse au XVIIᵉ siècle vue par un érudit dantzikois." *L'Auta* 51 (April 1941).

Goubert, Pierre. *Beauvais et les beauvaisis de 1600 à 1730: Contribution à l'histoire sociale de la France du XVIIᵉ siècle.* 2 vols. Paris, 1960.

———. *Louis XIV and Twenty Million Frenchmen.* Trans. Anne Carter. New York, 1970.

Graillot, Henri. *Nicolas Bachelier, imagier et maçon de Toulouse au XVIᵉ siècle.* Toulouse, 1914.

Greengrass, Mark. "The Anatomy of a Religious Riot in Toulouse in May 1562." *Journal of Ecclesiastical History* 34 (1983): 367–91.

———. *France in the Age of Henri IV.* London, 1984.

———. "The *Sainte Union* in the Provinces: The Case of Toulouse." *Sixteenth Century Journal* 14 (1983): 469–98.

Gutton, Jean-Pierre. *La société et les pauvres: L'exemple de la généralité de Lyon.* Paris, 1971.

Hamscher, Albert. "The Parlement of Paris and the Social Interpretation of Early French Jansenism." *Catholic Historical Review* 63 (1977): 392–410.

Harding, Robert R. *Anatomy of a Power Elite: The Provincial Governors of Early Modern France.* New Haven, 1978.

———. "Revolution and Reform in the Holy League: Angers, Rennes, Nantes." *Journal of Modern History* 53 (1981): 379–416.

Higgs, David. *Ultraroyalism in Toulouse.* Baltimore, 1973.

Hoffman, Philip T. *Church and Community: The Counter-Reformation in the Diocese of Lyons, 1500–1789.* New Haven, 1985.

Hsia, R. Po-chia. *Society and Religion in Münster, 1535–1618.* New Haven, 1984.

Hudson, David. "The Parlementary Crisis of 1763 in France and Its Consequences." *Canadian Journal of History* 7 (1972): 97–117.

Hufton, Olwen. *The Poor of Eighteenth-Century France, 1750–1789.* Oxford, 1974.

Huppert, George. *Les Bourgeois Gentilhommes: An Essay on the Definition of Elites in Renaissance France.* Chicago, 1970.

———. *Public Schools in Renaissance France.* Chicago, 1984.

Isherwood, Robert. *Farce and Fantasy: Popular Entertainment in Eighteenth-Century Paris.* New York, 1986.

Jacobet, Henri. "Les dix années d'amitié de Dolet et de Boyssone (Toulouse 1532–Lyon 1542)." *Revue du Dix-Septième Siècle* 12 (1925): 1–32.

James, Mervyn. "Ritual, Drama and Social Body in the Late Medieval English Town." *Past & Present,* no. 98 (1983): 2–29.

Jaudon, Henry. *Port-Royal à Toulouse ou le jansénisme au Parlement.* Toulouse, 1900.

Jeanroy, A. "Une Henriade gasconne: Le gentilhomme gascon de Guillaume Ader." *Revue des Pyrénées* 17 (1905): 271–91.

Jones, Colin. *Charity and "Bienfaisance": The Treatment of the Poor in the Montpellier Region, 1740–1815.* Cambridge, 1982.

Julien, R. D. *Toulouse chrétienne: Histoire de la paroisse Notre-Dame la Dalbade.* Toulouse, 1891.

Kaiser, Colin. "Les cours souveraines au XVIe siècle: Morale et contre-réforme." *Annales: ESC* 37 (1982): 15–31.

Kaplan, Steven L. *Bread, Politics and Political Economy in the Reign of Louis XV.* 2 vols. The Hague, 1976.

———. *Provisioning Paris.* Ithaca, 1984.

Kelley, Donald. *The Foundations of Modern Scholarship: Language, Law and History in the French Renaissance.* New York, 1970.

———. *François Hotman: A Revolutionary's Ordeal.* Princeton, 1981.

Kelly, George Armstrong. *Mortal Politics in Eighteenth-Century France.* Waterloo, Ontario, 1986.

Keohane, Nannerl O. *Philosophy and the State in France.* Princeton, 1980.

Kettering, Sharon. *Judicial Politics and Urban Revolt in Seventeenth-Century France: The Parlement of Aix, 1629–1659.* Princeton, 1978.

———. *Patrons, Brokers, and Clients in Seventeenth-Century France.* New York, 1986.

Lachèvre, Fréderic. *Le libertinage au XVIIe siècle, Mélanges.* Paris, 1920.

———. *Procès du poète Théophile de Viau.* 2 vols. Paris, 1909.

Lafont, Robert. *Renaissance du sud: Essai sur la littérature occitane au temps de Henri IV.* Paris, 1970.

Lahondès, Jules de. *Les monuments de Toulouse.* Toulouse, 1920.

———. "Simon de Laboubère." *Revue des Pyrénées* 7 (1895): 233–63.

———. "Les statues de la vierge au Musée de Toulouse." *Mémoires de la Société Archéologique du Midi de la France* 16 (1908): 270–87.

———. *Toulouse chrétienne: L'église Saint-Etienne.* Toulouse, 1890.

Lamouzèle, E. *La Famille de Guet à XVIe et XVIIe siècles.* Toulouse, 1906.

———. "Inventaire du mobilier de l'hôtel de Jean DuBarry, à Toulouse, 1794." *Bulletin de la Société Archéologique du Midi de la France,* 2d ser., no. 30 (1902): 197–208.

———. "Une ordre de chevalerie ecclésiastique en Languedoc au commencement du dix-septième siècle." *Revue des Pyrénés* 16 (1904): 565–90.

———. "Quelques fonctionnaires municipaux de Toulouse à la fin du dix-septième siècle." *Bulletin de la Société Archéologique du Midi de France* 32 (1904): 37–42.

Lancaster, Henry. *A History of French Dramatic Literature in the Seventeenth Century.* 9 vols. New York, 1929–42.

Lane, Frederic C. *Venice and History.* Baltimore, 1966.

Lapierre, M. "Les bout-rimes des Lanternistes." *MASIBL,* 8th ser., 9 (1887): 273.

Laurent, André. "Ce qu'on a dit de Toulouse: Elie Brackenhoffer, strasbourgeois." *L'Auta* 41 (May 1931).

Lavedan, P. *Histoire de l'urbanisme.* Vol. 3: *Renaissance et temps modernes.* 1926. Reprint. Paris, 1953.

Le Bras, Gabriel. *Etudes de sociologie religieuse.* 2 vols. Paris, 1955.

Le Goff, Jacques, ed. *Histoire de la France urbaine*. Vol. 2: *La ville médiévale*. Paris, 1980.

Le Roy Ladurie, Emmanuel. *Les paysans de Languedoc*. 2 vols. Paris, 1966.

———. *The Peasants of Languedoc*. Trans. John Day. Urbana, Ill., 1974.

Lestrade, Jean. "Le feu d'artifice de Saint-Etienne." *RHT* 2 (1915–19): 168.

———. "Frais d'un baptême à Toulouse en 1785." *RHT* 3 (1920): 134–35.

———. *Pierre Goudelin, see ancêtres, ses frères, ses amis*. Toulouse, 1896.

Limouzin-Lamouthe, Roger. *La commune de Toulouse et les sources de son histoire*. Toulouse, 1932.

Lis, C., and H. Soly. *Poverty and Capitalism in Pre-Industrial Europe*. Atlantic Highlands, N.J., 1979.

Lougee, Carolyn. *Le Paradis des Femmes: Women, Salons and Social Stratification in Seventeenth-Century France*. Princeton, 1976.

Lublinskaya, A. D. *French Absolutism: The Crucial Phase, 1620–1629*. Cambridge, 1968.

MacManners, John. *French Ecclesiastical Society under the Ancien Régime: A Study of Angers in the Eighteenth Century*. Manchester, 1960.

Mahoney, Michael. *The Mathematical Career of Pierre de Fermat, 1601–1665*. Princeton, 1963.

Major, J. Russell. "The Crown and the Aristocracy in the Renaissance." *Americal Historical Review* 88 (1983): 631–45.

———. "Noble Income, Inflation, and the Wars of Religion in France." *American Historical Review* 86 (1981): 21–48.

Maland, David. *Culture and Society in Seventeenth-Century France*. New York, 1970.

Mandrou, Robert. *Classes et luttes des classes en France au début du XVIIᵉ siècle*. Messina and Florence, 1968.

———. "Tragique XVIIᵉ siècle, à propos de travaux récents." *Annales: ESC* 12 (1957): 305–13.

Mentzer, Raymond A. "Heresy Suspects in Languedoc Prior to 1560: Observations on Their Social and Occupational Status." *Bibliothèque d'Humanisme et Renaissance* 39 (1977): 561–68.

———. "The Inquisitor as Heretic: The Pre-Reformation at Toulouse." *Wascana Review* 9 (1974): 156–65.

Mesnard, Pierre. "Jean Bodin à Toulouse." *Bibliothèque d'Humanisme et Renaissance* 12 (1950): 31–59.

———. "La place de Cujas dans la querelle de l'humanisme juridique." *Revue Historique du Droit Française et Etrangère* 28 (1950): 521–37.

Mésuret, Robert. *Evocation du vieux Toulouse*. Toulouse, 1960.

Meuvret, Jean. *Le problème des subsistances à l'époque de Louis XIV*. 2 vols. Paris, 1977.

Michel, Henri. "Urbanisme et société à Montpellier sous l'Ancien Régime." *ADM* 86 (1974): 21–43.

Moeller, Bernd. *Imperial Cities and the Reformation*. Trans. E. Midelfort and M. Edwards. Philadelphia, 1972.

Monin, Henri. *Essai sur l'histoire administrative du Languedoc pendant l'intendance de Basville*. Toulouse, 1884.

Morineau, Michel. "Y a-t-il une révolution agricole en France au XVIIIe siècle?" *Revue Historique*, no. 237 (1967): 299–326.

Mouflard, Marie-Madeleine. *Robert Garnier, 1545–1590. La vie.* La Ferté-Bernard, 1961.

Mousnier, Roland. *Les hiérarchies sociales de 1450 à nos jours.* Paris, 1969.

———. *The Institutions of France under the Absolute Monarchy, 1598–1789: Society and the State.* Trans. Brian Pearce. Chicago, 1979.

———. *La plume, la faucille et le marteau: Institutions et société en France du moyen âge à la Révolution.* Paris, 1970.

———. "Recherches sur les soulèvements populaires en France avant la Fronde." *Revue d'Histoire Moderne et Contemporaine* 4 (1958): 88–113.

———. *Les société française de 1770 à 1789.* Paris, 1967.

Muchembled, Robert. *Culture populaire et culture des élites dans la France moderne, XVe–XVIIIe siècles: Essai.* Paris, 1978.

Neale, J. E. *The Age of Catherine de' Medici.* New York, 1943.

Norberg, Kathryn. *Rich and Poor in Grenoble, 1600–1814.* Berkeley, 1985.

Noulet, J. B. "De la prétendue Pléiade Toulousaine." *MASIBL*, 4th ser., 3 (1853): 312–13.

Obelkevich, James, ed. *Religion and the People, 800–1700.* Chapel Hill, 1979.

Oulmont, Charles. "Etienne Forcadel: Un jurist, historien et poète vers 1550." *Revue des Pyrénées* 19 (1907): 547–83.

Ousset, P. E. *La Confrérie des Pénitents Bleus de Toulouse.* Toulouse, 1927.

———. "La Confrérie des Pénitents Bleus de Toulouse." *RHT* 11 (1924): 5–41, 103–15, 199–218, 273–92; 12 (1925): 113–37, 220–36, 256–76; 13 (1926): 41–64, 177–98.

Ozment, Steven. *The Reformation in the Cities.* New Haven, 1975.

Pagès, Georges. "Autour de grand orage. Richelieu et Marillac: Deux politiques." *Revue Historique* 79 (1937): 63–97.

Palmer, Robert R. *The Age of Democratic Revolution.* Vol. 1. Princeton, 1959.

Parker, David. *The Making of French Absolutism.* New York, 1983.

Paulhet, Jean-Claude. "Les parlementaires toulousains à la fin du XVIIe siècle." *ADM* 76 (1964): 37–51.

Pecquet, Marguerite. "La Compagnie des Pénitents Blancs de Toulouse." *ADM* 84 (1972): 213–24.

Perrot, J.-C. *Genèse d'une ville moderne: Caen au XVIIIe siècle.* Paris and La Haye, 1975.

Peyronnet, Pierre. "Le théâtre d'éducation des Jésuites," *Dix-Huitième siècle*, no. 8 (1976): 107–20.

Picot, Emile. "Les françaises à l'Université de Ferrare." *Journal des Savants* 67 (1902): 80–102, 141–58.

Pins, Jean de. "Autour des guerres: Une ambassade à Venise et à Rome (1515–1525), Jean de Pins, évêque de Rieux." *Revue d'Histoire Diplomatique* 61 (1947): 215–46.

Pintard, René. "Les adventures et la procès du chevalier de Roquelaure." *Revue d'Histoire de la Philosophie et d'Histoire Générale de la Civilisation* 17 (1937): 1–27.

———. *Le libertinage érudit dans la première moitié du XVIIe siècle.* Paris, 1943.

Pocock, J. G. A. *The Machiavellian Moment: Florentine Political Thought and the Atlantic Republican Tradition*. Princeton, 1975.

Porschnev, Boris. *Les soulèvements populaires en France de 1623 à 1648*. Paris, 1963.

Porte, T. "Esprit social et charité: Le tiers-ordre dominicain à Toulouse au XVIIᵉ siècle." *ADM* 70 (1958): 161–80.

Poutet, Y., and J. Roubert. *Les "assemblées" secrètes des XVIIIᵉ–XVIIᵉ siècles en relation avec L'AA de Lyon*. Piacenza, 1968.

Pullan, Brian. "Catholics and the Poor in Early Modern Europe." *Transactions of the Royal Historical Society*. 5th ser., 26 (1976): 15–24.

_____. *Rich and Poor in Renaissance Venice*. Cambridge, Mass., 1971.

Puybusque, G. A. de. "Le Confrérie de Sainte-Barbe à Toulouse." *RHT* 2 (1920): 14–16.

Rabb, T., and J. Seigel, eds. *Action and Conviction in Early Modern Europe*. Princeton, 1969.

Ramet, Henri. *Le Capitole et le Parlement de Toulouse*. Toulouse, 1926.

_____. *Histoire de Toulouse*. Toulouse, n.d.

Ranum, Orest. *Paris in the Age of Absolutism*. New York, 1968.

Raybaud, Leon-Pierre. "Le bureau de la miséricorde de Toulouse au XVIIᵉ et XVIIIᵉ siècles." In *Mélanges Roger Aubens*. Recueil de Mémoires et Travaux publié par la Société d'Histoire du Droit et des Institutions des Anciens Pays de Droit Ecrit. Fasc. IX. Montpellier, 1974.

Ribe, Marie-Louise, and Michelle Ribe. "La décadence de l'autonomie municipale toulousaine pendant les dernières années de la Ligue (1594–1596)." Mémoire maîtrise, Université de Toulouse-Mirail, 1974.

Richet, Denis. "Aspects socio-culturels des conflits religieux à Paris dans la seconde moitié du XVIᵉ siècle." *Annales: ESC* 22 (1977): 764–89.

Rives, Jean. "L'évolution démographique de Toulouse au XVIIIᵉ siècle." *Bulletin d'Histoire Économique et Sociale de la Révolution Française*, 1968, pp. 85–146.

Roche, Daniel. *Le peuple de Paris: Essai sur la culture populaire au XVIIIᵉ siècle*. Paris, 1981.

_____. *Le siècle des lumières en province: Académies et académiciens provinciaux, 1680–1789*. 2 vols. Paris, 1978.

Romier, Lucien, *Catholiques et huguenots à la cour de Charles IX*. Paris, 1925.

Root, Hilton. *Peasants and King in Burgundy*. Berkeley, 1987.

Roques, H. *L'administration municipale à Toulouse de 1693 à 1694*. Toulouse, 1908.

Roschach, Ernest. *Les archives de Toulouse*. Toulouse, n.d.

_____. "Documents inédits sur le voyage du roi Charles IX à Toulouse." *MASIBL*, 9th ser., 7 (1895): 20–46.

Rothkrug, Lionel. *Opposition to Louis XIV: The Political and Social Origins of the French Enlightenment*. Princeton, 1965.

Roucaud, Joseph. *La peste à Toulouse: Des origines au dix-huitième siècle*. Toulouse, 1918.

Roupnel, Gaston. *La ville et la campagne au XVIIᵉ siècle: Etude sur les populations des pays dijonnais*. Paris, 1955.

Roux, E. "La population de Toulouse de 1600 à 1650." Mémoire maîtrise, Université de Toulouse-Mirail, 1967.

Ruel-Albernhe, Huguette, and Philippe Gardy. "Le thème du carnaval dans la littérature occitane." In *Actes du VIᵉ Congrès International de Langues et Littérature d'Oc et d'Etudes Franco-Provinciales.* Montpellier, 1970.

Saint-Léon, Etienne-Martin. *Le compagnonnage.* Paris, 1901.

Saint-Raymond. "Les travaux d'utilité publique de l'Académie Royale des Beaux Arts." *MASIBL,* 11th ser., 2 (1914): 117–40, 349–83.

Saliès, Pierre. "Le grand incendie de Toulouse de 1463." *Mémoires de la Société Archéologique du Midi de la France.* 30 (1964): 131–66; 32 (1966): 70–85.

Salmon, J. H. M. *Cardinal de Retz: The Anatomy of a Conspirator.* New York, 1970.

_____. "The Paris Sixteen, 1584–94: The Social Analysis of a Revolutionary Movement." *Journal of Modern History* 44 (1972): 540–76.

_____. *Society in Crisis: France in the Sixteenth Century.* New York, 1975.

_____. "Venality of Office and Popular Sedition in Seventeenth-Century France." *Past & Present* 37 (1967): 21–43.

Salvan, Abbé. *Histoire générale de l'église de Toulouse.* 4 vols. Toulouse, 1861.

Salvat, Joseph. *Etude sur Pèire Godolin.* Toulouse, n.d.

Santi, M. L. "Madame Du Barry-Ceres." *MASIBL,* 11th ser., 5 (1917): 21–70.

_____. "La réaction universitaire à Toulouse à l'époque de la renaissance." *MASIBL,* 10th ser., 6 (1906): 27–68.

Schneider, Robert A. "The Ceremonial City: Toulouse Observed 1737–1780." Paper presented at the Annual Conference of the Western Society for French History, Los Angeles, 1988.

_____. "Mortification on Parade: Penitential Processions in Sixteenth- and Seventeenth-Century France." *Renaissance and Reformation* 10 (1986): 123–46.

_____. "Urban Sociability in the Old Regime: Religion and Culture in Early Modern Toulouse." Ph.D. diss., University of Michigan, 1982.

Sennet, Richard. *The Fall of Public Man.* New York, 1978.

Senot, Robert. "Analyse du rolle de la capitation de Toulouse (1695)." Mémoire maîtrise, Université de Toulouse-Mirail, n.d.

Sentou, Jean. *Fortunes et groupes sociaux à Toulouse sous la Révolution.* Toulouse, 1969.

Shibano, Marguerite-Marie. "Les débuts de la Congrégation des Filles de l'Enfance de N.S. J.-C.: Les fondateurs Gabriel de Ciron et Madame de Mondonville (1619–1657)." 3 vols. Mémoire présenté à l'Ecole Pratique des Hautes-Etudes. Paris, 1977.

_____. "Gabriel de Ciron (1619–1675), esquisse biographique." *Revue d'Histoire de la Spiritualité* 52 (1976): 89–124.

Shklar, Judith. *Men and Citizens: A Study of Rousseau's Social Theory.* Cambridge, 1969.

Sicard, Germain. *L'administration capitulaire sous l'Ancien Régime.* Toulouse, 1952.

Skinner, Quentin. *The Foundations of Modern Political Thought.* 2 vols. Cambridge, 1978.

Soriano, Marc. *Les contes de Perrault: Culture savante et traditions populaires.* Paris, 1968.

Stoye, John. *English Travellers Abroad.* New York, 1968.

Tackett, Timothy. *Priest and Parish in Eighteenth-Century France.* Princeton, 1977.

Taillefer, Michel. *Une académie interprète les lumières: L'Académie royale des Sciences, Inscriptions et Belle-Lettres de Toulouse au XVIIIᵉ siècle.* Paris, 1984.

——. *La franc-maçonnerie toulousaine: 1741–99.* Paris, 1984.

Tapié, V. L. *France in the Age of Louis XIII and Richelieu.* New York, 1974.

Taveneaux, René. *Jansénisme et politique.* Paris, 1965.

Teisseyre-Sallmann, Line. "Urbanisme et société: L'exemple de Nîmes aux XVIIᵉ et XVIIIᵉ siècles." *Annales: ESC* 35 (1980): 965–86.

Thomas, Jack. "La vie des foires et des marchés dans le Midi toulousain." Thèse de doctorat, Université de Toulouse-Mirail. 1989.

Thoumas-Schapira, Michele. "La bourgeoisie toulousaine à la fin du XVIIᵉ siècle." *ADM* 67 (1955): 312–29.

Tilly, Charles. *The Contentious French.* Cambridge, Mass., 1986.

——, ed. *The Formation of National States in Western Europe.* Princeton, 1975.

Tilly, Louise. "The Food Riot as a Form of Political Conflict in France." *Journal of Interdisciplinary History* 2 (1971): 23–57.

Tocqueville, Alexis de. *The Old Regime and the French Revolution.* Trans. Stuart Gilbert. Garden City, N.Y., 1955.

Tournier, Clément. *Histoire des séminaires toulousains.* Toulouse, 1942.

Trexler, Richard. *Public Life in Renaissance Florence.* New York, 1979.

Vaisse-Cibel, E. "Lucilio Vanini, sa vie, sa doctrine, sa mort, 1585–1619." *MASIBL*, 6th ser., 2 (1864): 113–42.

Vallette, G. *Jean-Jacques Rousseau, genevois.* Geneva and Paris, 1911.

Van Horn Melton, James. "From Image to Word: Cultural Reform and the Rise of Literate Culture in Eighteenth-Century Austria." *Journal of Modern History* 58 (1967): 95–124.

Van Kley, Dale. *The Jansenists and the Expulsion of the Jesuits from France.* New Haven, 1975.

Vedel, Jacques. "La consommation dans le Haute-Languedoc aux XVIIᵉ et XVIIIᵉ siècles." Thèse de doctorat, 3ᵉ cycle, Université de Toulouse-Mirail, n.d.

Venard, Marc. "Les confréries des pénitents au XVIᵉ siècle dans la province ecclésiastique d'Avignon." *Mémoires de l'Académie du Vaucluse*, 6th ser., 1 (1967): 55–79.

Viala, André. *Le Parlement de Toulouse et l'administration laïque, 1420–1525 environ.* 2 vols. Albi, 1953.

Vie, L. "Une incident à l'Université de Toulouse en 1645 à propos de la censure du livre *De Sciencia media.*" *Bulletin de la Société Archéologique du Midi*, 1912, pp. 303–19, 389–93.

Virieux, Maurice. "Une enquête sur le Parlement de Toulouse en 1718." *ADM* 87 (1975): 37–65.

Vovelle, Michel. *Piété baroque et déchristianisation en Provence au XVIIᵉ siècle.* Paris, 1973.

Walzer, Michael. *The Revolution of the Saints: A Study of the Origins of Radical Politics.* Cambridge, Mass., 1965.

Wolfe, Martin. *The Fiscal System of Renaissance France.* New Haven, 1972.

Wolff, Philippe. "Civitas et burgus: L'exemple de Toulouse." *Die Stadt in der europäischen Geschichte*. Bonn, 1922.

———, ed. *Histoire de Toulouse*. Toulouse, 1974.

———, ed. *Les toulousains dans l'histoire*. Toulouse, 1984.

Wood, James B. *The Nobility of the Election of Bayeux, 1463–1666: Continuity through Change*. Princeton, 1980.

Wrightson, Keith, and David Levine. *Poverty and Piety in an English Village: Terling, 1525–1700*. New York: 1979.

Yarrow, P. J. *A Literary History of France: The Seventeenth Century, 1600–1715*. New York and London, 1967.

Yates, Frances. *French Academies of the Sixteenth Century*. London, 1947.

Index

Library of Congress Cataloging-in-Publication Data

Schneider, Robert Alan.
   Public life in Toulouse, 1463–1789.

   Includes bibliographical references.
   1. Toulouse (France)—History.   2. Local government—
France—History.   3. Social classes—France—Toulouse—
History.   4. Toulouse (France)—Popular culture—History.
5. Elite (Social sciences)—France—Toulouse—History.
I. Title.
DC801.T726S36   1989   944'.862   89-42880
ISBN 0-8014-2191-8 (alk. paper)